'Trouble is brewing; all is not well in the land of customer management. Companies and customers often act deceitfully and amorally. This important book sounds the alarm about contemporary customer management practice, and suggests responses and remedies for businesses and public policy makers.'

Dr. Francis Buttle, *Principal, Francis Buttle & Associates – francisbuttle.com.au – and author 'Customer Relationship Management: Concepts and Technologies', 3rd edition.*

THE DARK SIDE OF CRM

Customers are treated badly. Not all customers. Not always. But many are and often. Some customers are bad. They treat firms badly. Firms have to react. Employees and customers endure the consequences. Such bad behaviours, by firms and customers, have consequences for perceptions of trust and fairness, for endorsements and referrals, for repeat purchasing and loyalty, and ultimately for a firm's profitability and return on investment. The management of customer relationships is core to the success and even survival of a firm. As *The Dark Side of CRM* explores, this is an area fraught with difficulties, duplicitous practice and undesirable behaviours. These need acknowledging, mitigating and controlling.

This book is the first of its kind to define this dark side, exploring also how firms and policy makers might address such behaviours and manage them successfully. With contributions from many of the leading exponents globally of customer relationship management and understanding customers, *The Dark Side of CRM* is essential reading for students, researchers and practitioners interested in managing customers, relationship marketing and CRM, as well as social media and marketing strategy.

Bang Nguyen, PhD, is a faculty member in the Marketing Department at the East China University of Science and Technology (ECUST), School of Business, China.

Lyndon Simkin, PhD, is Executive Director of the Centre for Business in Society and Professor of Strategic Marketing at the University of Coventry, UK.

Ana Isabel Canhoto, PhD, is a Principal Lecturer in Marketing at Oxford Brookes University, UK and the Alf Mizzi Chair in Digital Marketing at the University of Malta.

THE DARK SIDE OF CRM

Customers, relationships and management

Edited by Bang Nguyen, Lyndon Simkin and Ana Isabel Canhoto

Routledge
Taylor & Francis Group

LONDON AND NEW YORK

First published 2016
by Routledge
2 Park Square, Milton Park, Abingdon, Oxon OX14 4RN

and by Routledge
711 Third Avenue, New York, NY 10017

Routledge is an imprint of the Taylor & Francis Group, an informa business

British Library Cataloguing in Publication Data
A catalogue record for this book is available from the British Library

Library of Congress Cataloging in Publication Data
The dark side of CRM / edited by Bang Nguyen, Lyndon Simkin and
Ana Isabel Canhoto.
    pages cm.
Includes bibliographical references and index.
1. Customer relations–Management. I. Nguyen, Bang Xu?n. II. Simkin,
Lyndon, 1961- III. Canhoto, Ana Isabel.
HF5415.5.D1655 2016
658.8'12–dc23
            2015007787

ISBN: 978-1-138-80331-2 (hbk)
ISBN: 978-1-138-80332-9 (pbk)
ISBN: 978-1-315-75373-7 (ebk)

Typeset in Bembo
by Taylor & Francis Books

To: Jason
Sally, Becky, James, Abby, Mae, Samantha and Rosa
Joana and Martim

CONTENTS

LIST OF ILLUSTRATIONS

Figures

Tables

CONTRIBUTORS

Ibrahim Abosag is a Senior Lecturer in International Marketing at the School of Oriental and African Studies (SOAS), University of London. His research interests include cross-cultural business to business (B2B), brand relationships and online marketing. Ibrahim has published in various academic journals, including *Industrial Marketing Management, International Business Review, European Journal of Marketing, Journal of Marketing Management, Journal of TQM*, and others.

Michael Breazeale is an Assistant Professor of Marketing at Mississippi State University. His primary areas of research encompass consumer–brand connections, retail atmospherics, the consumption of experiences and emotional branding. He has published articles in the *Journal of Retailing, International Journal of Market Research, Marketing Management Journal* and the *Journal of Business Research*, and has won multiple awards for both teaching and research. He is also co-editor of the books *Consumer-Brand Relationships: Theory and Practice* (Taylor & Francis, 2012) and *Strong Brands, Strong Relationships* (Taylor & Francis, 2015).

Pennie Frow is Associate Professor in Marketing in the discipline of Marketing at the University of Sydney Business School. Her main research interests are managing customer relationships, employee commitment, customer retention, developing a customer-oriented culture and internal marketing. She serves on the review board of a number of international journals. Pennie has published in a range of academic publications, including the *Journal of Marketing, European Journal of Marketing, Journal of the Academy of Marketing Science, Industrial Marketing Management, Journal of Business Research* and the *Journal of Services Marketing*.

Venessa Funches is Associate Professor and Associate Dean for Undergraduate Studies at Auburn Montgomery University. She taught at numerous institutions before joining the AUM faculty, including the University of Alabama at Birmingham, Jefferson State Community College, Miles College and Stillman College. Her work experience includes several sales and marketing positions with companies such as Philip Morris USA, Prudential, SouthTrust and Nationwide Financial. Her teaching interests focus on personal selling, principles of marketing, new product development and retailing.

Mackenzie Harms is a doctoral student in Industrial and Organisational Psychology at the University of Nebraska at Omaha. She is also the lead graduate student on a project funded by the Department of Homeland Security Science and Technology directorate, investigating violent extremist organisations. Mackenzie plans to continue her research programme after graduate school, and is interested in the security and intelligence fields.

Martin Hickley is a Senior Associate at Customer Essential, where he is an expert in CRM systems and the use of data for customer management. Martin is noted for his ability to establish a path through data protection regulations for client companies. Martin's clarity of thinking enables the delivery of successful data strategy and management programmes.

Irina V. Kozlenkova is an Assistant Professor of Marketing at the Eli Broad College of Business at Michigan State University. Irina's research focuses on marketing strategy, channels and international marketing. Her research has been published in numerous internationally recognised academic journals.

Paul Laughlin helps customer insight and marketing leaders to maximise the value created by their teams, and coaches executives to help them sustain delivery. Formerly Head of Customer Insights for both Lloyds Banking Group Insurance and Scottish Widows, Paul has managed insight teams for 12 years and delivered value from data and analytics for 25 years.

Gina Scott Ligon is an organisational psychologist who applies leadership and innovation theory to examine the performance of violent extremist organisations. She has published over 30 peer-reviewed manuscripts in journals such as *Advances in Human Resources, Dynamics of Asymmetric Conflict* and *The Creativity Research Journal*. In 2009, Gina won the Best Paper Award from the Centre for Creative Leadership for her publication, 'The Development of Outstanding Leadership', in the *Leadership Quarterly Journal*. She is the only management faculty member of the National Consortium for Studies of Terrorism and Responses to Terrorism (START) and is Director of Research and Development for the University of Nebraska Omaha's Center for Collaboration Science.

Donald J. Lund is an Assistant Professor of Marketing at the Collat School of Business at the University of Alabama at Birmingham. Donald's research has been published in internationally recognised journals regarding business and consumer relationships, strategic marketing and service performance.

Liz Machtynger is Managing Director of Customer Essential Ltd and a leading expert in the area of customer management/CRM strategy evaluation and development, organisational development for customer management, customer proposition development, key account management, customer knowledge strategies and customer management programme design.

Gilles N'Goala is a Professor of Marketing at the University of Montpellier. Gilles's research focuses on customer relationship management in service organisations and in a digital environment (e-commerce, collaborative platforms). His research has been published in journals including the *Journal of the Academy of Marketing Science, Journal of Economic Psychology, Recherche et Applications en Marketing* (English edition), and the *Journal of Retailing and Consumer Services*. Gilles is currently Vice-President of the French Marketing Association (AFM) and a member of the Centre for Customer Management (CCM) in Paris.

Jessica Ogilvie is a doctoral candidate at the University of Alabama, with research focusing on front-line service and sales personnel. She has taught professional selling and sales management and has worked as a consultant and sales trainer in numerous corporate engagements with the University of Alabama Sales Program. She has published in multiple peer-reviewed journals, including the *Journal of Retailing, Industrial Marketing Management, Journal of Personal Selling and Sales Management* and *Business Horizons*.

Robert W. Palmatier is Professor of Marketing and holds the John C. Narver Chair of Business Administration at the University of Washington's Foster School of Business. He is also the Research Director of the University of Washington's Center for Sales and Marketing Strategy. Robert's research focuses on relationship marketing, loyalty programmes, channels and marketing strategy.

Adrian Payne is Professor of Marketing at the Australian School of Business at the University of New South Wales, and Visiting Professor at Cranfield School of Management, Cranfield University. His main research interests are relationship marketing, service marketing and CRM. He serves on the review board of a number of international journals. Adrian's publications have appeared in the *Journal of Marketing, Journal of the Academy of Marketing Science, European Journal of Marketing, Journal of International Business Studies, Journal of Business Research, Industrial Marketing Management* and *Marketing Theory*.

Erin G. Pleggenkuhle-Miles is an Assistant Professor in the Marketing and Management Department at the University of Nebraska at Omaha. Her areas of expertise include strategic management and entrepreneurship, with specific interest in how institutional or environmental factors influence firm strategy. Her research has been published in academic journals such as *Research Policy* and *Management Decision*. She acts as an ad hoc consultant for several start-up firms in Iowa and Nebraska, and sits on the board of directors for Plegg's Inc.

Adam Rapp is currently an Associate Professor of Marketing at Ohio University. His research examines factors influencing the performance of front-line service and sales personnel. Adam was awarded the 2015 Neil Rackham Research Dissemination Award for excellence in sales research. He has published over 25 articles since 2012 and his research has been published in many leading academic journals, including the *Journal of Marketing Research, Management Science, Journal of Applied Psychology, Journal of the Academy of Marketing Science* and the *International Journal of Research in Marketing*.

Denish Shah is a Marketing Professor at Georgia State University, with research focusing on substantive issues pertaining to linking marketing strategies to firm performance. Denish's research approach entails developing new conceptual frameworks and/or conducting rigorous quantitative analyses to develop novel data-driven managerial insights.

Merlin Stone is a Senior Associate at Customer Essential and a consultant, researcher and lecturer on CRM, direct and digital marketing. He is an Honorary Life Fellow of the Institute of Direct and Digital Marketing. He has pursued a full academic career and is now a Visiting Professor at Oxford Brookes University and Portsmouth University. Merlin is on the editorial board of several academic journals.

Caroline Tynan is Professor of Marketing at Nottingham University Business School, President of the Academy of Marketing, and a Fellow and Chartered Marketer of the Chartered Institute of Marketing. Her research interests focus on consumption meanings, experience marketing, relationship marketing, luxury goods marketing and managerial marketing practice.

Ian Wilkinson is an Honorary Professor of Marketing at the University of Sydney and a Visiting Professor in the Department of Entrepreneurship and Relationship Management at the University of Southern Denmark. His current research focuses on the development and management of inter-firm relations and networks in domestic and international business, and the dynamics of markets and industrial networks, including an interest in complexity. Ian's research has been published in leading journals, including the *Journal of Applied Psychology, European Journal of Marketing, Journal of the Academy of Marketing Science* and the *Journal of International Marketing*.

Lan Xia is Associate Professor in Marketing at Bentley University. Her areas of research include behavioural pricing, price fairness perceptions, service pricing, consumer information processing and retailing. Her work has appeared in the *Journal of Marketing, Journal of Retailing, Journal of Consumer Psychology, Journal of Interactive Marketing* and the *Journal of Service Research.*

Dorothy Ai-wan Yen is a Senior Lecturer in Marketing at Brunel University. She examines cross-cultural business relationships between Anglo-Saxon suppliers and Chinese buyers. She is also interested in studying young Chinese consumers' identity, acculturation and their consumption of food and brands. Her work has been published in journals including the *Journal of Business Research, Industrial Marketing Management, Journal of General Management, Total Quality Management* and *The Marketing Review.*

Louise Young is Professor of Marketing in the School of Business at the University of Western Sydney and a Visiting Professor at the University of Southern Denmark. Her main research interests are in the evolution of business relationships and networks, considering the processes and mechanisms that guide this with particular reference to the nature and role of interpersonal relationships. Louise's publications have appeared in a range of academic journals, including the *Journal of the Academy of Marketing Science, European Journal of Marketing, Industrial Marketing Management, Journal of Business Research, International Journal of Human Resource Management* and the *Journal of Services Marketing.*

Xiaoyu Yu is Professor and Head of the Department of Management at the School of Management at Shanghai University. He is Deputy Secretary-General of the Shanghai Behavioural Science Society, a member of the Expert Committee for the Shanghai MBA Case Development & Sharing Platform, and the Corresponding Reviewer Expert of One Hundred National Excellent Management Cases Selection in China. Xiaoyu's current research interests include informal entrepreneurship, effectuation behaviour and interdisciplinary research of entrepreneurship and marketing.

EDITORS' PROFILES

Bang Nguyen, PhD, is a faculty member in the Marketing Department at the East China University of Science and Technology (ECUST), School of Business, in Shanghai. Previously, he held positions at Oxford Brookes University and RMIT International University Vietnam, and was a Visiting Scholar at the China Europe International Business School (CEIBS). Bang's research interests include customer management, CRM, services marketing, consumer behaviour, branding and innovation management. Bang has published widely in journals such as the *Industrial Marketing Management, Journal of Marketing Management, Journal of Services Marketing, The Service Industries Journal, Harvard Business Review* (Chinese edition), *Journal of Strategic Marketing, International Journal of Technology Management, Information Technology & Management, Internet Research* and *Systems Research & Behavioural Science.* In addition, he has edited three other books: *Ethical and Social Marketing in Asia* (Elsevier), *Services Marketing Cases in Asia* (Springer) and *Asia Branding* (Palgrave Macmillan). Bang is an experienced consultant and advises on marketing and brand development for small and medium-sized enterprises and start-ups.

Lyndon Simkin, PhD, has recently moved from being Professor of Strategic Marketing at Henley Business School at the University of Reading in the UK to become the Executive Director of the Centre for Business in Society at the University of Coventry. Previously Lyndon was at Oxford Brookes University and the University of Warwick. Lyndon is Associate Editor of the *Journal of Marketing Management*, a member of the Academy of Marketing's Research Committee, and co-chairs two of the Academy's special interest groups: Market Segmentation and Targeting Strategy, and CRM and Services. Lyndon has published widely and authored numerous books, including *Marketing: Concepts and Strategies* (Cengage), *Marketing Planning* (Cengage), *Market Segmentation Success* (Routledge), *Marketing Essentials* (Cengage), *The Marketing Casebook* (Cengage) and *Marketing Briefs* (Routledge). Lyndon advises many blue-chip companies and mentors CEOs in strategy development and execution.

Ana Isabel Canhoto is a Principal Lecturer in Marketing at Oxford Brookes University. Ana co-chairs the Academy of Marketing's special interest group in customer relationship management (CRM). Her research focuses on the collection and uses of customer data, managing customers and the role of digital in customer management. Ana holds a PhD from the London School of Economics as well as an MBA from the London Business School. Before joining academia, she worked in the telecommunications, media and entertainment industries.

PART I

Introduction

1

INTRODUCTION

Bang Nguyen, Lyndon Simkin and Ana Isabel Canhoto

1 Introduction

Customer relationship management (CRM) is now adopted by most organisations and taught within the syllabi of all leading business schools. No one disputes the importance of managing customer relationships to extract value from customers over a protracted period of time and to create mutually beneficial relationships that increase customer satisfaction and transactions. There are reported benefits for both firms and their customers. However, there are also downsides attached to these practices and to the behaviours of managements deploying CRM. These are the focus of *The Dark Side of CRM*.

Concerns are often directed towards firms' use of customer tracking systems, perceived to induce both information mishandling and discrimination of certain customers. These are termed the 'dark side' of customer relationship management and link with unethical firm behaviours including manipulation, neglect and unfair treatment, often damaging firms' brand reputation. As CRM schemes continue to be implemented worldwide, customers' perceptions of CRM remain diverse, providing a perplexing environment to successful CRM development and organisation of customers, relationships and management. Differing industries, organisational cultures, development stages, resources, politics and consumption behaviours require multiple strategic directions emphasising different things in varying contexts. There is the belief that customising adverts to individual customers may not always be favourably viewed by those customers interested in privacy, and fairness and trust concerns exist about 'big data' such as how the data are collected, handled and stored. These are only some of the issues marketers and their partners should address.

Due to these complexities, the study of the dark side – towards customers, relationships and management – is a timely topic for further investigation. *The*

Dark Side of CRM includes practitioner views and the thoughts of leading academics. It is of interest to far more than just students, and aims to address the following:

- *Customers*: Readers are exposed to the CRM dark side's effects on consumption behaviour through extant consumer behavioural and psychological theories and research. This enables readers to understand customers' different characteristics and subsequent applications towards managing these.
- *Relationships*: Readers gain insights into relationship marketing (RM) from different perspectives. The book enables readers to compare, contrast and comprehend how relationships at different levels are created and managed in the context of CRM.
- *Management*: An exciting aspect of this book is a wide-ranging presentation of CRM dark side cases across commercial and non-commercial sectors. These cover business-to-business and business-to-consumer, encompassing industries such as manufacturing, fast-moving consumer goods (FMCG), hotels, airlines, financial services and information communications technology (ICT) sectors. Readers are exposed to differing management approaches, which, once applied to their business, will increase their chances of avoiding the dark side and successfully implementing CRM.

2 The dark side of CRM: customers, relationships and management

The growing interest in CRM and the subjects of customers, relationships and management lies in the belief that customer data provide an essential source for delivering and customising offerings that meet their needs better than the competition, over a prolonged and mutually beneficial relationship between the firm or brand and its priority customers (e.g. Nguyen et al., 2015). Building relationships enables firms to learn what customers want through continuous interaction, increasing customer intimacy and loyalty intentions. Firms find ways to add value, such that customers as well as businesses operating in those markets gain from increased competencies and skills, often referred to as win–win situations. These value added customer data contribute a coherent CRM strategy reflecting management, operations, distribution and marketing, providing an opportunity for cross-sales and up-selling. This in turn generates a significant future income stream and sustainable competitive advantages.

However, as CRM has, over recent decades, developed more advanced schemes for the benefit of firms, CRM technologies are progressively extracting customer surplus by exacerbating hidden fees and surcharges (Yu et al., 2015). Concerns are often directed towards firms' use of customer tracking systems, perceived to induce both information mishandling and discrimination of certain customers. These are termed the 'dark side' of customer relationship management and link with unethical firm behaviour, including manipulation, neglect and unfair treatment, often damaging firms' brand reputation (Nguyen, Lee-Wingate and Simkin, 2014).

To date, there are limited empirical studies in understanding the dark side of CRM, focusing on customers, relationships and management in a comprehensive text. Little is known about how the CRM dark side is perceived, the type of research methods used to understand relationships, and how companies and policy makers can manage the dark side successfully. How customers, relationships and management work in the CRM dark side context are issues still unanswered. Existing books primarily focus on general CRM applications with some practitioners' case study examples, which are insufficient and often outdated in this fast-changing environment.

Exploring and understanding the dark side of CRM is vital for developing and managing positively perceived products and services that help a company achieve higher levels of performance, including increased sales and profits (Nguyen, Klaus and Simkin, 2014). For example, investing enormous amounts on targeted advertising may not suffice if other areas such as privacy and fairness are not considered important. By understanding how customers respond to CRM schemes, firms can induce consumer patronage. For marketers, a greater understanding of customer relationships influences decisions towards efficient use of marketing resources, lowering costs and increasing profits. Finally, by exploring management, it is possible to benchmark best practices and avoid dark side behaviour, in order to achieve sustainable competitive advantages, contributing to higher levels of goodwill and improved reputation.

3 Target market and readership

The Dark Side of CRM provides final-year undergraduate students, Master's students and doctoral students in business and marketing with a comprehensive treatment of the nature of the dark side of customers, relationships and management in the CRM context. The book will also be of significant interest to practitioners involved with supplying CRM solutions, and their clients seeking to deploy CRM successfully. It explores current research and practices in different areas, industries, commercial and non-commercial sectors. The text serves as an invaluable resource for marketing academics and practitioners requiring more than anecdotal evidence of different CRM applications. Readers will find it interesting to compare and contrast different dark side situations covering important aspects related to customers, relationships and management. The text includes a valuable mix of theory, research findings and practices, which engenders confidence in academics, practitioners and students of marketing and management alike.

Of interest to a diversified audience, courses that could use the book include marketing management, services management, consumer behaviour, relationship marketing and customer relationship management, information systems and technology, to mention a few. These listed courses, at both postgraduate and undergraduate levels, are very widely taught globally.

4 Content of *The Dark Side of CRM*

Chapter 2 introduces customer relationship management and its dark side. It notes that, while CRM and RM bring considerable benefits when they work, as reports of success stories (e.g. Columbo, 2013) and case studies of companies (e.g. Duhigg, 2012) practising CRM or RM illustrate, not all is well and many RM and CRM practitioners manifest behaviour that damages or even destroys customer relationships. One report by Nucleus Research (2012) shows that 80% of the CRM returns are yet to be realised in companies, and 30% of companies have not achieved a positive return on this CRM investment. A study in 2012 of large CRM projects in five countries showed a 28% failure rate (Mieritz, 2012). The chapter focuses on customer management activity that can damage customer relationships and knowingly or deliberately exploit customers, and conceptualises this as the dark side of customer management including RM and CRM. While the focus is on service provider dark side behaviour in the business-to-consumer sector, many aspects are considered relevant to business-to-business contexts.

There is evidence that dark side practices are widespread and appear to be growing. For example, McGovern and Moon (2007, p. 80) point out that many companies infuriate customers by deliberately 'Binding them with contracts, bleeding them with fees [and] confounding them with fine print'. They observe that certain industries including mobile phone service providers, banks, video stores, book-purchasing clubs, car rental companies, health clubs and credit card companies seem especially prone to 'dark side' behaviour. Frequently, service providers find it profitable to confuse and mislead customers into making poor purchase decisions through use of complicated and detailed rules and conditions of sale. Common practices include confusing usage rates on mobile phones, high penalties when customers exceed credit limits, overdrafts and payment deadlines, or fall short of minimum balances in bank accounts. As a result, customer anguish and retaliation may contribute to service providers increasing their antagonistic strategies. This can create dysfunctional vicious cycles leading from 'Transparent, customer-centric strategies for delivering value ... [to] opaque, company-centric strategies for extracting it' (McGovern and Moon, 2007, p. 80). Two key reasons for poor customer management that may result in dark side service provider behaviour are identified (Frow et al., 2011). First, it is suggested that a poor understanding of the strategic focus of CRM may lead to inappropriate exploitation of customers, especially when service providers use intrusive technology. Second, maliciously motivated service providers can explicitly abuse customers, as CRM technology can equip them with powerful resources to do this (Payne and Frow, 2013).

Chapter 3 reviews major theories in the field of unfairness perceptions, examines sources of such perceptions, as well as consequences when perceptions of unfairness arise in the context of CRM. For example, *The Wall Street Journal* reported that Orbitz showed Mac users costlier hotels than Windows visitors see. Consequently, Apple users spent as much as 30% more a night on hotels (Mattioli, 2012). Even though the sites do not change the prices of hotels per se, the cry of unfairness is still loud and common in the marketplace, and has been shown both to constrain firms' pursuit of profit and to damage customer relationships (Kahneman et al., 1986; Xia et al., 2004). Pricing is a marketing element that can easily provoke such cries.

Why does fairness matter? From the incidents in which unfairness occurred, such as the Orbitz case, we can glimpse the consequences of the perception of unfairness. In general, perceptions of unfairness induce dissatisfaction (Herrmann et al. 2007; Van den Bos et al., 1998) and constrain firms' ability to maximise their profit when customers with a grudge leave the relationship and/or seek retribution through negative word-of-mouth (WOM) or revenge (e.g. Campbell, 1999; Kahneman et al., 1994).

Negative affect is an integral part of the perception of unfairness (Xia et al., 2004). Various negative emotions associated with these perceptions include, most commonly, anger and hostility. These emotions are evoked when customers attribute the responsibility to the seller and are considered outward emotions (Barclay et al., 2005). Perceptions of unfairness coupled with strong outward negative emotions lead to behaviours intended not only to restore financial equity but also to vent negative emotions, reinforce relationship norms, rebuild self-concept and damage the seller. These behaviours may include complaints, switching, negative WOM and/or boycott of the seller's product or service. Given the potential damage of the perceptions of unfairness on customer relationships and firms' profitability, it is important to understand how consumers form these perceptions and the sources of perceptions of unfairness.

Chapter 4 incorporates social media tools into CRM. Formally, social CRM has been defined by marketing scholars as the integration of social media applications into the traditional customer-facing activities of the firm to engage and collaborate with customers and enhance customer relationships (Greenberg, 2010; Trainor, 2012). When properly leveraged, social media technologies and tools can enhance CRM systems and boost efficiency and effectiveness of customer interactions and resultant customer relationships. Social CRM has provided companies with an array of benefits including low-cost customer interaction, increased response time, an extended number of communication platforms, and marked efficiencies in customer relationship processes. However, the growing emphasis on social media as a crux of customer-facing communications is forcing companies to embrace a shift from traditional CRM practices to a focus on collaborative experiences and facilitation of value-driven dialogue with their customers. With such a dramatic shift in control within the customer–firm relationship, firms have been plagued with many social media- and CRM-related shortcomings. The chapter examines the pitfalls associated with social media and explores ways to overcome the problems faced by many of today's firms in the social CRM process.

Without proper strategic implementation, firms are prone to social media failures and risk harming the customer relationship more often than enhancing it. The chapter discusses the many pitfalls to implementing social media actions without proper planning or strategic considerations. Notably, while hasty implementation of social media can hurt customer relationships, delay in establishing a social media presence can also have negative impacts on CRM. Active involvement on social media platforms is being increasingly demanded by customers and is becoming essential in the competitive marketplace. Considering the increase in customer demand for interaction in social media channels, this chapter also explores the pitfalls associated with delays and failure to launch social media strategies. Reconciling these pitfalls, this chapter further explores how to successfully shift necessary resources, train and empower employees, implement a top-down model of technology acceptance, and create a social CRM strategy that is both timely and effective.

Chapter 5 explains both the importance of negative WOM, misbehaviour and revenge behaviours in the marketplace, and the types of service failures leading consumers to engage in these behaviours. The chapter examines the various internal psychological processes that lead to these behaviours, their influence on consumer decision making, and implications for consumer–firm relationships.

While we know that negative WOM occurs more frequently, the ramifications in today's digitally connected world can be severe. The widespread occurrence of the consumer revenge phenomenon is particularly alarming. A Customer Rage Survey conducted in 2013 revealed that shoppers who received unsatisfactory service were seeking revenge for their suffering and many of them admitted having already exacted revenge (Customer Care Alliance, 2013). Consumers may now post their complaints online, call for boycotts, organise class-action lawsuits, along with a host of other options all driven to hurt the firm. When consumers are dissatisfied, their responses can range from doing nothing at all to suing for millions of dollars.

However, what distinguishes a merely dissatisfactory experience from one likely to end in one of the negative behaviours? The emotion of anger is the difference. Anger is a key and fundamental emotion. The concept of anger is a central element in social behaviour (Diaz et al., 2002). It is one of the most frequently experienced of all emotions. Studies have generally proposed one broad cause for anger. For example, prior research suggests that anger is caused by violations of the moral code of conduct or is the result of moral outrage (Diaz et al., 2002; Weiner, 2000). Anger is also thought to be caused by an inability to attain desired goals (Nyer, 1997). Additionally, feelings of anger are associated with individual perceptions of mistreatment (Rose and Neidermeyer, 1999).

In consumer–firm relationships, as in all relationships, we develop expectations. We learn what the other party expects us to contribute and we, in turn, develop notions about what we should receive from the relationship (Heath et al., 1993). The source of these expectations stems from a consumer's past experiences and social norms. Contract violation is more than a failure of the organisation to meet expectations; responses are more intense because respect and codes of conduct are called into question – because essentially a 'promise' has been broken and it is more personalised (Rousseau, 1989). Any changes in behaviour from expectations are typically perceived to violate the implicit contract and therefore seen as unjust and unfair (Heath et al., 1993, p. 76). These consumer assessments have consequences for the firm.

Chapter 6 provides the reader with an understanding of *which* factors can make business relationships more or less successful, and *when* these factors will be especially helpful or detrimental. This knowledge can help guide decision making when managing relationships with suppliers or customers, be they individuals or firms.

Just as certain behaviours can make or break interpersonal relationships, such as a marriage, theoretical and empirical research as well as anecdotal evidence from different companies show that in business-to-business or business-to-consumer relationships there exist certain mechanisms that either improve these relationships (positive mediating mechanisms), or severely damage them (negative mediating mechanisms) and even lead to their dissolution.

There are various drivers that have an impact on positive and negative mediating mechanisms of relationship performance. For instance, how well partners are able to communicate with each other, the dependence of business partners on each other, investments in the relationship, relationship duration, level of expertise and similarity all affect the development of positive and negative mediating mechanisms. Performance of a business relationship may be measured in a number of different ways. Some of the outcomes are more attitudinal in nature such as customer loyalty and satisfaction, whereas other desirable outcomes of business relationships have more direct financial consequences and include WOM, sales growth, market share and profit margins. Mechanisms that improve these performance outcomes include gratitude, trust, commitment and reciprocal norms of partners involved in the relationship. Some of these mechanisms, such as gratitude and trust, have more of a short-term effect on performance, while others have a lasting impact. Negative mechanisms that hurt performance include opportunism, conflict, unfairness and complacency. These behaviours can damage relationships over a relatively short period of time (opportunism and conflict) or long into the future (unfairness and complacency). The chapter summarises the most common theoretical underpinnings for these linkages, which include equity theory, social exchange theory, relationship marketing and transaction cost economics, synthesising decades of empirical results from seminal academic research.

Chapter 7 explores how companies can develop and/or restore trust through avoiding deceptive or manipulative marketing tactics and promoting transparency in the market. Of course, CRM is not deceptive and manipulative in itself, but its use by marketers may lead to wrong practices, harm customers and enhance distrust. Without trust, no long-lasting relationship between providers and customers is likely to develop. Indeed, trust is becoming more and more critical as partners' vulnerability, situation uncertainty and information asymmetry between providers and customers increase (Aurier and N'Goala, 2010).

While research in marketing has emphasised customer satisfaction, trust and commitment as top priorities, CRM may also lead to manipulative and deceptive tactics that are contrary to these priorities (e.g. N'Goala, 2010). Using CRM, companies may exploit relationship asymmetry and customers' vulnerabilities instead of developing a balance of power and win–win situations. Information asymmetry is increasing along with new technologies, which opaquely collect data via spyware without any explicit agreement by the concerned customers (e.g. Google, Yahoo, Facebook, etc.). Companies are increasingly pervasive and intrusive, multiplying the messages on computers, smartphones and tablets, staying constantly connected to their customers. They enter their customers' social networks, geo-localise them and send customised offers on several devices (social local mobile marketing). They also recruit community managers to manage their e-reputation.

Instead of enhancing full transparency over the Internet, the use of CRM creates new forms of information asymmetry (big data), new forms of vulnerability (privacy concern) and new potential causes of distrust. As a consequence, while investments in CRM still increase, trust in manufacturers (e.g. food industry, pharmaceuticals), retailers, service providers (e.g. retail banking, insurance companies) and media (e.g. press, advertising) is declining, in particular in Europe (Porter Lynch and Lawrence, 2012). For Nguyen (2011), opportunistic firm behaviour and lack of transparency reduce trust and cause negative perceptions, such as unfairness, and customer misbehaviour (vengeance, vandalism, aggressiveness, etc.). One can then imagine the potential hidden costs of distrust for companies (e.g. disloyalty, decrease of customer lifetime value, negative WOM, stress and absenteeism of contact persons, decrease of marketing effectiveness).

Chapter 8 aims to expand, clarify and develop a better understanding of the dynamic development and effect of the dark side of business relationships. Despite the conflicting findings and arguments about where in the development process darker elements are likely to occur in business relationships, studies of relationship development tend to rely on theories and models of the relationship development process that are not free from criticism.

Research on when and how the dark side emerges through the relationship development process has been very limited. From the handful of studies that examined where in the development process the dark side emerges, leading to serious challenges to the relationship, Moorman et al. (1992) were among the first to claim that there is a dark side of long-term relationships that dampens the positive influence of relational constructs like trust. Contrary to common belief, they suggest that the longer the relationship exists, the more likely it is to become prone to negative influences, resulting in a reduction of the positive impacts from relational constructs, such as trust and commitment. While the findings of Moorman et al. (1992) were later confirmed by Grayson and Ambler (1999), Barnes (2005) discovered that, in a dyadic context, some negativity is more likely to occur in medium-term rather than long-term relationships, as some degree of complacency creeps into such relationships. Research examining the dark side of relationships is scant and very little has been concluded on how such effects can influence future relationship dynamics.

Nonetheless, and despite the apparent lack of studies in this area, it is safe to argue that the dark side of a business relationship can emerge at any point in the development process, depending on relationship contexts, types, interaction dynamics and market conditions. It is also safe to argue that the dark side is likely to occur frequently in those relationships where uncertainty and a large distance between relational partners exist because of their cross-cultural/cross-national nature, as indicated by Leonidou, Barnes and Talias (2006). What is clear is that more studies are needed on the emergence of the dark side throughout the relationship development process.

Chapter 9 focuses on a very specific dark side of consumer–brand relationships – the relationship between violent extremist organisations (VEOs) and their sympathisers. The authors conducted research exploring these organisations' use of accepted branding and CRM techniques that further their causes, engage potential followers and enhance their reputations among existing supporters. This situation is unique in that the organisations in question are not trying to minimise the aspects of their practices that most would consider to be dark sided, but instead choose to highlight those aspects as 'selling points'. The chapter explores various brand-building and relationship management techniques currently employed by VEOs – primarily via social media, where recent estimates suggest that nearly 90% of VEO Internet activity takes place (Weimann, 2012). CRM techniques such as treating customers as partners, soliciting customer input, communicating proactively with customers and recognising the importance of service take on additional significance when the customer in question is potentially being asked to sacrifice more than financial resources and the product being promoted is terrorism. The customer of a VEO may actually be asked to give their own life to advance the cause; the product of the VEO is often destruction; and the more attention that destruction receives, the more profitable that product is for the VEO.

The authors find that even the most unlikely types of organisations employ CRM techniques and, when effectively implemented, these techniques produce desirable outcomes for the organisation. Whether the desired effect is a vocal cohort of brand advocates and a strong bottom line, or a willing band of volunteers and increasing donations from like-minded sympathisers, impactful CRM is a common thread. So the question becomes: if VEOs have adopted techniques utilised by successful businesses, will traditional businesses benefit from studying the dark-side implementation of those same techniques? This chapter explores the various social media tactics employed by VEOs to build and maintain a strong brand image, as well as the CRM strategies that allow them to customise these communications, ensuring a strong customer–brand relationship with their constituents. The unique nature of these strategies allows the authors to recommend some novel techniques that can be employed by more traditional organisations.

Chapter 10 questions four popular managerial beliefs: Are loyal customers profitable? Are the most profitable customers of the firm the most valuable? Is customer cross-buying beneficial for the firm? Does marketing uniformly influence customer behaviour over time? Drawing upon strong evidence from extant research, the author finds that the long-held conventional CRM beliefs do not hold true for a sizeable proportion of a firm's customers and can lead to adverse financial outcomes. Consequently, the author proposes tools and frameworks that firms can implement to measure and manage the 'problem' customers and refine their conventional CRM strategies to maximise customer profits and overall firm performance.

The key point to take away from this chapter is that it is now imperative for firms to rely on data analyses before implementing key CRM strategies. More specifically, data analyses should be first conducted at the customer level, so as to capture the nuances of each customer's behaviour. The recommended bottom–up approach would then entail aggregating unique nuances of customer behaviour to a customer-segment level. For example, each customer exhibiting unprofitable cross-buy can be grouped into a customer segment. Thereafter, firms can evaluate whether the segment of customers with unconventional (or unexpected) behaviour is substantially large with a significantly high impact on the firm's performance. If so, the firm needs to account for the behavioural nuance(s) of the new segment(s) of customers by making the necessary changes in its CRM practices and policies.

Chapter 11 explores a previously neglected area of the CRM literature on how firms can overcome the dark side, by exploring and linking varying CRM aspects with learning behaviour from failures. This chapter thus suggests that the CRM concept has potential to survive and regain its success despite initial failures, so extending the relationship marketing theories and with the outcome that successfully overcoming the dark sides may result in the stimulation of long-term relationships. There are reflections on this exploration and implications for CRM, marketing and management and the future of CRM strategy.

As various studies show high rates of failure when implementing CRM schemes, an urgent problem facing both academics and managers is to address how CRM expenditure can be more effectively and consistently translated into meaningful business and profits. Both the failure rates and lack of key success factors in organisations implementing CRM remain poorly conceptualised and understood. Previous work with organisations has demonstrated that the indicators of organisations' CRM performance can be developed through a number of factors, such as strategic emphasis, technology and the integration of market knowledge (e.g. Yu et al., 2014). To achieve effective results, firms are encouraged to combine the richness of information with the rigour of organisational learning and subsequent strategic implementation. Various studies show that, despite all its benefits, high rates of failure are in evidence when implementing CRM (Rigby et al., 2002). When analysing the return on investment of a CRM strategy, some researchers have obtained contradictory results, in that these seem to vary both within and between organisations (Bohling et al., 2006). In order to identify and verify what actionable factors are critical to the successful outcome of CRM initiatives, a significant body of research has emerged in the last decade (e.g. Sin et al., 2005). In this relationship, we suggest that firms adopting CRM should not abandon their efforts, but rather continue to overcome the damages caused by the dark side. We propose that firms need to learn from their past failures, as such awareness related to failure may provide a source of knowledge that is unique to the organisation. The chapter thus includes in its exploration of ways to overcome the dark side of CRM the construct of *learning from failure*.

Chapter 12 examines the issue of good and bad customers, followed by that of good and bad suppliers. The two are inter-related, as bad suppliers can cause poor behaviour in customers and vice versa. Good suppliers can encourage customers to be good, while good customers can encourage the formation and success of good suppliers. This subject is often discussed within suppliers and referred to, though not in the same language, by customers.

In this chapter, 'good' and 'bad' are defined mainly according to the supplier's objectives, rather than morally. However, there may be a correlation between the supplier-focused and moral definitions. 'Good' and 'bad' customer profiles differ by supplier and industry sector. Typically, when defining 'good' and 'bad', organisations use indicators that are unlinked to a moral position, but based on 'objective' data they have about the customer (e.g. whether a customer has required a very high level of customer service relative to what they have paid). Technology and data sources now make it possible for suppliers of all sizes (not just large) and government suppliers to differentiate much more accurately between 'good' and 'bad' individuals and groups, as they define them. These developments also make it much easier for these suppliers to predict likely 'goodness' or 'badness', using a range of statistical indicators. Where use of these indicators is not permitted for some reason, this initiates a search for surrogates for these indicators. Following this approach requires a supplier to define what it means by 'good' or 'bad', and to keep this definition under review according to the performance of individuals or groups. The conclusion is clear: identification and management of good customers brings rich rewards, but so does identifying and managing bad customers.

The concluding Chapter 13 explores how analytics, big data and digital/mobile marketing change what financial services customers and companies do. The increased competition for consumers and the erosion of profit margins led to information asymmetry, particularly between insurance and credit companies and bad customers, in which the latter could become bad without suffering legal or other consequences. This asymmetry is being redressed by shared databases, by use of many new sources of data, by much more rapid and accurate data analysis and forecasting (allowing financial services companies to predict fraud much more easily), and by closer cooperation with law enforcement authorities. As the consequences of much higher levels of internal migration in the European Union become clearer, governments will need to ensure that they do not handicap insurers and credit companies in their attempts to identify and deter bad customers. This is because there are clear benefits from this in terms of fighting crime. At the same time, they will need to ensure that the new capabilities of financial services companies are not abused, and that they observe the provisions of the various data protection laws. In an industry very much under the spotlight, particularly in terms of the appropriateness of selling certain products to certain consumers, this chapter explores the darker side of CRM and its consequences.

5 Conclusion

The Dark Side of CRM is an edited book that serves as a supplementary text for advanced undergraduates and postgraduates, and a key resource for academics and practitioners. It provides a topical set of thought-provoking insights in the field of CRM. This book is unique in its layout and focus in that it reveals the composite overview of customers, relationships and management through groundbreaking research and practitioner experiences. It combines theoretical and methodological aspects of CRM's dark side, in different contexts and across multiple industries, in a comprehensive review. Top researchers and users of relationship marketing and customer management converge to provide submissions that are grouped accordingly, drawing attention to the relevant context and from varying perspectives. Students and practitioners, therefore, may access information on trends, theory and practice about customers, relationships and management in the international arena.

The editors manage the Academy of Marketing's special interest group in CRM. This involves routinely running workshops for academics and practitioners regarding the practice and future of CRM, as well as guest editing special issues of well-known journals, such as a recent issue of the *Journal of Strategic Marketing* that looked at the impact of digital on CRM practice. Many of this book's contributors are part of this network. We wish to acknowledge the support of members of this special interest group in the creation of *The Dark Side of CRM*. Above all else, we are most grateful for our contributors' insightful, informative and highly directional chapters. We hope you enjoy the book.

TABLE 1.1 Chapter outline and authors

Chapters	Titles	Contributor(s)/author(s)
Part I: Introduction		
Sets the scene and provides a commentary on the separate contributions in *The Dark Side of CRM*		
1	Introduction	Bang Nguyen (East China University of Science and Technology), Lyndon Simkin (University of Coventry) and Ana Isabel Canhoto (Oxford Brookes University)
Part II: Customers		
Revolves around research studies focusing on customers' responses towards the dark side of CRM. Explores consumption behaviour and the psychological underpinnings in the customer decision-making process		
2	CRM and customer management: identifying and confronting dark side behaviours	Pennie Frow (University of Sydney), Adrian Payne (University of New South Wales), Ian Wilkinson (University of Sydney) and Louise Young (University of Western Sydney)
3	Perceptions of fairness and unfairness	Lan Xia (Bentley University)

Chapters	Titles	Contributor(s)/author(s)
4	CRM and social media	Adam Rapp (Ohio University) and Jessica Ogilvie (University of Alabama)
5	Negative word-of-mouth, misbehaviour and revenge	Venessa Funches (Auburn Montgomery University)

Part III: Relationships

Examines different relationship marketing and management studies from extant economic, consumer behavioural and psychological theories and research. Presents important aspects of social indicators influencing relationships in varying contexts

6	Good versus bad relationship framework	Donald J. Lund (University of Alabama), Irina V. Kozlenkova (Michigan State University) and Robert W. Palmatier (University of Washington)
7	Opportunism, transparency, manipulation, deception and exploitation of customers' vulnerabilities in CRM	Gilles N'Goala (University of Montpellier)
8	The dark side of business relationships: an overview	Ibrahim Abosag (SOAS, University of London), Dorothy Ai-wan Yen (Brunel University) and Caroline Tynan (Nottingham University)
9	The dark side of CRM: brand relationships and violent extremist organisations	Mike Breazeale (Mississippi State University), Erin G. Pleggenkuhle-Miles (University of Nebraska Omaha), Mackenzie Harms (University of Nebraska Omaha) and Gina Scott Ligon (University of Nebraska Omaha)

Part IV: Management

Covers the management perspective of CRM's dark side and includes companies from a wide range of industries. Focuses on identifying and overcoming the dark side at the management level

10	The right marketing to the wrong customers? Rethinking conventional CRM strategies	Denish Shah (Georgia State University)
11	Recovery from CRM implementation pitfalls: integrating learning behaviour from failure	Bang Nguyen (ECUST) and Xiaoyu Yu (Shanghai University)
12	The dark side: customers versus companies	Liz Machtynger (Customer Essential), Martin Hickley (Customer Essential), Merlin Stone (Customer Essential), and Paul Laughlin (Customer Essential)

Part V: Conclusion

Rounds off *The Dark Side of CRM*, suggesting some emerging themes and priorities

References

Aurier, P. and N'Goala, G. (2010). The differing and mediating roles of trust and relationship commitment in service relationship maintenance and development. *Journal of the Academy of Marketing Science*, 38(3), pp. 303–325.

Barclay, L.J., Skarlicki, D.P. and Pugh, S.D. (2005). Exploring the role of emotions in injustice perceptions and retaliation. *Journal of Applied Psychology*, 90(4), pp. 629.

Barnes, B.R. (2005). Is the seven-year hitch premature in industrial markets? *European Journal of Marketing*, 39(5/6), pp. 560–581.

Bohling, T., Bowman, D., LaValle, S., Mittal, V., Narayandas, D. and Ramani, G. (2006). CRM implementation: effectiveness issues and insights. *Journal of Service Research*, 9(2), pp. 184–194.

Campbell, M.C. (1999). Perceptions of price unfairness: antecedents and consequences. *Journal of Marketing Research*, 36(2), pp. 187–199.

Columbo, L. (2013). Gartner predicts CRM will be a $36B market by 2017. *Forbes*. www.forbes.com/sites/louiscolumbus/2013/06/18/gartner-predicts-crm-will-be-a-36b-market-by-2017/.

Customer Care Alliance (2013). *Customer Rage Survey*. www.customercaremc.com/the-2013-customer-rage-study.

Diaz, A., Casado, B. and Mas Ruiz, F.J. (2002). The consumer's reaction to delays in service. *International Journal of Service Industry Management*, 13(2), pp. 118–140.

Duhigg, C. (2012). How companies learn your secrets. *The New York Times* (16 February). www.nytimes.com/2012/02/19/magazine/shopping-habits.html?pagewanted=all&_r=0.

Frow, P.E., Payne, A., Wilkinson, I.F. and Young, L. (2011). Customer management and CRM: addressing the dark side. *Journal of Services Marketing*, 25(2), pp. 79–89.

Grayson, K. and Ambler, T. (1999). The dark side of long-term relationships in marketing services. *Journal of Marketing Research*, February, 36(1), pp. 132–141.

Greenberg, P. (2010). The impact of CRM 2.0 on customer insight. *Journal of Business & Industrial Marketing*, 25(6), pp. 410–419.

Heath, C., Knez, M. and Camerer, C. (1993). The strategic management of the entitlement process in the employment relationship. *Strategic Management Journal*, 14, pp. 75–93.

Herrmann, A., Xia, L., Monroe, K.B. and Huber, F. (2007). The influence of price fairness on customer satisfaction: an empirical test in the context of automobile purchases. *Journal of Product and Brand Management*, 16(1), pp. 49–58.

Kahneman, D., Knetsch, J.L. and Thaler, R. (1986). Fairness and the assumptions of economics . *Journal of Business*, 59(4), pp. 285–300.

Kahneman, D., Knetsch, J.L. and Thaler, R. (1994). 'Fairness as a constraint on profit seeking: entitlements in the market'. In *Quasi Rational Economics*. Russel Sage, New York, pp. 199–219.

Leonidou, L., Barnes, B. and Talias, M. (2006). Exporter–importer relationship quality: the inhibiting role of uncertainty, distance and conflict. *Industrial Marketing Management*, 35(4), pp. 576–588.

Mattioli, D. (2012). On Orbitz, Mac users steered to pricier hotels. *The Wall Street Journal*, 23 August.

McGovern, G. and Moon, Y. (2007). Companies and the customers who hate them. *Harvard Business Review*, June, pp. 78–84.

Mieritz, L. (2012). Survey shows why projects fail, Gartner Inc. http://my.gartner.com/portal/server.pt?open=512&objID=202&&PageID=5553&mode=2&in_hi_userid=2&cached=true&resId=2034616&ref=AnalystProfile.

Moorman, C., Zaltman, G. and Deshpande, R. (1992). Relationships between providers and users of market research: the dynamics of trust within and between organizations. *Journal of Marketing Research*, 29, August, pp. 314–328.

n.a. (2010) Rage over McNuggets sends woman to jail, 10 August. www.nbc4i.com/story/20749053/rage-over-mcnuggets-sends-woman-to-jail (8 September 2014).

N'Goala, G. (2010). Discovering the dark side of service relationships ... or why long-lasting and exclusive relationships are self-destructing. *Recherche et Applications en Marketing* (English edn), 25 (March), pp. 3–30.

Nguyen, B. (2011). The dark side of CRM. *The Marketing Review*, 11(2), pp. 137–149.

Nguyen, B., Klaus, P. and Simkin, L. (2014). It's just not fair: exploring the effects of firm customisation on unfairness perceptions, loyalty and trust. *Journal of Services Marketing*, 28(6), pp. 484–497.

Nguyen, B., Lee-Wingate, N. and Simkin, L. (2014). The customer relationship management paradox: five steps to create a fairer organisation. *Social Business Journal*, 4(3), pp. 207–230.

Nguyen, B., Simkin, L., Chen, J. and Klaus, P. (2015). Fairness quality: a conceptual model and multiple-item scale for assessing firms' fairness – An exploratory study. *Journal of Marketing Management*. Published online, doi: 10.1080/0267257X.2014.997273.

Nyer, P.U. (1997). A study of the relationships between cognitive appraisals and consumption emotions. *Journal of the Academy of Marketing Science*, 25(4), pp. 296–304.

Nucleus Research (2012). *CRM: 80% of the Returns are Yet to be Achieved*. Research Note M132, Nucleus Research Inc.

Payne, A. and Frow, P. (2013). *Strategic Customer Management: Integrating CRM and Relationship Marketing*. Cambridge University Press, Cambridge.

Porter Lynch, R. and Lawrence, P.R. (2012). The age of distrust: a European perspective, White Paper.

Rigby, D.K., Reichheld, F.F. and Schefter, P. (2002). Avoid the four perils of CRM. *Harvard Business Review*, 80 (February), pp. 101–109.

Rose, R.L. and Neidermeyer, M. (1999). From rudeness to roadrage: the antecedents and consequences of consumer aggression. *Advances in Consumer Research*, 26, pp. 12–17.

Rousseau, D.M. (1989). Psychological and implied contracts in organisations. *Employee Responsibilities and Rights Journal*, 2, pp. 121–139.

Sin, L.Y.M., Tse, A.C.B. and Yim, F.H.K. (2005). CRM: conceptualisation and scale development. *European Journal of Marketing*, 39(11/12), pp. 1264–1290.

Trainor, K.J. (2012). Relating social media technologies to performance: a capabilities-based perspective. *Journal of Personal Selling and Sales Management*, 3, pp. 317–331.

Van den Bos, K., Wilke, H.A.M., Lind, E.A. and Vermunt, R. (1998). Evaluating outcomes by means of the fair process effect: evidence for different processes in fairness and satisfaction judgments. *Journal of Personality and Social Psychology*, 74(6), pp. 1493.

Weimann, G. (2012). Terrorist groups recruiting through social media. CBC News, 10 January.   www.cbc.ca/news/technology/story/2012/01/10/tech-terrorist-social-media.html (accessed 4 September 2014).

Weiner, B. (2000). Attributional thoughts about consumer behaviour. *Journal of Consumer Research*, 27(3), pp. 382–387.

Xia, L., Monroe, K.B. and Cox, J.L. (2004). The price is unfair! A conceptual framework of price fairness perceptions. *Journal of Marketing*, 68(4), pp. 1–15.

Yu, X., Chen, Y. and Nguyen, B. (2014). Knowledge management, learning behaviour from failure and new product development in new technology ventures. *Systems Research and Behavioural Science*, 31(3), pp. 405–423.

Yu, X., Nguyen, B., Han, S.H., Chen, C.H.S. and Li, F. (2015). Electronic CRM and perceptions of unfairness. *Information Technology & Management*. Published online, doi: 10.1007/s10799-10014-0210-0214.

PART II

Customers

2

CRM AND CUSTOMER MANAGEMENT: IDENTIFYING AND CONFRONTING DARK SIDE BEHAVIOURS[1]

Pennie Frow, Adrian Payne, Ian Wilkinson and Louise Young

1 Introduction

Management of customer relationships is a key activity for the enterprise. Ways of more effectively managing relationships with customers are typically addressed under the headings of customer relationship management (CRM) and relationship marketing (RM), to name but two terms used to describe the management of customer relationships. Resources applied to such relationship management initiatives are substantial and growing. For example, global expenditure on CRM is expected to grow to US$36.5 billion by 2017 (Columbo, 2013).

CRM and RM bring considerable benefits when they work, as reports of success stories and case studies of companies practising CRM or RM illustrate. However, all is not well. Many RM and CRM practitioners manifest behaviour that damages or even destroys customer relationships. Further, there are high failure rates in CRM. A study by Nucleus Research (2012) shows 80% of the CRM returns are yet to be realised in companies and 30% of companies have not achieved a positive return on this CRM investment. A study in 2012 of large CRM projects in five countries showed a 28% failure rate (Mieritz, 2012).

In this chapter, we focus on customer management activity that can damage customer relationships and knowingly or deliberately exploit customers. We conceptualise this as the dark side of customer management, including RM and CRM. While our focus is on service provider dark side behaviour in the business-to-consumer sector, we consider many aspects are also relevant in business-to-business contexts.

Learning objectives

When you have read the chapter, you should be able to:

1. Discuss forms of dark side behaviour in customer management and their impact on customers.

2. Identify instances of dark side behaviour from service providers across different industries.
3. Analyse the role of key strategic processes in customer management.
4. Develop a plan to minimise negative outcomes for customers, from dark side behaviour.

2 Route map

RM and CRM have been the focus of much research, but the 'dark side' of service provider relationships has been given little attention. However, there is evidence that dark side practices are widespread and appear to be growing. For example, McGovern and Moon (2007, p. 80) point out that many companies infuriate customers by deliberately 'binding them with contracts, bleeding them with fees, [and] confounding them with fine print'. They observe that certain industries, including mobile phone service providers, banks, video stores, book-purchasing clubs, car rental companies, health clubs and credit card companies, seem especially prone to 'dark side' behaviour. Frequently, service providers find it profitable to confuse and mislead customers into making poor purchase decisions through use of complicated and detailed rules and conditions of sale. Common practices include confusing usage rates on mobile phones, high penalties when customers exceed credit limits, overdrafts and payment deadlines, or fall short of minimum balances in bank accounts. As a result, customer anguish and retaliation may contribute to service providers increasing their antagonistic strategies. This can create dysfunctional vicious cycles leading from 'transparent, customer-centric strategies for delivering value ... [to] opaque, company-centric strategies for extracting it' (McGovern and Moon, 2007, p. 80).

The objective of this chapter is to explore the dark side of service provider behaviour in terms of the abuse of relationships created through poor customer management. We identify two key reasons for poor customer management, which may result in dark side service provider behaviour. First, we suggest that a poor understanding of the strategic focus of CRM may lead to inappropriate exploitation of customers, especially when service providers use intrusive technology. Second, maliciously motivated service providers can explicitly abuse customers, as CRM technology can equip them with powerful resources to do this.

The chapter is structured as follows. First, we briefly describe the nature of relationship management and differentiate between CRM and the associated terms of relationship marketing, customer management and service management. Second, we consider the dark side of service provider behaviour and identify the different forms it can take. Third, we discuss how the negative outcomes of customer management can be addressed through a more holistic approach to CRM involving a focus on five key strategic processes. A consideration of these strategic CRM processes draws greater attention to key dark side issues and their potential for resolution. Finally, we identify key areas for future research.

3 CRM and the state of the art in research of the dark side

CRM and managing relationships

Over recent decades, RM, CRM and other ways of systematically managing relationships have developed significantly. However, there is considerable confusion in both the academic literature and managerial practice regarding how they differ and what the implications might be of using each approach for effective customer management. Often, the terms RM and CRM have been used interchangeably. However, they should be considered distinct, but interrelated (Shukla, 2010; Payne and Frow, 2013).

We define these terms and highlight key differences between them in Figure 2.1. Their definitions, developed from the academic literature and field-based research with executives, help clarify the distinction between these terms.

Relationship marketing involves the strategic management of relationships with multiple stakeholders – a view widely supported in the relationship marketing literature (e.g. Christopher et al., 2002; Gummesson, 2008).

Customer relationship management is a cross-functional strategic approach concerned with creating improved shareholder value through the development of appropriate relationships with key customers and customer segments. CRM typically involves identifying appropriate business and customer strategies, the acquisition and diffusion of customer knowledge, deciding appropriate segment granularity, managing the co-creation of customer value, developing integrated channel strategies, and the intelligent use of data and technology solutions to create superior customer experiences (Payne and Frow, 2013). Thus, CRM involves the strategic management of *customer* relationships utilising, where appropriate, technological tools.

Customer management represents that part of CRM that involves a more tactical management of customer interactions and transactions, as shown in Figure 2.1. A substantial amount of CRM failure can be attributed to a lack of clarity as to what

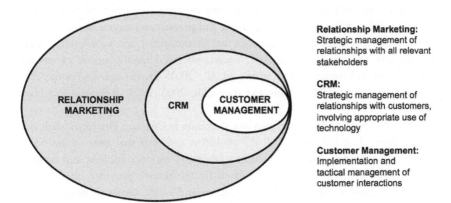

FIGURE 2.1 Relationship marketing, CRM and customer management

CRM encompasses, a failure to adopt a comprehensive definition that spells out its full scope and a lack of a strategic framework to guide its implementation. This can result in suppliers exploiting customers, mistaking tactically orientated customer management for CRM. This reason for the failure of CRM is distinct from maliciously motivated suppliers who abuse customers using powerful CRM technology.

We argue that many service providers are engaging in tactical customer management transactions without the overarching structure of a more holistic, strategic approach to customer relationships. Thus, their transactionally oriented customer management activities are masquerading as strategic CRM, opening up greater opportunities for both failure and dark side behaviour, and perhaps undermining the adoption by others of strategic CRM.

Payne and Frow (2013), building on their earlier work, develop a strategic process-based cross-functional conceptualisation of CRM derived from empirical research. They identify five key processes:

1.   A strategy development process
2.   A value creation process
3.   A multi-channel and customer experience process
4.   An information management process
5.   A performance assessment process

This framework, together with its detailing of component elements within these processes, permits a more thorough understanding of the multifaceted nature of CRM activities. We utilise this latter framework in the discussion section of this Chapter, where we consider how customer management activities can be managed more strategically and how dark side behaviours can be addressed.

The dark side of service provider relationships

Customers can also engage in dark side behaviour when they try to take advantage of service providers, e.g. excessive complaining and product and service misuse. Lovelock (1994) described misbehaving customers as 'jaycustomers', and subsequently several authors have considered the motives, characteristics and specific aspects of customer dysfunctional behaviour (e.g. Caruana et al., 2001; Harris and Ogbonna, 2002; Fullerton and Punj, 2003; Harris and Reynolds, 2003, 2004; Reynolds and Harris, 2006).

Our focus here is on service provider dark side behaviour. The term 'dark side', as used here, does not include all the problems and costs that arise in the normal course of conducting business, such as service and product failures, and time and money costs, unless they are manipulated by the service provider for their own benefit and against the interests of customers and other parties. Instead, the dark side of customer management and CRM discussed in this chapter refers to the deliberate behaviours of service providers, often undertaken in the name of CRM, that take advantage of customers in unfair ways. As we suggest above, deliberate dark side service provider behaviour may result from malicious intentions or sometimes may occur through poor understanding of CRM. The result is service provider actions that deliberately set out to abuse and exploit customers.

We used two sources of data to identify a representative depiction of service provider dark side behaviours linked to CRM. Our principal source was a detailed literature review on the topics of CRM and relationship marketing, linking these search terms with the term 'dark side' as well as a number of terms relating to dark side behaviours. Working independently, the four authors identified key themes of dark side service provider behaviour from this literature and categorised them. A process of consensus was then used to consider and develop initial categories. The dark side behaviour identified reflected practices across a wide range of industry sectors. While this discussion is essentially a conceptual one, we supplemented this detailed literature review with insights drawn from an ongoing longitudinal study of CRM, which utilised an 'interaction research' (Gummesson, 2002) approach. This research included a day-long workshop with a panel of highly experienced CRM practitioners and a separate set of interviews with CRM, marketing and IT executives from the financial services sector.

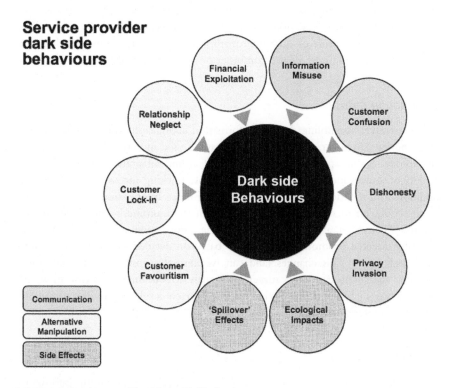

FIGURE 2.2 Service provider 'dark side' behaviours

The four researchers progressively discussed, extended and refined the initial categories until final consensus was reached on important forms of dark side behaviour. Figure 2.2 shows the main forms of dark side behaviour identified from our investigations. Given the almost unlimited possibilities of potential dark side activity, we do not claim this list is fully exhaustive. Rather, we seek to identify principal manifestations of dark side behaviours. The ten types of behaviour have been grouped in three broader categories based on the means used to produce and the target of the dark side behaviour. They are explained further in the following discussion.

Communication-based dark side behaviour

Information flows play an essential role in CRM systems and markets generally. As Alderson (1965, p. 30) commented: 'The heterogeneous market, it can be said to be cleared by information'. Information flows are the means by which buyers and sellers identify each other and evaluate alternative market offerings. They are also the means by which relationships are established and developed and implementation tasks are managed. Timely and reliable information flows help customers make better marketing decisions but poorly timed, confusing and biased information can distort decision making, leading to mismatches in the marketplace, dissatisfaction and misuse of resources. Various forms of dark side behaviour result when service providers hinder, distort or otherwise manipulate information flows for their own interests and against those of the consumer or other interested parties.

Information misuse

CRM involves assembling detailed information about customers in order to serve them better. However, this information may be used in ways of which customers disapprove. Service providers are able to collect and integrate information from a variety of sources including the web and in-store tracking and supplement this with additional information purchased from data brokers. Information about customers is often sold on to other firms to use without the customer's knowledge or permission (Turow et al., 2005). The resulting information provides the basis for carefully targeted promotional campaigns based on detailed knowledge of a customer's behaviour. This changes (and can weaken) the position of the consumer: 'because marketers can now survey and analyze consumer behavior in such a detailed way that they achieve what has been unachievable heretofore: turning the consumer's interior inside out' (Zwick and Dholakia, 2004, p. 31).

Customer confusion

This dark side behaviour refers to the use of misleading or confusing information and/or the hiding of relevant information from customers, which can encourage customers to make decisions that disadvantage them. For example, complex pricing alternatives generated by CRM systems can make comparisons among service providers very difficult (e.g. mobile phone services). Vulnerable groups such as the young, the elderly and the poor are particularly susceptible to this type of dark side behaviour (Sheth and Sisodia, 2006). Many consumers find it increasingly difficult to make reasonably well-informed decisions in today's complex market-place. Customers are presented with ever greater choice but the degree of actual differentiation has shrunk, making the return on any search and shopping beha-viour more marginal (Sheth and Sisodia, 2006). Another way of confusing the customer is through frequent price and rate changes such that the customer does not have enough time to adapt fully to the new tariffs.

Dishonesty

In addition to the practices outlined above (at least some of which could be described as dishonest), there are further categories of dark side behaviours that fall under the heading of dishonesty. For example, CRM systems frequently place pressure on staff to up-sell and cross-sell. Management pressure, CRM perfor-mance measurement systems and employee reward structures may result in custo-mers being sold products or services that they do not need. There are also instances of fraudulent activity. Car servicing firms charge for replacement parts and repairs not needed, and doctors charge for 'blanket' medical screening when it is not called for. Certain sectors, including bars and restaurants, are notorious for per-mitting staff illicitly to overcharge customers (Varzhabedian, 2007). Sale of products or services with known defects, or 'lemons' (Akerlof, 1970), is another example of such dark side behaviour.

Privacy invasion

Dark side behaviour can arise as a result of the flow of information from customers to service providers. Firms can access information about customers from many sources, not all of which customers are aware they are using, for example, trans-action records and observations of customer behaviour. This ready access to detailed information leads to complaints that providers can learn more about them than the customer wishes. For example, hotels keep records of clients' expenditure and may even check a guest's room and waste bins for clues as to customers' likes and dislikes (Jaipuria, 2006). This is done in the name of better serving the custo-mer in the future, but collecting information about such behaviour may exceed the information that some customers are comfortable with the provider knowing. Sensitive information could include personal details, such as whether pornographic movie channels were watched. The central issue here is that, in the pursuit of implementing CRM, firms may desire to develop closer relations with their customers than is agreed to or desired by the customer.

Dark side behaviour through manipulating alternatives

The second type of dark side behaviours concerns situations in which inferior products and/or services are deliberately provided to some customers or their choices are constrained or misdirected in some way. This may be done by restricting the alternatives available, offering the customer products and services with 'hidden' and unexpected costs and conditions, treating some customers more favourably than others, or ignoring the needs of some customers.

Customer favouritism

CRM involves segmenting customers based on characteristics of their buying behaviour and their economic attractiveness. High-priority customers are then offered additional and superior services. This can have adverse effects on customers who have not been prioritised and who observe the ways other customers are treated better, for example with priority service lines or dedicated personnel. When there are no obvious differences in pricing, yet groups are treated differently, there is the potential for dissent. Ramkumar and Saravanan (2007) identify a number of drawbacks to long-term relationship maintenance and preferential treatment to the most profitable customers. For example, CRM systems can punish loyal and highly valuable customers whose circumstances temporarily change. This could occur if an airline gold card holder, who travels overseas frequently on business, has a temporary in-country reassignment and is demoted to the bottom level of the airline's frequent flyer hierarchy by their CRM system.

Customer 'lock-in'

In order to retain customers, service providers can make it difficult and costly for customers to change service providers. Switching costs can arise naturally in a relationship as the parties get to know each other and invest in the relationship – but these are not dark side costs as they arise as a natural by-product of business transactions and represent relationship-specific assets that have value to those involved. However, customer 'lock-in' can be a manifestation of the dark side. Gummesson (1994) points to the 'hooking' of customers into captive relationships and punishing their escape with high switching costs. CRM predictive models can help identify where firms can profit from such behaviour. 'Price gouging' is a further example of dark side behaviour linked to consumer lock-in. This happens, for example, when a consumer commits to a service from a particular service provider and is forced to buy upgrades, repair services and replacement parts from the same provider at much higher prices than they might otherwise pay.

Relationship neglect

Anderson and Yap (2005) point to how seemingly good relationships can go bad and how close relationships, which seem stable, can also be vulnerable to decline and destruction. Researchers such as Moorman et al. (1992) and Grayson and Ambler (1999) point to the dark side of long-term relationships where service providers may lose their ability to be objective or become too stale to design and add further value, or where customers come to believe that the service provider may take advantage of the trust between the two parties and act opportunistically against the interests of the customer. This can be institutionalised in customer management and CRM where bad behaviour does not matter because long-time customers cannot leave (are locked in) or will not (customer inertia) and receive lesser quality of service as a result. A further source of relationship neglect is the 'corner-shop dilemma'. Small organisations, such as the corner shop, typically serve their customer base well. However, once a service provider's customer base reaches a certain size, it may invest heavily in CRM systems to improve its 'management' of customer relationships. Customers can become increasingly remote to such service providers, customer service and customer commitment may degenerate, and dark side behaviours occur as a result.

Financial exploitation

Another example of dark side behaviour is deliberate financial exploitation of customers and the use of unfair financial penalties as a source of revenue. For example, people returning rental cars who have failed to pay a road toll are charged a large fee for not paying the road toll, plus the toll, or when customers not making a payment on time are charged a disproportionate penalty. Often these penalties are buried in the 'small print' because service providers stand to make significant revenue from them (McGovern and Moon, 2007). In particular, the pensions industry has been home to dark side financial practices. This is highlighted by an example of a customer who purchased an 'adaptable pension plan' from a UK financial services company. The customer made payments into the pension plan of £3,227 and had 65% of his contributions deducted in the first two years (Kirby, 2004).

Side effects and dark side behaviour

So far we have focused on dark side behaviour that involves service providers deliberately manipulating market conditions, so as to advantage their firm, while disadvantaging the customer. However, customers and service providers are not the only ones affected by service providers' marketing behaviour. Customers are connected to other people and other firms and, more generally, market transactions take place in a society with particular norms and values and in a world with finite resources. The last forms of dark side instances we identify concern the negative impacts of product and service providers' dark side behaviour on third parties and the environment more generally.

'Spillover' effects

In both CRM and other marketing activity, a service provider's focus on certain targeted consumer groups can have undesirable 'spillover' effects on other groups, such as annoying or invasive promotion. For example, broadcast advertising targeted at particular consumer groups reaches non-targeted groups as well, becoming an unwanted intrusion. The rise of the Internet has led to new forms of communication and intrusion, including the pop-up ad and unsolicited email offering various unwanted services. These can become annoying, especially if you are not part of the intended target audience (Edwards et al., 2002). Spillovers can spread beyond customers, with the dark side practices directed towards customers impacting on other members of a service provider's network. For example, dissatisfied customers might retaliate and the impacts of such activity could spread throughout the firm's network, impacting on other service providers, distributors and industry bodies (Holmlund-Rytkönen and Strandvik, 2005).

Ecological impacts

Customer management and other marketing activity may have a negative impact on the environment. These activities include deliberate waste and pollution that firms may shift to other countries with more lax regulations. Another example is encouraging undesirable behaviour among particular groups in society, such as the consumption of high-sugar-content foods, tobacco and alcohol among the young. Encouraging poor dietary habits through the sale and promotion of junk food and confectionery is an example of this, perhaps not always unintended, that has resulted in high rates of obesity in the West (Lemon and Seiders, 2006). As is the case with 'spillover' effects, this is dark side behaviour when it knowingly exploits other groups, including those in other countries, customers acting in other roles and/or the planet.

Conclusions and solutions

In this chapter, we have considered the neglected area of dark side service provider practices, highlighting a key downside of poorly implemented relationship management and in particular CRM – the increased potential for exploitation of customers. We suggest that dark side behaviour may occur not only when suppliers are maliciously motivated to abuse customers, but also when they mistake customer exploitation for CRM. Here, suppliers may use CRM technology with the intention of extracting value from customers, misunderstanding that the overall aim of CRM is to achieve the strategic goals of the firm through enhanced customer relationships. The dark side manifestations outlined above represent an area that should be of great concern to service providers, consumers, policy makers and researchers.

These dark side behaviours often exist because, despite the word 'relationship' in its name, poorly practised CRM paradoxically often focuses on transactions rather than on building and maintaining relationships. This is reflected in Sheth and Sisodia's (2006, p. 3) characterisation of modern marketing practices: 'Instead of acting as partners engaged in mutually rewarding co-destiny relationships, too many marketers and consumers continue to be locked into mistrustful, adversarial relationships in which there is a constant tug-of-war to determine which side can benefit disproportionately and unfairly.'

We believe that many types of dark side behaviour can be addressed through a more enlightened and holistic approach to CRM. However, high levels of profitability and widespread prevalence of dark side practices do little to encourage service providers to address their use in a timely, socially responsible and ethical manner. Research on the dark side of customer management and CRM has been given little attention. In particular, researchers do not appear to have examined the long-term economic and customer impact of dark side activities. As there is little or no systematic evidence as to the scope of its impact, it is easier for service providers to ignore.

Figure 2.3 illustrates the way in which a holistic use of CRM processes can help guide service providers away from the 'dark side' and towards a more 'enlightened' practice of CRM. The five key strategic processes of CRM, proposed by Payne and Frow (2005, 2013) and discussed earlier, are used as a structure to consider how various dark side behaviours can be addressed. At the centre of this figure, more enlightened CRM strategy is shown to develop from addressing the ongoing cross-functional processes of strategy development; value creation; multi-channel integration and customer experience; information management; and performance

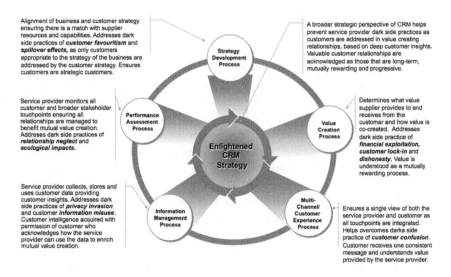

FIGURE 2.3 Addressing 'dark side' service provide practices – towards 'enlightened' CRM

assessment. The figure provides some examples of how successful implementation of each process can facilitate more effective CRM and militate against dark side practices.

Strategy development is the first process in the CRM strategy framework shown in Figure 2.3. At the heart of this process is the goal of matching the needs of the customer with the resources and capabilities of the service provider. Issues of customer favouritism and spillover effects are addressed. This process provides important inputs to the value creation process.

The value creation process determines the value the supplier provides and receives from the customer and how value is co-created (e.g. Prahalad, 2004). The focus in this process is on developing a mutually rewarding relationship. This process addresses dark side practices including financial exploitation, customer lock-in and dishonesty, as it is in both parties' interests (service provider and customer) to co-create a mutually beneficial exchange of value over the duration of the relationship.

The multi-channel/customer experience process seeks to ensure an integration of customer touchpoints and communication channels to give a single view of the service provider for the customer, and the customer for the service provider. The service provider aims to interact with the customer in the channels the customer prefers (for each type of activity), and to capture and utilise details of these customers' interactions in different channels. This process seeks to avoid customer confusion. The objective of this process is to provide a consistently superior customer experience.

The information management process refers to the service providers' collection, storage and use of customer information. Here there is the potential for dark side behaviour related to information use and customer communication – i.e. information misuse, customer confusion, dishonesty and privacy invasion. A strategic approach seeks to use information acquired, with the permission of the customer, to enhance mutual value creation. This involves seeking to have the same, or a better, memory of previous transactions as that held by the customer and to use this proactively during customer interactions to deliver high levels of service quality.

The final process, the performance assessment process, involves monitoring all relevant touchpoints to ensure all relationships are managed for mutual value creation. This includes assessing the firm's performance across a broader range of stakeholders than just customers. This process addresses issues of relationship neglect and ecological impacts on both customers and other relevant stakeholders.

We have included illustrations of each of the ten forms of dark side behaviour that can be addressed within specific CRM processes in Figure 2.3. However, some of these manifestations of dark side behaviour can also be addressed within more than one process. Each of these cross-functional processes interacts with the other processes. Collectively, as a consequence of adoption of a strategic and holistic approach, they have the potential to contribute to the recursive development of more enlightened CRM practices. We now conclude by considering how future academic research can contribute to a better understanding of overcoming dark side behaviour in customer management and CRM.

4 New research directions

The subject of dark side behaviour requires further research. Our review of the dark side of customer management and CRM has some limitations that also point to specific opportunities for further work.

First, our research has distinguished between the intended (dark side) and the unintended (poor or ineffective) consequences of customer management and CRM. We have focused primarily on intended consequences. The consequences of poor or ineffective practices versus dark side practices will often appear identical to customers who may react in similar ways, irrespective of the motives of the vendor. Future research should focus on the implications of different motivations, both in terms of customer response and in managing an organisation to achieve better CRM practice. For example, the poorly functioning CRM practitioner needs to develop managerial skills to improve implementing CRM, while dark side practitioners may already have excellent implementation skills, but require changes in strategic orientation, ethical values and/or in the culture of their organisation.

Second, the forms and classification scheme for dark side behaviours developed in this chapter may not be exhaustive. More systemic dark side behaviours may remain to be identified or may emerge in the future. Empirical research is needed to seek to identify any further forms of dark side behaviour and to test, and possibly extend, the proposed classification described in this chapter.

Third, we do not seek to identify how widespread these dark side practices are and their longer-term social and economic impacts. We suggest future research should identify the scope, scale and economic and social impact of dark side practices. Part of this work should consider the service provider addressing the broader ramifications of multiple stakeholders, including more generally connected third parties as well as societal impacts.

Fourth, there is a need to identify those industries where dark side practices are most prevalent. Sectors that have a high level of dark side practices need greater attention. We have cited literature that indicates industries in which the incidence of dark side practices appears to be greater and more widespread, but this is anecdotal and may relate only to obvious and high-profile cases.

Fifth, we have not fully considered the processes by which dark side practices emerge or the inter-relationships between them. Some causes include opportunism and greed but there are other possibilities. For example, we describe the practice of complex pricing. This may begin as a means to combat competitive activity, but can deteriorate into dark side abuses. Certain dark side activity may be driven by other underlying dark side behaviour. Deeper examination of dark side practices will allow comparison with the results of best practices in CRM and customer management, identification of deviation from them and potential remedy for dark side practices.

Finally, we propose that greater attention needs to be directed at making dark side practices more visible and vivid. Lakoff and Johnson (1980) and O'Malley and Tynan (1999) suggest the use of metaphors to further understanding and to illuminate and 'vivify' the subject under consideration. Given existing metaphors in relationship marketing, such as marriage, have lost their relevance (e.g. Tynan, 2008), we suggest new metaphors need to be identified that make dark side behaviour more vivid and visible. One such metaphor that we consider to have considerable promise is that of animal husbandry. Negligent practitioners of customer management often treat customers much as some farmers treat their animals – as property to provide benefit to them. The rearing, growing and even 'fleecing' of customers have interesting and discomforting parallels that are worthy of further examination.

In summary, we need more research that seeks to understand how service providers can avoid damaging dark side behaviour during their interactions with customers, and the dysfunctional economic, social and ethical consequences of dark side behaviour. Then we will be on our way to address further some of the negative outcomes of CRM that we have considered in this chapter.

5 Practising marketing – a case study: exploitation of customers

As large supermarkets diversify, for example by selling insurance, offering banking and legal services, in-store pharmacies, surgeries and post offices, their ability to collect and analyse consumer data to understand better their preferences and target them with personalised offers becomes more prevalent. These organisations are using advanced CRM systems to connect great amounts of data in different ways that will save them money and increase up- and cross-selling. However, at the same time the organisations risk intruding in the customer's privacy, health, finances or lifestyle choices.

For example, a Ryanair customer recently claimed on Twitter that, when he looked up a fare on a particular day, it was £123, but on the next day the fare had risen to £237. When he then 'flushed cookies' from his Internet browser, the fare returned to £123 (Shah, 2012).

Are retailers overstepping their mark and exploiting customers' trust by using their data for reasons other than those they disclose? Many customers expect companies and organisations to gather data, especially from their preferred suppliers, to target and reward them with services and products and to improve overall service levels with better relationships.

For example, former Tesco boss Philip Clarke admitted that the retailer uses Clubcard data to target consumers according to their wealth. On the Tesco website, relevant promotions are highlighted to the customer who is browsing the site. With Clubcard data, Tesco can show offers of the 'Everyday Value' range to price-sensitive customers, and offers of the 'Finest' range to more upmarket customers (Shah, 2012). In another example, Tesco was able to use Clubcard data to learn whether a customer would be more swayed by price or quality. They would then display the type of mattress that best reflected that shopper's characteristic. Sales grew by 10%.

However, at what point might the use of such tactics cross the line and be perceived as exploitation? Rumours have circulated of retailers gathering data about unhealthy eating, smoking or excessive alcohol consumption from a customer's purchases and using it to increase their insurance premiums (Shah, 2012). Other, perhaps fictional, stories include the customer who injured himself after slipping on a wet floor in a US supermarket. According to industry lore, he tried to sue the store only to be told that the company's records of his shopping habits suggested he was a heavy drinker and this was the real reason he had fallen over, the store claimed.

Examples are plentiful. A Whitehall unit called the 'Behavioural Insight Team' was in talks with supermarkets over using their databases of customers' shopping habits in a bid to improve the nation's health. They suggested that customers deemed to have 'unhealthy' shopping habits (in terms of food, alcohol or tobacco, etc.), might be contacted directly by the government in a form of social control via the checkout. Of course, the health secretary swiftly ruled out any government involvement, but perhaps only because ministers are thought to be wary of 'Big Brother' accusations (Shah, 2012). According to a recent *New York Times* article, the US retailer Target was found to have predicted a high school girl's pregnancy by analysing her shopping habits and, with the use of predictive analytics, identifying a pattern of products that are typically bought in early pregnancy. The retailer reportedly sent out coupons for other products that she might need for her new baby. The girl's father, meanwhile, was unaware of his daughter's situation (Duhigg, 2012; Shah, 2012).

While the use of such data in the UK is governed by the Data Protection Act, and the basic principle of the act is transparency and fairness, within the law retailers can alter their privacy policies as they like, which means that the onus rests on the customer to stay informed of the details. If a policy states that a company uses a customer's data across all of its operations, then consumers need to consider the implications of this. There is nothing to suggest they cannot do that, but then, do customers think this is fair?

Discussion questions

1. In each of the above examples, which seem fair to you, and which do not seem fair? Why/why not?
2. Which industries are more prone to experience exploitation than others?
3. Are there any other examples of consumer exploitation with which you have had experience? What happened?
4. There seems to be a paradox between the collection of more and more data to increase service levels and personalise offerings and offers, and the issues of crossing the line also increasing. What do consumers want and how might marketers solve this potential issue?
5. While some argue that customers are gaining more power in the markets due to increased transparency with peer ranking and testimonials, others claim that organisations are winning due to their advanced data systems. What are your views on this discussion?

6 Further investigation

1. What are the most prevalent instances of dark side behaviour in the following industry sectors and what should be done by companies to address them: telecommunications; Internet providers; utilities, e.g. electricity, gas and water supply; fast-moving consumer goods; professional services, e.g. legal services; healthcare services; insurance; banking; car sales; retail fast food services; department store retailing.

2. For a group project, participants can all focus on just one of these sectors, or each member of the group can select one of the sectors. Either a report or a presentation should be compiled, highlighting: the most prevalent instances of dark side behaviour; and what should be done to address them and avoid future occurrences.

3. For the company you work for/have recently worked for, or for a company with which you are very familiar, undertake a review of their CRM practices. Rate each of the ten potential dark side behaviours identified in this chapter on a 1–5 scale, where 0 = no evidence of this dark side behaviour, and 5 = strong evidence of this dark side behaviour. The behaviours are: information misuse; customer confusion; dishonesty; privacy invasion; customer favouritism; customer 'lock-in'; relationship neglect; financial exploitation; 'spillover' effects; and ecological impacts.

4. For each dark side behaviour that ranks between 2 and 5, identify: negative effects on the customer and company actions needed to address them; and negative effects on the firm and company actions needed to address them. Develop a practical action plan to address these negative effects on your selected company.

Note

1 This chapter is an updated reproduction of the following article: Pennie Frow, Adrian Payne, Ian F. Wilkinson, Louise Young (2011), Customer management and CRM: addressing the dark side, *Journal of Services Marketing*, 25(2), 79-89. Reproduced with permission from Emerald.

References

Akerlof, G.A. (1970). The market for "lemons": quality uncertainty and the market mechanism. *Quarterly Journal of Economics*, 84(3), pp. 488–500.
Alderson, W. (1965). *Dynamic Marketing Behaviour*. Irwin, Homewood, IL.
Anderson, E. and Yap, D.S. (2005). The dark side of close relationships. *MIT Sloan Management Review*, 46(3), pp. 75–82.
Caruana, A., Ramaseshan, B. and Ewing, M. (2001). Anomia and deviant behaviour in marketing: some preliminary evidence. *Journal of Managerial Psychology*, 16(5), pp. 322–338.
Christopher, M., Payne, A. and Ballantyne, D. (2002). *Relationship Marketing: Creating Stakeholder Value*. Butterworth-Heinemann, Oxford.
Columbo, L. (2013). Gartner predicts CRM will be a $36B market by 2017. www.forbes.com/sites/louiscolumbus/2013/06/18/gartner-predicts-crm-will-be-a-36b-market-by-2017/.

Duhigg, C. (2012). How companies learn your secrets. *The New York Times*, 16 February. www.nytimes.com/2012/02/19/magazine/shopping-habits.html?pagewanted=all&_r=0.

Edwards, S.M., Li, H. and Lee, J.H. (2002). Forced exposure and psychological reactance: antecedents and consequences of the perceived intrusiveness of pop-up advertising. *Journal of Advertising*, 31(3), pp. 83–95.

Fullerton, R. and Punj, G. (2003). Repercussions of promoting an ideology of consumption: consumer misbehaviour. *Journal of Business Research*, 57(11), pp. 1230–1249.

Grayson, K. and Ambler, T. (1999). The dark side of longterm relationships in marketing services. *Journal of Marketing Research*, 36, February, pp. 132–141.

Gummesson, E. (1994). Making relationship marketing operational. *International Journal of Science Industry Management*, 5(5), pp. 5–20.

Gummesson, E. (2002). Practical value of adequate marketing management theory. *European Journal of Marketing*, 36, March, pp. 325–349.

Gummesson, E. (2008). *Total Relationship Marketing*, 3rd edn. Butterworth Heinemann, Oxford.

Harris, L. and Ogbonna, E. (2002). Exploring service sabotage: the antecedents, types, and consequences of frontline, deviant, anti-service behaviours. *Journal of Service Research*, 4(3), pp. 163–183.

Harris, L. and Reynolds, K. (2003). The consequences of dysfunctional customer behaviour. *Journal of Services Research*, 6(2), pp. 144–161.

Harris, L. and Reynolds, K. (2004). Jaycustomer behaviour: an exploration of types and motives in the hospitality industry. *Journal of Services Marketing*, 18(5), pp. 339–357.

Holmlund-Rytkönen, M. and Strandvik, T. (2005). Stress in business relationships. *Journal of Business & Industrial Marketing*, 20(1), pp. 12–22.

Jaipuria, A. (2006). 'The dark side of customer relationship management in the luxury segment of the hotel industry'. MA dissertation, University of Nottingham.

Kim, H. and Kim, Y. (2008), A CRM performance measurement framework: its development process and application. *Industrial Marketing Management*, 38, pp. 477–489.

Kirby, S. (2004). My Allied Dunbar pension isn't very good. Multi-media complaint prepared by Simon Kirby for the Boards of Allied Dunbar and Zurich Financial Services.

Lakoff, G. and Johnson, M. (1980). *Metaphors we Live By*. University of Chicago, Chicago, IL.

Lemon, K.N. and Seiders, K. (2006). 'Making marketing accountable: a broader view'. In Sheth, J.N. and Sisodia, R.S. (Eds), *Does Marketing Need Reform?*M.E Sharpe, Armonk, NY, pp. 201–208.

Lovelock, C. (1994). *Product Plus: How Product + Service = Competitive Advantage*. McGraw-Hill, New York, NY.

McGovern, G. and Moon, Y. (2007). Companies and the customers who hate them. *Harvard Business Review*, June, pp. 78–84.

Mieritz, L. (2012). Survey shows why projects fail. Gartner Inc. http://my.gartner.com/portal/server.pt?open=512&objID=202&&PageID=5553&mode=2&in_hi_userid=2&cached=true&resId=2034616&ref=AnalystProfile.

Moorman, C., Zaltman, G. and Deshpande, R. (1992). Relationships between providers and users of market research: the dynamics of trust within and between organizations. *Journal of Marketing Research*, 29, August, pp. 314–328.

Nucleus Research (2012). *CRM: 80% of the returns are yet to be achieved*. Research Note M132, Nucleus Research Inc.

O'Malley, L. and Tynan, C. (1999). The utility of the relationship metaphor in consumer markets: a critical evaluation. *Journal of Marketing Management*, 15.

Payne, A. and Frow, P. (2005). A strategic framework for customer relationship management. *Journal of Marketing*, 69, October, pp. 167–176.

Payne, A. and Frow, P. (2013). *Strategic Customer Management: Integrating CRM and Relationship Marketing*. Cambridge University Press, Cambridge.

Prahalad, C.K. (2004). The co-creation of value. *Journal of Marketing*, 68(1), p. 23.

Ramkumar, D. and Saravanan, S. (2007). The dark side of relationship marketing. Conference Proceedings of the International Conference on Marketing and Society, Part VI Consumer Markets & Marketing, Indian Institute of Management, Kozhikode, pp. 453–457. http://dspace.iimk.ac.in/handle/2259/340 (accessed 20 March 2009).

Reynolds, K. and Harris, L. (2006). Deviant customer behaviour: an exploration of frontline employee tactics. *Journal of Marketing Theory and Practice*, 14(3), pp. 95–111.

Shah, S. (2012). How Tesco and co are testing the limits of customer data exploitation. *Computing* (4 July). www.computing.co.uk/ctg/feature/2188626/tesco-testing-limits-customer-exploitation.

Sheth, J.N. and Sisodia, R.S. (2006). *'Marketing's final frontier: the automation of consumption'*. In J.N. Sheth and R.S. Sisodia (Eds), *Does Marketing Need Reform?*, M.E Sharpe, Armonk, NY, pp. 180–190.

Shukla, P. (2010). 'Relationship marketing and CRM'. In H. Bidgoli (Ed.) *The Handbook of Technology Management, Volume 2: Supply Chain Management, Marketing and Advertising, and Global Management.* Wiley, pp. 462–472.

Turow, J., Feldman, L. and Meltzer, K. (2005). *Open to Exploitation: American Shoppers Online and Offline.* Annenberg Public Policy Center, University of Pennsylvania, Philadelphia, PA.

Tynan, A.C. (2008). 'Metaphors and marketing: some uses and abuses'. In P.J. Kitchen (Ed.) *Marketing Metaphors and Metamorphosis.* Palgrave Macmillan, Basingstoke.

Varzhabedian, R. (2007). *Status Quo.* Wheatmark, Tucson, AZ.

Zwick, D. and Dholakia, N. (2004). Whose identity is it anyway? Consumer representation in the age of database marketing. *Journal of Macromarketing*, 24(1), pp. 31–43.

Further reading

Ambler, T. (2007). Call centres, CRM and cows: why modern service marketing is not like cattle farming'. *Market Leader*, 39, Winter, pp. 33–37.

Fisk, R., Grove, S., Harris, L.C., Keeffe, D.A., Daunt, K.L., Russell-Bennett, K. and Wirtz, J. (2010). Customers behaving badly: a state of the art review, research agenda and implications for practitioners. *Journal of Service Marketing*, 24(6), pp. 417–429.

Friend, L.A., Costley, C.L. and Brown, C. (2010). Spirals of distrust vs. spirals of trust in retail customer service: consumers as victims or allies. *Journal of Service Marketing*, 24(6), pp. 458–467.

Grönroos, C. (2009). 'Relationship marketing as promise management'. In P.M. MacLaran, M. Saren, B. Stern and M. Tadajewski (Eds) *The Sage Handbook of Marketing Theory*, pp. 397–412. Sage, Los Angeles, CA.

Homburg, C. and Fürst, A. (2007). See no evil, hear no evil, speak no evil: a study of defensive organizational behavior towards customer complaints. *Journal of the Academy of Marketing Science*, 3(4), pp. 523–536.

Nguyen, B. and Simkin, L. (2013). The dark side of CRM: advantaged and disadvantaged customers. *Journal of Consumer Marketing*, 30(1), pp. 17–30.

Reibstein, D.J., Day, G. and Wind, J. (2009). Is marketing losing its way? *Journal of Marketing*, 73 (4), pp. 1–3.

Steinle, C., Schiele, H. and Ernst, T. (2014). Information asymmetries as antecedents of opportunism in buyer-supplier relationships: testing Principal-Agent Theory. *Journal of Business-to-Business Marketing*, 21(2), pp. 123–140.

3

PERCEPTIONS OF FAIRNESS AND UNFAIRNESS

Lan Xia

1 Introduction

In 1999, Coca-Cola announced a smart vending machine that would raise the price when the weather was hot. Following negative feedback from the public, the company was forced to give up the idea and issue a public statement that the machine would not be introduced (at least in the US market).

In September 2000, an Amazon.com customer deleted the cookies on his computer and found that the price of a DVD he had just bought for US$26.24 had dropped to $22.74. As more customers discovered the price discrepancy, they were outraged. Amazon claimed that it was a random price test. Pressured by negative publicity, they apologised, refunded the price difference and promised not to repeat their mistake.

In September 2007, the iPhone price dropped by $200 66 days after its launch, leaving many new owners seething. In response to a flood of complaints, Apple's CEO apologised and offered $100 in-store credit to all customers who had bought the iPhone before the price slash.

More recently, *The Wall Street Journal* reported that Orbitz showed Mac users costlier hotels than Windows visitors see. Consequently, Apple users spent as much as 30% more a night on hotels (Mattioli, 2012). Even though the site did not change the prices of the hotels per se, the cry of unfairness was still loud.

These pricing practices are not illegal, but to many consumers they feel wrong. Perception of unfairness is the critical issue in all these incidents. So, what makes a price difference fair or unfair? What makes a price fair or unfair? Is it the price differences among the hotels listed, although the individual hotels offer the same prices to everyone? Or are consumers offended by being labelled as a 'Mac user' or a 'Windows user'? Or is it that the manipulation constrains consumers' choices? The issue does involve price, but it is not only about money.

The cry of unfairness is common in the marketplace and has been shown both to constrain firms' pursuit of profit and to damage customer relationships (Kahneman et al., 1986b; Xia et al., 2004). Pricing is a marketing element that can easily provoke such cries.

In this chapter, we will review major theories in the field, examine sources of such perceptions as well as consequences when perceptions of unfairness arise in the context of customer relationship management (CRM). Implications for management and practices to minimise perceptions of unfairness and subsequent damages will also be discussed.

Learning objectives

When you have read the chapter, you should be able to:

1.   Discuss the background to pricing strategies and subsequent perceptions of fairness and unfairness.
2.   Identify the source of unfairness perceptions in various scenarios.
3.   Anticipate the consequences of differential pricing strategies for CRM.
4.   Develop a plan to minimise perceptions of unfairness and associated damage to the relationship between the customer and the firm.

2 Route map: perceptions of fairness and unfairness

Price fairness is defined as a consumer's assessment of whether the difference (or lack of difference) between a seller's price and that of a comparable other party is reasonable, acceptable or justifiable (Bolton et al., 2003; Xia et al., 2004). Conceptually, fairness and unfairness are different. Xia et al. (2004) specified several unique features of the concept of unfairness. First, our notions of unfairness are typically clearer, sharper and more concrete than those of fairness. Consumers tend not to evaluate a price as fair voluntarily, but they recognise it and cry out loud when it is unfair. We know what is unfair when we see it, but it is difficult to articulate what is fair (Finkel, 2001). Second, perceptions of unfairness are formed based on comparisons. Consumers would either implicitly or explicitly compare the price they get with that of another consumer, another seller or a past price they had been offered. Third, although unfairness judgement is rooted in equity, consumer judgement of fairness is biased by self-interest, which means that, given an equivalent magnitude of price inequality, consumers will perceive a smaller degree of perceived unfairness when the inequality is to their advantage than when it is to the other's advantage (Ordonez et al., 2000; Xia and Monroe, 2010). Finally, although cognitively defined, a perception of unfairness is usually accompanied by negative emotions such as disappointment and anger.

Why does fairness matter? From the incidents in which unfairness occurred, such as the Amazon or Coca-Cola cases, we can glimpse the consequences of the perception of unfairness. In general, perceptions of unfairness induce dissatisfaction (Herrmann et al., 2007; Van den Bos et al., 1998) and constrain firms' ability to maximise their profit when customers with a grudge leave the relationship and/or seek retribution through negative word-of-mouth or revenge (e.g. Campbell, 1999; Kahneman et al., 1994).

Negative affect is an integral part of the perception of unfairness (Xia et al., 2004). Various negative emotions associated with these perceptions include, most commonly, anger and hostility. These emotions are evoked when customers attribute the responsibility to the seller and are considered outward emotions (Barclay et al., 2005). Perceptions of unfairness coupled with strong outward negative emotions lead to behaviours intended not only to restore financial equity but also to vent negative emotions, reinforce relationship norms, rebuild self-concept and damage the seller. These behaviours may include complaints, switching, negative word-of-mouth and/or boycott of the seller's product or service.

Given the potential damage of the perceptions of unfairness on customer relationships and firms' profitability, it is important to understand how consumers form these perceptions and the sources of perceptions of unfairness.

3 State of the art in research on unfairness

What makes a price fair or unfair? Over the years, researchers have developed and adapted various theories in an attempt to understand when and how buyers form judgements that price is unfair. We briefly review them here.

Dual entitlement

The dual entitlement principle emphasises the influence of supply-demand changes and a seller's profit orientation (Kahneman et al., 1986c). The principle of dual entitlement suggests that price increases designed to cover costs and maintain sellers' profits should be considered fair, while those aimed at boosting profit by taking advantage of higher demand are not (Kahneman et al., 1986a). Hence, it is fair to increase the price of lettuce due to shortage in supply associated with a natural disaster, but it is not fair to increase the price of a snow shovel after a snowstorm.

Equity theory and attribution theory

Equity theory emphasises the importance of equality of input and output ratios between two parties in an exchange (Adams, 1965; Homans, 1961). Equity theory argues that individuals are entitled to receive a reward that is proportional to what they have invested in the relationship (Homans, 1961). For example, a seller's cost could be considered his/her input, and a buyer's money outlay could be considered his/her input. However, not all costs are the same in consumers' eyes. Legitimate cost increases typically refer to those that are caused by factors external to the firm (Aggarwal and Vaidyanathan, 2003). Attribution theory adds that, when price deviates from (i.e. is higher than) one's expectation, people tend to make external attributions. If a cost increase is due to the seller's own deficiency, people consider it unfair to shift the cost increase to consumers. Equity theory also broadens the concept of the comparative other to include not only the seller but also another customer, a group of customers, or the buyer himself relative to his experiences from an earlier point in time (Jacoby, 1976). The reference selected for comparison plays a crucial role in forming perceptions of unfairness.

Justice theory

Judgement of fairness is typically concerned with price (i.e. an outcome), although the reasons behind the unfair outcome influence the judgement. Justice theory, however, explicitly separates justice into distributive justice, procedural justice and interactional justice. While distributive justice concerns an individual's perception of resource allocation or the outcome of an exchange, procedural justice focuses on the influence of the procedures or means used to determine the outcomes on perceptions of fairness (Thibaut and Walker, 1975). Procedural justice relates to the processes, methods and rules used to derive outcomes (Lind and Tyler, 1988), and it affects the attribution process to some extent. Given a price inequality (i.e. outcome), the process or reasons behind such price inequity may significantly influence the formation or adjustment of a judgement of unfairness. For example, perceived firm motives in determining prices have been found to be very influential in determining customers' perceptions of fairness (e.g. Campbell, 1999).

Interactional justice refers to fairness in the exchange of information and communication of outcomes. Interactional justice focuses on the two-way flow between customers and marketers, including the manner in which the customer is treated in terms of respect, interest, friendliness, honesty and politeness. Interactional justice adds yet another layer of information to a transaction and further emphasises the relational nature of the transaction and the psychological inferences the consumer makes.

A comprehensive conceptual framework

While all the theories above have been reasonably successful in explaining and predicting perceptions of unfairness, each theory has its own focus. The dual entitlement principle and equity theory focus on analysis of costs and social norms, while attribution and social justice theory focus on individuals' psychological experiences and inferences. Xia et al. (2004) presented a conceptual framework for price fairness that integrates these conceptualisations and organises existing price fairness research. They identified four groups of factors influencing perceptions of fairness. At the transaction level – when perceived price discrepancies occur – the degree of similarity between the transactions is an important element of judgements of price fairness. Haws and Bearden (2006) showed that, with the same price differential, transaction characteristics vary by purchase situation (seller, consumer, time, price setter), and they all influence perceptions of unfairness. A judgement of fairness depends on the comparative parties involved in the transactions. Of all comparable parties, another customer has the greatest impact on perceptions of fairness, not only for disadvantaged price inequity (Haws and Bearden, 2006), but also for advantaged inequity (Xia and Monroe, 2010).

Information that provides reasons why a certain price is set may influence perceptions of price fairness through attributions and various inferences. Consistent with the dual entitlement principle and justice theory, consumers consider whether those reasons can legitimately justify the price change or price differential (Bolton et al., 2003; Kahneman et al., 1986b). Finally, consumers may also rely on their general knowledge or beliefs about sellers' practices to adjust their judgements of price fairness. For example, Wirtz and Kimes (2007) showed that familiarity with the business practice moderated perceptions of unfairness.

Unfairness in customer relationship management

Earlier theoretical conceptualisations of unfairness mostly focus on a one-shot transaction between the buyer and the seller, and examine the influence of social norms, seller costs and responsibilities, while more recent research has attempted to broaden the scope by incorporating different references of comparison and examining psychological in addition to economic sources of unfairness (Lind and Van den Bos, 2002; Xia et al., 2004). Although perceptions of unfairness have been extensively researched in social psychology, very little research has specifically examined issues of unfairness in CRM.

In the context of CRM, perception of unfairness reveals a more complex picture. First, while social comparison processes are central to most theories of justice and outcome satisfaction (Major and Testa, 1989), the 'social' aspect manifests most in the context of CRM. Factors characterising a relationship – such as loyalty and relationship strength, trust in a relationship, and different types of relationships and the norms associated with them – are all potential factors that may influence consumers' perceptions of unfairness when they are confronted with discrepancies in price. In addition, the relationship to be managed includes not only that between the buyer and the seller, but also that between the buyer and other buyers. As consumers have adopted various social media and new technology, they are increasingly influenced by what others do and get, adding to the complexity of perceptions of unfairness.

The buyer–seller relationship and perceptions of unfairness

In CRM, what is to be managed is the long-term relationship, which is developed through multiple transactions. Consumers' perceptions of price fairness in one transaction are influenced by the relationship built and developed based on previous transactions. Relationship stage, strength, as well as type may all moderate the effect of price differentials on perceptions of unfairness.

First, relationships vary in duration. Some customers are new to the seller, while others are long-term loyal customers. It is a common practice for firms to vary prices among customers with different loyalty status. For example, airlines set up different tiers of frequent flyer membership and give customers in different tiers different privileges and prices. On the other hand, telecommunications companies tend to offer better deals to new customers to encourage them to switch from another company. Research has shown that consumers' loyalty status influences their reaction to price differentials. An existing relationship primes customers' expectations of a commensurate level of benefits. Loyal customers perceive certain relationship benefits (e.g. confidence, social and special treatment) and are willing to endure obstacles to maintain these benefits (Gwinner et al., 1998). Their orientation is more long term, and they would try to some extent to maintain the relationship by forgoing their own interests (Gilliland and Bello, 2002). Martin, Ponder and Lueg (2009) showed that loyalty has a positive effect on perceptions of fairness at least when price increases are low. However, loyal customers may have higher expectations of benefits as reciprocation for their loyalty; hence, they may react more strongly to harsh price increases. For example, frequent customers tend to perceive a price as more unfair than less frequent customers when high price inequity occurs.

Related to loyalty status, experiences from previous consumption episodes also influence reactions to price increases in the subsequent consumption episodes. For example, Homburg et al. (2005) identified the moderating effect of customer satisfaction with previous consumption experience. Satisfaction moderates the negative effect of a price increase in that satisfied customers are more likely to infer positive motives of the seller, which mitigates perceptions of unfairness. The effects are consistent with most of the fairness theories such as equity theory, except that the assessments of input, output and equity are based on accumulated experiences over a long period of time rather than a one-time transaction.

Second, trust is a central element in a relationship, which takes different forms in different relationship stages. Perception of whether a price offer is fair is also influenced by the nature of the trust and stage of the relationship (Xia et al., 2004). According to Lewicki and Bunker (1995), at an early stage of a buyer–seller relationship the two parties are regulated by the potential benefits of doing what they promised and/or the costs of cheating. *Calculus-based trust* is thus developed. Over repeated interactions, the two parties begin to know each other and can anticipate and predict what the other party should and will do in certain circumstances. *Knowledge-based trust* is developed. Finally, when the relationship is fully developed, the two parties have a clear understanding of each other's desires and intentions and will act accordingly. They are confident that their interests will be fully protected by the other party. Hence, *identification-based trust* is developed.

Xia et al. (2004) suggest that the nature of trust and its influence on perceptions of price fairness are associated with the specific stage of a buyer–seller relationship. For new customers, calculus-based trust is more salient; calculated cost/benefit may have a greater influence on fairness perceptions. As the relationship develops, the emphasis is placed more on the benevolence dimension. The buyer is more likely to take the seller's actions 'personally' and make additional inferences. When the price is as expected or lower, the buyer may attribute it to a benefit of the relationship. However, when the price is higher than the reference, they may judge that the seller has betrayed their good relationship (Sirdeshmukh et al., 2002), leading to a perception of a more unfair price. Huppertz, Arenson and Evans (1978) found that, when perceived price and service inequity were high, buyers judged the situation as less fair when they had a close and frequent exchange relationship with the seller than when the buyer–seller exchanges were infrequent. Similarly, Grewal, Hardesty and Iyer (2004) showed that price advantage provided to existing customers was perceived as fairer than that provided to new customers. Overall, research consistently showed that a stronger relationship has a polarising effect. The influence of trust on perceptions of price fairness depends on the direction of the inequality as well as the nature of the trust, which varies depending on the stage of the buyer–seller relationship.

Third, the type of relationship also matters. Clark and Mills distinguish between exchange and communal relationships (Clark and Mills, 1979; Mills and Clark, 1982). Exchange relationships are primarily based on economic factors. They provide benefits and lead to the expectation of a comparable benefit in return. On the other hand, in communal relationships, people give benefits to others out of concern and care. Strangers and people who interact for mere business purposes typically form exchange relationships, while family relationships and friendships tend to be communal. Relationship type does not necessarily signal relationship length or strength. A long-term relationship can be either transactional or communal. For example, a customer can be a loyal customer to Walmart or Apple, but the nature of the customer–company relationship could vary. The customer could have a more transaction-oriented relationship with Walmart and a more communal relationship with Apple. Using a brand relationship context, Aggarwal and Larrick (2012) showed that consumers in communal and exchange relationships are sensitive to different aspects of fairness. When a customer is faced with an unfair outcome, the presence of interactional fairness has a larger cushioning effect in a communal than in a transactional relationship. However, facing a favourable outcome, the pattern is reversed.

Overall, in the context of relationship management, theoretical and empirical research point out that, when price differentials occur, whether and to what degree they lead to perceptions of unfairness depend on the stage and strength of the relationship as well as the type of relationship developed over time in addition to degree of price variation. Consumers make various inferences based on these factors. They infer how firms value their relationships and whether the firms comply with relationship norms.

The dynamics between customers and customers

CRM is social in nature, and social comparisons are closely related to fairness judgements (Austin et al., 1980). While the centre of CRM is the relationship between the provider and the customer, the actual relationships to be managed go beyond and can include those between different customers or customer segments. While a comparable other party could be another seller, one's past experience or another customer, social comparison theory has identified 'similar others' as the most important comparative reference due to its salience (Major, 1994; Wood, 1989). When multiple comparative others are available, others similar to the self are more likely to be chosen as the comparative other party over intrapersonal (self/self) comparisons. Research shows that social comparisons (i.e. comparisons with others) explain more variance in satisfaction than an individual's expected outcomes (Major and Testa, 1989).

Xia et al. (2004) suggest that, given the same transaction characteristics, comparison with other customers produces a larger effect on feelings of entitlement and will have the largest effect on perceived price unfairness (Major and Testa, 1989). The proposition has been supported by empirical tests (Campbell, 2007; Haws and Bearden, 2006). Given a price discrepancy, a comparison with a similar other customer led to the highest perceptions of unfairness (Haws and Bearden, 2006; Xia and Monroe, 2004b), even for advantaged inequity (Xia and Monroe, 2010). A higher price communicated by the store salespeople is perceived as more unfair than the same price printed on a price tag (Campbell, 2007). In online segmented pricing, tactics based on buyer identification are perceived as more unfair than those based on purchase timing (Grewal et al., 2004).

On the other hand, when there was no price discrepancy, a comparison with a similar other customer led to the highest perceptions of fairness relative to the self/self comparison (Xia and Monroe, 2004b). Furthermore, while perceptions of unfairness mostly stem from being disadvantaged (Xia et al., 2004), when the comparative reference is another customer, research showed that being advantaged actually also led to perceptions of unfairness. Xia and Monroe (2010) distinguish preference for a good deal and a fair price. They show that when a customer is explicitly advantaged over another customer, although perceived value is higher than the equity condition, consumers actually perceive that explicit advantage as unfair. Jiang et al. (2013) demonstrated the same effect in the context of preferential treatment. They showed that unearned preferential treatment, such as receiving a surprise discount or getting a free upgrade, is not always perceived as fair, although it generates positive reactions. When other customers are present, the positive feelings of obtaining an advantage are accompanied by feelings of social discomfort due to concerns about negative judgement by others. These feelings of discomfort can reduce satisfaction with a shopping experience and affect purchasing behaviours in certain conditions.

With technological development and consumer adoption of various social media, the opportunity for such peer comparison is ever increasing. How is consumer–consumer comparison different from other types of comparison? More recent research has begun to pinpoint the mechanisms behind such comparisons. Ashworth and McShane (2012) suggest that firms charging customers different prices not only produce inequitable outcomes, but also lead consumers to infer firms' opinions of them. Customers paying more perceive that they are not respected by the firm. The price inequity exacerbates the perception of unfairness, as they may feel what they deserve has been violated. This intention could be inferred even when there is no evidence of the accuracy of this perception. In addition, consumers also make inferences that reflect their self-concept – e.g. Am I incompetent? Am I inferior to others? Such inferences are evidently based on research that showed that perceptions of unfairness are also influenced by the relationship between the consumers. For example, Bolton et al. (2010) found that, for Chinese consumers, paying a higher price compared with a friend (vs. a stranger) evokes a stronger perception of unfairness because they experience a greater loss of face. Peters and Van den Bos (2008) showed that, when the reference has a communal relationship with the focal customer, they are more satisfied with being underpaid and less satisfied with being overpaid compared with the same situations when their interaction partners are unknown others.

Overall, what makes it unfair – and why?

While perceptions of price unfairness typically stem from an unexpected price change, actual perceptions of fairness are formed in the context of a transaction within a relationship that is influenced by a variety of social inferences and perceptions. The research studies discussed above reveal four major sources of perceptions of unfairness.

First, perceptions of fairness are closely related to perceptions of value. Thaler (1985) defined a fair price as a good price (i.e. transaction value). A price offer that is higher than expected or higher than a comparative reference is associated with perceived higher sacrifice; hence, this decreases perceived value (Martins and Monroe, 1994). The strength of the perception of unfairness is highly associated with the level of price disadvantage. Although a price offer that is lower than a comparable reference may also be considered unfair, the effect is much smaller compared with when the consumer personally experiences a price disadvantage (Xia and Monroe, 2010).

While perceptions of value provide the financial basis for perceptions of unfairness, the non-financial basis for perceptions of unfairness is equally important. First, consumers search for information and make inferences about whether the seller breaks social norms. For example, the dual entitlement principle posits that sellers are entitled to their profit and it is fair to increase prices when costs increase but not to reduce prices when costs fall (Kahneman et al., 1994). Violation of this expectation (e.g. increased price of a shovel after a snowstorm) leads to perceptions of unfairness. Second, prices are set for two parties within a relationship. Consumers look for information regarding the procedure that leads to the price and the manner in which the seller interacts with them. Whether consumers feel they are respected and whether the seller values their relationship confirms or disconfirms their relational identity, further influencing perceptions of fairness. Finally, a comparison with another customer incentivises consumers to search for information regarding their personal identity. Inequity says something about how they stand relative to their peers. When the inequity is interpreted as a threat to personal identity, it will further negatively influence perceived relational identity with the seller and exacerbate perceptions of unfairness.

Overall, both financial and non-financial sources contribute to perceptions of unfairness. While it is easier to understand that consumers perceive an offer as unfair when they are financially disadvantaged, relative to the comparative reference, reasons other than the financial aspect are equally important, especially in the context of CRM. Consumers will make inferences regarding the seller's moral identity, their relationship identity with the seller, as well as their own personal identity. Hence, fairness is not only business, but is also very personal.

Managerial implications of perceptions of unfairness in CRM

Segmentation and targeting are fundamental to marketing and CRS is based on customisation and personalisation. It automatically implies that one price does not fit all and customised price is the way to go. However, price differentials can easily evoke perceptions of unfairness. While value-based pricing has been shown to be profitable to the firm and may also benefit customers, the potential impact on perceptions of unfairness should be carefully thought through.

First, although perceived value is closely related to consumer willingness to pay, segmentation should not be driven solely by customer willingness to pay. Price differentials should be a natural by-product of different values delivered. Price should be a quality cue instead of a vehicle of taking advantage. Focusing on values provided will help to switch consumers' attention away from price. Value is multi-dimensional and is embedded not only in price, but also in what is provided, where and how it is provided, and how it is communicated. As Xia et al. (2004) suggest, product differentiation is a dominant factor in decreasing transaction similarity and tendency to compare prices. Companies should leverage multiple marketing stimuli together with price to satisfy customers with the best value delivered.

Second, consumers care about what others get (Feinberg et al., 2002) and have a natural tendency to compare. Either a (price) disadvantage or advantage may lead to perceptions of unfairness. Therefore, carefully setting up price screens will help to minimise social comparison and reduce perceptions of unfairness. A screen does not mean to hide the price differences and keep consumers in the dark about what others get, which is impossible anyway. The price screen has to be built carefully into the segmentation process. Social comparison research has reported a similarity bias, demonstrating that people tend to pay attention to the similarity between the two parties or entities being compared. Observable similarities between the two comparison entities induce people to access information selectively supporting these similarities, leading to an assimilation effect (Mussweiler, 2003). Such an assimilation effect enhances the saliency of the outcome differences, leading to a strong feeling of entitlement (Major, 1994; Major and Testa, 1989). The assimilation effect leads consumers to expect or feel they are entitled to equal prices, and the price discrepancy likely will be judged as unfair. However, when the dissimilarity between the two entities is obvious, people will selectively access information supporting these dissimilarities, leading to a contrast effect (Mussweiler, 2003). Such a contrast effect leads to judgements that the comparative transactions or parties are not similar, offering a natural explanation for the perceived price differences. Therefore, customer segments should be accompanied with clear profiles that are sufficiently distinctive, delineating the characteristics of each segment. The dissimilarities will help to form the screens that reduce the propensity to compare.

Third, providing a certain degree of control to consumers helps to reduce perceptions of unfairness. Price differentials do not naturally lead to perceptions of unfairness. Transaction characteristics such as how prices are presented make a significant difference in perceptions. For example, Haws and Bearden (2006) found that, for the same price disadvantage, consumers perceive the price as more unfair if it is given/posted, rather than if they discover it on their own through bidding. Campbell (2007) showed that the same higher prices are perceived to be more unfair when communicated by the sales associate than when consumers discover them on a price tag themselves. Companies can reduce the potential for perceptions of unfairness by offering different price options, having customers customise their own prices and delivering price increases in a less personal way.

Fourth, CRM is about long-term relationships. Carefully building and managing customer expectations from the relationships not only help to design price variations that are less likely to be perceived as unfair, but also minimise the impact when illegitimate price variations occur. Consumers make different inferences based on the relationship. Procedural fairness has been analysed as a relational construct – that is, as a signal of the social bonds between individuals and the groups they belong to. It conveys feelings of individual self-esteem and self-respect (Koper et al., 1993; Lind and Tyler, 1988). Therefore, in designing the price structure and prices, it is important to pay attention to procedural fairness. Making the price structure transparent and information regarding price differentials accessible will help.

Fifth, a crucial element in a relationship is trust. Trust and fairness influence each other. On one hand, trust influences perceptions of fairness. Consumers tend to give firms the benefit of the doubt and are less likely to infer a disadvantaged price as unfair when trust is high because they are more confident that the price-setting procedure is fair. They focus on the future and are not too concerned with current favourability (Brockner, 2002). On the other hand, fairness (especially procedural and interactional fairness) can help to build trust in the long run. Whether the procedure is fair influences consumers' judgement of whether the seller is trustworthy, especially when consumers are facing uncertainties (Lind and Van den Bos, 2002). Perceptions of greater fairness lead people to be more trusting of the other party, which, in turn, satisfies their social/psychological needs for esteem, identity and affiliation (Blodgett et al., 1997).

Sixth, providing an appropriate amount of price-setting information with price differentials is important to guide inferences. Consumers make inferences and further form judgements of fairness based on these. When no information is provided, the default is a negative motive on the part of the seller, especially when a strong relationship does not exist. Thus, providing information related to price offerings lends prices more transparency, hence reducing the chances of evoking perceptions of unfairness. For example, consumers prefer partitioned price in addition to the total due to their clarity and transparency (Xia and Monroe, 2004a). Presumably, this tactic will also enhance perceptions of fairness (Carlson and Weathers, 2008). In addition, providing appropriate information is also a good tactic that helps prevent consumers from taking price differentials personally. However, sellers should be cautious in using this tactic. While price partitioning offers clarity and transparency, it also adds to processing load. When transparency becomes complexity, price partitioning may actually decrease perceptions of fairness (Carlson and Weathers, 2008; Homburg et al., 2013).

Finally, while it is important to prevent perceptions of unfairness in the first place, it is equally important to mend a relationship when transgressions occur. The different role of distributive, procedural and interactional fairness offers implications for minimising the consequences of perceptions of unfairness, especially for different types of relationships. Research showed that, while the three elements of fairness are highly linked and jointly influence satisfaction with service recovery, interactional fairness has the largest impact (Blodgett et al., 1997). Therefore, successful service recovery may require appropriate financial compensation according to a procedure that gives consumers voice and control, as well as courtesy and helpfulness from service employees during the interaction.

4 New research directions

As the review of literature and the above discussion suggested, perceptions of unfairness can originate from various sources. Each of these sources warrants further research, to provide us with a better understanding of unfairness. First, perceptions of unfairness could be due to perceptions of inadequate value offered. Dual entitlement principle provided the general idea that the nature of vendors' costs influences value and unfairness perceptions. Research has investigated the effect of different types of costs (Bolton et al., 2003), as well as different costs associated with goods versus services (Bolton and Alba, 2006). Future research could further investigate the effect of different types of costs in different industries. For example, the Internet typically decreases variable costs of doing business, although fixed costs could be substantial. However, variable costs are more tangible and consumers may associate fairness more with variable costs while being reluctant to pay for fixed costs. Companies' investment in corporate social responsibility (CSR) is on the rise. While CSR investment may elicit a positive attitude towards the company, some companies have customers shoulder all or part of the costs through increased prices of products or services. It is for a good cause and companies do not necessarily profit from it, but do consumers perceive this as fair? These issues could be further investigated.

Second, research has shown that perceptions of unfairness are based on price comparisons. The selection of the reference transaction is crucial in the formation of this perception (Xia et al., 2004). One particular reference that warrants further research is other customers, which puts unfairness in the context of social comparison. Perceptions of unfairness are also very personal, helping individuals to assess whether they are respected by their relational partners and how they stand relative to their peers. Both the choice of the comparative reference and response to the comparison could be culturally rooted. For example, Bolton et al. (2010) examined how consumers in China and the United States perceive the fairness of charging different prices for identical goods. They found that the Chinese are more sensitive to the type of social comparison and judge it unfair to pay a higher price than a friend, but are indifferent to the price paid by a stranger, while US consumers are insensitive to this distinction. The authors attributed this difference to the collectivism versus individualism culture and the concern for 'face' of the Chinese. In more recent research, Jin et al. (2014) showed that high-power consumers perceive stronger price unfairness when paying more than other consumers do, whereas low-power consumers perceive stronger unfairness when paying more than they themselves paid in previous transactions. The distinction occurs because consumers experience a threat to their self-importance from different types of disadvantaged comparisons, depending on their power states. Such research provides new insights in understanding why consumers perceive prices as being unfair under certain conditions. Future research should continue in this direction and explore how cultural factors, different social norms and individual consumer characteristics influence their perceptions of unfairness and why consumers pick one reference over another in price comparisons.

Finally, as companies strive to foster and build life-long relationships with their customers, perceptions of unfairness may influence as well as be influenced by the nature of the relationship. While Xia et al. (2004) outlined the potential influences of different relationship stages and the role of trust on perceptions of unfairness, not much research has empirically examined the effects. Limited research seems to suggest that relationship norms do influence perceptions of unfairness. For example, in a working paper, Chen et al. (2014) tested the dual entitlement principle in different cultures and showed that consumers react to asymmetric pricing differently due to different social norms held. People held or primed in the Western culture are more accepting of asymmetric pricing than those of Eastern culture. Future research could explore the dynamics of relationship type, relationship strength and perceptions of unfairness.

5 Practising marketing – the case of targeted promotion

The practice of dynamic pricing – which is adjusting prices based on supply and demand changes in real time or near-real time – is on the rise. Targeted promotion is one form of dynamic pricing where sellers provide price breaks to selective customers based on consumer profiles, search habits and demographic data. The practice has been proven profitable.

While it is typically price increases that evoke perceptions of unfairness, price promotions may produce the same result. When some customers are advantaged with a discounted price, it means other customers will be relatively disadvantaged. Given the expanded use of social networks, smartphone apps and various other forms of communication, it is not difficult for consumers to find out that other consumers have gained a better price. As a result, the practice is controversial and unfairness is one of the associated issues.

Imagine that one customer learns that another customer received a price discount. The price differential will prompt the customer to consider whether the price s/he paid is fair and to be interested in learning why. According to fairness research, it would make a difference in perceptions of unfairness whether the discount is because the other customer is a loyal customer, the other customer got lucky when the seller randomly sent coupons to consumers, the other customer is knowledgeable about the product and the seller gives him/her a price break so s/he can spread the word, the seller monitors which websites buyers browse and provides the other customer with a discount because s/he visited price comparison sites, or the other customer is familiar with various sites to search for price discounts.

Applying the various fairness theories we discussed above, companies can use several tactics in order to reduce potential perceptions of unfairness. First, the basis of offering targeted price promotion is clear segmentation. Whether to offer a promotion to a certain customer segment and how the promotion should be offered should be based on segmentation profiles. How do they trade off between price and quality? Where do they look for information? Utilise multiple characteristics instead of singling out one particular feature. Try to avoid very personal identification that does not contribute to 'deservingness', or which leaves other customers feeling exploited (e.g. just because I am not price sensitive does not mean I should pay a higher price than others).

Second, set up effective pricing screens. Screens based on what consumers do tend to be more effective in avoiding perceptions of unfairness than screens based on merely who they are. Loyal customers deserve a price break because of their purchase record. Other customers would recognise that these customers with a strong purchase record deserve a price break – hence, they would be unlikely to consider the promotion as unfair. They may be even inspired to think 'if I were to … I would get the better price, too'.

Third, reduce price compatibility. Transaction similarity enhances perceptions of unfairness. Companies can reduce customers' tendency to compare by applying different price metrics and/or framing the discount differently from the original price. Instead of an instant discount that consumers can use to integrate with the product price and arrive at a lower price, offer the incentive in different forms such as points and rewards, free shipping or bonus products. This way, the comparison with the base price of the product will not yield a significant discrepancy.

Fourth, give customers control. Customer-discovered prices are fairer than seller-imposed ones. If the customer attributes the price discrepancy to the other customer, such as his/her knowledge or his/her effort, it will be perceived as fairer than seller-granted prices. Therefore, companies may want to understand target customers' search behaviours and media preferences. Also, it is helpful to offer tiered promotions or different types of promotions that consumers can self-select. For example, offer $1 off $10, $5 off $30, or $10 off $40. Targeted promotion often works with contextual targeting through online tracking or smartphone apps. When consumers are targeted with different levels or types of promotions (e.g. small vs. larger gains), perception of unfairness is less likely to be an issue compared with receiving a promotion or not (gain vs. no gain).

Fifth, preferential treatment could be perceived as unfair even for the advantaged customers in the presence of others. Hence, targeted promotion works better when communicated and offered to the targeted customer in private rather than a public context. Finally, while the objective of price promotion is typically short-term sales and profit, firms should carefully consider its impact on the long-term relationship.

Overall, advances in technology and availability of increased computing power to analyse large amounts of data give companies an unprecedented opportunity to know their customers. This enables better segmentation, better product or service offers, better value communicated and delivered. At the same time, it also offers opportunities to exploit customers. Targeted promotion can benefit both firms and customers, but at the same time may evoke perceptions of unfairness and customer resentment. Firms should carefully design the targeted promotion programme in order to capitalise effectively on the technical capability to differentiate price without jeopardising perceptions of fairness

Discussion questions

1. Why would targeted promotion be considered unfair? What makes targeted promotion fair or unfair?
2. What are the underlying sources for unfairness perception in the context of targeted promotion?
3. How can perceptions of unfairness be anticipated and how can successful promotional programmes be designed?
4. What could companies do to handle consumer perceptions of unfairness when such situations arise?

6 Further investigation

To investigate perceptions of price unfairness further, these are the key questions to keep in mind:

1. How do consumers select reference transactions in their assessment of unfairness among all available references?

2.   How do perceptions of unfairness vary in different cultures and with different social norms?

3.   How do consumers perceive price increases associated with companies' CSR activities?

4.   How do perceptions of unfairness vary by different product categories, such as hedonic versus utilitarian, necessities versus luxuries?

5.   How should price fences be set for different target markets (e.g. loyal versus new customers), to minimise the danger of potential unfairness perception?

6.   Are there any differences in the nature of perceptions of unfairness when these originate from different sources, such as those due to a lack of value versus those accompanied by damage of personal identity?

7.   How can damage be minimised and how can a company recover from the damage of perceptions of unfairness? What are the best remedies?

References

Adams, J.S. (1965). 'Inequity in social exchange'. In L. Berkowitz (ed.) *Advances in Experimental Social Psychology*, Vol. 2. New York: Academic Press.

Aggarwal, P. and Larrick, R.P. (2012). When consumers care about being treated fairly: the interaction of relationship norms and fairness norms. *Journal of Consumer Psychology*, 22(1), pp. 114–127.

Aggarwal, P. and Vaidyanathan, R. (2003). 'The perceived effectiveness of virtual shopping agents for search vs. experience goods'. In P.A. Keller and D.W. Rook (eds) *Advances in Consumer Research*, Vol. 30. Valdosta, GA: Association for Consumer Research, pp. 347–348.

Ashworth, L. and McShane, L. (2012). Why do we care what others pay? The effect of other consumers' prices on inferences of seller (dis)respect and perceptions of deservingness violation. *Journal of Retailing*, 88(1), pp. 145–155.

Austin, W., McGinn, N.C. and Susmilch, C. (1980). Internal standards revisited: effects of social comparisons and expectancies on judgments of fairness and satisfaction. *Journal of Experimental Social Psychology*, 16(5), pp. 426–441.

Barclay, L.J., Skarlicki, D.P. and Pugh, S.D. (2005). Exploring the role of emotions in injustice perceptions and retaliation. *Journal of Applied Psychology*, 90(4), pp. 629.

Blodgett, J.G., Hill, D.J. and Tax, S.S. (1997). The effects of distributive, procedural, and interactional justice on postcomplaint behavior. *Journal of Retailing*, 73(2), pp. 185–210.

Bolton, L.E. and Alba, J.W. (2006). Price fairness: good and service differences and the role of vendor costs. *Journal of Consumer Research*, 33(2), pp. 258–265.

Bolton, L.E., Hean, T.K. and Alba, J.W. (2010). How do price fairness perceptions differ across culture? *Journal of Marketing Research*, 47(3), pp. 564–576.

Bolton, L.E., Warlop, L. and Alba, J.W. (2003). Consumer perceptions of price (un) fairness. *Journal of Consumer Research*, 29(4), pp. 474–491.

Brockner, J. (2002). Making sense of procedural fairness: how high procedural fairness can reduce or heighten the influence of outcome favorability. *Academy of Management Review*, 27(1), pp. 58–76.

Campbell, M.C. (1999). Perceptions of price unfairness: antecedents and consequences. *Journal of Marketing Research*, pp. 187–199.

Campbell, M.C. (2007). 'Says who?!' How the source of price information and affect influence perceived price (un) fairness. *Journal of Marketing Research*, 44(2), pp. 261–271.

Carlson, J.P. and Weathers, D. (2008). Examining differences in consumer reactions to partitioned prices with a variable number of price components. *Journal of Business Research*, 61 (7), pp. 724–731.

Chen, H.A., Bolton, L.E., Ng, S. and Lee, D. (2014). *Cultural Differences in Asymmetric Price Adjustment*. University of Texas A&M.

Clark, M.S. and Mills, J. (1979). Interpersonal attraction in exchange and communal relationships. *Journal of Personality and Social Psychology*, 37(1), pp. 12.

Feinberg, F.M., Krishna, A. and Zhang, Z.J. (2002). Do we care what others get? A behaviorist approach to targeted promotions. *Journal of Marketing Research*, 39(3), pp. 277–291.

Finkel, N.J. (2001). *Not fair!: The typology of commonsense unfairness*. American Psychological Association.

Gilliland, D.I. and Bello, D.C. (2002). Two sides to attitudinal commitment: the effect of calculative and loyalty commitment on enforcement mechanisms in distribution channels. *Journal of the Academy of Marketing Science*, 30(1), pp. 24–43.

Goodwin, C. and Ross, I. (1992). Consumer responses to service failures: influence of procedural and interactional fairness perceptions. *Journal of Business Research*, 25(2), pp. 149–163.

Grewal, D., Hardesty, D.M. and Iyer, G.R. (2004). The effects of buyer identification and purchase timing on consumers' perceptions of trust, price fairness, and repurchase intentions. *Journal of Interactive Marketing*, 18(4), pp. 87–100.

Gwinner, K.P., Gremler, D.D. and Bitner, M.J. (1998). Relational benefits in services industries: the customer's perspective. *Journal of the Academy of Marketing Science*, 26(2), pp. 101–114.

Haws, K.L. and Bearden, W.O. (2006). Dynamic pricing and consumer fairness perceptions. *Journal of Consumer Research*, 33(3), pp. 304–311.

Herrmann, A., Xia, L., Monroe, K.B. and Huber, F. (2007). The influence of price fairness on customer satisfaction: an empirical test in the context of automobile purchases. *Journal of Product & Brand Management*, 16(1), pp. 49–58.

Homans, G.C. (1961). *Social Behavior: Its Elementary Forms*. Harcourt, Brace & World, New York.

Homburg, C., Hoyer, W.D. and Koschate, N. (2005). Customers' reactions to price increases: do customer satisfaction and perceived motive fairness matter? *Journal of the Academy of Marketing Science*, 33(1), pp. 36–49.

Homburg, C., Totzek, D. and Krämer, M. (2013). How price complexity takes its toll: the neglected role of a simplicity bias and fairness in price evaluations. *Journal of Business Research*.

Huppertz, J.W., Arenson, S.J. and Evans, R.H. (1978). An application of equity theory to buyer-seller exchange situations. *Journal of Marketing Research*, 15, pp. 250–260.

Jacoby, J. (1976). 'Consumer and industrial psychology: prospects for theory corroboration and mutual contribution'. In M.D. Dunnette (ed.) *Handbook of Industrial and Organizational Psychology*, Rand McNally, Chicago.

Jiang, L., Hoegg, J.A. and Dahl, D.W. (2013). Consumer reaction to unearned preferential treatment. *Journal of Consumer Research*, 40(3), pp. 412–427.

Jin, L., He, Y. and Zhang, Y. (2014). How power states influence consumers' perceptions of price unfairness. *Journal of Consumer Research*, 40(5), pp. 818–833.

Kahneman, D., Knetsch, J.L. and Thaler, R. (1986a). Fairness as a constraint on profit seeking: entitlements in the market. *The American Economic Review*, pp. 728–741.

Kahneman, D., Knetsch, J.L. and Thaler, R.H. (1986b). Fairness and the assumptions of economics. *Journal of Business*, pp. S285–300.

Kahneman, D., Knetsch, J.L. and Thaler, R. (1986c). Fairness as a constraint on profit seeking entitlements in the market. *The American Economic Review*, 76 (September), pp. 728–741.

Kahneman, D., Knetsch, J.L. and Thaler, R. (1994). Fairness as a constraint on profit seeking: entitlements in the market. *Quasi Rational Economics*, pp. 199–219.

Koper, G., Van Knippenberg, D., Bouhuijs, F., Vermunt, R. and Wilke, H. (1993). Procedural fairness and self-esteem. *European Journal of Social Psychology*, 23(3), pp. 313–325.

Lewicki, R.J. and Bunker, B.B. (1995). *Trust in Relationships: A Model of Development and Decline*. Jossey-Bass.

Lind, E.A. and Tyler, T.R. (1988) *The Social Psychology of Procedural Justice*. Springer.

Lind, E.A. and Van den Bos, K. (2002) When fairness works: toward a general theory of uncertainty management. *Research in Organizational Behaviour*, 24, pp. 181–223.

Major, B. (1994). From social inequality to personal entitlement: the role of social comparisons, legitimacy appraisals, and group membership. *Advances in Experimental Social Psychology*, 26, pp. 293–355.

Major, B. and Testa, M. (1989). Social comparison processes and judgments of entitlement and satisfaction. *Journal of Experimental Social Psychology*, 25(2), pp. 101–120.

Martin, W.C., Ponder, N. and Lueg, J.E. (2009). Price fairness perceptions and customer loyalty in a retail context. *Journal of Business Research*, 62(6), pp. 588–593.

Martins, M. and Monroe, K.B. (1994). Perceived price fairness: a new look at an old construct. *Advances in Consumer Research*, 21(1).

Mattila, A.S. and Cranage, D. (2005). The impact of choice on fairness in the context of service recovery. *Journal of Services Marketing*, 19(5), pp. 271–279.

Mattioli, D. (2012). On Orbitz, Mac users steered to pricier hotels. *The Wall Street Journal*, 23 August.

McColl-Kennedy, J.R. and Sparks, B.A. (2003). Application of fairness theory to service failures and service recovery. *Journal of Service Research*, 5(3), pp. 251–266.

Mills, J. and Clark, M.S. (1982). Exchange and communal relationships. *Review of Personality and Social Psychology*, 3, pp. 121–144.

Mussweiler, T. (2003). 'Everything is relative': comparison processes in social judgment. The 2002 Jaspars Lecture. *European Journal of Social Psychology*, 33(6), pp. 719–733.

Ordonez, L.D., Connolly, T. and Coughlan, R. (2000). Multiple reference points in satisfaction and fairness assessment. *Journal of Behavioral Decision Making*, 13(3), pp. 329–344.

Peters, S.L. and Van den Bos, K. (2008). When fairness is especially important: reactions to being inequitably paid in communal relationships. *Social Justice Research*, 21(1), pp. 86–105.

Sirdeshmukh, D., Singh, J. and Sabol, B. (2002). Consumer trust, value, and loyalty in relational exchanges. *Journal of Marketing*, 66(1), pp. 15–37.

Thaler, R. (1985). Mental accounting and consumer choice. *Marketing Science*, 4(3), pp. 199–214.

Thibaut, J.W. and Walker, L. (1975). *Procedural Justice: A Psychological Analysis*. Erlbaum Associates, Hillsdale, NJ.

Van den Bos, K., Wilke, H.A.M., Lind, E.A. and Vermunt, R. (1998). Evaluating outcomes by means of the fair process effect: evidence for different processes in fairness and satisfaction judgments. *Journal of Personality and Social Psychology*, 74(6), pp. 1493.

Wirtz, J. and Kimes, S.E. (2007). The moderating role of familiarity in fairness perceptions of revenue management pricing. *Journal of Service Research*, 9(3), pp. 229–240.

Wirtz, J. and Mattila, A.S. (2004). Consumer responses to compensation, speed of recovery and apology after a service failure. *International Journal of Service Industry Management*, 15(2), pp. 150–166.

Wood, J.V. (1989). Theory and research concerning social comparisons of personal attributes. *Psychological Bulletin*, 106(2), p. 231.

Xia, L. and Monroe, K.B. (2004a). Price partitioning on the internet. *Journal of Interactive Marketing*, 18(4), pp. 63–73.

Xia, L. and Monroe, K.B. (2004b). 'Comparative Others, Trust, and Perceived Price Fairness'. Annual Conference of Society of Consumer Psychology, San Francisco.

Xia, L., Monroe, K.B. and Cox, J.L. (2004). The price is unfair! A conceptual framework of price fairness perceptions. *Journal of Marketing*, 68(4), pp. 1–15.

Xia, L. and Monroe, K.B. (2010). Is a good deal always fair? Examining the concepts of transaction value and price fairness. *Journal of Economic Psychology*, 31(6), pp. 884–894.

Further reading

Nguyen, B. (2011). The dark side of CRM. *The Marketing Review*, 11(2), pp. 137–149.

Nguyen, B. (2012). The dark side of customer relationship management: exploring the underlying reasons for pitfalls, exploitation and unfairness. *Journal of Database Marketing and Customer Strategy Management*, 19(1), pp. 56–70.

Nguyen, B. and Klaus, P. (2013). Retail fairness: exploring consumer perceptions of fairness in retailers' marketing tactics. *Journal of Retailing and Consumer Services*, 20(3), pp. 311–324.

Nguyen, B., Klaus, P. and Simkin, L. (2014). It's just not fair: exploring the effects of firm customization on unfairness perceptions, loyalty, and trust. *Journal of Services Marketing*, 28(6), pp. 484–497.

Nguyen, B. and Mutum, D.S. (2012). Customer relationship management: advances, dark sides, exploitation and unfairness. *International Journal of Electronic Customer Relationship Management*, 6(1), pp. 1–19.

Nguyen, B. and Simkin, L. (2013). The dark side of CRM: advantaged and disadvantaged customers. *Journal of Consumer Marketing*, 30(1), pp. 17–30.

4

CRM AND SOCIAL MEDIA

Adam Rapp and Jessica Ogilvie

1 Introduction

The incorporation of social media tools into customer relationship management (CRM) has provided companies with an array of benefits including low-cost customer interaction, increased response time, an extended number of communication platforms and marked efficiencies in customer relationship processes. However, the growing emphasis on social media as a crux of customer-facing communications is forcing companies to embrace a shift from traditional CRM practices to a focus on collaborative experiences and facilitation of value-driven dialogue with their customers. With such a dramatic shift in control within the customer–firm relationship, firms have been plagued with many social media- and CRM-related shortcomings. By exploring the phases of social media-enabled CRM – from adoption of social media through successful integration into CRM practices – we examine the pitfalls associated with social media and explore ways to overcome the problems faced by many of today's firms in the social CRM process.

With the explosion of social media platforms in recent years, as well as mounting stress from customers and competitors to establish a social media presence, firms are under increased pressure to incorporate social media successfully into their CRM processes. Often the time pressure to implement social media tools pushes companies into adoption of the new technology without considering the shift in CRM strategy and training necessary for successful implementation. Without proper strategic implementation, firms are prone to social media failures and risk harming the customer relationship more often than they enhance it. Thus, this chapter discusses the many pitfalls to implementing social media actions without proper planning or strategic considerations. Notably, while hasty implementation of social media can hurt customer relationships, delay in establishing a social media presence can also have negative impacts on CRM. Active involvement on social media platforms is being increasingly demanded by customers and becoming essential in the competitive marketplace. Considering the increase in customer demand for interaction in social media channels, this chapter also explores pitfalls associated with delays and failure to launch social media strategies. Reconciling these pitfalls, this chapter further explores how to successfully shift necessary resources, train and empower employees, implement a top-down model of technology acceptance, and create a social CRM strategy that is both timely and effective.

Finally, when firms adopt social CRM strategies but maintain the tendency of *managing* the customer (as associated with traditional CRM practices), the related consequences can be vast. Significant gaps exist between what customers desire from social media interactions and what businesses believe they should be providing. Accordingly, this chapter explores the negative consequences of using social media tools to maintain a marketing 'push' of information to customers and discusses the shift towards expanding customer value co-creation through the unprecedented reach, transparency and information immediacy associated with social media. Additional problems associated with the implementation of social CRM strategies are also outlined, including the growing pains associated with new technology, engaging customers without providing tangible benefits, mismanaging interactions and treating social media as a 'one-way street'. Insights into an array of solutions for improved social media strategies are provided as well as discussion of proper leveraging of social media as a key constituent in the CRM process throughout the chapter.

Learning objectives

When you have read the chapter, you should be able to:

1. Define social CRM and recognise unique aspects of social media in the customer relationship.
2. Identify key differences in traditional CRM and social CRM.
3. Recognise where social CRM fits within the broader marketing mix of a firm.
4. Understand the common pitfalls (or dark side) associated with the implementation of social CRM.
5. Develop a strategy for leveraging the opportunities of social CRM and form implementable solutions to avoid social CRM pitfalls.

2 Route map

Social media and the new customer relationship

While consumers have flocked to social media outlets and have begun using these tools to engage in the online flow of information, many organisations have been slow in responding to and adopting these new technologies (Andzulis et al., 2012).

However, under the cumulative pressure of ever-increasing customer use, many organisations have begun to put in place hurried social media campaigns, resulting in a vast amount of failure in this social media push. As many continue their push towards a social media presence, despite setbacks, it is clear that firms recognise the potential of these new channels; however, in attempting to adapt social media to their CRM operations, many organisations often fail to recognise the necessary resource allocation, planning, training and strategic operations involved in a successful social media component of CRM activity. Social media do not represent a minor extension of CRM technologies. In fact, the nature of social media represents a shift in power within the customer relationship (cf. Labrecque et al., 2013). This shift of power affects what information is shared, how it is shared within the relationship and who controls the flow of information (Malthouse et al., 2013). Indeed, this shift has been so paramount as to result in a fundamentally different customer paradigm (Mosadegh and Behboudi, 2011), which considers an evolved customer with greater knowledge, new perceptions and increased expectations.

In traditional CRM, information is gathered, processed and controlled by the firm. With the social CRM evolution, information is now user generated (by customers) and flows freely from customer to customer and between customers, employees and the firm, as in Figure 4.1.

Despite this paradigm shift, social media should not be confused with a new substitute for traditional CRM strategies (Weinberg and Pehlivan, 2011). Instead, social media capabilities should be acknowledged for the vast opportunities they afford for enriching customer interactions *within* the CRM strategy. With the addition of social media tools and a social CRM strategy, firms can influence and expand their traditional CRM capabilities and enhance customer engagement, relationship management and customer retention. Social media have impacted many functional areas of today's firms. However, the customer-facing functions of the organisation have the potential to see dramatic impacts with the technology

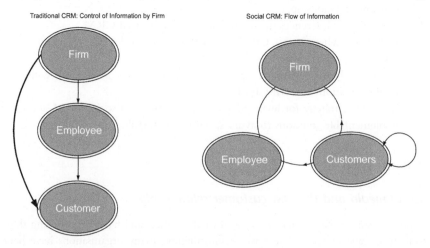

FIGURE 4.1 From information control to information flow

advances brought on by social media (Trainor, 2012). Firms must recognise and leverage the distinctions in elements of social CRM in translating organisational objectives into tactical relationship management activities. Importantly, the customer empowerment that exists in social media channels has shifted the state of marketing communications (Castronovo and Huang, 2012).

3 Defining social CRM

CRM strategies are designed to manage customer relationships and, in doing so, extract the greatest value over the customer's lifetime with the firm. With the addition of social media technology to the marketing mix, a social strategy has become a key piece of successful CRM systems. Formally, social CRM has been defined by marketing scholars as the integration of social media applications into the traditional customer-facing activities of the firm to engage and collaborate with customers and enhance customer relationships (Greenberg, 2010; Trainor, 2012). When properly leveraged, social media technologies and tools can enhance CRM systems and boost efficiency and effectiveness of customer interactions and resultant customer relationships.

Traditional vs. social CRM: the networked effect

CRM activities have long been informed by processes and technologies (Baird and Parasnis, 2011). However, while past CRM technology advances offered new tools to enhance a firm's CRM capabilities, social media technology has altered many fundamental characteristics of the CRM process itself. As customers increasingly demand valuable interactivity with firms via social medial channels (Baird and Parasnis, 2011), academics and practitioners alike have been forced to re-evaluate the notion of customer relationship management in light of the unique characteristics brought about by social media tools (Greenberg, 2010; Berthon et al., 2012; Trainor et al., 2014).

Drilling down, social CRM differs from traditional CRM in the very nature of the relationship. Traditional CRM activities involved a multitude of dyadic relationships – between each individual customer and the firm. With social CRM, activities are no longer just dyadic relationships but instead include the network of relationships associated with the customer's interaction with the firm. This network includes the customer's relationships outside the firm (e.g. family, friends, or other individuals from whom the consumer may seek advice), as well as the network of other consumers (e.g. discussions among buyers, product reviews and ratings, or featured posts from other consumers). In this way, social CRM introduces a network characteristic that must be considered. Customers are now leveraging 'the power of relationships and the collective wisdom of many' (Berthon et al., 2012). By shifting from the individual to the collective, social networking provides opportunities that are unique to a new social customer and reaffirm the emergence of a new customer paradigm.

TABLE 4.1 Characteristics of traditional versus social CRM

	Traditional CRM	Social CRM
Control of information	Firms track customer transactions and information is gathered	Customers generate content and information is exchanged
Concept of customer value	Focus on customer transactions and purchase-based calculations	Considers customer transactions, interactions and additional social elements (e.g. referrals)

To be successful in an ever-increasing digital marketplace, companies must recognise the shifting CRM landscape and consider the strategic changes necessary to engage effectively. With social media, the firm can no longer simply manage the customer's information but instead must manage its role in the customer's conversation. We offer an overview of social CRM and traditional CRM activities in Table 4.1, which illustrates the unique characteristics of social media as a new and dynamic tool for the enrichment and expansion of CRM activities.

4 The state of the art of social CRM

Evolution of social media and revolution of CRM

Social media in CRM has followed an evolutionary path in organisational adoption very similar to that of the first adoption of Internet and website usage in organisational marketing strategy (Andzulis et al., 2012). Thus, there is much to learn from a developmental process standpoint when considering the future of social CRM. By identifying similarities in the adoption process, we can outline a parallel

Why Social Media?

■ Social media use has become a part of daily life for a growing percentage of the consumer population.

■ Customer activity is increasingly viral – social media channels represent enormous potential for companies to better understand and influence their customers.

■ Advances in technology and digital platforms have given today's customers ever-increasing power within the buyer–seller relationship – this can be detrimental to companies if they fail to listen to, and engage with, their customers.

FIGURE 4.2 Key points in the future of CRM

understanding of customer expectations in firm social media presence. These expectations must be clearly defined in order to understand where and why social CRM pitfalls emerge.

When businesses first began adopting an Internet presence as a way to extend their marketing mix, the attempt most often resulted in an 'information only' website (Andzulis et al., 2012). Then, as e-commerce developed and became prominent, many firms were forced to add an element of purchasing capabilities to their websites, allowing customers to make purchases from the company but still not allowing a platform for interaction. Finally, as the Internet evolved and technology strengthened, firms were able to interact with customers through their website in live chats, interactive product displays, and information posting and sharing among the brand community.

Social media thus far have followed a similar path of adoption by organisations. Slowly and painfully, customers are forcing movement away from an information push towards a conversation and network interaction (Agnihothri et al., 2012). Unfortunately, it appears in many cases that history is merely repeating itself, as organisations take action in social media channels without aligning and integrating these new channel opportunities with their CRM strategy. Many of the resulting social media activities fail to consider customer expectations, customer knowledge and the new landscape of marketing communication. Adoption of social media applications must be treated as an evolving and dynamic process within the firm's CRM strategy (Andzulis et al., 2012).

With this evolution of social media, the CRM process has seen a great revolution as well. Customers and organisations have increased levels of real-time information (Marshall et al., 2012) and expect interactions to occur at equivalent speeds. With social CRM, relationships are now driven by information access and availability, and results are expected to be immediate. These increasing demands can result in relationship tension or employee burnout if not handled properly. Buyers are inclined to increase social media interactions to function more efficiently and many consider virtual relationships a more efficient and effective means of working.

Social CRM is indeed changing the nature and symmetry of buyer–seller interaction and the selling tools involved within. Specifically, there exists not only a reformation of sales execution, but a noticeable evolving and condensing of the traditional *Seven Steps of Selling*. With the proper integration of social media tools, firms can provide a more cohesive customer experience with greater value co-creation. The agility, ease of use and cost benefits (to name a few) of social media tools will continue to entice firms to incorporate social media into their customer-facing actions.

The social customer

In this chapter, we have discussed the paradigm shift resulting from the evolution of the social customer. Importantly, two fundamental shifts in the customer relationship inform many of the benefits and pitfalls of social CRM processes. First, we consider the knowledgeable consumer. Customers are more informed than ever and require transparency and authenticity from the companies they deal with (Greenberg, 2010). Product information is readily available and easy to gather, while consumers are more informed in their purchase decisions than ever before. Second, social media have impacted the expectations of today's consumers. Consumers expect information to be available on demand (Greenberg, 2010) and expect interactivity with their business counterparts (Trainor et al., 2014). This 'always on' expectation associated with social media interaction (Marshall et al., 2012) can create problems for firms that implement social CRM activities without the proper planning and resource allocation to support demands. Ultimately, many firms remain unable to develop effective implementation strategies, resulting in mismanagement of the opportunities and threats presented by social media technologies in the marketplace (Kietzmann et al., 2012).

Opportunities

Social media and the evolution of the social customer present many opportunities for organisations. Social media can help create positive exchange experiences and engage customers through superior information exchange, reciprocity and problem solving (Hennig-Thurau et al., 2010). Social media tools provide an array of platforms for efficient communication, information exchange and relationship development (Gupta et al., 2011; Trainor, 2012).

In today's marketplace, traditional boundaries pose no real limitations as customers and companies form relationships despite physical or international borders. Organisations that can successfully manage the communication capabilities and customer opportunities created by the billions of people currently connected to the Internet worldwide (Kandampully, 2002) can create an unparalleled advantage. Social media platforms provide the means to manage customers with ease and the opportunity to establish superior customer relationships through properly leveraged and managed social media use within the front lines of the organisation. Specifically, increased availability of detailed customer information creates an opportunity for organisations to create more focused and effective marketing campaigns, sales initiatives and customer interactions (Scullin et al., 2004).

Further, while advances in technology in general have influenced the growth and importance of services, cost-effective social media tools are unique in their ability to provide increased service performance at a lower cost to firms than traditional technologies (Rigby and Ledingham, 2004). This creates an outlet for firms seeking to implement and expand service networks without financial risk or large monetary investments. There also exists a variety of social media platforms that allows firms to identify those outlets that complement their CRM strategies and best extend their current CRM capabilities.

The dark side of social CRM

With the introduction of a technological shift in any process, a firm will face inevitable growing pains that result from adoption, learning and implementation performance lags. Social CRM practices demand resource allocation and management to implement and maintain successfully. Introducing social media into business strategy represents 'one of the most disruptive forces facing businesses today' (Baird and Parasnis, 2011, p. 32). That being said, the implications of implementing social media technology without proper strategic alignment has the potential for far-reaching and expensive consequences. New media channels are threatening long-established business models and corporate strategies (Hennig-Thurau et al., 2010). Academic research has recognised the power of social media, yet many organisations remain reluctant or unable to implement effective social media strategies (Kietzmann et al., 2012). Because social media give companies a means of constant communication with customers (Mangold and Faulds, 2009), mismanagement of this technology can result in consequences beyond mere lost opportunities for the firm. With such a prominent shift in customer thinking and behaviour, a variety of pitfalls associated with social media implementation plague today's organisations.

Pitfalls

Too often, companies begin spending money without first establishing a comprehensive strategy. Pitfalls of social CRM often relate to an inconsistency in organisational understanding of customer expectations. Extant literature maintains that benefits of technology use are realised when firms couple technology investments with changes in strategy and organisational support processes to best leverage technological value (Agnihothri et al., 2012). Unlike the financial challenges of traditional technology implementation that have long tested managers (Rigby and Ledingham, 2004), social media technology does not require a big monetary investment from the organisation. However, the stakes of implementing social media technology are still high considering the impact of improper technology use on customer expectations, consumer concerns of privacy, confidentiality and unsolicited communication. Such negative aspects of technology infusion have left some firms wary of new applications.

Failure to understand customer expectations

A gap exists between what customers want and expect from social media interactions with the firm and what firms think customers care about in their social media interactions (Baird and Parasnis, 2011). When firms use social media channels merely as an outlet to push information towards customers, valuable information is missed and customers are driven away. When firms fail to listen and respond to their customers' needs, a deviation from customer expectations often results, which can damage customer relationships. Social CRM must be treated as a two-way street (Andzulis et al., 2012), meaning that organisations must engage in the information exchange if they hope to gain customer support. For example, businesses often overestimate consumers' desires to engage with the brand (Baird and Parasnis, 2011) and assume customers will appreciate and cooperate in their social CRM activities simply for the sake of interaction. Instead, customers maintain pragmatic preferences in sharing their time and information with firms, placing value on those interactions that deliver tangible value or rewards for their attention (Greenberg, 2010).

Failure to integrate

This occurs when firms consider social media activities apart from CRM strategy. The result is often a static presence in digital channels. Within proper integration and alignment of social media, communication can be inconsistent, customer interactions are sporadic and add little value, and the relationships may be viewed as inauthentic by customers (Greenberg, 2010). Inconsistency in marketing communications and customer interactions becomes more readily apparent as customers share their experiences and knowledge with others in the network. Indeed, social media platforms facilitate the democratisation of knowledge (Berthon et al., 2012), which necessitates organisational transparency of information. With increased transparency, companies find it increasingly difficult to manage the message consumers receive about their products and services (Malthouse et al., 2013). Inconsistent interactions may be perceived as unfair, damaging the customer relationship value, trust and satisfaction.

Failure to allocate

When resources are not properly anticipated, allocated or aligned with the processes necessary for successful social CRM systems, the customer can be left upset and the organisation's capabilities and competence may be questioned. Success in social CRM is contingent upon organisational support and requires a significant shift in resources to meet new demands (Agnihothri et al., 2012). Remembering again the network effects of social media, when customer interactions are not satisfactory, far-reaching negative word-of-mouth can result (Nguyen and Mutum, 2012) and the firm may be worse off than had they never interacted with the customer in the first place. The social media realm operates much faster than more traditional means of customer interaction. When technology, staff or capabilities are lacking, the resulting frustration of the customer can be detrimental. The 'always on' environment can quickly result in unanswered customer engagement and missed opportunities.

Failure to train

The literature emphasises the need to manage technology effectively in the buyer–seller exchange (cf. Agnihothri et al., 2012). In a situation where the company fails to redirect resources to support technology adoption and use initiatives, there is a greater possibility of reduction in performance and productivity with increased technology use (Ahearne et al., 2005; Ahearne et al., 2008). Many employees remain uncertain about implementation of new technologies in the service delivery process, as infusion of new technologies forces employees to adjust to the changing nature of service activities (Andzulis et al., 2012). Organisational facilitating conditions, such as training, can not only help avoid such consequences but also positively impact technology use.

Failure to monitor and adapt

Social media technology is still in a process of evolution. Thus, an overarching pitfall of social media technology use in the organisation is its dynamic future. In the business landscape, it is still a new and evolving tool that is in an early stage of its lifecycle (Andzulis et al., 2012). Consistent monitoring of CRM activities is important to the success of any customer process, but importantly the newness of social CRM warrants additional support in consistently evaluating the performance of social networking decisions.

Organisational implications

Social CRM requires organisations to establish, communicate, facilitate and consistently evaluate and enforce a social media policy. Social CRM failures result from poor organisational culture, absence of managerial support, insufficient staffing and lack of customer engagement (Myron, 2013). Avoidance of the many pitfalls associated with social networks occurs when a firm has aligned, fully integrated and strategically developed social media capabilities to expand and enhance CRM processes. Table 4.2 summarises the common pitfalls of social CRM and strategic considerations that can be used to combat this dark side of social CRM.

To overcome the pitfalls of social CRM, we must establish and maintain a customer-centric CRM strategy. Relationship management is no longer about simply extracting information from customer transactions, but involves the co-creation of value with consumers through social media. To do this, firms must set appropriate goals for social media interactions (Andzulis et al., 2012). These customer-centric goals should derive from an understanding of the customer expectations and appropriate integration of social networking into the CRM strategy in conjunction with those expectations. Then, for success in reaching those goals, strategic allocation of resources must be considered thoroughly and employees must be trained to perform the tasks necessary for CRM goal attainment. Finally, to maintain goal actualisation, constant evaluation of social CRM effectiveness must occur through monitoring and adapting of social media implementation as the technologies associated with this phenomenon continue to evolve.

TABLE 4.2 Strategic considerations in preventing social CRM pitfalls

Common pitfalls of social CRM	Strategic considerations
Failure to understand customer expectations	What information are customers seeking? What do customers expect in their interactions with the organisation? How do customers prefer to be rewarded for engagement?
Failure to integrate	How do these tools complement the existing strategy? Where can they be used to leverage customer relationships? How can current CRM activities be extended with these new capabilities?
Failure to allocate	What resources will be required? Which employees are best suited for this role? How many personnel are needed for smooth interactions across customers? Does customer interaction have any high-volume times? Do we have the proper tools to provide the interaction expected from our customers?
Failure to train	What new abilities will employees need to use these technologies? How intensive are these tools for the average employee? What are the most effective ways to educate employees in social CRM activities?
Failure to monitor and adapt	Are we using the most effective social media tools on the market? Are we meeting customer expectations? Are employees proficient in their CRM activities? Can efficiency be improved in any CRM processes?

5 New research directions

Social CRM requires an organisational strategy involving substantial commitment from the top levels of the organisation and continuous monitoring at the more tactical levels of implementation and usage. Digital considerations are increasingly important as consumers and businesses alike continue to rely more and more on technology in all aspects of everyday life. Technological advances and shifting paradigms can no longer be ignored or simply managed by firms; these changes must be embraced and integrated into the very core of a firm's marketing strategy. With this in mind, we conclude this chapter with a look at the developing role of digital marketing and the resulting challenges for social media-enabled CRM.

Social media provide many new outlets for firms to increase CRM benefits and resulting performance but – due in large part to their new and evolving nature – they also incur a learning curve. Interestingly, given the popularity of social media platforms, firms should also be aware of their potential as a distraction to employees. Research reports growing popularity among younger Internet users (who

FIGURE 4.3 Overcoming pitfalls with a customer-focused strategy

notably are currently entering or will be entering the workforce) as well as the majority of adults (Kaplan and Haenlein, 2010). This popularity may posit benefits of interface and operational familiarity of employees, which could reduce the amount of necessary employer training. However, the popularity of social media outlets can easily lead to employees spending 'too much time networking instead of working' (Kaplan and Haenlein, 2010, p. 66). Future research should consider this growing popularity and explore the extent of distraction and improper use of work time and tools with the inclusion of social media tools in the CRM process.

Employee-specific impacts of social CRM should also be considered in future research. These tools create an opportunity for 'always-on' customer interactions. Typically, employees have time to prepare for customer interactions and have specific times of scheduled or expected customer interface. With social CRM, the customer has the opportunity to interact with the firm and with the employee at any time and across multiple platforms. Such a system requires constant monitoring and can create problems for the employee if s/he is working with too many customers simultaneously. Employees may not have enough time to prepare for customers or may be unable to research responses as customers expect immediate attention and information. This means that increased connectivity requires the management of customer connectivity expectations. Customers and organisations have increased levels of real-time information (Marshall et al., 2012) and expect interactions to occur at equivalent speeds. With social CRM, relationships are now driven by information access and availability, and results are expected to be immediate. These increasing demands can result in relationship tensions or employee burnout if not handled properly.

Finally, further research needs to explore the industry-specific boundaries of social CRM. By nature, this addition to the CRM strategy is of a higher technology calibre and requires more intensive understanding of social media tools, platforms and customer preferences across platforms. Specific industries may differ in the benefits presented by social CRM. For example, the impact of social media use in a complicated technology industry may or may not be beneficial. One could argue that these technological customers would prefer a technologically advanced form of communication with the firm. However, the products sold in such an industry will be information intensive and require more interaction with the customer. If the products sold require a high level of expertise and product knowledge to sell, service and operate, then these customers may prefer traditional face-to-face interactions with the firm to maintain a more in-depth understanding. While social media provide a new outlet for customer interaction, when managing information-heavy products, the ability of social media tools to provide a platform for the employee may no longer be as beneficial as sales calls – for example, situations in which the employee can provide extensive product knowledge in face-to-face customer interactions. Social media 'is a very active and fast-moving domain' (Kaplan and Haenlein, 2010, p. 64), and timely academic research is vital to implement this strategic tool successfully.

6 Practising marketing – case study

Firm XYZ was in desperate need of a social media presence. All of the firm's top competitors now interacted with and managed their customers through social media channels. Top management had been watching these changes occur over the last ten years but thought the social media frenzy was just a phase. Thus, they had neglected to establish a social media presence to engage and interact with their customers.

Annie's firm has been a customer of XYZ for almost five years now. She manages the account and makes all of the purchase decisions for her firm. She has enjoyed doing business with XYZ, but wishes her interactions with the company were more efficient and productive. She could not seem to make her voice heard at any point when dealing with the employees of the firm lately.

Recently, Annie had noticed that many firms now allowed their customers to interact with them over social media channels – even some of the same social media platforms she already used regularly. Learning more about products, making purchases, sharing information, interacting with the brand and communicating with organisational members would be much easier in social media channels and would provide Annie with a means of interacting with the firm that she enjoyed.

At the next board meeting, Annie brought up her concern with XYZ and proposed considering dealing with a new company to fulfil their purchasing needs. With the time and resources saved through social media interactions, Annie made a strong argument for the switching costs of terminating their contract with XYZ. With the board's approval, she planned to speak with her contact at XYZ the next day.

When Annie discussed ending the relationship with XYZ the next day, she was informed that they had recently adopted a social media element into their CRM process and she now had the option to communicate with the firm through a selected few of these channels. While she was slightly concerned about the newness of XYZ's initiative and the relegation to only certain social media channels, she decided to give them a chance based on her long relationship with the firm.

With the new system in place at XYZ, Annie expected to have increased contact with the firm and a greater number of touchpoints to gather information before purchasing. However, she still found herself uninformed of shipments, unable to interact with her representative or the firm, and constantly awaiting a response to an email, post or message she had shared with the firm. Any contact she did receive from the firm was almost always a blatant sales pitch that had no relevance to her usual orders with the company. Instead of saving her time, the new social media element of her interactions with XYZ was wasting more of her precious time and increasing her irritation with the relationship daily.

Mark is the sales representative that manages Annie's account at XYZ and he could understand his customers' frustrations with the current relationship management practices at his firm. He had been informed by his manager that social media tools were being incorporated into the CRM processes utilised by the employees, but no one had explained how or why these were now a part of their CRM tools.

Without understanding the role played by these new technologies, most of the sales representatives abandoned them or fumbled through customer interactions as they experimented with the new tools.

As more and more customers spread word of XYZ's social media failures, the company tried desperately to fix all of the holes in their social CRM activities. As XYZ scrambled just to react to new issues, Annie and hundreds of other customers were already giving up on the social media interactions with the firm, getting frustrated and moving to the competition. Just like that, XYZ lost all of the 'followers' whom they had devoted so much money to attracting.

Discussion questions

1. Where did the breakdown in expectations and delivery occur?
2. In what ways could XYZ better integrate their social media capabilities with their strategic outlook?
3. In what industries would this scenario most likely occur (i.e. consider which industries might be less likely to adopt social media as a tool for customer interaction)?
4. How would strategic planning have altered the outcomes of this situation for XYZ?

7 Further investigation

1. What do expanding social networks mean for current CRM activities?

    *   Businesses must continue to monitor their CRM practices and provide the resources necessary to evolve with changes in the social media lifecycle.

2. What are the trade-offs associated with adopting a social networking element into CRM strategy?

    *   In adopting social networking activities, an organisation sacrifices control of information and information flow to the customer. However, it is important to understand that customer networks operate outside organisational interaction. In today's digital age, customers own information and a firm that chooses not to participate in the social media realm has no voice or influence in the conversation. Firms cannot run from social media, as future growth will depend on the shift in control being embraced, incorporated, leveraged and properly managed.

3. Choose a firm and consider its current CRM strategy. Evaluate the effectiveness of its current strategy in co-creating value with customers.
4. Identify opportunities for leveraging social media platforms in the firm's CRM strategy. In what ways should they adapt their CRM strategy to increase value with their customers?

5. Consider the resource allocation necessary to align this new strategy with tactical execution by front-line employees of the chosen firm. Outline all resources that would be necessary for success and determine the feasibility of this new strategy.

References

Agnihothri, R., Kothandaraman, P., Kashyap, R. and Singh, R. (2012). Bringing 'social' into sales: the impact of salespeople's social media use on service behaviors and value creation. *Journal of Personal Selling & Sales Management*, 32(3), pp. 333–348.

Ahearne, M., Jelinek, R. and Rapp, A. (2005). Moving beyond the direct effect of SFA adoption on salesperson performance: training and support as key moderating factors. *Industrial Marketing Management*, 34(4), pp. 379–388.

Ahearne, M., Jones, E., Rapp, A. and Mathieu, J. (2008). High touch through high tech: the impact of salesperson technology usage on sales performance via mediating mechanisms. *Management Science*, 54(3), pp. 671–685.

Andzulis, J.M., Panagopoulos, N.G. and Rapp, A. (2012). A review of social media and implications for the sales process. *Journal of Personal Selling and Sales Management*, 3, pp. 305–316.

Baird, C.H. and Parasnis, G. (2011). From social media to social customer relationship management. *Strategy & Leadership*, 39(5), pp. 30–37.

Band, W. and Petouhoff, N.L. (2009). Topic overview: social CRM goes mainstream. *Future*.

Berthon, P.R., Pitt, L.F., Plangger, K. and Shapiro, D. (2012). Marketing meets Web 2.0, social media and creative consumers: implications for international marketing strategy. *Business Horizons*, 55(3), pp. 261–271.

Castronovo, C. and Huang, L. (2012). Social media in an alternative marketing communication model. *Journal of Marketing Development and Competitiveness*, 6(1), pp. 117–134.

Fisher, T. (2009). ROI in social media: a look at the arguments. *Journal of Database Marketing & Customer Strategy Management*, 16(3), pp. 189–195.

Greenberg, P. (2010). The impact of CRM 2.0 on customer insight. *Journal of Business & Industrial Marketing*, 25(6), pp. 410–419.

Gupta, S., Armstrong, K. and Clayton, Z. (2011). Social media. Harvard Business School Case no. 9-510-095, Boston.

Hennig-Thurau, T., Malthouse, E.C., Friege, C., Gensler, S., Lobschat, L., Rangaswamy, A. and Skiera, B. (2010). The impact of new media on customer relationships. *Journal of Service Research*, 13(3), pp. 311–330.

Kandampully, J. (2002). Innovation as the core competency of a service organisation: the role of technology, knowledge and networks. *European Journal of Innovation Management*, 5(1), pp. 18–26.

Kaplan, A.M. (2012). If you love something, let it go mobile: mobile marketing and mobile social media 4x4. *Business Horizons*, 55(2), pp. 129–139.

Kaplan, A.M. and Haenlein, M. (2010). Users of the world, unite! The challenges and opportunities of social media. *Business Horizons*, 53(1), pp. 59–68.

Kietzmann, J.H., Silvestre, B.S., McCarthy, I.P. and Pitt, L.F. (2012). Unpacking the social media phenomenon: towards a research agenda. *Journal of Public Affairs*, 12(2), pp. 109–119.

Kim, A.J. and Ko, E. (2012). Do social media marketing activities enhance customer equity? An empirical study of a luxury fashion brand. *Journal of Business Research*, 65(10), pp. 1480–1486.

Labrecque, L.I., Mathwick, C., Novak, T.P. and Hofacker, C.F. (2013). Consumer power: evolution in the digital age. *Journal of Interactive Marketing*, 27(4), pp. 257–269.

Malthouse, E.C., Haenlein, M., Skiera, B., Wege, E. and Zhang, M. (2013). Managing customer relationships in the social media era: introducing the social CRM house. *Journal of Interactive Marketing*, 27(4), pp. 270–280.

Mangold, W.G. and Faulds, D.J. (2009). Social media: the new hybrid element of the promotion mix. *Business Horizons*, 52(4), pp. 357–365.

Marshall, G.W., Moncrief, W.C., Rudd, J.M. and Lee, N. (2012). Revolution in sales: the impact of social media and related technology on the selling environment. *Journal of Personal Selling and Sales Management*, 32(3), pp. 349–363.

Mosadegh, M.J. and Behboudi, M. (2011). Using the social network paradigm for developing a conceptual framework in CRM. *Australian Journal of Business and Management Research*, 1(4), pp. 63–71.

Myron, D. (2013). CRM – What lies ahead in 2014?, *CRM Magazine*, December.

Nguyen, B. and Mutum, D.S. (2012). A review of customer relationship management: successes, advances, pitfalls and futures. *Business Process Management Journal*, 18(3), pp. 400–419.

O'Brien, C. (2011). The emergence of the social media empowered consumer. *Irish Marketing Review*, 21(1/2), pp. 32–40.

Rigby, D.K. and Ledingham, D. (2004). CRM done right. *Harvard Business Review*, 82(11), pp. 118–129.

Sashi, C.M. (2012). Customer engagement, buyer-seller relationships, and social media. *Management Decision*, 50(2), pp. 253–272.

Scullin, S.S., Fjermestad, J. and Romano, N.C., Jr (2004). e-Relationship marketing: changes in traditional marketing as an outcome of electronic customer relationship management. *Journal of Enterprise Information Management*, 17(6), pp. 410–415.

Trainor, K.J. (2012). Relating social media technologies to performance: a capabilities-based perspective. *Journal of Personal Selling and Sales Management*, 3, pp. 317–331.

Trainor, K.J., Andzulis, J.M., Rapp, A. and Agnihotri, R. (2014). Social media technology usage and customer relationship performance: a capabilities-based examination of social CRM. *Journal of Business Research*, 67(6), pp. 1201–1208.

Weinberg, B.D. and Pehlivan, E. (2011). Social spending: managing the social media mix. *Business Horizons*, 54(3), pp. 275–282.

Further reading

Greenberg, P. (2009). *CRM at the Speed of Light: Social CRM 2.0 Strategies, Tools and Techniques for Engaging Your Customers*. McGraw-Hill Osborne Media.

IBM Global Business Services (n.d.) From social media to social CRM – what customers want. http://www-935.ibm.com/services/us/gbs/thoughtleadership/ibv-social-crm-whitepaper.html.

IBM Global Business Services (n.d.) From social media to social CRM – reinventing the customer relationship. http://www-935.ibm.com/services/us/gbs/thoughtleadership/ibv-social-crm-whitepaper.html.

Marketo (2010a). *The Definitive Guide to B2B Social Media*. McGraw-Hill Osborne Media.

Marketo (2010b). The definitive guide to B2B social media: a Marketo workbook. www.scrantongillette.com/ sites/default/files/tabs/guide-b2b-social-media-all.pdf.

5

NEGATIVE WORD-OF-MOUTH, MISBEHAVIOUR AND REVENGE

Venessa Funches

1 Introduction

In today's business environment, consumer relationships are a prize to be sought. In fact, firms are actively seeking to establish, grow and capitalise on those relationships. Although good consumer–firm relationships can be extremely profitable, few recognise the potential costs and ramifications of poor, mismanaged or dysfunctional relationships. These potential costs are much broader than a reduction in purchase behaviours, and in some cases include negative word-of-mouth (WOM), misbehaviour and revenge.

The widespread occurrence of the consumer revenge phenomenon is particularly alarming. A Customer Rage Survey conducted in 2013 revealed that a significant number of customers are angry and the situation is worsening. In fact, the number of households reported experiencing 'customer rage' increased by eight percentage points from 2011 to 2013 (Customer Care Alliance, 2013). Consumers may now post their complaints online, call for boycotts, organise class-action lawsuits, along with a host of other options, all driven to hurt the firm. When consumers are dissatisfied, they have a wide range of responses available to them.

Unfortunately, not a great deal of research has been conducted on these types of behaviour. At one time consumers who participated in such behaviours were viewed as dysfunctional and abnormal. This type of consumer behaviour is becoming more widespread and must be understood. The consequences of these behaviours affect both consumers and firms. Typically these consumers are angry and as a result behave in ways that cost firms money and damage the consumer–firm relationship (Huefner and Hunt, 2000). Therefore, understanding this behaviour is in the best interest of firms. Researchers are working to answer the question of when and why consumers choose responses such as negative word-of-mouth, misbehaviour and revenge.

Learning objectives

When you have read the chapter, you should be able to:

1. Explain the importance of these behaviours and their role in the marketplace.
2. Define what negative word-of-mouth, misbehaviour and revenge behaviours are and differentiate between them.
3. Understand various internal psychological processes that lead to these behaviours, their influence on consumer decision making and implications for consumer–firm relationships.
4. Understand the theoretical context used to explain these behaviours.
5. Examine the typical nature of firm responses to these behaviours.

2 Route map

Consumer decisions to engage in behaviours such as negative word-of-mouth, misbehaviour and revenge are generally preceded by a dissatisfactory service encounter. This has significant consequences for the customer–firm relationship. While a considerable amount of research has been done on the dissatisfied consumer, today's marketplace further complicates the experience. Today's consumers are very powerful. They have more product and service alternatives and information than ever before. Consumers are communicating their displeasure in a variety of ways, many of which firms are ill-equipped to anticipate or handle. This chapter seeks to explain the importance of negative WOM, misbehaviour and revenge behaviours in the marketplace, and the types of service failures that lead consumers to engage in these behaviours. The chapter examines the various internal psychological processes that lead to these behaviours, their influence on consumer decision making and implications for consumer–firm relationships. The chapter presents multiple theoretical contexts used to explain these behaviours. In addition, the typical firm response processes to these behaviours are presented and new research directions are discussed.

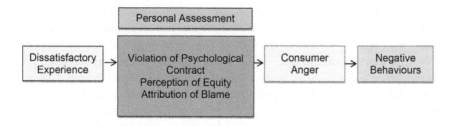

FIGURE 5.1 Conceptual framework of the consumer anger process

3 State of the art in negative WOM, misbehaviour and revenge behaviours

Consumer negative word-of-mouth, misbehaviour and revenge each represent distinct and separate behaviours. Each of these behaviours has its own definition, characteristics and research streams. Therefore, we begin by defining and providing an example of each one.

Negative word-of-mouth

Negative word-of-mouth (WOM) communication is defined as 'all negatively valenced, informal communication between private parties about goods and services and the evaluation thereof' (Wetzer et al., 2007, p. 661). The extent to which consumers engage in negative WOM behaviours depends on two factors: perceived justice (Blodgett et al., 1993) and severity of the problems (Richins, 1983).

While we know that negative WOM occurs frequently, the ramifications in today's digitally connected world can be severe. For example, DoubleTree Club Hotel experienced the impact of negative WOM from two Internet consultants from Seattle. Tom Farmer and Shane Atchison were refused rooms at the hotel despite having received their credit card confirmations and staff having noted their late-night arrival in Houston. Enraged, the two men created a set of PowerPoint slides describing everything that happened that night at the DoubleTree Club Hotel. The two men included approximately how much money the Houston branch would lose, quotes from the employee at the front desk, odds of the two men returning to the DoubleTree Club Hotel, and more. At the end of the PowerPoint presentation, the two men urged people who received the presentation via email to 'share it with their friends'. As a result, thousands of people have seen it. In the end, the firm offered an apology to the affected customers and made sizable donations to Houston's Toys for Tots campaign, but the damage from the spread of the presentation had been done (www.hyperorg.com).

Consumer misbehaviour

Consumer misbehaviour is defined as 'behavioural acts by consumers, which violate the generally accepted norms of conduct in consumption situations' (Fullerton and Punj, 1997, p. 336). Behaviours such as shoplifting, vandalism, financial fraud, coupon fraud, abuse of return policies and the purchase of counterfeit goods, along with many others, would be classified as consumer misbehaviour. According to CNN, an example of consumer misbehaviour occurred in the early morning hours of New Year's Day in 2010, when a 24-year-old female customer from Toledo in Ohio pulled up to the McDonald's drive-thru and ordered chicken nuggets. She was told no McNuggets were available. A verbal argument ensued between the employees and the customer. In the end, the young woman verbally and physically assaulted employees and damaged property because she could not have chicken nuggets. As punishment she spent two months in jail, a year on probation and was forced to pay restitution for the broken window (Sowa, 2009; n.a., 2010).

Consumer revenge

Consumer revenge is defined as the actions taken by a customer to cause harm to a firm for the damage it has caused (Bechwati and Morrin, 2003). Similarly, others have defined consumer revenge as customers causing harm to firms after unacceptable service (Zourrig et al., 2009). Revenge is a key driver of negative WOM, vindictive complaining and switching for a suboptimal alternative (Bechwati and Morrin, 2003; Grégoire and Fisher, 2008).

While these behaviours are distinct, they share some commonalities. Each indicates a breakdown in the customer–firm relationship. In many cases, the breakdown in the relationship begins with a core service failure or inappropriate expectations. Research suggests that these behaviours are occurring more frequently, costing businesses substantial money, inconvenience and distress (Huefner et al., 2002). Many questions regarding these behaviours remain. What types of consumers participate in these behaviours? What situational factors are likely to lead consumers to participate in these behaviours? Why do consumers decide to engage in these behaviours? The answers to these questions hold important information for firms in terms of creating procedures to prevent these behaviours and in recovering from them. In order to manage customer relationships effectively, the process of relationship breakdown must also be understood.

Dissatisfactory experience

Dissatisfaction is the root cause that leads many consumers to participate in negative WOM, misbehaviour and revenge. Seminal research conducted by Hirschman (1970) concluded that dissatisfaction in any relationship could be addressed with three different responses: exit, voice and loyalty. Exit is the termination of the exchange relationship. Exit decisions are perceived as 'painful' for both parties since they involve some effort such as switching costs and searching for alternatives for consumers, and loss of profitability for firms. In the exchange relationship, voice is seen as complaint behaviour. Loyalty is defined as actively doing nothing, but hoping for eventual resolution of the issue. According to Hirschman (1970), complaint behaviour and exit were the only appropriate ways for consumers to communicate displeasure with undesirable market behaviour by firms.

As a result, behaviours outside voice and exit were characterised as negative, ascribed to deviant individuals and were not thought to represent 'normal' consumer behaviour. However, evidence suggests that 'normal' consumers do engage in negative behaviours. The perpetrators of most acts of deviant consumer behaviour are ordinary-seeming people who cannot be differentiated from other consumers on sexual, genetic, socioeconomic, racial, educational or lifestyle grounds (Fullerton and Punj, 1993). So now that we know that consumers who participate in these behaviours are indistinguishable, we must gain a better understanding of what situational factors typically lead otherwise normal consumers to engage in these behaviours.

Typically, but certainly not always, consumers who decide to participate in negative WOM behaviours, misbehaviours and/or revenge behaviours have experienced a service failure. 'Service failure and recovery encounters represent critical moments of truth for organizations in their efforts to satisfy and keep customers' (Smith and Bolton, 2002, p. 5). Consumer responses to dissatisfaction involve both cognitive and affective components (Westbrook, 1987; Westbrook and Oliver, 1991; Oliver, 1997). Hence, cognitive models are limited in their ability to account for satisfaction evaluations and subsequent behaviours (Bagozzi, 1997; Smith and Bolton, 2002). In other words, emotions are important drivers of these behaviours (Bigne et al., 2008; Liljander and Strandvik, 1997; Wirtz and Bateson, 1999). As a result, poor service recovery could potentially turn minor situations into major problems (Hoffman et al., 1995).

Dissatisfying experiences are potentially stressful events that consumers evaluate using the cognitive appraisal process, according to Stephens and Gwinner (1998). This process begins with the consumer perceiving that the action taken by the service provider is harmful or wrong (Aquino et al., 2001), hence the dissatisfactory service evaluation (see Figure 5.1). Next, there is the assignment of blame. Blame is assigned when an individual feels that they have been wronged and that a response is warranted (Felstiner et al., 1980–81). It then triggers emotional responses. The last step in the cognitive process is determining the type of action that will be taken and who will be the target of that action (Aquino et al., 2001; Beugre, 2005).

Consumer anger

However, what distinguishes a merely dissatisfactory experience from one likely to end in negative WOM, misbehaviour or revenge? Typically, the answer is based in emotions – more specifically, anger is the difference. Behaviours that typically follow anger include aggression, hostility and revenge. Consumers engage in these types of behaviours to discourage the service provider from doing what caused the anger and to recover the service failure (Bougie et al., 2003). The experience of anger for the consumer differs from other interpersonal anger experiences in its causes and consequences. The consumption setting is special because it involves specific roles and expectations of its members. Consumer anger is defined as 'an emotional state, which stems from a consumer's perceived loss of entitlement due to an unfair, threatening or harmful consumption experience. These consumption experiences involve interactions with the firm, its products or services, and or its employees' (Funches, 2008, p. 1).

Researchers have proposed various causes for anger. Studies have generally proposed one broad cause. For example, prior research suggests that anger is caused by violations of the moral code of conduct or is the result of moral outrage (Diaz et al., 2002; Weiner, 2000). Anger is also thought to be caused by an inability to attain desired goals (Nyer, 1997). Additionally, feelings of anger are associated with individual perceptions of mistreatment (Rose and Neidermeyer, 1999). Bougie et al. (2003) found that dissatisfaction was an antecedent to anger. Finally, Weiner (2000) suggests that anger is a result of social transgression. More specific knowledge of anger in the consumption setting is needed.

Research conducted by Funches (2011) developed a listing of specific situational causes of consumer anger. The qualitative study employed the critical incident technique to review over 700 anger-evoking service encounters. The incidents revealed three broad causes of consumer anger: broken promises, unfair treatment and expressed hostility. Broken promises were defined as situations where promises or obligations went unfulfilled by the firm or its employees. Unfair treatment situations involved occurrences that excessively favoured the firm. Expressed hostility was defined by an individual's belief that social norms were violated. Since consumer anger experiences are pivotal moments in the consumer–firm relationship, understanding the causes could allow firms to prevent or control consumer anger as well as better manage the recovery process.

Internal psychological processes

In consumer–firm relationships, as in all relationships, we develop expectations. We learn what the other party expects us to contribute and we, in turn, develop notions about what we should receive from the relationship (Heath et al., 1993). The source of these expectations is consumers' past experiences and social norms. Social norms of economic exchange are the understood rules of behaviour for both buyers and sellers, and they serve as guides to behaviours of parties in exchanges (Maxwell, 1999). These repeated interactions with products, brands or employees of the firm lead consumers to form psychological contracts.

Psychological contract

A psychological contract is a set of beliefs held by a person regarding the terms of an exchange agreement to which that person is a party (Robinson and Morrison, 1995). The psychological contract represents a set of unwritten reciprocal expectations between an individual and the firm (Schein, 1978). The psychological contract involves agreements, promises or obligations between the firm and the employee, and is defined by the individual (Lemire and Rouillard, 2005). These contracts are informal, subject to interpretation and evolve over the course of the relationship between the employee and the firm (Lemire and Rouillard, 2005).

Contract violation is more than failure of the organisation to meet expectations; responses are more intensive because respect and codes of conduct are called into question because essentially a 'promise' has been broken and it is more personalised (Rousseau, 1989). Therefore, a violation involves an emotional state, which stems from the belief that the organisation has failed to maintain the psychological contract adequately (Morrison and Robinson, 1997). Any changes in behaviours from expectations are typically perceived to violate the implicit contract and, therefore, are perceived to be unjust and unfair (Heath et al., 1993). These consumer assessments have consequences for the firm. A study conducted by Kalamas et al. (2008) found that, as anger increased, consumers were more likely purposefully to levy consequences against firms.

Customers are no longer just receptacles for firm messages. They can now easily communicate their opinions and evaluations to large audiences (Schultz et al., 2012). The Internet and social media make such communications possible. Today's individual consumer is more powerful than ever. In the typical consumer–firm relationship, the firm has traditionally been viewed as the more powerful entity. However, the tide is changing. Lee (2010) discusses the power asymmetry between firms and consumers, suggesting that many customers indeed enact the proactive, leading roles in their interactions with businesses because of the resources that they possess and the alternative choices readily available to them for their purchase needs (Lancaster, 1990). These occurrences of power asymmetry in favour of the consumer are increasing in both number and frequency.

Theoretical contexts

Traditionally, marketers have addressed passive consumers through television and radio, and their ability to respond to the company's efforts has been mainly limited to their purchase behaviour (Malthouse et al., 2013). However, changing media habits by consumers have reduced the effectiveness of these media. Consumers dramatically shifted their media habits in the early 2000s. They have reduced the amount of time they spend with music, broadcast TV and newspapers, and they have increased the amount of time they spend on the Internet and mobile devices (Vollmer and Precourt, 2008). These types of media allow consumers to control their media experience.

As a result of this new ability to control the media experience, consumers are no longer content just to be spoken to; now they want true interaction. By seeking and developing relationships with consumers, firms have introduced new and greater expectations on the part of consumers. 'Expectations constitute the perceived or psychological contract in a relationship and the benefits we believe we deserve constitute our entitlements' (Heath et al., 1993, p. 75). Expectations and reciprocity are key elements in the concept of entitlement. Entitlements are the benefits that people believe they deserve under the implicit contract (Heath et al., 1993). Any inability of the firm to fulfil consumer-perceived entitlements is viewed as a breach or violation of the psychological contract. In terms of customer relationship management, the development and maintenance of the psychological contract is crucial to healthy profitable exchange relationships.

The idea of a relationship suggests reciprocity, fairness and equity (see Figure 5.2 for an illustration). So the question becomes, what do consumers expect and what happens when firms fail to deliver? Consumers expect not only to receive better and more highly customised products and services from their relationships with firms, but also deeper and more meaningful interactions.

As consumers invest more time, effort and other irrecoverable resources in a relationship, psychological ties and expectations of reciprocation are formed (Blau, 1964). Reciprocity is identified as a key feature explaining the duration and stability of exchange relationships (Larson, 1992). Reciprocity evokes obligation towards others on the basis of past behaviour. The principle of reciprocity states that people should return good for good, in proportion to what they have received (Bagozzi, 1995). Therefore, actions taken by one party in an exchange relationship are expected to be reciprocated in kind by the other party. This principle fosters a positive atmosphere, removes barriers of risk and enables relationships to move forward (Barclay and Smith, 1997).

Through repeated interactions with the firm, customers are able to assess what is fair and equitable in terms of inputs and outcomes. In other words, individuals gauge 'what is right' or 'what they deserve'. Fairness has been defined as a judgement of whether an outcome and/or the process used to reach that outcome are reasonable, acceptable or just (Bolton et al., 2003). These assessments are based on equity theory.

Equity theory is a social comparison theory in which consumers evaluate the ratio of the investments they make to a firm against the benefits they derive from it. According to the principle of distributive justice, people in an exchange relationship with others are entitled to receive a reward that is proportional to what they have invested in the relationship (Homans, 1961). According to equity theory, consumers compare the inputs and outcomes of firms in comparison to their own inputs and outcomes, based on role expectations (Oliver and Swan, 1989). Inequity exists when the perceived inputs and outcomes in an exchange relationship are psychologically inconsistent with some referent (Huppertz et al., 1978).

Perceived inequity in relationships leaves individual participants feeling anxious and tense. The extent to which the consumer believes the encounter to be inequitable determines the type of negative affect experienced (Oliver and Swan, 1989). Then, consumers' perceptions of the fairness of the situation become a key component in their post-purchase response and in how – or if – the relationship is maintained (Blodgett and Anderson, 2000; Maxham, 2001). Another important component in consumer post-purchase response is the element of blame or attribution.

'Attribution theory focuses upon the universal concern with explanation – why a particular event, or state or outcome has come about – and the consequences of phenomenal causality' (Weiner, 2000, p. 382). In the context of service failure, consumers ask why an event was dissatisfactory, whether it will occur again, and who or what is to be blamed. Attribution theory addresses these thoughts, their accompanying emotions and how both influence subsequent behaviours (Weiner, 2000). Attribution theory provides some important insight into the antecedents and consequences of consumer anger. Previously conducted research suggests that emotional responses vary depending on how consumers attribute blame (Machleit

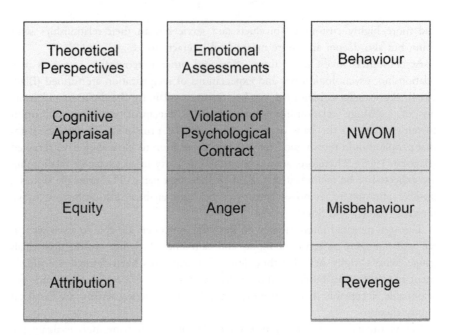

FIGURE 5.2 Theoretical framework

and Mantel, 2001). Blame attribution is believed to affect a variety of emotional experiences, including anger (Machleit and Mantel, 2001; Weiner, 1985). The assignment of responsibility following an unfavourable event affects the intensity of an individual's emotional reaction (Ortony et al., 1988). Therefore, consumer perceptions of psychological contract violation are accompanied by intensive emotional response. In other words, the consumer's perception of causality plays a critical role in the anger experience. This aspect of anger is particularly interesting, because the theory suggests that proper blame assignment provides a guide for future behaviour or remedy (Weiner, 1985).

In fact, consumer research conducted by Nyer (1997) found that different appraisals influenced respondents' emotions – particularly anger – and linked anger to negative WOM behaviour. In addition, Chebat and Slusarczyk (2005) supported the notion that different attributions impact on consumers' behavioural responses. They discussed the differing emotional and behavioural results from attributing blame to the firm or the individual. Likewise, Ruth et al. (2002) investigated how individuals' appraisals of situations correspond to the emotions they experience in those situations. Their work demonstrated that, although consumption emotions are individual experiences, they are not idiosyncratic. Therefore, specific appraisals lead to specific emotions. For instance, anger is thought to be associated with externally placed blame and control (Folkes, 1984).

In terms of customer relationship management, it is important for firms to realise that reciprocity and equitableness are constantly being assessed by consumers. Negative WOM, misbehaviour and revenge behaviours are often enacted in response to perceived injustices. When consumers assign blame to firms for negative experiences, they become angry and seek to damage the firm as a way to bring balance and equity back to the relationship. As a result, the firm's response becomes crucial to the future of the relationship.

Firm responses

Firms are seeking appropriate strategies to reduce or prevent consumer participation in negative WOM, misbehaviour and revenge behaviours. Unfortunately, a great deal of consumer participation in these behaviours is fuelled by the lack of firm response. According to the Customer Rage Survey (Customer Care Alliance, 2013), the number of complaining consumers who received nothing as a result increased by nine percentage points to 56%. Furthermore, the primary causes of consumer anger identified by Funches (2011) were broken promises and unfair treatment. The author delved deeper into these categories, revealing that most of the anger was due to unresponsiveness of the firm. Consumers reported a total lack of firm response to their requests for redress or very time-consuming processes. Such occurrences are incredibly damaging to the customer–firm relationship, costing both parties time and money and preventing both from fully realising the highest potential of their investments.

Addressing negative consumer behaviour is a tricky and sensitive process for firms. Some firms have responded by trying to curtail consumers' ability to convey negative information (such as buying up domain names for potential hate sites), with little success. Other firms have ignored consumer negative behaviours, often with disastrous consequences. Other firms have been overwhelmed by trying to respond to consumer negative behaviours. 'Retailing practitioners have long wrestled with the possibility of controlling – if not eradicating – misbehaviour by customers' (Fullerton and Punj, 1997, p. 340).

Some of the research into consumer misbehaviour and revenge has provided suggestions to firms regarding appropriate responses. For example, Funches et al. (2009) state that companies can avoid acts of retaliation if interactional justice is maintained throughout the front-line employee–customer interface. In addition, the authors suggest service providers should establish and communicate their procedures for managing key contact employees who provide poor customer service. Customers are less likely to engage in retaliatory behaviour if they feel mechanisms are in place to punish offending employees (Aquino et al., 2006).

However, very few studies have examined the role firm responses play in deffusing consumer anger situations. One such study conducted by Menon and Dube (2004) explored the role that provider responses can play in the relationship between consumer anger and subsequent satisfaction judgements. Menon and Dube's paper was based on the idea that consumer satisfaction could be improved by employing appropriate provider responses to specific consumer emotions. They found that firms seemed to have a difficult time responding appropriately to consumer anger. This is not surprising, given the highly contagious nature of anger. Front-line employees must be trained to deal with consumer anger effectively.

A study conducted by Funches and Foxx (2009) examined whether the intent of the individual posting impacted on the influence of negative online message postings. The results suggested that these communications, although influential, may not be as damaging as once thought. Consumers appear to discern intentions fairly well and then weigh the information accordingly. So extremely negative online postings with the intent of damaging the firm were discounted and seen as less valid by other consumers than less negative postings with the intent of warning other consumers.

The primary means for addressing negative behaviours have been education and deterrence. The educational approach seeks to change attitudes and subsequently behaviours through the use of messages designed to strengthen moral constraints. The deterrence approach uses formal and informal sanctions in order to heighten the perceived risks of misbehaviour, thereby reducing opportunism. Unfortunately, there exists very little information as to which approach is the best to use in specific situations. As a result, firms are still trying to determine the best ways to respond, through trial and error.

4 New research directions

Despite the breadth of research that has been conducted, there are many questions left unanswered. As academics and practitioners seek to manage better the customer-firm relationship process, more focus must be placed on the dissolution and termination of relationships. As our understanding of the demise process grows, so too will our ability to foresee and prevent such a demise.

An inordinate amount of research has been conducted regarding the benefits of relationships for firms and the role that firms should play in developing those relationships. However, this has left a huge gap in the understanding of the customer's role. This role is much broader than simply communicating satisfaction or dissatisfaction through purchase behaviour. In the quest to create relationships with customers, their expectations have been largely ignored. This omission is illustrated in ever-growing customer rage levels.

The customer–firm relationship has been forever altered in terms of power and expectations. These changes are the core issues that must be examined and understood in order to address behaviours such as negative WOM, misbehaviour and revenge. The first questions that must be addressed are: When consumers enter into relationships, rather than mere exchanges, what are their expectations? What role do firms play in shaping those expectations?

Gaining insight into these issues will require deeper interactions with customers. The hallmark of relationships is dialogue. Historically, marketers have engaged in one-way communication. Today's marketing media – the Internet, Facebook, Twitter and so forth – allow for more true communication and today's customers require this.

Subsequent research should also focus on the design of appropriate preventative measures and responses to various forms of consumer negative behaviours. These behaviours are far more expansive than detailed here. In fact, consumers are now hijacking firms' hashtags and sabotaging marketing efforts. As technology provides more means of communicating with customers, firms will need to be more vigilant and responsive to what consumers are communicating back.

Firms are collecting a great deal of data from consumers at various touchpoints. Could these data be used proactively to identify relationships between situational factors and the occurrence of consumer negative behaviours? In other words, could employees be trained to flag potentially problematic exchanges (late deliveries, multiple returns, numerous contacts with customer service representatives, etc.) with customers and offer redress, without the customer even initiating such a response?

Of course, further understanding of cultural factors might determine different rules of engagement and, therefore, lead to consumers engaging in negative behaviours. In addition, insight may also be gained by understanding the moderating roles of relationship duration, loyalty and power distance on consumer participation in negative behaviours.

5 Practising marketing – a case study

Dave Carroll and a few of his fellow band members were flying United Airlines from Halifax in Nova Scotia to Omaha in Nebraska. During the layover at Chicago's O'Hare Airport, the debacle occurred. Another passenger commented, 'My God! They're throwing guitars out there!' As suspected, Carroll later discovered that his US$3,500 Taylor guitar was broken.

What occurred next was a customer service nightmare. For the next nine months Carroll contacted multiple United representatives by phone and email about the incident, only to be told repeatedly that he had waited more than the allowable 24 hours to make his claim, so his request for $1,200 in damages would not be paid.

Frustrated and out of viable options, Carroll turned to his natural talents and decided to write a song about his experience. The song was titled 'United Breaks Guitars'. He went even further. With a group of friends he created three songs with accompanying videos, which he posted on YouTube to enormous success. The videos went viral in a big way. Fellow consumers loved the video trilogy and frequently passed them on. The 'United Breaks Guitars' video trilogy received over 12.5 million views. Carroll did over 200 interviews relaying his tale of woe and performing his song for radio and TV shows across the United States. In addition, numerous newspapers and media broadcasts ran the story. Pretty soon the story was everywhere.

United decided to give in and offered Carroll compensation for the damages, but it was too late: the video had taken on a life of its own and Carroll refused the offer. United's stock price declined by 10% in the first month the video appeared, resulting in a devaluation of nearly $180 million. Taylor guitars replaced Carroll's guitar for free and his song-writing and performing career exploded (*Huffington Post*, 2009).

Discussion questions

1. Did Dave Carroll really exhaust all options of redress available to him? What would you have done in this case?
2. What key opportunities did United miss? In hindsight, what should they have done?
3. Is United's reputation still damaged today by Dave Carroll's case?
4. What strategy should firms pursue in response to consumer negative behaviours – education or deterrence – and why?
5. While it worked out well for Dave Carroll, are public shaming and other types of revenge a good idea in your opinion?

6 Further investigation

Questions

1. What are the expectations of customers in the customer–firm relationship?
2. Technology now allows firms to monitor consumer communications online. How should firms utilise this capability to respond to negative word-of-mouth online?
3. Should firms use education or deterrence to dissuade consumer participation in misbehaviour? Why? Develop an appropriate strategy a firm could use to discourage consumers from participating in misbehaviour.
4. Consumer efforts to seek revenge can be disastrous for firms. Find a current example of consumer revenge and identify all the missed opportunities the firm had to de-escalate the situation.

Projects

1. Students should divide into teams. Review the latest Customer Rage Survey and develop insights for firms.
2. Firms face significant challenges in deciding which consumer communications to respond to. Develop a plan for classifying consumer communications based on damage potential and create a response strategy for each classification.
3. Pick a firm and identify how it could use customer data to identify gaps in its customer service plan. How can firms address these gaps?

References

Aquino, K., Tripp, T.M. and Bies, R.J. (2001). How employees respond to personal offense: the effects of blame attribution, victim status, and offender status on revenge and reconciliation in the workplace. *Journal of Applied Psychology*, 86(1), pp. 52–59.

Aquino, K., Tripp, T.M. and Bies, R.J. (2006). Getting even or moving on? Power, procedural justice, and types of offense as predictors of revenge, forgiveness, reconciliation, and avoidance in organizations. *Journal of Applied Psychology*, 1(5), pp. 653–668.

Averill, J.R. (1982). *Anger and Aggression: An Essay on Emotion*. Springer-Verlag, New York.

Bagozzi, R.P. (1995). Reflections on relationship marketing in consumer markets. *Academy of Marketing Science Journal*, 23(4), pp. 272–278.

Bagozzi, R.P. (1997). Goal-directed behaviours in marketing: cognitive and emotional perspectives. *Psychology & Marketing*, 6(14), pp. 539–543.

Barclay, D.W. and Smith, J.B. (1997). The effects of organizational differences and trust on the effectiveness of selling partners relationships. *Journal of Marketing*, 61(1), pp. 3–21.

Bechwati, N.N. and Morrin, M. (2003). Outraged consumers: getting even at the expense of getting a good deal. *Journal of Consumer Psychology*, 13(4), pp. 440–453.

Beugre, C.D. (2005). Reacting aggressively to injustice at work: a cognitive stage model. *Journal of Business Psychology*, 20, pp. 291–301.

Bigne, J.E., Mattila, A.S. and Andreu, L. (2008). The impact of experiential consumption cognitions and emotions on behavioural intentions. *Journal of Services Marketing*, 22(4), pp. 303–315.

Blau, P.M. (1964). *Exchange and Power in Social Life*. Wiley, New York.

Blodgett, J.G. and Anderson, R.D. (2000). A Bayesian network model of the consumer complaint process. *Journal of Service Research*, 2(4), pp. 321–338.

Blodgett, J.G., Granbois, D.H. and Walters, R.G. (1993). The effects of perceived justice on complainants' negative word-of-mouth behaviour and repatronage intentions. *Journal of Retailing*, 69(4), pp. 399–427.

Bolton, L.E., Warlop, L. and Alba, J.W. (2003). Consumer perceptions of price (un)fairness. *Journal of Consumer Research*, 29(4), pp. 474–492.

Bougie, R., Pieters, R. and Zeelenberg, M. (2003). Angry customers don't come back, they get back: the experience and behavioural implications of anger and dissatisfaction in services. *Journal of the Academy of Marketing Science*, 31(4) (Fall), pp. 377–394.

Chebat, J. and Slusarczyk, W. (2005). How emotions mediate the effects of perceived justice on loyalty in service recovery situations: an empirical study. *Journal of Business Research*, 58(5), pp. 664–673.

Customer Care Alliance (2013). Customer Rage Survey. www.customercaremc.com/the-2013-customer-rage-study.

Diaz, A., Casado, B. and Mas Ruiz, F.J. (2002). The consumer's reaction to delays in service. *International Journal of Service Industry Management*, 13(2), pp. 118–140.

Felstiner, W., Abel, R. and Sarat, A. (1980–81). The emergence & transformation of disputes: naming, blaming, claiming. *Law & Society Review*, 15(3/4), pp. 631–654.

Folkes, V.S. (1984). Consumer reactions to product failure: an attributional approach. *Journal of Consumer Research*, 11, pp. 398–409.

Fullerton, R.A. and Punj, G. (1993). Choosing to misbehave: a structural model of aberrant consumer behaviour. *Advances in Consumer Research*, 20, pp. 570–574.

Fullerton, R.A. and Punj, G. (1997). 'Can consumer misbehavior be controlled? A critical analysis of two major control techniques'. In M. Brucks and D.J. MacInnis (eds) *Advances in Consumer Research*, Vol. 24. Provo, UT: Association for Consumer Research, pp. 340–344.

Funches, V. (2008). *Shoppers Scorned*. VDM Publishing.

Funches, V. (2011). The consumer anger phenomena: causes and consequences. *Journal of Services Marketing*, 25(6), pp. 420–428.

Funches, V. and Foxx, W. (2009). Electronic word-of-mouth: should firms be concerned? Society of Marketing Conference, New Orleans, La.

Funches, V., Markley, M. and Davis, L. (2009). Reprisal, retribution, requital: investigating customer retaliation. *Journal of Business Research*, 62(2), pp. 231–238.

Grégoire, Y. and Fisher, R.J. (2008). Customer betrayal and retaliation: when your best customers become your worst enemies. *Journal of the Academy of Marketing Science*, 36(2), pp. 247–261.

Heath, C., Knez, M. and Camerer, C. (1993). The strategic management of the entitlement process in the employment relationship. *Strategic Management Journal*, 14, pp. 75–93.

Hirschman, A.O. (1970). *Exit, Voice and Loyalty: Responses to Decline in Firms, Organizations and States*. Harvard University Press, Cambridge, MA.

Hoffman, K.D., Kelley, S.W. and Rotalsky, H.M. (1995). Tracking service failures and employee recovery efforts. *Journal of Services Marketing*, 9(2), pp. 49–61.

Homans, G.C. (1961). *Social Behaviour: Its Elementary Form*. Harcourt Brace Jovanovich, New York.

Huefner, J.C. and Hunt, H.K. (2000). Consumer retaliation as a response to dissatisfaction. *Journal of Consumer Satisfaction, Dissatisfaction and Complaining Behaviour*, 13, pp. 61–82.

Huefner, J.C., Parry, B.L., Payne, C.R., Otto, S.D., Huff, S.C., Swenson, M.J. and Hunt, H.K. (2002). Consumer retaliation: confirmation and extension. *Journal of Consumer Satisfaction, Dissatisfaction and Complaining Behaviour*, 15, pp. 114–127.

Huffington Post (2009). 'United breaks guitars': did it really cost the airline $180 million? www.huffingtonpost.com/2009/07/27.

Huppertz, J.W., Arenson, S.J. and Evans, R.H. (1978). An application of equity theory to buyer-seller exchange situations. *Journal of Marketing Research*, 15(5), pp. 250–260.

Kalamas, M., Laroche, M. and Makdessian, L. (2008). Reaching the boiling point: consumer's negative affective reactions to firm-attributed service failures. *Journal of Business Research*, 61, pp. 813–824.

Lancaster, K. (1990). The economics of product variety: a survey. *Marketing Science*, 9(3), pp. 189–206.

Larson, A. (1992). Network dyads in entrepreneurial settings: a study of the governance of exchange relationships. *Administrative Science Quarterly*, 37(1), p. 76–105.

Lee, J. (2010). Perceived power imbalance and customer dissatisfaction. *The Service Industries Journal*, 30(7), pp. 1113–1137.

Lemire, L. and Rouillard, C. (2005). An empirical exploration of psychological contract fulfillment and individual behaviour. *Journal of Managerial Psychology*, 20(2), pp. 150–163.

Liljander, V. and Strandvik, T. (1997). Emotions in service satisfaction. *International Journal of Service Industry Management*, pp. 148–169.

Machleit, K.A. and Mantel, S.P. (2001). Emotional response and shopping satisfaction moderating effects of shopper attributions. *Journal of Business Research*, 54, pp. 97–106.

Malthouse, E.C., Haenlein, M., Skiera, B., Wege, E. and Zhang, M. (2013). Managing customer relationships in the social media era: introducing the social CRM house. *Journal of Interactive Marketing*, 27, pp. 270–280.

Maxham, J.G. III (2001). Service recovery's influence on consumer satisfaction, positive word-of-mouth, and purchase intentions. *Journal of Business Research*, 54(1), pp. 11–24.

Maxwell, S. (1999). The social norm of discrete consumer exchange: classification and quantification. *The American Journal of Economics and Sociology*, 58(4), pp. 999–1019.

Menon, K. and Dube, L. (2004). Service provider responses to anxious and angry customers: different challenges, different payoffs. *Journal of Retailing*, 80, p. 229–237.

Morrison, E.W. and Robinson, S.L. (1997). When employees feel betrayed: a model of how psychological contract fulfilment develops. *Academy of Management Review*, 22, pp. 226–256.

n.a. (2010). Rage over McNuggets sends woman to jail. 10 August. www.nbc4i.com/story/20749053/rage-over-mcnuggets-sends-woman-to-jail (accessed 8 September 2014).

Nyer, P.U. (1997). A study of the relationships between cognitive appraisals and consumption emotions. *Journal of the Academy of Marketing Science*, 25(4), pp. 296–304.

Oliver, R.L. (1997). *Satisfaction: A Behavioural Perspective on the Consumer*. McGraw Hill, New York.

Oliver, R.L. and Swan, J.E. (1989). Equity and disconfirmation perceptions as influences on merchant and product satisfaction. *Journal of Consumer Research*, 16(12), pp. 372–383.

Ortony, A., Clore, G.L. and Collins, A. (1988). *The Cognitive Structure of Emotions*. Press Syndicate of the University of Cambridge, New York.

Richins, M. (1983). Negative word-of-mouth by dissatisfied consumers: a pilot study. *Journal of Marketing*, 47(1), pp. 68–78.

Robinson, S.L. and Morrison, E.W. (1995). Psychological contract and OCB: the effects of unfulfilled obligations. *Journal of Organizational Behaviour*, 16, pp. 289–298.

Rose, R.L. and Neidermeyer, M. (1999). From rudeness to roadrage: the antecedents and consequences of consumer aggression. *Advances in Consumer Research*, 26, pp. 12–17.

Rousseau, D.M. (1989). Psychological and implied contracts in organizations. *Employee Responsibilities and Rights Journal*, 2, pp. 121–139.

Rousseau, D.M. (1995). *Psychological Contracts in Organizations: Understanding Written and Unwritten Agreements*. Sage Publications, Thousand Oaks, CA.

Ruth, J.A., Brunel, F.F. and Otnes, C.C. (2002). Linking thoughts to feelings: investigating cognitive appraisals and consumption emotions in a mixed-emotions context. *Journal of the Academy of Marketing Science*, 30(1), pp. 44–58.

Schein, E.H. (1978). *Career Dynamics: Matching Individual and Organizational Needs*. Addison-Wesley, Reading, MA.

Schultz, D., Malthouse, E. and Pick, D. (2012). 'From CM to CRM to CN2: a research agenda for the marketing communications transition'. In Tobias Langner, Shitaro Okazaki, Martin Eisend (Eds) *Advances in Advertising Research, 3*, pp. 421–432. European Advertising Academy.

Smith, A.K. and Bolton, R. (2002a). The effect of customers' emotional responses to service failures on their recovery effort evaluations and satisfaction judgments. *Journal of the Academy of Marketing Science*, 30(1), pp. 5–23.

Sowa, C. (2009) Wanted: reputation killer – negative word-of-mouth. America's best companies. www.americasbestcompanies.com (accessed August 2014).

Stephens, N. and Gwinner, K.P. (1998). Why don't some people complain? A cognitive-emotive process model of consumer complaint behaviour. *Journal of the Academy of Marketing Science*, 26(3), pp. 172–189.

Vollmer, C. and Precourt, G. (2008). *Always On: Advertising, Marketing, and Media in an Era of Consumer Control*. McGraw Hill Companies, New York.

Weiner, B. (1985). An attributional theory of achievement motivation and emotion. *Psychological Review*, 92(4), pp. 548–573.

Weiner, B. (2000). Attributional thoughts about consumer behavior. *Journal of Consumer Research*, 27(3), pp. 382–387.

Westbrook, R.A. (1987). Product/consumption-based affective responses and postpurchase processes. *Journal of Marketing Research*, 24(8), pp. 258–270.

Westbrook, R.A. and Oliver, R.L. (1991). The dimensionality of consumption emotion patterns and consumer satisfaction. *Journal of Consumer Research*, 18(6), pp. 84–91.

Wetzer, I.M., Zeelenberg, M. and Pieters, R. (2007). 'Never eat in that restaurant, I did!': exploring why people engage in negative word-of-mouth communication. *Psychology and Marketing*, 24(8), pp. 661–680.

Wirtz, J. and Bateson, J.E.G. (1999). Consumer satisfaction with services: integrating the environment perspective in services marketing into the traditional disconfirmation paradigm. *Journal of Business Research*, 44, pp. 55–66.

Zourrig, H., Chebat, J.C. and Toffoli, R. (2009). Consumer revenge behavior: a cross-cultural perspective. *Journal of Business Research*, 62, pp. 995–1001.

Further reading

Funches, V. (2009) *Shoppers Scorned*. VDM Verlag.
Vollmer, C. and Precourt, G. (2008) *Always On: Advertising, Marketing, and Media in an Era of Consumer Control*. McGraw-Hill.

PART III
Relationships

6

GOOD VERSUS BAD RELATIONSHIP FRAMEWORK

Donald J. Lund, Irina V. Kozlenkova and Robert W. Palmatier

1 Introduction

Just like certain behaviours can make or break interpersonal relationships such as a marriage, theoretical and empirical research as well as anecdotal evidence from different companies shows that, in business-to-business or business-to-consumer relationships, there exist certain mechanisms that either improve (positive mediating mechanisms) or severely damage (negative mediating mechanisms) these relationships and even lead to their dissolution. Here we will discuss the drivers of both positive and negative mediating mechanisms. We will then review the effects of positive and negative mediating mechanisms on relationship performance. Finally, we will summarise research findings on situations in which these mechanisms are especially helpful or detrimental to a business relationship.

There are various drivers that have an impact on positive and negative mediating mechanisms of relationship performance – for instance, how well partners are able to communicate with each other, the dependence of business partners on one other, investments in the relationship, relationship duration, level of expertise and similarity all affect the development of positive and negative mediating mechanisms. We summarise the most common theoretical underpinnings for these linkages, which include equity theory, social exchange theory, relationship marketing and transaction cost economics, synthesising decades of empirical results from seminal academic research.

Learning objectives

When you have read the chapter, you should be able to:

1.   Describe the seven drivers of exchange relationship performance.

2. Explain the process through which relational drivers impact on relationship performance.
3. Describe the positive and negative relational mediating mechanisms.
4. Identify conditions that enhance the impact of relational drivers on exchange relationship performance.
5. Apply relationship marketing concepts to a real marketing problem.
6. Identify and explain the four theories commonly applied to describe negative and positive effects in exchange relationships.

2 Route map

Performance of a business relationship may be measured in a number of different ways. Some of the outcomes are more attitudinal in nature, such as customer loyalty and satisfaction, whereas other desirable outcomes of business relationships have more direct financial consequences and include word-of-mouth, sales growth, market share and profit margins. Mechanisms that improve these performance outcomes include gratitude, trust, commitment and reciprocal norms of partners involved in the relationship. Some of these mechanisms, such as gratitude and trust, have more of a short-term effect on performance, while others have a lasting impact. Negative mechanisms that hurt performance include opportunism, conflict, unfairness and complacency. These behaviours can damage relationships over a relatively short period of time (opportunism and conflict), or long into the future (unfairness and complacency).

Overall, the aim of this chapter is to provide the reader with an understanding of *which* factors can make business relationships more or less successful, and *when* these factors will be especially helpful or detrimental. This knowledge can help guide decision making when managing relationships with suppliers or customers, be they individuals or firms. In the following sections, we review the relational drivers that impact positive and negative relational mediators and contingency factors that make these mediators more or less impactful on relationship performance. Figure 6.1 illustrates the framework discussed in this chapter.

3 State of the art in good versus bad relationships

Drivers of positive and negative relational mediators

Firms expend substantial effort to build stronger relationships with customers. Often these efforts positively impact on customers and build commitment, trust, gratitude and reciprocal norms, which deepen the relationship and lead to greater value creation for both parties. These relational drivers may be actively pursued, or could be more passive characteristics of the relationship or environment. In this section, we first summarise common theories (see Table 6.1 below) employed to describe this process and then review the relationship management strategies that impact both positive and negative relational mediators.

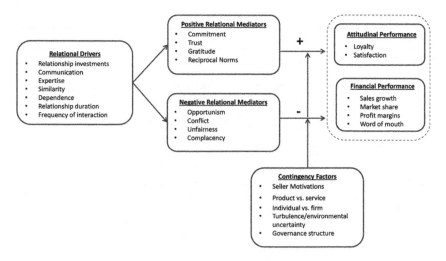

FIGURE 6.1 Conceptual framework

Relationship investments

Sellers invest time, effort and financial resources into building stronger relationships with their customers, with the goal of creating value and benefits for both parties. These benefits may include time savings, convenience, interpersonal relationships, greater financial rewards and more efficient decision-making processes. Gifts, personalised communications, preferential treatment and loyalty programmes are all examples of ways sellers may invest in relationships with their customers. These seller-generated investments are designed to create value for one or both parties, but they have the added benefit of building a psychological debt based on norms of reciprocity (Gouldner, 1960). Paying off this reciprocal debt benefits the relationship through two distinct processes: first, when seller relational investments benefit the customer, customers are more likely to increase purchases to avoid feelings of guilt caused by this reciprocal debt (Dahl et al., 2005; Palmatier et al., 2009); second, the reciprocal debt indirectly benefits both parties by deepening psychological bonds and strengthening commitment to the relationship over time (Becker, 1956; De Wulf et al., 2001). This process may even result in the customer investing in the relationship by affording preferential status to the seller, expanding his or her breadth of purchases, or promoting the seller directly or indirectly through social media outlets to potential customers.

Relationship investments can be classified as financial, social or structural in nature (Berry, 1995). Financial relationship investments can include discounts, free products and other financial benefits that reward customer purchases. Although Bolton et al. (2000) find that financial programmes can result in adequate returns for companies, these programmes are likely to be unsustainable as competitive strategies due to the ease with which they can be replicated by competitors (Day

TABLE 6.1 Common theories of relational drivers

Theory	Description	Key findings	Representative papers
Equity theory	Equity in exchange relationships is desired such that one's own ratio of outcomes/inputs is similar to one's partner's ratio of outcomes/inputs	When inequity is perceived in exchange relationships, efforts will be made to adjust either the inputs or outcomes (or both) such that equity is achieved	Adams 1965; Frazier 1983; Huppertz et al. 1978
Social exchange theory	A theory of social interaction based on the idea that people seek equitable responses for their inputs into social exchanges	Social exchange theory views efforts made at social interaction (whether they are financial or otherwise) as inputs into a relationship. When people feel undervalued or poorly treated, they are likely to retaliate or exit a relationship	Homans 1950, 1961; Macneil 1986
Relationship marketing theory	The process of identifying, developing, maintaining and terminating relational exchanges with the purpose of enhancing performance	Efforts and investments in the relationship impact key mediating mechanisms (e.g. commitment, trust and others), which in turn drive attitudinal and behavioural outcomes	Dwyer et al. 1987; Morgan and Hunt 1994; Palmatier et al. 2006a
Transaction cost economics	Focuses on the 'make or buy' decision based on the goal of reducing transaction costs (safeguarding and monitoring costs)	Demonstrates that relationship governance can serve many of the same functions as vertical integration to suppress opportunism and reduce transaction costs, thereby enhancing relationship performance	Heide 1994; Williamson 1998, 1979

and Wensley, 1988). Social relationship investments include entertainment, meals and special treatment of customers. Social investments develop bonds that are difficult for other firms to imitate and create close ties with the customer, resulting in repeat business, recommendations to others and increased loyalty by building commitment in the relationship. When firms make social investments in relationships with customers, customers are also more likely to ignore competitive offers (Blau, 1964; De Wulf et al., 2001). Structural relationship investments are designed to enhance relationship productivity and/or efficiency by introducing specialised processes or procedures that customers are unlikely or unable to develop themselves. Customised order processing systems, dedicated personnel and integrated distribution systems are all examples of structural relationship investments. For example, Delta Airlines rewards its frequent flyers by providing them with a dedicated customer service telephone number. These customers are then able to resolve any travel issues with Delta faster than other customers. Such investments involve substantial setup costs and are typically customised for each relationship, offering the customer a unique value proposition that decreases the likelihood of the customer switching to a competitor (Berry, 1995).

The nature and magnitude of impact from these various relationship investments may vary (Palmatier et al., 2006b); however, when successful, all three types of relationship investment can benefit the customer. It is widely recognised that the receipt of any type of benefit causes people to feel indebted to reciprocate, and further that failure to fulfil that obligation can lead to feelings of guilt (Becker, 1986; Dahl et al., 2005). It is said that people are 'hard-wired' not only to recognise these reciprocal obligations, but also to repay those who provide them with any type of benefit through some beneficial action of their own. Thus, relationship investments not only impact trust and commitment by signalling the seller's interest in supporting the success of the customer, but also create feelings of gratitude and encourage reciprocal norms as customers perceive, internalise and repay benefits gained through the actions of the seller. The most effective relationship investments tap into this reciprocal process to help strengthen the relationship over time.

Communication

Communication, defined as the amount, frequency and quality of information shared between exchange partners (Mohr et al., 1996), builds many of the positive relational mediators to help develop stronger relationships. Information shared through bilateral communication increases trust, as parties become confident that their partner intends to uphold their end of the relationship. Communication develops a better understanding of the goals and intentions of the other party, allowing relationship partners to identify new value-creating possibilities and help develop commitment within the relationship (Joshi, 2009; Mohr et al., 1996). Frequent communications early in a relationship not only build initial levels of trust (Morgan and Hunt, 1994), but also increase the speed at which trust develops (Palmatier et al., 2013).

Because communication involves the sharing of quality information between partners, effective communication reduces many negative relational mediators. For example, communication will reduce relationship conflict (LaBahn and Harich, 1997), as shared information aids in the effective resolution of disagreements throughout a relationship (Morgan and Hunt, 1994). Additionally, because communication is built on open and factual sharing of information, the ability to engage in deceptive behaviour is diminished, thus reducing the prevalence of opportunism (Macneil, 1982; Williamson, 1975). Finally, open lines of communication help increase awareness of potential obstacles and challenges, thus reducing the likelihood that either relationship partner will become complacent.

Overall, effective bilateral communication is one of the most impactful relational drivers (Palmatier et al., 2006a) as it not only boosts many of the positive relational mediators, but also helps eliminate (or at least decrease) many of the negative relational mediators.

Expertise

Vargo and Lusch (2004, p. 3) argue that, 'skills and knowledge are the fundamental unit of exchange'. Seller expertise is defined as the knowledge, experience and overall competence of the seller (Palmatier et al., 2006a). Information shared by sellers with greater expertise is perceived as more reliable, valuable and persuasive – all attributes that translate into the partner being perceived as more trustworthy (Dholakia and Sternthal, 1977). Additionally, dealing with a competent seller results in greater value creation, which encourages customers to become more committed, evidenced by greater investments to strengthen and maintain their relationship (Lagace et al., 1991).

It should be expected that seller expertise will lead to success; however, the magnitude of this impact may be surprising. Palmatier et al. (2006a) found that seller expertise, which can include industry and product-specific expertise, process knowledge, overall customer knowledge and creativity, has a greater positive impact on relationship quality than communication, relationship investments or similarity. Based on this, the authors argue that proper training of boundary-spanning personnel is imperative, because incompetent front-line employees can drastically undermine other firm efforts to build strong customer relationships.

Similarity

Similarity of business partners on an individual level is evident by commonalities in appearance, lifestyle and status, while on an organisational level similarity relates to the coordination of firms' cultures, values and goals (Nicholson et al., 2001). Similarity strengthens relationships by indicating that exchange partners share and understand common goals (Johnson and Johnson, 1972). Common goals and perspective help reduce uncertainty about the partner's actions, which increases trust and commitment in a relationship (Boles et al., 2000; Doney and Cannon, 1997; Nicholson et al., 2001). Common perspectives and expectations between partners reduce opportunism (Wong et al., 2005), and also help norms of reciprocity develop within the relationship, as both partners have similar expectations for acceptable reactions to relationship investments. While exchange relationships can persist with little similarity between partners, it is likely that some degree of similarity is required in order to advance beyond transactional exchange into being more relational in nature. For example, consumers may purchase utilitarian items, such as paper towels from Walmart, but if they are seeking organic products, they are more likely to develop feelings of trust and commitment to a specialised seller, like Whole Foods, with which they perceive more similarity. Similarity also reduces conflict as shared understanding of the partner's needs and expectations results in fewer opportunities for differences in perspective to disrupt the relationship.

Similarity between the buyer and seller is an important aspect of the branding process. Both consumer and organisational product and service companies invest substantial resources to position their brands to appeal to their target market. One way to create that appeal is to build the perception that the brand shares similarities with the target audience. Evidence for this can be seen in advertising strategies across the automobile industry. For example, marketing messages for Kia are designed to appeal (create the perception of similarity) to a younger urban and hip crowd, while those for Cadillac strive to relate to a more established and wealthier audience.

Dependence

Dependence is the reliance of one party on another due to a lack of available alternatives (Morgan and Hunt, 1994). Unlike the other relational drivers discussed up to this point, dependence can have both positive and negative effects on relationships. When two parties depend on each other (interdependence), the relationship prospers through greater levels of commitment and the potential to develop relational norms, while also reducing opportunism (Gundlach and Cadotte, 1994); however, when there are dependence asymmetries (one party is highly dependent on its partner, while the partner is much less so), conflict and unfairness are likely to result (Bucklin and Sengupta, 1993; Gassenheimer et al., 1998; Hibbard et al., 2001). For example, Procter & Gamble likely has a healthier relationship (less conflict, unfairness and opportunism) with Walmart than do many of Walmart's smaller suppliers (which are very dependent on Walmart), as both Walmart and P&G would have a very difficult time replacing each other should their highly interdependent relationship end.

Dependence does have a strong impact on commitment because, with few alternatives available, exchange partners are likely to desire to continue their relationship. However, we do not see the same effect on trust (or other affective relational measures), because as one partner grows more dependent on the other, they become more prone to opportunistic actions by their partner. Due to this double-edged effect of dependence in exchange relationships, it is important that marketers ensure that their relationship strategies do not result in large dependence asymmetries, increased switching costs and customer lock-in, as these strategies may not be effective and, in some cases, may actually lead to the deterioration of the relationship.

Relationship duration and frequency of interactions

The relationship duration (the length of the relationship between exchange part-ners) and the frequency of interactions (the number of interactions per unit of time between exchange partners) both increase trust and signal that commitment may exist within the relationship as well. However, these are not primary drivers of relationship success. Relationships will only endure if both parties experience some measure of success; however, duration by itself may be an indication of high levels of dependence and a lack of viable alternatives. Further, as relationships progress, parties become more comfortable with each other and thus are more likely to become complacent, missing opportunities and threats in the market or the rela-tionship itself (Chowdhury and Lang, 1996). The impact of interaction frequency on trust is relatively larger than the impact of relationship duration, as frequent interactions build confidence in the partner's reliability and integrity. Greater interaction frequency reduces the risk of opportunism and more frequent interac-tions also allow parties to gain a better understanding of their partner, which reduces uncertainty about their future behaviour. Interaction frequency may also encourage the development of relational norms, although interaction frequency alone would not drive satisfaction or commitment. Other relationship drivers would need to work in conjunction with interaction frequency in order to result in high-quality relationships.

Summary

In this section, we have reviewed various strategies or drivers of relational media-tors. These strategies may be controlled by the selling firm (e.g. relationship investments), dictated by the industry or other characteristics outside the control of the selling firm (e.g. interaction frequency), or some combination of the two (e.g. dependence). Many of the drivers can impact as both positive and negative rela-tional mediators, depending on the quality of their implementation and how they are perceived by the customer. To be most effective, firms need to develop seller expertise, make sure their relationship investments result in customer benefits, encourage effective bilateral communication, and highlight similarities of both boundary spanning and organisational-level characteristics with those of targeted customers. Additionally, customer dependence, relationship duration and interac-tion frequency are more effective when combined with other relationship drivers that impact affective relational mediators.

TABLE 6.2 Relational drivers

Constructs	Definitions	Theories	Key findings	Representative papers
Relationship investment	Seller's investment of time, effort, spending and resources focused on building a stronger relationship	Relationship marketing theory	Social and structural investments have positive direct effects on customer return, and structural investments are enhanced by interaction frequency. Financial investments positively interact with buyer commitment and ownership interest, and a negative interaction with existence of a customer relationship management system	De Wulf et al. 2001; Ganesan 1994
Communication	Amount, frequency and quality of information shared between exchange partners	Information processing theory	Communication has a positive impact on trust, commitment, trust velocity and relational norms, and a negative impact on conflict, opportunism and complacency	Anderson and Weitz 1992; Mohr et al. 1996; Morgan and Hunt 1994
Expertise	Knowledge, experience and overall competency of seller	Service dominant logic; resource-based theory	Positive impact on trust, commitment and satisfaction	Crosby et al. 1990; Lagace et al. 1991

Constructs	Definitions	Theories	Key findings	Representative papers
Similarity	Commonality in appearance, lifestyle and status between individual boundary spanners, or similar cultures, values and goals between buying and selling organisations	Social identity theory	Positive impact on trust, commitment and the development of relational norms	Crosby et al. 1990; Doney and Cannon 1997; Morgan and Hunt 1994
Dependence	Customer's evaluation of the value of seller-provided resources for which few alternatives are available from other sellers	Power-dependence framework; bilateral deterrence theory	Interdependence leads to commitment and relational norms; dependence asymmetry leads to conflict, opportunism and unfairness	Hibbard et al. 2001; Morgan and Hunt 1994
Relationship duration	Length of time that the relationship between the exchange partners has existed	Social exchange theory	Positive impact on trust and complacency	Anderson and Weitz 1989; Doney and Cannon 1997; Kumar et al. 1995a, 1995b
Frequency of interactions	Number of interactions or number of interactions per unit time between exchange partners	Social exchange theory; transaction cost economics	Positive impact on trust and relational norms, reduces chances of opportunism	Crosby et al. 1990; Doney and Cannon 1997

Source: Adapted from Palmatier et al., 2006a

Positive relational mediating mechanisms

Relational drivers ultimately impact on relationship success through positive relational mediators. Marketers have traditionally focused on developing commitment and trust – two necessary positive relational mediators – in order to develop strong customer relationships (Morgan and Hunt, 1994). Recent research has uncovered other mediators, gratitude and reciprocal norms, which also positively impact relationship outcomes (Palmatier et al., 2006a). In this section, we review these four relational mediators and their role in the relationship marketing process.

Commitment and trust

Commitment refers to an enduring desire to maintain a valued relationship (Moorman et al., 1992), while trust is defined as having confidence in an exchange partner's reliability and integrity (Morgan and Hunt, 1994). Committed partners are motivated to preserve their relationship and will expend extra effort and resources in order to maintain and strengthen their relationship. For example, Toyota's Japanese parts suppliers locate their headquarters in the same city as Toyota's primary manufacturing plant. Similarly, commitment reduces the chance that a partner will respond to competitive offers. While commitment can result from dependence asymmetry, it is generally viewed as being more affective in nature. Thus, commitment leads to greater loyalty and satisfaction, as well as increased financial performance within the exchange relationship (Hibbard et al., 2001; Morgan and Hunt, 1994). Committed customers are also more likely to expand the seller's market by informing their friends, co-workers and family members through direct or virtual (social media) word-of-mouth communications.

Trust and commitment tend to go hand in hand. It is unlikely that an individual will remain committed to a partner that they do not trust. Exceptions may exist when one party is highly dependent on its partner, but in general trust is a necessary requirement for commitment. Trust and commitment are critical for an exchange relationship to endure (Morgan and Hunt, 1994). Because some level of trust must exist before commitment can develop, trust has a more complex impact on the overall relationship, as it not only directly drives financial outcomes, but also indirectly enhances them through its positive impact on commitment (Ambler et al., 1999; Crosby et al., 1990; Mohr and Spekman, 1994). The combination of trust and commitment enhances relationship outcomes by increasing loyalty, satisfaction, market share, profit, sales growth and word-of-mouth.

Gratitude

Gratitude includes both affective and behavioural characteristics. Both occur in response to the realisation that an exchange partner has provided some benefit to the individual or firm. The affective component of gratitude is defined as feelings of gratefulness, thankfulness or appreciation for a benefit received. Research from a vast number of disciplines agrees that these feelings of gratitude create psychological pressure to repay the source of the benefit received (Cialdini, 2009; Gouldner, 1960; Macneil, 1986), which leads to the behavioural aspect of gratitude – defined as actions to repay or reciprocate benefits received due to feelings of gratefulness (Emmons and McCullough, 2003; Morales, 2005; Palmatier et al., 2009). These two components of gratitude combined create a cycle of reciprocity between parties which contributes not only to financial performance in exchange relationships, but also to the development of reciprocal norms, which strengthen the relationship over time (Bartlett and DeSteno, 2006; Emmons and McCullough, 2003). It has even been suggested that people subconsciously pay back slightly more or less than they owe to their partner, such that a gratitude obligation remains, which helps ensure relationship continuation, as both parties alternately feel grateful and act to repay something that approximates the balance of the benefits received (Becker, 1986; Schwartz, 1967).

Customers who are grateful reward firms for extra efforts (Morales, 2005), and in fact feel guilty when they are unable to repay the firm for benefits received. For example, in a retail environment, grateful consumers repay friendly salespeople by making a purchase; however, if they are unable to purchase right then, they feel guilty and are likely to return in the future to rectify those feelings (Dahl et al., 2005). This suggests that relationship investments instil feelings of gratitude, which result in a behavioural response. The guilt implies that people are 'psychologically hard-wired' with emotional systems to respond favourably to feelings of gratitude, and supports the idea that gratitude is an 'imperative force' that ensures people repay the benefits they receive (Komter, 2004; Meyer, 2002).

The effects of gratitude are more far reaching than simply encouraging immediate purchasing behaviour. By prompting reciprocity norms in the mind of the customer, gratitude is a platform to initiate pro-social behaviours, including the development of trust, and the first step to creating an ongoing cycle of reciprocity. Thus, gratitude benefits exchange relationships through three distinct processes: first, customers engage in beneficial behaviours to repay the obligation resulting from feelings of gratitude; second, gratitude increases trust and commitment, which in turn positively impact relationship outcomes; and finally, gratitude promotes the development of reciprocity norms, which have long-term positive effects on the relationship.

Reciprocal norms

The norm of reciprocity is defined by two important components: first, people should help those who have helped them; and second, people should not injure those who have helped them (Gouldner, 1960). It is important to recognise that, while the affective feelings of gratitude will often lead to reciprocal responses, the norm of reciprocity is distinct in that gratitude is not necessary to trigger a reciprocal reaction. For example, a consumer may not feel gratitude towards Southwest Airlines for consistently offering the lowest fares; however, s/he may still feel they owe Southwest their business because of the financial benefits afforded by their pricing structure. Becker (1986, p. 73) argues that, 'people everywhere do "feel" such obligations ... the mere recognition of a benefit seems to generate a sense of obligation to repay' – with or without a feeling of gratitude.

So ingrained is the norm to reciprocate that it has been credited as the essential component in the development of all civilisations – some illustrations include children caring for their ageing parents to repay the benefits they received growing up, employers recognising successful labourers with advancement opportunities, citizens paying taxes for the numerous services provided by their government, among others (Becker, 1956). The fact that the recipient of a benefit feels an obligation to repay that benefit results in positive relational outcomes as the cycle of reciprocity continues over time.

The norm of reciprocity is an integral component of exchange relationship performance and is one of the basic psychological principles underlying successful influence strategies (Cialdini and Rhoads, 2001). It impacts customer decisions and has a positive effect on revenue, cooperative behaviours and other beneficial relational outcomes (Diekmann, 2004; Whatley et al., 1999). Recent research shows that including reciprocity as a positive relational mediator helps to clarify the impact of relationship investments on performance outcomes, suggesting that social pressure to repay benefits generated by relationship investments enhances relationship performance regardless of the level of trust or commitment (Palmatier et al., 2006a). As this norm impacts both parties and encourages an ongoing cycle of reciprocity, the effect on performance should be more long term than those derived from trust or gratitude.

Summary

Commitment, trust, gratitude and reciprocal norms take a central role in the development of successful exchange relationships. Trust and gratitude have shorter-term effects on relational outcomes, while commitment and reciprocal norms have enduring effects that promote lasting relationship success. Commitment and trust have long been recognised as key mediating variables in the relationship marketing process, while gratitude and reciprocal norms are more recent additions to this framework. While all four mediators positively impact relationship performance, there are often complex relationships among these mediators. For example, trust helps drive commitment, gratitude impacts trust and reciprocal norms, and reciprocal norms have a positive impact on trust. In order to be most effective, relationship marketing programmes must create clear benefits for the customer. In so doing, all four positive relational mediators will be activated, ensuring the largest impact on relationship performance.

Negative relational mediating mechanisms

Marketers actively invest in strategies geared towards building positive relational mediators; however, it is critical that they also work towards reducing actions and perceptions that are detrimental to the relationship, or negative relational mediators. Research from behavioural economics shows that a few negative events may overshadow the combined effects of many beneficial actions, such that relationship success over time may be impacted more by reducing the negative influences than by investing in the positive (Baumeister et al., 2001; Gottman, 1994). Relationship marketing research supports this contention, that people pay more attention to the bad than the good, as a recent meta-analysis shows that the largest single effect in the relationship marketing framework is the negative impact of conflict on all

TABLE 6.3 Positive relational mediators

Constructs	Definitions	Theories	Key findings	Representative papers
Commitment	An enduring desire to maintain a valued relationship	Social exchange theory; marriage and organisational behaviour	Positive effect on satisfaction, loyalty, sales growth, market share, profit margins and word-of-mouth	Anderson and Weitz 1992; Jap and Ganesan 2000; Moorman et al. 1992; Morgan and Hunt 1994
Trust	Confidence in an exchange partner's reliability and integrity	Social exchange theory; marriage and organisational behaviour	Positive effect on financial performance along with an indirect effect through commitment	Doney and Cannon 1997; Hibbard et al. 2001; Sirdeshmukh et al. 2002
Gratitude	Affective – feelings of gratitude, thankfulness, or appreciation for a benefit received. Behavioural – actions to repay or reciprocate benefits received due to feelings of gratitude	Social exchange theory; relationship marketing theory	Positive effect on sales growth, loyalty, satisfaction, market share, word-of-mouth and reciprocal norms	Dahl et al. 2005; Dawson 1988; Morales 2005; Palmatier et al. 2009
Reciprocal norms	Either people should help those who have helped them, or people should not injure those who have helped them	Social exchange theory; reciprocity theory	Positive effect on sales growth, market share, loyalty and satisfaction	Gouldner 1960; Palmatier et al. 2009; Perugini et al. 2003

aspects of relationship quality (Palmatier et al., 2006a). Given the prominent role of these negative actions for the success of the relationship, it is critical that marketers know how these negative relational mediators impact on relationships, so that strategies to avoid them (or reduce their impact) can be pursued. In this section, we review the background of four such negative mediators: opportunism, conflict, unfairness and complacency.

Opportunism

The study of opportunism, defined as self-interest seeking with guile, is tied most strongly to transaction cost economics (TCE) theory (Williamson, 1975). TCE is primarily concerned with relationship governance strategies to reduce transaction costs between exchange partners, and argues that governance structures should be organised with the goal of clarifying roles and expectations between partners, thus resulting in a reduction of the costs associated with conflict and opportunism (Williamson and Ghani, 2012). These costs can be dire for exchange relationships as opportunism leads to decreased performance and often relationship dissolution because it undermines the foundational components of trust and commitment upon which many exchange relationships are built.

Opportunism refers to many actions, including intentional distortion of information, lying, cheating, stealing, misrepresenting information and failing to fulfil promises and obligations (Jap and Anderson, 2003). The intentionality of these actions is one essential component of opportunism that distinguishes it from other negative relational mediators (Macneil, 1982). People engage in opportunistic behaviours to improve their own financial outcomes, and while they may be successful in the short term, over time these actions result in decreased value for both sides of the relationship (Ghosh and John, 1999; Wathne and Heide, 2000). Opportunism reduces trust, cooperation, commitment and future purchase intentions (Bell and Anderson, 2000; Lancastre and Lages, 2006; Skarmeas, 2006). Additionally, opportunism leads to retaliation, the breakdown of relational norms and eventually to the dissolution of the relationship (Bacharach and Lawler, 1980; Gundlach et al., 1995; Morgan and Hunt, 1994).

While TCE looks at formal mechanisms to help reduce opportunistic actions (e.g. monitoring and the use of contracts), the relational perspective argues that strategies aimed at building interdependence, trust, reciprocity, commitment and equity are possibly more successful at reducing or eliminating opportunism from the relationship (Dwyer et al., 1987). When a person perceives a relationship to be both financially and socially rewarding, they will likely avoid opportunistic behaviours that break down the trust and commitment, and eventually cause the dissolution of that beneficial exchange. Whether firms focus on formal or informal mechanisms, there is general agreement that efforts to reduce opportunism are critical for the long-term success of the relationship.

Conflict

Conflict arises from the perception that a relational partner is engaging in behaviours that prevent or impede one's own goal achievement. Like opportunism, conflict has a negative impact on relationship performance (Anderson and Weitz, 1992; Frazier, 1983). A recent meta-analysis reveals that the negative effect of conflict is more impactful than the combined effects of all positive relational mediators (Palmatier et al., 2006). Conflict has been defined in various ways, with some arguments positioning it as a dynamic process rather than a specific behaviour. The conflict process occurs over five distinct stages: latent conflict, perceived conflict, affective conflict, manifest conflict and conflict aftermath (Pondy, 1967).

Conflict in exchange relationships can occur as the result of incompatible goals, conflicting perceptions (especially regarding the equitable distribution of outcomes), and differing expectations of the responsibilities of each party (Palmatier et al., 2014). Additionally, when power and dependence asymmetries exist in a relationship, conflict is a likely result (Frazier et al., 1989). At the same time, cooperation may require partners to make adaptations to align better with expectations for their role in the relationship. These adaptations may not always be easy, and can cause conflict as relationship partners each strive to reach their own goals. Whatever the cause, unresolved conflict has similar detrimental effects to those of opportunism, including the dissolution of trust, commitment, loyalty, satisfaction, cooperation and communication (Anderson and Narus, 1990; Frazier et al., 1989; Plank and Newell, 2007). Ultimately, as these critical positive relational mechanisms break down, relational outcomes suffer and eventually the relationship will likely be terminated (Brown et al., 1991). Thus, marketers need to be especially vigilant to make efforts to resolve conflict before it begins to erode the relational ties (Palmatier et al., 2006a).

Some level of conflict is likely to occur at different points in any exchange relationship (Loomis and Loomis, 1965). Importantly, there are strategies that can be used to resolve conflict. Joint problem solving is one such approach, where both parties actively seek a constructive solution to the situation such that neither party feels unjustly burdened by the result. In cases where the conflict has surpassed the abilities for a collaborative solution, arbitration is an option that could save the relationship (Mohr and Spekman, 1994). Whatever strategy is employed, it is imperative that conflict is resolved before its effects threaten to destroy the relationship.

Unfairness

Relationship partners consciously or unconsciously compare the ratio of their own rewards and investments to that of their partners, to decide whether they are being treated fairly. Unfairness exists when one party perceives that their partner's ratio of investments to rewards is better than their own (Adams, 1965). Despite its importance in exchange relationships, the topic of unfairness is not as well researched as conflict or opportunism. However, research in other academic fields has paid more attention to unfairness because people will go out of their way, possibly at a financial cost to themselves, to punish actions they perceive as unfair (Fehr and Gachter, 2000; Offerman, 2002). This emotional response often results in a greater backlash than do other negative actions (Turillo et al., 2002). Therefore, it is important that managers avoid situations that will result in perceptions of unfairness.

benefit (Becker, 1956; Cialdini, 2009). Second, while the buyer's perception of the salesperson is distinct from that of the selling firm, their relationship with the salesperson (as a representative of the selling firm) influences their feelings towards the firm. Therefore, interactions at an individual level may have a greater impact on relationship performance as they impact trust and commitment to both the salesperson and the selling firm. Sellers can leverage this fact by designing programmes that highlight the role of the salesperson in providing the benefits to the customer.

Turbulence/environmental uncertainty

As environmental uncertainty increases, greater levels of adaptation and flexibility are needed to succeed in the turbulent conditions. In this situation, relational components become even more important, providing confidence in the partner's ability to continue to create value (Cannon and Perreault, 1999; Dahlstrom and Nygaard, 1995). Relational bonds also reduce conflict, which is critical when partners need to interact more frequently to coordinate and make adjustments to deal with the rapidly changing conditions of the environment. Therefore, higher environmental uncertainty enhances the positive impact of commitment, trust and reciprocal norms on relationship outcomes (Cannon et al., 2000; Joshi and Stump, 1999; Palmatier et al., 2007a).

Governance structure

Relationship governance is a continuum that ranges from purely formalised contractual relationships (e.g. the franchisee–franchisor relationship) to purely relational exchanges (e.g. a customer's close relationship with a trusted hair stylist), although most exchange relationships are governed using some combination of the two. Relational governance structures are often more successful at solving conflict and increasing relationship performance than contract-based structures (Heide and John, 1988).

Summary

In this section, we have briefly covered five characteristics that may impact the effectiveness of common relationship strategies. There are many other possible contingencies that can make relationship investments more or less successful depending on the specific context of the relationship. For example, firms can sell products across a wide variety of channels, including online (Amazon.com), remote (through telephone orders), and bricks and mortar stores. Additionally, combinations of these channels exist in a number of consumer and organisational industries (e.g. placing an order online to be picked up at a store). The specifics of any given exchange context may impact on the importance of developing closer relationships with customers. Managers need to analyse their specific situation carefully to adapt their strategies to optimise returns on their relationship development efforts.

4 New research directions

There are numerous opportunities to further our understanding of the positive and negative effects of investments in managing customer relationships:

1. More effort is needed to quantify the potential negative performance implications of relationship marketing efforts (e.g. inefficiencies due to price erosion and consumer preferences for a transactional relationship).
2. Investigating which performance drivers (other than price) are most important for exchange contexts that are more transactional (rather than relational) in nature.
3. Answering the following questions about gratitude and reciprocity: Do customers reciprocate based on feelings of gratitude over multiple or single exchange transactions? If over multiple exchanges, for how long will the feelings of gratitude drive customer purchase behaviour? If the customer is unable to reciprocate immediately, does the gratitude-based response decay over time?
4. Very few researchers have measured a comprehensive set of either positive or negative relational mediators in the same study. Therefore, research is needed to understand better the relative effects of positive and negative relational mediators.
5. Examining effective strategies to identify the existence of complacency – prior to realising the potential negative consequences.
6. While there has been extensive research investigating strategies to mitigate the negative impact of conflict and opportunism, more research is needed regarding strategies to limit the impacts of unfairness and complacency.
7. Investigating how unique aspects of the relationship context (e.g. e-commerce) impact on the effectiveness of relationship marketing in consumer and organisational contexts.

5 Practising marketing – a case study

Recent worldwide recalls of almost 30 million General Motors vehicles illustrate the dire consequences of low expertise and mismanagement of the communication process. During the first five months of 2014, GM issued 30 different recalls, beginning with a flawed ignition system that resulted in 13 deaths. GM was aware of this problem for over a decade but did not communicate this to its dealers or consumers. This created problems for all involved parties. In 2014 alone, GM recalled more vehicles than it had sold since its restructuring in 2009. Because of GM's failure to communicate these problems, in 2014 the company faced a US$35 million federal fine for covering up information regarding the engineering flaws, over $1.7 billion in estimated costs for fixing the vehicles, and a resulting 18% decrease in stock prices. In addition, the future economic consequence of their tarnished reputation is difficult to project (Isidore, 2014). It is possible that their damaged reputation will be the most detrimental outcome for the company.

GM dealers are not happy about this unfair situation. They, after all, were not the ones responsible for the engineering problems and the failure to inform consumers. Heading into the Memorial Day weekend – a big weekend for car sales with many planned promotions – dealers were told by GM that they could not allow consumer test drives or sell any of the vehicles until the recalls were fixed. This meant lost revenues and increased costs due to extra inventory at each showroom (Colias and LaReau, 2014). Dealers also incurred the costs of providing extra service staff to accommodate the repairs of numerous panicked customers. GM also asked dealers to provide loan or courtesy cars to consumers waiting for the repairs.

Consumers, even those who have not personally experienced any issues with their GM vehicles, are not happy either. They had been able to trust the expertise of the automaker giant to make a safe and high-quality product, yet all but four GM models faced recalls in 2014. One consumer mentioned that, even with trade-in incentives, he would think twice about buying from GM again: 'I don't really know how I can trust them' (Rogers, 2014). Once trust is broken, it is very difficult to repair. The result is diminished brand loyalty, dissatisfaction and negative word-of-mouth. 'Whether it's a TV spot on CBS's *60 Minutes*, a YouTube video or a full-page ad in the *Wall Street Journal* or *New York Times*, GM needs to start communicating. Without that, the story will shift to a "GM is back in trouble" meme', one PR expert commented (McCarthy, 2014). While the ending of this story is yet to be told, one thing is clear: a lack of communication and expertise, among other things, can decrease positive relational mediators while increasing the negative, and seriously damage all aspects of performance.

Discussion questions

1. Focusing on the relationship between a manufacturer (e.g. GM) and its distributors (e.g. dealerships), what strategies could be used to promote positive relational mediators when production problems occur? What strategies would be more effective at reducing the negative relational mediators?
2. Following the situation described in the case, discuss how the feelings of a typical GM consumer would be affected with respect to the dealership from which s/he purchased the vehicle. How would the consumer reaction impact on dealer performance?
3. From the dealership's perspective, how would that anticipated consumer reaction impact on perceptions of fairness and trust in their relationship with GM?
4. Compare and contrast the expected outcomes for the relationship in the case example with a relationship that is less contractually binding (e.g. a toy manufacturer and Toys 'R' Us).

6 Further investigation

1. Compare and contrast social, financial and structural relationship investments.
2. Explain the link between gratitude and reciprocal norms.
3. Describe how building trust and commitment can lead to unintended negative consequences.
4. What are the causes of complacency and how can firms guard against the onset of complacency in exchange relationships?
5. Explain how seller motivations can impact the effectiveness of relationship investments.
6. Discuss the similarities and differences between social exchange theory, equity theory and relationship marketing theory.

References

Adams, J.S. (1965). *Inequity in Social Exchange*. Academic Press, New York.
Ambler, T., Styles, C. and Xiucun, W. (1999). The effect of channel relationships and guanxi on the performance of inter-province export ventures in the People's Republic of China. *International Journal of Research in Marketing*, 16, pp. 75–87.
Anderson, E. and Jap, S. (2005). The dark side of close relationships. *MIT Sloan Management Review*, 46, pp. 75–82.
Anderson, E. and Weitz, B. (1989). Determinants of continuity in conventional industrial channel dyads. *Marketing Science*, 8, pp. 310–323.
Anderson, E. and Weitz, B. (1992). The use of pledges to build and sustain commitment in distribution channels. *Journal of Marketing Research*, 29, pp. 18–34.
Anderson, J.C. and Narus, J.A. (1990). A model of distributor firm and manufacturer firm working partnerships. *Journal of Marketing*, 54, pp. 42–58.
Bacharach, S.B. and Lawler, E.J. (1980). *Power and Politics in Organizations: The Social Psychology of Conflict, Coalitions and Bargaining*. San Francisco, Jossey-Bass Inc.
Bartlett, M.Y. and DeSteno, D. (2006). Gratitude and prosocial behavior: helping when it costs you. *Psychological Science*, 17, pp. 319–325.
Baumeister, R.F., Bratslavsky, E., Finkenauer, C. and Vohs, K.D. (2001). Bad is stronger than good. *Review of General Psychology*, 5, pp. 323–370.
Baumol, W.J., Litan, R.E. and Schramm, C.J. (2007). *Good Capitalism, Bad Capitalism, and the Economics of Growth and Prosperity*. New Haven, CT, Yale University Press.
Becker, H. (1956). *Man in Reciprocity: Introductory Lectures on Culture, Society and Personality*. New York, Praeger Publishers, Inc.
Becker, L.C. (1986). *Reciprocity*. New York, Routledge & Kegan Paul.
Bell, G.G. and Anderson, M. (2000). *Trust, Positional Security and Information Transfer in Four Network-Ideal Types: Exploring the Linkages Between Forms of Social Capital*. Toronto, Academy of Management.
Berry, L.L. (1995). Relationship marketing of services – growing interest, emerging perspectives. *Journal of the Academy of Marketing Science*, 23, pp. 236–245.
Blau, P.M. (1964). Justice in social exchange. *Sociological Inquiry*, 34, pp. 193–206.
Boles, J.S., Johnson, J.T. and Barksdale, H.C., Jr (2000). How salespeople build quality relationships: a replication and extension. *Journal of Business Research*, 48, pp. 75–81.
Bolton, R.N., Kannan, P.K. and Bramlett, M.D. (2000). Implications of loyalty program membership and service experiences for customer retention and value. *Journal of the Academy of Marketing Science*, 28, pp. 95–108.

Brennan, R. (1997). Buyer/supplier partnering in British industry: the automotive and telecommunications sectors. *Journal of Marketing Management*, 13, pp. 759–775.

Brown, J.R., Cobb, A.T. and Lusch, R.F. (2006). The roles played by interorganizational contracts and justice in marketing channel relationships. *Journal of Business Research*, 59, pp. 166–175.

Brown, J.R., Lusch, R.F. and Smith, L.P. (1991). Conflict and satisfaction in an industrial channel of distribution. *International Journal of Physical Distribution & Logistics Management*, 21, pp. 15–26.

Bucklin, L.P. and Sengupta, S. (1993). Organizing successful co-marketing alliances. *Journal of Marketing*, 57, pp. 32–46.

Cannon, J.P., Achrol, R.S. and Gundlach, G.T. (2000). Contracts, norms, and plural form governance. *Journal of the Academy of Marketing Science*, 28, pp. 180–194.

Cannon, J.P. and Perreault, W.D.J. (1999). Buyer-seller relationships in business markets. *Journal of Marketing Research*, 36, pp. 439–460.

Chowdhury, S.D. and Lang, J.R. (1996). The decline of small firms: a preliminary investigation into the concept of complacency. *Revue Canadienne des Sciences de l'Administration*, 13, pp. 321–331.

Cialdini, R.B. (2009). *Influence: Science and Practice*. Boston, MA, Pearson Education, Inc.

Cialdini, R.B. and Rhoads, K.V.L. (2001). Human behavior and the marketplace. *Marketing Research*, 13, pp. 8–13.

Colias, M. and LaReau, J. (2014). GM dealers grapple with stop-sale orders on busy weekend. *Automotive News*. www.autonews.com/article/20140521/RETAIL01/140529963/gm-dealers-grapple-with-stop-sale-orders-on-busy-weekend (accessed May 28 2014).

Crosby, L.A., Evans, K.R. and Cowles, D. (1990). Relationship quality in services selling: an interpersonal influence perspective. *The Journal of Marketing*, 54, pp. 68–81.

Crosno, J.L. and Dahlstrom, R. (2008). A meta-analytic review of opportunism in exchange relationships. *Journal of the Academy of Marketing Science*, 36, pp. 191–201.

Dahl, D.W., Honea, H. and Manchanda, R.V. (2005). Three Rs of interpersonal consumer guilt: relationship, reciprocity, reparation. *Journal of Consumer Psychology*, 15, pp. 307–315.

Dahlstrom, R. and Nygaard, A. (1995). An exploratory investigation of interpersonal trust in new and mature market economies. *Journal of Retailing*, 71, pp. 339–361.

Dawson, S. (1988). Four motivations for charitable giving: implications for marketing strategy to attract monetary donations for medical research. *Journal of Health Care Marketing*, 8, pp. 31–37.

Day, G.S. and Wensley, R. (1988). Assessing advantage: a framework for diagnosing competitive superiority. *Journal of Marketing*, 52, pp. 1–20.

De Wulf, K., Odekerken-Schröder, G. and Iacobucci, D. (2001). Investments in consumer relationships: a cross-country and cross-industry exploration. *Journal of Marketing*, 65, pp. 33–50.

Dholakia, R.R. and Sternthal, B. (1977). Highly credible sources: persuasive facilitators or persuasive liabilities? *Journal of Consumer Research*, 3, pp. 223–232.

Diekmann, A. (2004). The power of reciprocity fairness, reciprocity, and stakes in variants of the dictator game. *Journal of Conflict Resolution*, 48, pp. 487–505.

Doney, P.M. and Cannon, J.P. (1997). An examination of the nature of trust in buyer-seller relationships. *Journal of Marketing*, 61, pp. 35–51.

Dwyer, F.R., Schurr, P.H. and Oh, S. (1987). Developing buyer-seller relationships. *Journal of Marketing*, 51, pp. 11–27.

Emmons, R.A. and McCullough, M.E. (2003). Counting blessings versus burdens: an experimental investigation of gratitude and subjective well-being in daily life. *Journal of Personality and Social Psychology*, 84, pp. 377–389.

Fehr, E. and Gachter, S. (2000). Fairness and retaliation: the economics of reciprocity. *The Journal of Economic Perspectives*, 14, pp. 159–181.

Frazier, G.L. (1983). Interorganizational exchange behavior in marketing channels: a broadened perspective. *Journal of Marketing*, 47, pp. 68–78.

Frazier, G.L., Gill, J.D. and Kale, S.H. (1989). Dealer dependence levels and reciprocal actions in a channel of distribution in a developing country. *Journal of Marketing*, 53, pp. 50–69.

Ganesan, S. (1994). Determinants of long-term orientation in buyer-seller relationships. *Journal of Marketing*, 58, pp. 1–19.

Gassenheimer, J.B., Davis, J.C. and Dahlstrom, R. (1998). Is dependent what we want to be? Effects of incongruency. *Journal of Retailing*, 74, pp. 247–271.

Ghosh, M. and John, G. (1999). Governance value analysis and marketing strategy. *Journal of Marketing*, 63, pp. 131–145.

Gottman, J.M. (1994). 'An agenda for marital therapy'. In S.M. Johnson and L.S. Greenberg (Eds) *The Heart of the Matter: Perspectives on Emotion in Marital Therapy*. Brunner/Mazel Publishers, New York.

Gouldner, A.W. (1960). The norm of reciprocity: a preliminary statement. *American Sociological Review*, 25, pp. 161–178.

Gundlach, G.T., Achrol, R.S. and Mentzer, J.T. (1995). The structure of commitment in exchange. *Journal of Marketing*, 59, pp. 78–92.

Gundlach, G.T. and Cadotte, E.R. (1994). Exchange interdependence and interfirm interaction: research in a simulated channel setting. *Journal of Marketing Research*, 31, pp. 516–532.

Harris, J. and Taylor, K.A. (2003). The case for greater agency involvement in strategic partnerships. *Journal of Advertising Research*, 43, pp. 346–352.

Haytko, D. (2004). Firm-to-firm and interpersonal relationships: perspectives from advertising agency account managers. *Journal of the Academy of Marketing Science*, 32, pp. 312–328.

Heide, J.B. (1994). Interorganizational governance in marketing channels. *Journal of Marketing*, 58, pp. 71–85.

Heide, J.B. and John, G. (1988). The role of dependence balancing in safeguarding transaction-specific assets in conventional channels. *Journal of Marketing*, 52, pp. 20–65.

Hibbard, J.D., Kumar, N. and Stern, L.W. (2001). Examining the impact of destructive acts in marketing channel relationships. *Journal of Marketing Research*, 38, pp. 45–61.

Homans, G.C. (1950). *The Human Group*. London, Routledge & Kegan Paul Ltd.

Homans, G.C. (1961). *Social Behavior: Its Elementary Forms*. London, Routledge & Kegan Paul Ltd.

Huppertz, J.W., Arenson, S.J. and Evans, R.H. (1978). An application of equity theory to buyer-seller exchange situations. *Journal of Marketing Research*, 15, pp. 250–260.

Isidore, C. (2014). GM cars sold: 12 million. Recalled: 13.8 million. CNN Money. http://money.cnn.com/2014/05/21/news/companies/gm-recall-nightmare/ (accessed 10 June 2014).

Jap, S.D. and Anderson, E. (2003). Safeguarding interorganizational performance and continuity under ex post opportunism. *Management Science*, 49, pp. 1684–1701.

Jap, S.D. and Ganesan, S. (2000). Control mechanisms and the relationship life cycle: implications for safeguarding specific investments and developing commitment. *Journal of Marketing Research*, 37, pp. 227–245.

Johnson, D.W. and Johnson, S. (1972). The effects of attitude similarity, expectation of goal facilitation, and actual goal facilitation on interpersonal attraction. *Journal of Experimental Social Psychology*, 8, pp. 197–206.

Joshi, A.W. (2009). Continuous supplier performance improvement: effects of collaborative communication and control. *Journal of Marketing*, 73, pp. 133–150.

Joshi, A.W. and Stump, R.L. (1999). The contingent effect of specific asset investments on joint action in manufacturer-supplier relationships: an empirical test of the moderating role of reciprocal asset investments, uncertainty, and trust. *Journal of the Academy of Marketing Science*, 27, pp. 291–305.

Kaufmann, P.J. and Stern, L.W. (1988). Relational exchange norms, perceptions of unfairness, and retained hostility in commercial litigation. *Journal of Conflict Resolution*, 32, pp. 534–552.

Komter, A.E. (2004). 'Gratitude and gift exchange'. In R.A. Emmons and M.E. McCullogh (Eds) *The Psychology of Gratitude*. Oxford University Press, New York.

Koshland, D.E. (1989). Low probability-high consequence accidents. *Science*, 244, pp. 405–405.

Koza, K.L. and Dant, R.P. (2007). Effects of relationship climate, control mechanism, and communications on conflict resolution behavior and performance outcomes. *Journal of Retailing*, 83, pp. 279–296.

Kumar, N., Scheer, L.K. and Steenkamp, J.-B.E.M. (1995a). The effects of perceived interdependence on dealer attitudes. *Journal of Marketing Research*, 32, pp. 348–356.

Kumar, N., Scheer, L.K. and Steenkamp, J.-B.E.M. (1995b). The effects of supplier fairness on vulnerable resellers. *Journal of Marketing Research*, 32, pp. 54–65.

LaBahn, D.W. and Harich, K.R. (1997). Sensitivity to national business culture: effects on US-Mexican channel relationship performance. *Journal of International Marketing*, pp. 29–51.

Lagace, R.R., Dahlstrom, R. and Gassenheimer, J.B. (1991). The relevance of ethical sales-person behavior on relationship quality: the pharmaceutical industry. *Journal of Personal Selling & Sales Management*, 11, pp. 39–47.

Lancastre, A. and Lages, L.F. (2006). The relationship between buyer and a B2B e-market-place: cooperation determinants in an electronic market context. *Industrial Marketing Management*, 35, pp. 774–789.

Loomis, C.P. and Loomis, Z.K. (1965). *Modern Social Theories: Selected American Writers*. Princeton, NJ, Van Nostrand Company, Inc.

Luo, Y. (2007). Are joint venture partners more opportunistic in a more volatile environment? *Strategic Management Journal*, 28, pp. 39–60.

Macneil, I.R. (1982). *Comments to the Workshop on Transaction Cost Analysis in Marketing*. Evanston, Il.

Macneil, I.R. (1986). Exchange revisited: individual utility and social solidarity. *Ethics*, 96, pp. 567–593.

McCarthy, M. (2014). How GM can steer through crisis of ignition-switch recall. *AdAge*. http://adage.com/article/cmo-strategy/general-motors-steer-recall/292149/ (accessed 28 May 2014).

Meyer, P. (2002). 'Ethnic solidarity as risk avoidance'. In F.K. Salter (Ed.) *Risky Transactions: Trust, Kinship, and Ethnicity*. Berghahn Books, Oxford.

Mohr, J.J., Fisher, R.J. and Nevin, J.R. (1996). Collaborative communication in interfirm relationships: moderating effects of integration and control. *Journal of Marketing*, 60, pp. 103–115.

Mohr, J.J. and Spekman, R. (1994). Characteristics of partnership success: partnership attributes, communication behavior, and conflict resolution techniques. *Strategic Management Journal*, 15, pp. 135–152.

Moorman, C., Zaltman, G. and Deshpande, R. (1992). Relationships between providers and users of market research: the dynamics of trust within and between organizations. *Journal of Marketing Research*, 29, pp. 314–328.

Morales, A.C. (2005). Giving firms an 'e' for effort: consumer responses to high-effort firms. *Journal of Consumer Research*, 31, pp. 806–812.

Morgan, R.M. and Hunt, S.D. (1994). The commitment-trust theory of relationship marketing. *Journal of Marketing*, 58, pp. 20–38.

Nicholson, C.Y., Compeau, L.D. and Sethi, R. (2001). The role of interpersonal liking in building trust in long-term channel relationships. *Journal of the Academy of Marketing Science*, 29, pp. 3–15.

Offerman, T. (2002). Hurting hurts more than helping helps. *European Economic Review*, 46, pp. 1423–1437.

Palmatier, R., Stern, L. and el-Ansary, A. (2014). *Marketing Channel Strategy*. Upper Saddle River, Pearson Higher Ed.

Palmatier, R.W., Dant, R.P. and Grewal, D. (2007a). A comparative longitudinal analysis of theoretical perspectives of interorganizational relationship performance. *Journal of Marketing*, 71, pp. 172–194.

Palmatier, R.W., Dant, R.P., Grewal, D. and Evans, K.R. (2006a). Factors influencing the effectiveness of relationship marketing: a meta-analysis. *Journal of Marketing*, 70, pp. 136–153.

Palmatier, R.W., Gopalakrishna, S. and Houston, M.B. (2006b). Returns on business-to-business relationship marketing investments: strategies for leveraging profits. *Marketing Science*, 25, pp. 477–493.

Palmatier, R.W., Houston, M.B., Dant, R.P. and Grewal, D. (2013). Relationship velocity: toward a theory of relationship dynamics. *Journal of Marketing*, 77, pp. 13–30.

Palmatier, R.W., Jarvis, C.B., Bechkoff, J.R. and Kardes, F.R. (2009). The role of customer gratitude in relationship marketing. *Journal of Marketing*, 73, pp. 1–18.

Palmatier, R.W., Scheer, L.K. and Steenkamp, J.-B.E.M. (2007b). Customer loyalty to whom? Managing the benefits and risks of salesperson-owned loyalty. *Journal of Marketing Research*, 44, pp. 185–199.

Parasuraman, R. and Manzey, D.H. (2010). Complacency and bias in human use of automation: an attentional integration. *Human Factors: The Journal of the Human Factors and Ergonomics Society*, 52, pp. 381–410.

Perugini, M., Gallucci, M., Presaghi, F. and Ercolani, A.P. (2003). The personal norm of reciprocity. *European Journal of Personality*, 17, pp. 251–283.

Plank, R. and Newell, S. (2007). The effect of social conflict on relationship loyalty in business markets. *Industrial Marketing Management*, 36, pp. 59–67.

Pondy, L.R. (1967). Organizational conflict: concepts and models. *Administrative Science Quarterly*, 12, pp. 296–320.

Rogers, C. (2014). GM, dealers aim to blunt impact of recall. *The Wall Street Journal*. http://online.wsj.com/news/articles/SB10001424052702304688104579463731521548204 (accessed 28 May 2014).

Samaha, S.A., Palmatier, R.W. and Dant, R.P. (2011). Poisoning relationships: perceived unfairness in channels of distribution. *Journal of Marketing*, 75, pp. 99–117.

Schwartz, B. (1967). The social psychology of the gift. *American Journal of Sociology*, 73, pp. 1–11.

Sirdeshmukh, D., Singh, J. and Sabol, B. (2002). Consumer trust, value, and loyalty in relational exchanges. *Journal of Marketing*, 66, pp. 15–37.

Skarmeas, D. (2006). The role of functional conflict in international buyer-seller relationships: Implications for industrial exporters. *Industrial Marketing Management*, 35, pp. 567–575.

Skinner, S.J., Gassenheimer, J.B. and Kelley, S.W. (1992). Cooperation in supplier-dealer relations. *Journal of Retailing*, 68, pp. 174–193.

Tax, S.S., Brown, S.W. and Chandrashekaran, M. (1998). Customer evaluations of service complaint experiences: implications for relationship marketing. *Journal of Marketing*, 62, pp. 60–76.

Turillo, C.J., Folger, R., Lavelle, J.J., Umphress, E.E. and Gee, J.O. (2002). Is virtue its own reward? Self-sacrificial decisions for the sake of fairness. *Organizational Behavior and Human Decision Processes*, 89, pp. 839–865.

Vargo, S.L. and Lusch, R.F. (2004). Evolving to a new dominant logic for marketing. *Journal of Marketing*, 68, pp. 1–17.

Wathne, K.H. and Heide, J.B. (2000). Opportunism in interfirm relationships: forms, outcomes, and solutions. *Journal of Marketing*, 64, pp. 36–51.

Whatley, M.A., Webster, J.M., Smith, R.H. and Rhodes, A. (1999). The effect of a favor on public and private compliance: how internalized is the norm of reciprocity? *Basic & Applied Social Psychology*, 21, pp. 251–259.

Williamson, O. and Ghani, T. (2012). Transaction cost economics and its uses in marketing. *Journal of the Academy of Marketing Science*, 40, pp. 74–85.

Williamson, O.E. (1975). Markets and hierarchies: analysis and antitrust implications: a study in the economics of internal organization. *University of Illinois at Urbana-Champaign's Academy for Entrepreneurial Leadership Historical Research Reference in Entrepreneurship*.

Williamson, O.E. (1979). Transaction-cost economics: the governance of contractual relations. *Journal of Law & Economics*, 22, pp. 233–261.

Williamson, O.E. (1998). The institutions of governance. *American Economic Review*, pp. 75–79.

Wong, A., Tjosvold, D. and Yu, Z.-Y. (2005). Organizational partnerships in China: self-interest, goal interdependence, and opportunism. *Journal of Applied Psychology*, 90, pp. 782–791.

Zeithaml, V.A., Parasuraman, A. and Berry, L.L. (1985). Problems and strategies in services marketing. *Journal of Marketing*, 49, pp. 33–46.

Further reading

Anderson, J.C. and Narus, J.A. (1990). A model of distributor firm and manufacturer firm working partnerships. *Journal of Marketing*, 54, pp. 42–58.

Brown, J.R., Dev, C.S. and Lee, D.-J. (2000). Managing marketing channel opportunism: the efficacy of alternative governance mechanisms. *Journal of Marketing*, 64, pp. 51–65.

Hibbard, J.D., Kumar, N. and Stern, L.W. (2001). Examining the impact of destructive acts in marketing channel relationships. *Journal of Marketing Research*, 38, pp. 45–61.

Inkpen, A.C. and Ross, J. (2001). Why do some strategic alliances persist beyond their useful life? *California Management Review*, 44, pp. 132–148.

Jap, S.D. and Ganesan, S. (2000). Control mechanisms and the relationship life cycle: implications for safeguarding specific investments and developing commitment. *Journal of Marketing Research*, 37, pp. 227–245.

Liker, J.K. and Choi, T.Y. (2004). Building deep supplier relationships. *Harvard Business Review*, 82, pp. 104–113.

Mohr, J.J. and Spekman, R. (1994). Characteristics of partnership success: partnership attributes, communication behavior, and conflict resolution techniques. *Strategic Management Journal*, 15, pp. 135–152.

Nyaga, G.N., Lynch, D.F., Marshall, D. and Ambrose, E. (2013). Power asymmetry, adaptation and collaboration in dyadic relationships involving a powerful partner. *Journal of Supply Chain Management*, 49, pp. 42–65.

7

OPPORTUNISM, TRANSPARENCY, MANIPULATION, DECEPTION AND EXPLOITATION OF CUSTOMERS' VULNERABILITIES IN CRM

Gilles N'Goala

1 Introduction

The relationship marketing literature has been emphasising trust for more than 30 years (Dwyer and Lagace, 1986; Dwyer et al., 1987). Companies also tend to consider trust building – and not just customer satisfaction – as a top priority. However, when making decisions, marketers may feel some role ambiguity and may be subjected to the paradoxical requirements of their CEO and shareholders, such as having to comply with a high level of performance in the short term (sales, margins and profits), whilst building trust and relationships in the long term (loyalty, positive word-of-mouth, etc.). In e-commerce, for instance, CEOs often speak in public about customer relationships and trust building, but in private they mostly focus on customer acquisition and short-term performance indicators, such as conversion rates, click-through rates and return on investment (ROI) for each campaign.[1] Managers also face ethical dilemmas, such as choosing between their own interests (incentives, objective achievement, elevation on the corporate ladder, etc.), their organisation's interests (profits, market share, etc.) and their customers' interests (cheaper products, better services, etc.).

While marketing has emphasised customer satisfaction, trust, commitment and engagement (word-of-mouth, etc.) as top priorities, customer relationship management (CRM) may also lead to manipulative and deceptive tactics contrary to these priorities. In this technology-driven era, information asymmetry is increasing, and ethics – which involves perceptions regarding right or wrong – is an even more critical issue. Customers are increasingly transparent to companies and are required to disclose personal information to their suppliers. For example, spyware, surveys and 'big data' solutions allow companies collecting, analysing and using personal data (behaviours, satisfaction, preferences, opinions) to adapt communication and offers effectively, such as real-time-bidding offers and discounts (Searls,

2012). The temptation for firms to exploit this asymmetry and to behave opportunistically is, therefore, very high. Instead of enhancing full transparency over the
Internet, the use of CRM capabilities creates new forms of information asymmetry
(big data, connected objects), new forms of opportunism, new forms of vulnerability (privacy concerns), new potential causes of distrust, new unfair situations,
and thus new customer misbehaviours (disloyalty, vengeance, vandalism, aggressiveness,
etc.) (Nguyen, 2011).

CRM practices are sometimes contrary to the ethical and legal foundations of
relationship marketing (Macneil, 1978) and may cause its premature death (Fournier et
al., 1998). In 1993, Gundlach and Murphy urged the need for more equality, for
keeping promises, for a morality of duty and aspiration, and for increased equity, trust,
responsibility and commitment of partners in relational exchanges. However, what
about ethics in CRM decision making today, in our connected world?

CRM refers to an extensive use of qualitative and/or quantitative data to market
customised offers to customers through various points of contact (call centres,
points of sale and sales force, direct marketing, Internet and smartphones, connected objects, etc.). While its initial promise is highly valuable (value creation and
satisfaction), its concrete application has led to an industrialisation of several
organisational processes (Stevens et al., 2012):

- Centralisation (decisions, power, data)
- Automation (sales force, marketing campaigns, call centres, e-CRM)
- Rationalisation (cost efficiency, economies of scale)
- Externalisation (crowdsourcing, customer participation, self-service).

Amazon, for example, claims that it can – almost completely – anticipate and
predict its customers' future behaviour, raising the issue of behavioural determinism
and consumer alienation. This company wants to ship customers' packages before
they buy them! Given that CRM brings several opportunities to manipulate and
deceive customers, managers must better understand which of their actions might
be considered opportunistic, opaque, manipulative, deceptive or immoral by their
customers or by society at large (governments, consumerists, etc.). The objective of
this chapter is also better to understand how companies can develop and/or restore
trust and fairness through avoiding deceptive or manipulative marketing tactics and
promoting transparency in the market.

Learning objectives

When you have read the chapter, you should be able to:

1. Define the key concepts of opportunism, transparency, manipulation,
   deception and exploitation of customers' vulnerabilities and weaknesses.
2. Address different ethical and strategic issues when making CRM decisions –
   What is right? What is wrong? What is risky? What is worth doing?

3.   Imagine disruptive CRM strategies that use CRM technological capabilities while restoring customer trust.

2 Route map

This chapter highlights the potential dark side of CRM. In fact, most CRM books, scientific papers and teaching courses underline its bright side, explaining that data collection and utilisation processes are implemented with good intentions and lead to efficiency, improved decision making and protection of intellectual property (McKinley, 2011).

The objective of this chapter is to understand better how companies can develop and/or restore trust through avoiding deceptive or manipulative marketing tactics and promoting transparency in the market. The aim is to enable readers to comprehend the ethical issues raised by CRM. We do not develop a normative perspective on CRM, prescribing for managers guidelines and rules for behaving in an ethical fashion (Hunt and Vitell, 1986). We develop a positive approach of CRM, which strives to describe and explain the issues that managers must address when making their decisions. In other words, we do not judge CRM managers, trying to force them to comply with the law or ethical principles. Instead, we explain the decision-making process and address ethical and strategic issues. We also discuss the potential boomerang effects of unethical CRM practices on companies' performance (disloyalty, negative word-of-mouth, decrease of customer value, financial loss, etc.) and explain why ethical CRM practices can pay off in the long run.

Of course, CRM is not deceptive and manipulative in itself, but its use by marketers may lead to wrong practices, harm customers and create distrust and inequity. We present different aspects of the way in which firms can overcome the dark side of CRM, including their decision-making processes. Furthermore, we address different ethical issues and underline new research avenues, since empirical studies on opportunism, transparency, manipulation, deception and exploitation of customers' vulnerabilities and weaknesses are still lacking in the CRM area. Theories are reviewed and extant research is presented.

3 State of the art in opportunism, transparency, manipulation, deception and exploitation of customers' vulnerabilities and weaknesses

Given that CRM brings several opportunities to manipulate and deceive customers (tracking, data gathering, promotions, etc.), managers must understand which of their actions might be considered opportunistic, opaque, manipulative, deceptive or immoral by their customers. Otherwise, they will face strong difficulties in customer acquisition and retention. Distrust and mistrust have many hidden costs, which impact on companies' profitability: customer disloyalty, decrease of customer lifetime value, negative word-of-mouth, stress and absenteeism of employees, decrease of marketing effectiveness, etc. (Aurier and N'Goala, 2010; Nguyen,

2011). As Harford (2006) explains, '[t]rust enables people to do business with each other, and doing business is what creates wealth'. In a context where trust is declining (media, financial services, pharmaceuticals, food industry, retailing, etc.), these ethical issues are particularly relevant (Porter Lynch and Lawrence, 2012). Hereafter, we will address different issues, such as opportunism, transparency, manipulation, deception, exploitation of customers' vulnerabilities, and weaknesses and immorality in CRM.

Opportunism and trust in customer relationship management

Trust is one of the most abstract and powerful concepts of CRM. Without trust, no exchange between economic actors is possible, and no long-lasting relationship between providers and customers is likely to develop. Indeed, trust becomes more and more critical as partners' vulnerability, situation uncertainty, and information asymmetry between providers and customers increase. For example, parents who look for a babysitter are highly vulnerable and feel uncomfortable in such an uncertain and risky situation. Limited by their bounded rationality, they are unable to predict accurately their new babysitter's competence, intentions and integrity. What could they do in such a situation? Either they trust her/him or they stay at home.

Many other situations in our day-to-day lives imply trust and risk (food, retail, medicine, transport, etc.). Imagine someone – Mr Dupont – takes his old car to a garage, since he is experiencing problems with the brakes. He will have to cope with three risks:

1. Adverse selection: The garage mechanic is unable to repair the car correctly, contrary to his previous promises. As Mr Dupont is not an expert, he does not detect the mechanic's incompetence and lack of reliability. Information in the market is imperfect. In agency theory, this risk is called adverse selection, as the most competent mechanic – who delivers more expensive service – is less likely to be selected in the market (Akerlof, 1970).
2. Moral hazard: The mechanic suggests Mr Dupont replace his car's brake system while the car is still in a good condition for its age. He then acts opportunistically, 'seeking his self-interest with guile' (Williamson, 1985). Information asymmetry between the garage mechanic (expert) and his client (novice) gives birth to opportunistic temptation. In such a frequent situation, companies and persons can withhold or distort important product/service information, and fail to fulfil promises and obligations. In agency theory, this risk is called moral hazard, as the customer cannot be sure of his service provider's benevolence.
3. Hold-up: The mechanic deliberately breaks the car's braking system, preventing Mr Dupont from using his car anymore. He then suggests Mr Dupont change his car, as the price of the repair exceeds the price of his car on the market. The garage owner shows Mr Dupont a new second-hand

car. Exploiting their customer's vulnerability, dependence and information asymmetry, the garage owner and mechanic are not just opportunistic but also immoral, causing harm to their customer. They demonstrate a lack of integrity, honesty and probity. In agency theory, this situation is referred to as a 'hold-up'.

Many exchange relationships imply – at different levels – these kinds of risks, as each partner depends on the performance of another actor. Williamson (1985, p. 47) argues that opportunism is a part of human nature and defines it as '[t]he incomplete or distorted disclosure of information, especially to calculated efforts to mislead, distort, disguise, obfuscate, or otherwise confuse'. Opportunism is not just self-interest seeking, which can be morally good, but may be accompanied by deceptive and manipulative tactics, which are morally wrong. In economics, trust is then similar to risk, as an agent assesses or calculates the subjective probability that another agent or group of agents will perform a particular action that is beneficial or, at least, not detrimental to him (Williamson, 1993). To prevent opportunism in exchange relationships, one must then implement different processes, such as contractual arrangements and governance mechanisms.

The literature in sociology, social psychology and marketing proposes another view of human nature. It considers that trust is not just a calculus, but also results from personal relations and social structures that develop over time. For Granovetter (1985, p. 489), opportunism and malfeasance are averted, '[b]ecause clever institutional arrangements make it too costly to engage in opportunistic behaviours', and because a generalised morality is 'essential to the survival of the society or at least contribute[s] greatly to the efficiency of its working'. Thus, trust is made possible. It goes beyond risk assessment and integrates affective and social meanings, such as intimacy and friendliness in interpersonal relationships. Taking into account the exchange's economic and social dimensions (Gurviez and Korchia, 2002), a customer apprehends the brand, retailer or service provider's *reliability* (i.e. ability to meet their expectations – competence, reputation and know-how), *benevolence* (i.e. willingness to act in the customer's interests and avoid doing anything detrimental), and *integrity* (i.e. moral traits that prevent them from doing anything immoral or illegal). When the exchange relationship develops, trust – especially its ethical dimensions, such as benevolence and integrity – becomes more and more critical to companies and consumers (N'Goala, 2010). In other words, to build trust over time, companies should not exploit information asymmetry and behave opportunistically. On the contrary, they must demonstrate their sincerity, honesty and good intentions, and enhance transparency in the exchange relationship.

Transparency in customer relationship management

Full transparency is not necessary to all business relationships. Williamson (1993) considers that economic agents will not '[c]andidly disclose all pertinent information on inquiry and reliably discharge all covenants'. In competitive markets, companies can avoid opportunistic behaviours and build trust over time, but cannot be fully transparent for their competitors, suppliers and customers. They must, however, determine to what extent they can be transparent and what information they can disclose to the markets. For example, a manufacturer cannot disclose all information to its customers and competitors concerning its strategy and its disruptive innovations, but it can provide customers with information about the origins and composition of its products to enhance customer trust. A retailer can also disclose information about its suppliers and ensure transparency in food chains to show how it guarantees food safety, but it has no duty to provide full information about its costs and margins, expecting that its customers could demand excessive discounts, which would cause financial difficulties. In other words, full transparency is neither necessary nor desirable, especially when the existence of the company is at stake. Managers must determine the level and types of transparency they should promote to develop trusting relationships.

Transparency can be defined from the customer's or the supplier's perspective. Eggert and Helm (2003) define relationship transparency as 'an individual's subjective perception of being informed about the relevant actions and properties of the other party in the interaction'. In a business-to-business (B2B) setting, they demonstrate that transparency delivers value to the customer, increases customer satisfaction and ultimately leads to favourable behavioural intentions. From the supplier's perspective, transparency refers to the 'process of making explicitly and openly available (disclosing) some information that can then be exploited by potential users for their decision-making processes' (Turilli and Floridi, 2009, pp. 105–106).

Four types of transparencies have to be managed in exchange relationships:

1. Cost transparency: CRM is often associated with dynamic pricing strategies, which aim at exploiting temporary scarcity situations. In the tourism industry (air transport, hotel, etc.), for example, prices change from one day to the next, even though the product/service cost is fixed. CRM is also associated with customer prioritisation strategies, which propose different prices for the same product, depending on the status of the customer. In contractual service industries for instance (insurances, phone companies), new customers often obtain better discounts than loyal customers, because customer acquisition is more difficult to achieve than customer retention. This leads to inequity situations. In reverse, cost (or price) transparency enhances a fair distribution of benefits between the customers and the suppliers. The company can then demonstrate its price fairness and build trust (Bolton et al., 2003).

2. Using controlled experiments in multiple product categories with diverse sampling frames, Carter and Curry (2010) show that transparent pricing, where information about revenues and costs in the supply chain is revealed, triggers a social component of utility that adds value to the same option priced opaquely, thus increasing the option's reservation price. For example, consumers are prepared to buy more expensive products (music CDs) when

artists are strong enough to deserve the premium. This research raises the issue of deservingness and fairness (Kivetz and Simonson, 2002): which company really deserves margins and profits? Will customers cooperate with the companies to share value fairly with them, or will they opportunistically compete with companies, through negotiation, to maximise their utility?

3. Supply transparency: Consumers often want to know the origins of the products they consume (country of origin, names of the manufacturers, etc.), so as to make rational and safe decisions. In business-to-business contexts, transparency is also expected. Examining agri-food supply chains, Bastian and Zentes (2013) show that transparency is a prerequisite or a basic indicator of good management in sustainable supply chain management. Transparency enhances social, ecological and operational performance, as well as long-term relationship success. Even in consumer goods, the country of origin is increasingly becoming a decision criterion. Customers want to know where and how the product has been manufactured, as they feel responsible for the social, ecological and economic consequences of their buying decisions (Folcher and N'Goala, 2014). However, they often have no ability to determine the percentage of the product that really comes from their country and are particularly sceptical concerning these claims.

4. Organisational transparency: Organisations are particularly opaque to their customers. In consumer goods, for instance, consumers buy and consume brands but often are unfamiliar with the manufacturer that markets them (P&G, Unilever, Kraft, etc.). Large organisations tend, however, to communicate regarding their corporate social responsibility (CSR) – e.g. their 'status and activities with respect to [their] perceived societal obligations' (Brown and Dacin, 1997, p. 68). They claim that they respect their social (employment, non-discrimination, etc.), ecological (environment) and/or economic (enriching the local economy) obligations. In other words, they communicate on the bright side of the organisation but of course they do not disclose information on the dark side. Customers are then sceptical regarding these claims and may distrust brands when the claims do not fit the reality. For instance, 'greenwashing' communication can enhance boomerang effects for firms. Some companies also strive to avoid overseas taxes, although they make millions in sales and profits. For instance, Google paid a tax rate of 2.6% on US$8.1 billion in non-US income in 2012, because it channelled almost all of its overseas profits to a subsidiary in Bermuda, which levies no corporate income tax (Bergin, 2013). However, Google claims on its corporate website that the company is 'firmly committed to active philanthropy and to addressing the global challenges of climate change, education and poverty alleviation'.

5. Technological transparency: As Turilli and Floridi (2009, p. 105) note, 'transparency' has two irreconcilable meanings. It can refer to 'forms of information visibility and to the possibility of accessing information, intentions or behaviours that have been intentionally revealed through a process of

disclosure', but in the disciplines of computer science and IT, transparency refers to 'a condition of information invisibility, such as when an application or computational process is said to be transparent'. The spyware used by firms to track customer behaviour is then transparent in the latter meaning (invisibility for users), but not the former (voluntary disclosure of information). Customers often do not know they are watched, identified and targeted by robots and marketers. Without transparency, 'big data' allow companies to collect huge volumes and varieties of personal data and use them in real time (velocity).

6. Big data matter to all of us and have a significant impact on the economy and the society. As Nguyen (2011) explains, this has led to a general distrust in online shopping and a desire for more consumer privacy. In our technological era, information asymmetry is increasing. Customers tend to be more transparent to companies and are required to disclose personal information to their suppliers. For example, spyware, surveys and big data solutions allow companies collecting, analysing and using personal data (behaviour, satisfaction, preferences, opinions) to adapt communication and offers effectively (real-time-bidding offers and discounts). However, while information is highly valuable for companies, most customers do not feel they benefit from personal data use and dissemination by companies. Moreover, despite the numerous possibilities to enhance transparency (websites, blogs, forums, etc.), companies are often reluctant to disclose information (costs, organisation, technology, supply) and want to control their online reputation effectively. They have invested in the recruitment of community managers and in their online reputation management. This may lead to deceptive and manipulative tactics, such as posting false comments or deleting negative evaluations.

Contrary to manipulation or deception, transparency is not an ethical principle but a strategic decision. Turilli and Floridi (2009, p. 107) explain that information transparency '[c]an be ethically neutral, but it can easily become an ethically "enabling" or "impairing" factor, that is a pro-ethical condition, when the disclosed information has an impact on ethical principles'. In other words, the incomplete disclosure of information is not morally wrong in itself. There is no general obligation for companies, as well as customers and citizens, to disclose information fully. However, if managers make calculated efforts to mislead, distort, disguise, obfuscate or otherwise confuse their customers, they can be blamed for manipulative and deceptive tactics.

Transparency might be an effective strategy and presents opportunities and pitfalls. In a connected world, transparency in data collection and use might be an effective strategy. The explosion of spyware – used by firms to track customer behaviour – has led to a general distrust of e-commerce. The development of connected objects that transfer data to manufacturers in real time also raises new issues in many areas: quantified self (health, sport), home automation (security, utilities, domestic appliances, etc.), gaming, connected cars (Tesla, for instance), and use of drones in sport, leisure and private life.

While personal data create value for companies (e.g. Google, Facebook or Amazon), customers do not always perceive the incremental value they obtain in terms of service quality, customisation and satisfaction. To succeed, a firm must then adequately consider fair value creation for both the firm and the customer, or it may lose access to the data required for the dual value-creation process. This collaborative approach of privacy is now extending. For instance, the vendor relationship management (VRM) perspective, as a natural counterpart of CRM, gives means to customers for engaging with vendors and for controlling their personal data (Searls, 2012). Customers are enabled to share data selectively and voluntarily. In this case, they are more likely to accept their supplier's offers and to engage in a more positive relationship.

To be effective, transparency requires a consensus between the company and its customers and implies that they both think in terms of long-term collaboration rather than short-term competition. Managers often think in terms of value distribution (competition to gain advantage over their customers), instead of focusing on value co-creation (cooperation in a win-win situation). Current pricing policies are thus inappropriate in an economy where relationships, value co-creation and intangible resources are critical in firm performance. As Bertini and Gourville (2012) suggest, to create a shared value with their customers, managers must then focus on relationships (not on transactions), be proactive, put a premium on flexibility, promote transparency and manage the market's standard for fairness. For Sinha (2000), in contrast, price (or cost) transparency can be a threat in the Internet age: it will result in lower margins for sellers, turn products into commodities, lower consumer loyalty and increase perceptions of unfairness.

According to classical economic principles, customers will often compete to obtain better discounts and will be increasingly demanding. For example, when the e-tailer BrandAlley launched its 'pay what you want' campaign in France in 2009, 85% of customers only paid €1. When the hotel chain Best Western did the same, the customers – even the most satisfied – only paid 40% to 60% of the normal price. Research on loyalty programmes also tends to support this hypothesis: customer prioritisation (exclusive offers, elevated customer status and preferential treatment), as well as prioritisation transparency, induce prioritised members to become overly demanding, through an entitlement-driven process (Wetzel et al., 2014). This increases service costs and reduces profits. By disclosing full information about their costs and margins, companies may then face an escalation of demands that could cause a crisis in the entire industry. Thus, to develop an effective transparency strategy, managers as well as customers must first change their mind and develop a long-term, collaborative perspective. For companies, transparency is a risky gamble that may pay off.

Manipulative tactics in customer relationship management

CRM – like other marketing practices – is often seen as manipulative, as it can potentially neglect or violate consumer autonomy, needs, desires and personhood, and widen the asymmetries of power between the company and the customers (Rudinow, 1978). Sher (2011, p. 97) suggests that '[a] marketing tactic is manipulative if it is intended to motivate by undermining what the marketer believes is his/her audience's normal decision making process either by deception or by playing on a vulnerability that the marketer believes exists in his/her audience's normal decision-making process'. Three types of tactics have been particularly criticised: persuasion, coercion and seduction.

Persuasion

Persuasion is not manipulative in itself, especially when the marketer attempts to persuade its customers through rational discourse (information, arguments and evidence), but some advertising strategies, using emotions or classical conditioning, are likely to manipulate consumers. For example, the increased use of neurosciences or eye-tracking technologies in advertising raises new ethical issues, as consumers are subconsciously controlled by the marketers. Other tactics are also subject to scrutiny. In e-commerce, for example, many marketers are using promotional techniques such as reduced prices (−10%, −20%, etc.) to display attractive discounts on their website. Without any knowledge of the market price for an item, customers often use the reduced prices as their reference price and are persuaded by a 'good deal', while in fact they are just paying the normal price for this item.

Sensorial marketing is also subject to scrutiny. For example, several points of sale diffuse specific fragrances to subconsciously influence consumers' mood and purchases. This sensorial marketing can be seen as a way to increase hedonic perceived value and consumer satisfaction, but it may also be a tactic to alter their decision-making process in the vendor's favour (Biehl-Missal and Saren, 2012). For instance, Starbucks coffee shops develop a seductive consumption atmosphere to augment aesthetic pleasure and manipulation. Schwartz (2005) argues, however, that aesthetic seduction is admissible in retailing, since the consumer is free to shop and does it with a certain level of purpose.

Coercion

Coercion is an objectionable tactic, as it tends to force customers' hands. Persuasion techniques can become coercive when they suppress an individual's ability to reason and make choices in their own best interest. Some marketing tactics that manipulate the individual's need for consistency or for reciprocity can be used to obtain customer compliance. Two tactics in particular are frequently used:

1.   The 'foot-in-the-door' technique: since a customer first agrees to a modest request (visit the store, accept a meeting with the sales rep, test the product or service for one week, answer a questionnaire), s/he will tend to agree to a large request in the future (buy a useless product or service, sign up to an

overly long-term contract, etc.). The customer will feel obliged to act consistently with their earlier act to reduce their cognitive dissonance. These tactics are also effective in online environments (e-commerce, media, etc.), and are more effective than external pressure (threats, etc.) (Guéguen, 2002). Moreover, when the marketer claims that the customer can refuse the offer, the customer is more likely to comply.

2.   The 'door-in-the-face' technique: the marketer first makes a large offer (a very high price, for example) that the customer will turn down. In a second step, the marketer makes a much more reasonable offer – in comparison with the earlier one – that the customer is more likely to accept. Because the marketer has accepted a large sacrifice, through a reciprocity mechanism the customer will feel obliged to accept the new offer. The customer will then maintain a positive self-presentation and will feel less guilty.

A firm may also put external pressure on its customers or suppliers to obtain their compliance. In distribution channels, coercive strategies (threats, humiliation, etc.) are often used to obtain partners' compliance. In consumer markets, companies may also develop switching costs to retain their customers, sometimes against their will. In retail banking, for example, customers who want a mortgage are strongly 'encouraged' to buy additional products, services packages and additional insurance. Thus, they cannot easily exit the relationship for a long time period. These 'forced sales' and lock-in strategies are particularly frequent in contractual services (banks, insurance, telephone, utilities, etc.).

Seduction

By seduction, Deighton and Grayson (1995, p. 660) mean '[i]nteractions between marketer and consumer that transform the consumer's initial resistance to a course of action into willing, even avid, compliance'. For them, seduction is 'something more voluntary than fraud and more collaborative than entertainment, a playful, gamelike social form'. They then describe four steps in seduction that may be applied to loyalty programmes or other CRM tactics:

1.   Enticement: the marketer presents a very desirable final goal and implicitly pledges to help the customer achieve it. For instance, the marketer underlines the numerous rewards of having a loyalty card (money savings, preferential treatment, etc.).
2.   Enrolment: the marketer elicits information from the consumer without reciprocal candour and designs a role for the consumer. For instance, loyalty programmes are used to collect personal data, to cross-sell products and to motivate electronic word-of-mouth (viral marketing).
3.   Entrapment: the unbalanced relationship becomes more so because exit for the consumer is increasingly costly (financial or social switching costs). Loyalty programmes often include financial or non-financial rewards that customers

do not want to lose (customer status, access to services, discounts, accrued points, etc.). They may also receive penalties when they are disloyal (decrease of status, loss of air miles with airlines, deactivation of the loyalty card in case of insufficient usage, etc.).

4. Confirmation: this involves small acts of commitment or fulfilment by the marketer in lieu of the fulfilment of the initial promise. For instance, supermarkets often provide loyalty card owners with small rewards, such as coupons (1% or 2% of discount on their total purchase) and insufficient services (special cash desks for loyalty card owners).

Deighton and Grayson (1995) consider that direct marketing often borrows from this enrolment process. Direct selling also aims to enrol customers to make them present, demonstrate and sell products and services to consumers, usually in their homes or at their jobs. For example, German company Vorwerk sells its leading product for cooking, Thermomix, through a network of seduced consumers. Several customers have transformed themselves into fanatic sellers and promoters of the product. This enticement process differs from the traditional relationship-development process, as it does not always result from a rational calculus of the costs and benefits associated with the relationship: awareness, exploration, expansion, commitment and dissolution (Dwyer et al., 1987). Seduction is more an emotional or irrational compliance with the company's requirements. It becomes unethical when the marketer violates its customers' trust and cynically uses its superior knowledge to take advantage of them. However, seduction may also be ethical if the marketer considers that the customer will finally gain from the transactions, even though the business relationship collapses (Deighton and Grayson, 1995).

Some persuasion, coercion and seduction tactics may be seen as manipulative, as they undermine the customer's normal and rational decision-making process. However, to be considered manipulative and morally objectionable, they have to be determined with a specific intention to violate consumer autonomy, needs, desires and personhood. The question is, does the marketer consciously intend to manipulate their customers? As Sher (2011, p. 99) suggests, people '[o]ften act with little awareness of their intentions sometimes even lying to themselves about them'. Through a powerful socialisation process, in their organisation or in their profession marketers learn to use the most effective CRM tactics (personal data use, promotional tactics, etc.). They are often unaware of their intentions, because of organisational norms – 'it's normal in my company or in my industry' – and strong personal incentives – 'I have to reach my sales objectives otherwise I lose my job and my financial rewards'. They may also lie to themselves to maintain their self-esteem, believing that the product or the tactic may finally benefit the customers. They may attribute the entire responsibility to external causes (their colleagues, their customers, their competitors, etc.), rather than to internal causes (themselves). For example, sales representatives are sometimes trained to use manipulative tactics (foot in the door, door in the face, etc.), but ethical issues are rarely addressed in their seminars. The marketers become aware of their manipulative acts after long reflection (seminars, discussions with colleagues, etc.) or when they change job or position.

Deceptive tactics in customer relationship management

As Deighton and Grayson (1995) noticed, deception has often been defined as '[t]hose instances in which a consumer changes his or her behaviour for reasons grounded not on "fact" or "reality" but on "beliefs" or "impressions"'. In other words, in prior literature (Gardner, 1975, p. 43), marketing tactics that emphasise 'non-objective' attributes or non-functional benefits of the product/service are considered deceptive. Thus, with this definition, almost all marketing is deceptive. In contrast, Sher (2011, p. 104) proposes a narrower definition of deception: a marketing tactic is deceptive, '[i]f it intends to bring about consumer misconception by providing what the marketer believes is false evidence, omitting key evidence, or mis-representing what the evidence means'. Buller et al. (1994) also distinguish three types of deception: concealment (withhold, omit or disguise relevant information), equivocation (information presented vaguely and/or ambiguously) and falsification (presentation of false or exaggerated information). Deception shares common meaning with the concept of opportunism (calculated efforts to mislead, disguise, obfuscate, etc.).

For Xiao and Benbasat (2011), the Internet is fertile ground for deception because of the digital environment (information can be easily manipulated in real time), low entry barriers (a website requires a low investment in comparison with a store), spatial/temporal separation, and anonymity in the exchange. Investigating deceptive tactics in e-commerce, they distinguish possible deceptive techniques that concern:

1. Information content: the e-tailer may alter the availability and quality of information on the product/service.
2. Information presentation: the e-tailer may alter the features of a medium to inhibit correct product understanding, manipulate the level of vividness of a presentation to distract customers' attention from relevant information (emotionally interesting, imagery provoking and inherently appealing), present conflicting information (text contrary to image, for instance), or develop a disorganised website to limit customers' information processing strategies.
3. Information generation: this refers to the 'dynamic production of product-related information at an eCommerce website, based on consumer interests, needs, and/or preferences obtained explicitly or implicitly' (Xiao and Benbasat, 2011, p. 174). The e-tailer can alter search engines, product catalogues and online product recommendation agents to achieve its objectives (sales and margins), even though it does not fit the customers' interests. In 2002, Amazon admitted they have used fake suggestions to promote a new clothing store (Wingfield and Pereira, 2002), while, in 2004, Amazon Canada revealed that a number of book reviews had been written by authors of their own

books or of competing books (*The New York Times*, 14 February 2004). Amazon also does not permit negative comments on their website to 'let truth loose'.

CRM and e-CRM are not deceptive in themselves. To be considered deceptive, a tactic must be a marketer's intentional act that aims at manipulating information to create false beliefs in the customer's mind. Deception thus has three characteristics:

1. Deception is an intentional or deliberate act. In this sense, it differs from misinformation, which is an unintentional distortion of a message. The marketer may be unaware that s/he is creating a misconception and thus altering the customer's decision-making process. This may be due to the marketer's self-deception, wishful thinking, intellectual laziness, recklessness or negligence of certain foreseeable consequences of her/his action. While negligence, recklessness and the harm caused to customers are morally condemnable, they do not characterise deception.

2. Deceptive marketing tactics imply acting on an intention. For example, a supermarket that re-sells fresh food without making sure there is no break in the cold chain is negligent or reckless, but not deceptive. If the retailer does not even control the composition of its ready-made meals provided by its manufacturers, it cannot be considered responsible for the harm it causes. For example, some manufacturers in Europe have consciously added horsemeat in their ready-made meals to save costs, without providing any information to retailers and consumers. In 2013, a medium-sized company from the southwest of France, Spanghero, was involved, going bankrupt in six months. Whereas the retailers were probably negligent, the manufacturers involved in this scandal were clearly deceptive (BBC News, 2013).

3. Deception is accomplished by manipulating information in some way. For instance, some companies may manipulate information content on web pages, design a product recommendation agent that provides biased product recommendations, broadcast false comments and opinions on forums and blogs, and/or employ multimedia technologies (e.g. Flash, animations) to facilitate impulse buying that customers may regret later.

4. Deception has '[a]n instrumental end goal – that is, to create or maintain a belief in another that the communicator herself believes to be false' (Xiao and Benbasat, 2011, p. 172). In tourism for instance, firms whose products are being discussed in Internet forums are tempted to manipulate consumer perceptions by posting costly anonymous messages that praise their products.

Misinformation – and not disinformation – is inherent in many exchange situations. On the one hand, the customers and the marketers have just a bounded rationality and have no cognitive ability to evaluate all the attributes, benefits and risks of the product. For instance, when the product is complex and/or when the customer is a novice in the product category, the customer uses heuristics to perform her (his) buying task.

On the other hand, marketers can spread unintentionally false or inaccurate information and often have no possibility to disclose full information to their customers. They just have to deliver the most relevant information (price, functions, brand, etc.) to help and persuade them. For example, an e-tailer that sells many thousands of products to millions of customers cannot be blamed for providing incomplete information on its website. As previously suggested, delivering too much information on a webpage can be the best way to mislead customers. Thus, information can be perceived as incomplete, vague, ambiguous and/or exaggerated by a customer, despite the sincere efforts of the marketer. To determine if a tactic is deceptive, the lines of responsibility must be defined for the marketer and the customer in this misinformation. The marketer must especially arrive at an unbiased view of the knowledge and responsibilities consumers possess in comparison with them. When a customer buys a service (travel, perhaps, or car hire), customers often do not have sufficient time and competence to read and understand the contract they sign owing to its length and complexity. In this context, companies probably expect that their customers usually ignore the detail and that creates a misconception and information asymmetry. When a problem occurs, the company can then underline terms and conditions that were often unknown to customers. To avoid deceptive action, the company should strongly urge customers to read and understand the terms of the contract, notify them of their responsibility to do so, and alert them that failure to do so does not annul their consent. If the customer signs a contract without paying attention to its clauses, s/he can be considered responsible and the marketer is not deceptive.

For Xiao and Benbasat (2011), companies must develop anti-deception mechanisms, such as:

1. Deterrence mechanisms, which aim to reduce companies' propensity to deceive (punishment and severe sanctions) and victims' propensity to engage in risky behaviours (consumer education).
2. Prevention measures, such as secure protocols, encryption and authentication online, which prevent certain forms of deception.
3. Detection mechanisms, such as warning and training consumers to recognise deception cues.

When customers become aware of these deceptive tactics, they believe that their supplier has violated their trust and they feel betrayed. Deception is then unacceptable and often leads to relationship dissolution. In comparison with deceptive tactics, tactics that play on customers' vulnerabilities can succeed even though customers are aware of them. For example, smokers know that the tobacco industry exploits their physiological and psychological dependence on the product, but they still smoke and do not attribute their harmful behaviour to the manufacturers, but to themselves instead.

Exploiting customers' vulnerabilities and weaknesses in CRM

As Shultz and Holbrook (2009) suggest, marketing both reduces and contributes to consumer vulnerability. On the one hand, it enhances customer satisfaction, social welfare and consumer well-being. On the other hand, marketers are suspected of exploiting and taking advantage of vulnerable customers. Baker et al. (2005, p. 134) define consumer vulnerability as a 'state of powerlessness that arises from an imbalance in marketplace interactions or from the consumption of marketing messages and products ... It occurs when control is not in an individual's hands, creating a dependence on external factors (e.g. marketers) to create fairness in the marketplace'.

There has been a long debate to determine whether to use marketing for vulnerable customers. On the one hand, Smith and Cooper-Martin (1997) address the ethical issues of targeting vulnerable consumers with products (tobacco, guns, alcohol, high-interest rate credit cards, etc.) that have adverse social and economic consequences and no respect or concern for the welfare of consumers. They show that this strategy enhances negative word-of-mouth, boycotts and complaints. On the other hand, for Palmer and Hedberg (2013), it is not morally wrong to market products to customers who have special physical vulnerabilities (e.g. allergies, sensitivity to chemicals), cognitive vulnerabilities (e.g. cognitive immaturity, senility), motivational vulnerabilities (e.g. grave illness, grief), or social vulnerabilities (e.g. poverty). For them, the wrong does not come from marketing – or CRM – but from the potential deliberate exploitation of these vulnerabilities by marketers.

Shultz and Holbrook (2009) distinguish two types of consumer vulnerability:

1. Cultural vulnerability: a lack of knowledge of beneficial means–ends relationships (they do not know what is good for them). Companies may then act opportunistically by selling excessive junk food or broadcasting poor reality shows on television to culturally vulnerable consumers. Some consumers are ignorant of the potential risks resulting from the consumption of certain products (infected vegetables, over-promoted medicines, tyre-exploding sports utility vehicles, ear-damaging headphones, flammable pyjamas, non-biodegradable containers, etc.).
2. Economic vulnerability: a lack of access to beneficial means, as they do not have the resources, funds, abilities and skills to achieve their goals. For example, a firm may deliver mortgages and sell expensive technological products to economically vulnerable consumers who cannot afford them.

Consumer vulnerability is relative, on a continuum from low to high vulnerability, and person specific, as an individual can be vulnerable in one area, but not in another (medicine, technology, etc.). It is also context specific and varies from one consumption situation to another (medical prescription in case of illness for instance), and evolves over time, as '[a]ll people, young or old, healthy or ill, rich or poor, domestic or foreign, have found or will find themselves, at one time or another, in a position of vulnerability' (Shultz and Holbrook, 2009, p. 126). Consumer vulnerability is not synonymous with moral rectitude, since some vulnerable consumers are not innocent victims. For instance, some insolvent consumers may take on excessive debt for conspicuous consumption, such as luxury products.

A customer's vulnerability can stem from his or her physiological, cultural or economical characteristics and also from the long-term business exchange in which s/he is involved. When a customer buys a product, acquires a service or signs a long-term contract, s/he is not fully sure that his/her supplier (product, brand, retailer, service provider) will keep its promises, which might cause her/him some negative consequences (physical harm, waste of money, useless product, etc.). In these exchange situations, trust becomes necessary, as it allows customers to overcome the exchange uncertainty and accept a certain level of vulnerability to their suppliers' opportunism (Moorman et al., 1992).

In long-term relationships, trust is even more critical. Customers become increasingly dependent and, in consequence, vulnerable to their suppliers by making implicit pledges and contractual arrangements that make relationship dissolution difficult to achieve (insurance, retail banking, B2B partnerships, etc.). To increase customer retention and customer lifetime value, many companies use 'lock-in' tactics, develop switching costs or exit barriers and reduce their customers' freedom. For example, Klemperer (1995) identified switching costs giving firms a degree of market power over their repeat purchasers in consumer markets: the need for compatibility with existing equipment (Apple, Microsoft, Gillette), transaction costs of switching suppliers (termination fees to pay, administrative tasks to accomplish), costs of learning to use new brands (new banking products, a new website environment), uncertainty about the quality of untested brands (new medicines), loss of discount coupons or advantages in loyalty programmes (loss of miles in frequent-flyer programmes), costs of returning loaned or rented devices (routers from Internet providers), and psychological costs of switching (pain or regret associated with relationship dissolution). This dependence may result from companies' decisions (termination fees, incompatibility of devices, long-term contracts, etc.) and also from decisions by customers to buy loyalty-generating products (mortgages in retail banking, for instance). Some customers are, therefore, particularly dependent on and vulnerable to their supplier's opportunism.

Relationship asymmetry is not wrong in itself, but companies' exploitation of customers' weakness and vulnerability becomes morally wrong when a company extracts excessive benefits from customers who are unable to reasonably refuse its offer. In other words, unfairness is even more immoral when it concerns dependent and vulnerable populations. For example, in a situation where a customer faces difficulty in switching supplier or finding an alternative – in regulated markets, such as utilities or air transport, for instance – companies may charge a high price instead of the normal price, exploiting their customers' temporary or ongoing vulnerability.

However, a CRM strategy that enhances unfairness will not be effective in the long term (N'Goala, 2007). As Bendapudi and Berry (1997, p. 28) note, '[w]hen customers stay in relationships because of the constraints against leaving, the relationship tends to last only as long as the constraints do; when the constraints no longer apply, the customer feels no compelling reason to continue in the relationship'. Furthermore, the development of switching costs along with unfair business exchanges lead to negative word-of-mouth, online vengeance and/or dysfunctional behaviour (aggressiveness, vandalism, etc.) which could create hidden costs for companies, such as stress and absenteeism of employees, loss of new potential customers, a decrease in cross-selling opportunities, a decrease in customer share of requirement, etc. In such a situation, customers would react and strive to recover their freedom (N'Goala, 2010).

Relationship asymmetry is inherent in many business exchanges (B2B and business to consumer – B2C), and each individual has weaknesses and vulnerabilities. However, dependence and relationship asymmetry are relative concepts. While customers become dependent on their suppliers, the suppliers are increasingly dependent on their customers. First, companies' profits strongly depend on their ability to keep their customers, especially the most profitable ones (20% of their customer portfolio). To maintain and develop customer relationships, CRM is used to improve the customisation of offers and thus customer satisfaction. Second, along with CRM development, customer empowerment is developing: dissatisfied or exploited customers can post comments or negative ratings on opinion platforms, express negative views offline, complain on different platforms (call centres, social media, etc.), or defend their rights in court. CRM becomes wrong when there is excessive and cynical exploitation of customer vulnerability that could create customer alienation.

Conclusion: the immorality of CRM?

From a business ethics perspective, customer relationship management is very likely to lead to manipulative and/or deceptive tactics, which opportunistically attempt to exploit relationship asymmetries and customer vulnerability. Following Sher's (2011) analysis, CRM becomes immorally manipulative when marketers violate their customers' autonomy and dignity, violate the trust that their customers place in them, take advantage of their customers' weaknesses and vulnerabilities, and/or violate the general obligation not to harm others.

This chapter has focused on this dark side of CRM. As a result, its bright side has been ignored. It is probably unfair to provide an unbalanced view of CRM and to attribute the negative responsibilities to managers. First, CRM contributes to customer satisfaction and value creation, since companies are better able to understand customers' expectations and preferences. Data collection and utilisation are necessary to achieve this objective. Second, in the new economy customers are empowered, even though their power is relative, and have several possibilities to spread positive and negative word-of-mouth and to co-create value with companies (co-innovation, co-production, co-conception, collaboration). Third, not all customers are innocent victims of CRM. They often understand and/or voluntarily participate in CRM programmes and strive opportunistically to exploit their status as a client. It may be a consequence of a reciprocity mechanism – 'the company is opportunistic, so I am' – but it is also part of human nature, as previously explained by Williamson (1993). Fourth, managers cannot always be blamed for doing their job and for achieving their objectives. As a Cheyenne proverb says, do not judge your neighbour until you walk two moons in his moccasins.

CRM is not deceptive, manipulative or immoral in itself. Let us come back to Grönroos's (1990, p. 138) definition, that relationship marketing is to '[e]stablish, maintain and enhance relationships with customers and other partners, at a profit, so that the objectives of the parties involved are met … This is achieved by a mutual exchange and fulfilment of promises'. No marketer can be blamed for developing long-lasting, win–win and cooperative relationships with their custo-mers. However, its actual use by companies is subject to much critical scrutiny. CRM technologies raise many issues in terms of transparency (increased informa-tion asymmetry), privacy (personal data collection and use), persuasion (intensive use of promotional techniques), seduction (enrolment, sensorial marketing), coer-cion (threats, constraints, psychological commitment), deception (false evidence) or exploitation of vulnerability (increased dependence, marketing products to vulnerable consumers).

Obviously, all marketers who manage a customer portfolio cannot be blamed for using customer data and for marketing products and services based on these insights. However, marketers can be blamed for their intentions to manipulate, deceive or exploit their customers. For Sher (2011), manipulation, deception and exploitation of customers are immoral, even though marketers do not harm cus-tomers, use invasive or aggressive tactics and remain within the law. The 'wrong' comes from marketers' intentions and attempts to manipulate. Most marketers are probably unaware of the ethical issues raised by their manipulative behaviour, but this excuse is less and less admissible, as CRM is taught, widely applied and debated in meetings, universities and the media. For instance, the issue of personal privacy has been addressed for a long time by governments, lawyers, journalists and con-sumerists. Furthermore, most managers know that remaining within the law – for instance for personal data collection and use – is not a sufficient condition for morality.

Marketers can also be blamed for the harm caused to customers or other parties: everyone has a general obligation not to harm others. From the customer's point of view, harm can be a waste of money, a bad experience with a service provider, a physical disease caused by poor food or drugs, the dissemination of their personal data, etc. Sometimes misinformation and consumer misconception occur without the marketer's intention, but marketers may be morally blameworthy because:

1. The marketers are negligent: they should devote much effort to extensively and clearly informing their customers, on data collection/dissemination, and on the potential negative consequences of their choices (types of risk, varia-bility of their services, legal constraints, long-term engagements, etc.). For example, customers are sometimes 'over-insured' in their personal life, as

insurance companies fail to explain that they are already protected by law, by the insurances included in their credit card services, by the guarantees paid for or from other insurance products already purchased. If this is not deliberate deception, it could be negligence.

2.   The marketers are reckless: the marketers may recognise that an act or a product might harm some customers but act anyway. For instance, a new drug might be made available without having full certainty of its consequences. Although there is no manipulation, the medicine is blameworthy.

3.   The marketers commit a harmful or egregious act to various parties. A company may commit an egregious act, which is intolerable, monstrous, shocking, outrageous, highly reprehensible and/or harmful to various parties (employees, consumers, society in general). For example, in December 2009, H&M and Zara were suspected of using cotton supplies from Bangladesh and raw materials from Uzbekistan that had been picked and manufactured by children (The Free Library, 2014). Customers may then decide if the brand deserves to be punished, through a boycott for example. Individuals can thus decide to boycott, even if this means making personal sacrifices (refraining from consumption) that outweigh the potential benefits received in return (the end of child labour, respect for human rights, preservation of the environment, etc.). Cissé-Depardon and N'Goala (2009) show, however, that customers' commitment to the brand generates an assimilation effect, which leads them to minimise the perceived egregiousness of the company's act (minimisation of the fault).

Finally, marketers can be blamed for the insufficient positive consequences of their decisions. The negative of manipulation has to be '[o]utweighed by other considerations with positive moral value related to the interests of consumers, society in general, or the marketer herself' (Sher, 2011, p. 111). CRM can be largely beneficial:

1.   To customers. In several companies, huge efforts are devoted to customer satisfaction, trust and commitment. The marketers indeed consider customer satisfaction, customer loyalty and customer referral as key antecedents of firm performance. In most companies, many relational indicators are surveyed and monitored, such as customer satisfaction (CSAT), net promoter score (NPS) or customer effort score (CES) (Dixon et al., 2010). CRM gives them the opportunity to deliver the right product (health insurance, vaccines, etc.), to the right place (multi-channel distribution), to the right customer (needs satisfaction, good deals, pleasure and fun, etc.). Companies are then more customer oriented than ever, and they collect and use data to customise their offers. Customers are then in a double privacy paradox: first, they must accept their personal data collection and use by marketers in order to obtain customised, valued and real-time offers, even though they have concerns about their privacy; second, they want to keep their life private but they overtly broadcast their photos, personal life and opinions on blogs, social networks or

in brand communities. To be good, CRM must imply a sort of reciprocity between the marketer and the customer, enhance fairness and win-win situations, and develop more balanced relationships (Dwyer et al., 1987). Along with technology development and marketer training, CRM has the potential to succeed, but it mainly depends on managers' strategic and financial decisions giving priority to long-term objectives (fairness, satisfaction, loyalty, collaboration, etc.), instead of short-term performance (competition, sales incentives, market share, etc.).

2.   To the companies. One of the key functions of a firm is to make margins and profits. Without them, no stakeholder or employee will exist. In addition, thousands of people are working in CRM roles. However, this is not an excuse for making unethical decisions. Customers tend to infer marketers' motives when they are exposed to CRM tactics and may believe that CRM will lead to unfair practices that are not beneficial to them (in comparison with the company) or are detrimental to them. Customers are often likely to accept that companies have extrinsic motives for using CRM (sales and profits), but they also want companies to have intrinsic motives, such as customer and employee well-being. In other words, CRM is legitimate when it leads to a shared value co-creation, such as a fair distribution of value between the different stakeholders (employees, suppliers, customers, marketers, etc.). In contrast, CRM becomes morally objectionable when marketers exploit information asymmetry and take advantage of other stakeholders. Marketers must deserve the value they obtain. Companies must explain their costs and better justify their decisions, in order to develop perceptions of fairness (Nguyen, 2011).

3.   To society. CRM is used in many settings, such as non-governmental organisations, which, for example, use CRM and direct mail to collect donations and support different social or environmental causes (ecology, fight against poverty). In these cases, the wrong of manipulation is outweighed by the positive moral value related to society in general.

Developments in CRM are extending, including technological capabilities in terms of data collection and utilisation, along with connection and pervasive/intrusive communication. Contrary to the ethical principles of relationship marketing (Gundlach and Murphy, 1993), CRM leads to many negative effects. Research is needed to create a new form of social contract between buyers and sellers, to enhance more transparency and symmetry.

4 New research directions

Relationship maintenance (customer retention) and development (increased service usage, cross-buying and share of the wallet) are top priorities in CRM. In the long run, companies can effectively influence customer patronage behaviours by leveraging overall customer satisfaction, trust and relationship commitment (Aurier and

N'Goala, 2010). While these concepts have been extensively studied in the relationship marketing literature, deception, manipulation and opacity have not received much attention. The literature in ethics addresses issues in marketing in general (advertising, sales, public relations, etc.), but does not focus on CRM in particular, except for privacy concerns. Thus, empirical studies are still missing in CRM concerning the antecedents and consequences of information asymmetry, deception, manipulation and the exploitation of customer vulnerability. For instance, research is still needed to better understand:

1.   The potential benefits and pitfalls of transparency in long-term relationships.
2.   The attribution mechanisms in situations of deception or manipulation (lines of responsibility for misinformation or misconception).
3.   The customer's inferences concerning the marketer's motives in CRM activities (intrinsic versus extrinsic motives).
4.   The perceived deservingness in long-term relationships from the customer's and the marketer's points of view.
5.   The decision-making process by customer relationship managers, which may include ethical considerations.

5 Practising marketing – a case study: CRM and ethical dilemmas in the food industry

Obesity is a leading global concern. The World Health Organization provides alarming figures: around 3.4 million adults die each year as a result of being overweight or obese – a figure that has nearly doubled since 1980. In 2008, more than 1.4 billion adults, aged 20 and over, were overweight. Of these, over 200 million men and nearly 300 million women were obese. Some 35% of adults aged 20 and over were overweight in 2008, and 11% were obese. Some 65% of the world's population lives in countries where obesity kills more people than malnutrition. More than 40 million children under the age of five were overweight or obese in 2012.

The food industry has a part to play in these results. Many food businesses put potentially unhealthy ingredients in their products (saturated fat, excessive sugar and salt, genetically modified ingredients, etc.), and market their products to economically or culturally vulnerable populations. In the United States, for instance, one in every three American teenagers is currently overweight or obese, with rates significantly higher for African-American and Hispanic adolescents.

Many food industry giants have been denounced for making false, ambiguous or exaggerated claims concerning their products. For instance, Wesson cooking oils (Simon, 2011a) and Frito-Lay's snack products (Simon, 2011b) sport the natural label in the United States, although they contain genetically engineered ingredients. General Mills put images of strawberries on their products that contained none (Center for Science in the Public Interest, 2011), while Coca-Cola's vitaminwater brand positions the product as a health tonic despite some varieties containing 33 grams of sugar (in 20 ounces), among other unhealthy ingredients such as colourings (Center for Science in the Public Interest, 2010; Simon, 2013, 2011c).

The food industry is also criticised for '[t]argeting teens with a variety of interactive techniques that take advantage of their vulnerabilities ... Some of these techniques are unfair and deceptive and are purposely designed to operate under the radar of parents and policy makers' (Chester and Montgomery, 2011, n.p.). For example, PepsiCo has been accused of using deceptive digital techniques, such as '[d]isguising its marketing efforts as entertaining videogames, concerts and other "immersive" experiences, making it more difficult for teens to recognise such content as advertising; Claiming to protect teen privacy while collecting a wide range of personal information, without meaningful notice and consent; Using viral marketing techniques that violate the Federal Trade Commission's endorsement guidelines' (Shayon, 2011, n.p.). Chester and Montgomery (2011) point to the use of digital immersive techniques (augmented reality, online gaming, virtual environments) and neuromarketing, which trigger subconscious, emotional arousal and foster impulsive behaviour. They also condemn the extensive use of location targeting and mobile marketing, which follow young people's movements and link point of influence to point of purchase.

Transparency, manipulation, deception and the exploitation of customers' vulnerabilities remain critical issues in the food industry. Thankfully, many food industry giants are now changing their minds and strategies, striving to recover their legitimacy and morality in society. This is also due to external pressure from customers, consumerists, governments and investors. As Oxfam (2013) noted, 33 major investment funds, representing nearly $1.4 trillion of assets under management, have called on food industry giants to improve their supply chain policies and transparency. For example, through its transparency campaign, McDonald's in Australia and Canada offered customers the opportunity to ask anything related to the brand and receive an honest answer, with its website 'Our Food, Your Questions'. Restoring trust has become a top priority in the entire food industry. Without trust, no sale is made possible.

Transparency of marketing tactics is less obvious. In a connected world, many food industry giants now have the opportunity to stay in contact with their customers, to collect personal data and to build consumer networks and communities. The advent of 'social local mobile' marketing allows companies to remain constantly connected to their customers anytime, anywhere, on any device (smartphones, tablets, etc.). For instance, KFC has installed early mobile payments in restaurants to help consumers order, pay for and collect their food faster. McDonald's offers an application facilitating online orders to be retrieved based on geolocation. Since smartphone adoption and mobile access to the Internet are exploding, especially among teenagers, one can imagine the potential consequences on firm performance (loyalty, online word-of-mouth, sales, etc.) and potentially on consumer health (overweight and obesity).

Connected objects are also emerging in the food industry. Many businesses can already collect personal data and influence their customers in real time (Alcimed,

2014). For example, the connected Nutricook Connect cooker made by SEB guides the consumer during the preparation of the recipe to prevent any missteps. Pernod Ricard has reinvented the experience of the 'home bar' by developing a connected spirits library, which provides information on alcohol stocks, suggests cocktail recipes according to the quantities available, and can also order alcohol online. Evian Water has developed a device connected to the home Wi-Fi that transmits new orders from the fridge door (the smart drop project). The next generation of connected devices will draw conclusions from data and spontaneously provide recommendations to consumers (e.g. a refrigerator offering recipes according to the food stored or a consumer's nutritional needs). According to Alcimed (2014), we are entering the era of food personalisation at home through connected devices. These might even one day be integrated into our body (embeddable technologies) to meet our needs instantly. Are marketers and consumers really prepared for the consequences and responsibilities?

Discussion questions

1. Customer relationship management is developing in fast-moving consumer goods (FMCG), with companies aiming to identify and retain their customers. What are the new managerial and ethical issues that managers should address in FMCG?
2. The food industry is inherently concerned by consumers' pleasure (taste) and health (obesity). How could managers reflect these complementary or contradictory objectives and enhance consumers' well-being?
3. Is it unethical – or even immoral – to use CRM tactics on children and teenagers? Why?
4. In a connected world, companies and their brands have an opportunity to stay in contact constantly with their customers (social media, big data, etc.). Will this evolution lead to a better balance of power between consumers and companies, or will this generate new asymmetries of information and power?
5. Connected objects revolutionise the way that data are collected and used. Machine-to-machine (M2M) data exchanges are usually invisible to customers. What are the benefits and drawbacks for companies, customers and society at large? What recommendations would you make to managers who develop connected objects?

6 Further investigation

Key questions relevant to the topic:

1. Why is trust necessary to long-term relationships?
2. Are buyers and sellers opportunistic in long-term relationships? What does opportunistic mean?

3. What are the promises and pitfalls of transparency in customer relationship management?
4. To what extent can we say that CRM is a manipulative strategy? Why?
5. Should companies avoid using persuasive, coercive or seductive tactics to market their products and services? What can make these strategies ethically admissible?
6. What kind of deceptive tactics can be developed in electronic customer relationship management (e-CRM)? How could companies overcome customers' possible misinformation?
7. Most companies market products to and develop relationships with vulnerable populations. To what extent is it morally objectionable and legally allowable?
8. What are the lines of responsibility between the marketer and the customer in personal data dissemination and use?

Note

1 In a survey of nearly 1,000 digital marketers and e-commerce professionals, carried out in April and May 2014, *econsultancy* note that 34% of them indicated that they would increase their investment in acquisition, while only 18% would focus on retention (see: http://econsultancy.com/blog/65339-marketers-more-focused-on-acquisition-tha n-retention/).

References

Akerlof, G.A. (1970). The market for 'lemons': quality uncertainty and the market mechanism. *Quarterly Journal of Economics*, 89, pp. 488–500.
Alcimed (2014). Connected objects: what are the challenges and opportunities for players in the agri-food industry?11 July, Paris. www.alcimed.com.
AurierP. and N'Goala, G. (2010). The differing and mediating roles of trust and relationship commitment in service relationship maintenance and development. *Journal of the Academy of Marketing Science*, 38(3), pp. 303–325.
Baker, S.M., Gentry, J. and Rittenburg, T. (2005). Building understanding of the domain of consumer vulnerability. *Journal of Macromarketing*, 25(2), pp 128–139.
Bastian, J. and Zentes, J. (2013). Supply chain transparency as a key prerequisite for sustainable agri-food supply chain management. *International Review of Retail, Distribution & Consumer Research*, 23(5), pp. 553–570.
BBC News (2013). Horsemeat scandal: Spanghero licence ban partially lifted. 18 February. www.bbc.co.uk/news/world-europe-21499290.
Bendapudi, N. and Berry, L.L. (1997). Customers' motivations for maintaining relationships with service providers. *Journal of Retailing*, 73(1), pp. 15–37.
Bergin, T. (2013). Google taxes overseas. www.huffingtonpost.com (accessed 30 September 2013).
Bertini, M. and Gourville, J.T. (2012). Pricing to create shared value. *Harvard Business Review*, June http://hbr.org/2012/06/pricing-to-create-shared-value.
Biehl-Missal, B. and Saren, M. (2012). Atmospheres of seduction: a critique of aesthetic marketing practices. *Journal of Macromarketing*, 32(2), pp. 168–180.
Bolton, L.E., Warlop, L. and Alba, J.W. (2003). Consumer perceptions of price (un)fairness. *Journal of Consumer Research*, 29(4), pp. 474–491.

Brown, T.J. and Dacin, P.A. (1997). The company and the product: corporate associations and consumer product. *Journal of Marketing*, 61(1), pp. 68–84.

Buller, D.B., Burgoon, J.K., White, C.H. and Ebesu, A.S. (1994). Interpersonal deception: behavioral profiles of falsification, equivocation, and concealment. *Journal of Language and Social Psychology*, 13(4), pp. 366–395.

Carter, R. and Curry, D. (2010). Transparent pricing: theory, tests, and implications for marketing practice. *Journal of the Academy of Marketing Science*, 38(6), pp. 759–774.

Center for Science in the Public Interest (2010). Lawsuit over deceptive vitaminwater claims to proceed. http://cspinet.org/new/201007231.html (accessed 28 January 2015).

Center for Science in the Public Interest (2011). General mills facing class action lawsuit over 'fruit snacks' full of sugars, partially hydrogenated oil, & dyes. http://cspinet.org/new/201110141.html (accessed 28 January 2015).

Chester, J. and Montgomery, K. (2011). Digital food marketing to children and adolescents: problematic practices and policy interventions. 19 October. National Policy & Legal Analysis Network to Prevent Childhood Obesity: Public Health Law & Policy. http://ca sestudies.digitalads.org/ftc-complaint/.

Cissé-Depardon, K. and N'Goala, G. (2009). The effects of satisfaction, trust and brand commitment on consumers' decision to boycott. *Recherche et Applications en Marketing* (English edition), 24(1), pp. 43–67.

Deighton, J. and Grayson, K. (1995). Marketing and seduction: building exchange relationships by managing social consensus. *Journal of Consumer Research*, 21 (March), pp. 93–109.

Dixon, M., Freeman, K. and Toman, N. (2010). Stop trying to delight your customers. *Harvard Business Review*. July–August, pp. 1–15.

Dwyer, F.R. and Lagace, R.R. (1986). On the nature and role of buyer-seller trust. AMA Summer Educators Conference Proceedings. 3–6 August. American Marketing Association, Chicago. pp. 40–45.

Dwyer, F.R., Schurr, P.H. and Oh, S. (1987). Developing buyer-seller relationships. *Journal of Marketing*, 51 (April), pp. 11–27.

Eggert, A. and Helm, S. (2003). Exploring the impact of relationship transparency on business relationships: a cross-sectional study among purchasing managers in Germany. *Industrial Marketing Management*, 32(2), pp. 101–108.

Folcher, P. and N'Goala, G. (2014). Le Consommateur et le 'made in France': conceptualisation et mesure de la responsabilité economique du consommateur. *Congrès de l'Association Française du Marketing*. Montpellier. 14–16 May.

Fournier, S., Dobscha, S. and Mick, D.G. (1998). Preventing the premature death of relationship marketing. *Harvard Business Review*, Jan./Feb., 76(1), pp. 42–51.

The Free Library (2014). Stores urged to stop using child labour cotton. Al Bawaba (Middle East) Ltd. www.thefreelibrary.com/Stores+urged+to+stop+using+child+labour+cotton. -a0215260181 (accessed 28 January 2015).

Gardner, D.M. (1975). Deception in advertising: a conceptual approach. *Journal of Marketing*, 39 (January), pp. 40–46.

Granovetter, N. (1985). Economic action and social structure: the problem of embeddedness. *American Journal of Sociology*, 91, pp. 481–510.

Grönroos, C. (1990). *Service Management and Marketing: Managing the Moments of Truth in Service Competition*. Lexington, MA: Free Press.

Guéguen, N. (2002). Foot-in-the-door and computer-mediated communication. *Computers in Human Behavior*, 18(1), pp. 11–15.

Gundlach, G.T. and Murphy, P.E. (1993). Ethical and legal foundations of relational marketing exchanges. *Journal of Marketing*, 57, pp. 35–46.

Gurviez, P. and Korchia, M. (2002). Proposition d'une échelle de mesure multi-dimensionnelle de la confiance dans la marque. *Recherche et Applications en Marketing*, 17(3), pp. 41–61.

Harford, T. (2006). The economics of trust, *Fortune*, 3 November.

Hunt, S. and Vitell, S. (1986). The general theory of marketing ethics: a revision and three questions. *Journal of Macromarketing*, 26, pp. 143–153.

Kivetz, R. and Simonson, I. (2002). Earning the right to indulge: effort as a determinant of customer preferences toward frequency program rewards. *Journal of Marketing Research*, 39 (2), pp. 155–170.

Klemperer, P. (1995). Competition when consumers have switching costs: an overview with applications to industrial organization, macroeconomics, and international trade. *The Review of Economic Studies*, 62(4), pp. 515–539.

Macneil, I.R. (1978). Contracts: adjustment of long term economic relations under classical, neo-classical, and relational contract law. *Northwestern Law Review*, 72, pp. 854–905.

McKinley, M.M. (2011). *Ethics in Marketing and Communications: Towards a Global Perspective*. Palgrave Macmillan, Business & Management Collection.

Moorman, C., Zaltman, G. and Deshpande, R. (1992). Relationships between providers and users of market research: the dynamics of trust within and between organizations. *Journal of Marketing Research*, 29(3), pp. 314–328.

N'Goala, G. (2007). Customer switching resistance (CSR): the effects of perceived equity, trust and relationship commitment. *International Journal of Service Industry Management*, 18 (5), pp. 510–533.

N'Goala, G. (2010). Discovering the dark side of service relationships … or why long-lasting and exclusive relationships are self-destructing. *Recherche et Applications en Marketing* (English edition), 25 (March), pp. 3–30.

Nguyen, B. (2011). The dark side of CRM. *The Marketing Review*, 11(2), pp. 137–149.

Oxfam (2013). Investors push food industry giants for urgent action on transparency. 17 September.

Palmer, D. and Hedberg, T. (2013). The ethics of marketing to vulnerable populations. *Journal of Business Ethics*, 116(2), pp. 403–413.

Porter Lynch, R. and Lawrence, P.R. (2012). The age of distrust: a European perspective. White Paper.

Rudinow, J. (1978). Manipulation. *Ethics*, 88(4), pp. 338–347.

Schwartz, M. (2005). What Gewirth is worth at the department store. *Journal of Business Ethics*, 58(1–3), pp. 27–35.

Searls, D. (2012). 'The intention economy: when customers take charge'. In *The Intention Economy*. Harvard Business Review Press.

Shayon, S. (2011). PepsiCo refutes consumer watchdogs' deceptive marketing complaint. 20 October. www.brandchannel.com.

Sher, S. (2011). A framework for assessing immorally manipulative marketing tactics. *Journal of Business Ethics*, 102(1), pp. 97–118.

Shultz, C.J. and Holbrook, M.B. (2009). The paradoxical relationships between marketing and vulnerability. *Journal of Public Policy & Marketing*, 28(1), pp. 124–127.

Simon, M. (2011a). ConAgra sued over GMO '100% natural' cooking oils. *Food Safety News*. www.foodsafetynews.com/2011/08/conagra-sued-over-gmo-100-natural-cooking-oils/#.VMmCcd5hzTB (accessed 28 January 2015).

Simon, M. (2011b). Lawsuit alleges Frito-Lay's GMO snacks aren't 'natural'. *Eat Drink Politics*. www.eatdrinkpolitics.com/2011/12/27/lawsuit-alleges-fritolays-gmo-snacks-arent-natural/ (accessed 28 January 2015).

Simon, M. (2011c). Court not buying Coke's defense of its deceptive marketing of vita-minwater as lawsuit proceeds. *Eat Drink Politics*. www.eatdrinkpolitics.com/2010/08/08/court-not-buying-cokes-defense-of-its-deceptive-marketing-of-vitaminwater-as-lawsuit-proceeds/ (accessed 28 January 2015).

Simon, M. (2013). Fighting big food's deceptive marketing campaign. 3 June. http://ecowatch.com.

Sinha, I. (2000). Cost transparency: the net's real threat to prices and brands. *Harvard Business Review*. March–April. pp. 43–50.

Smith, C.N. and Cooper-Martin, E. (1997). Ethics and target marketing: the role of product harm and consumer vulnerability. *Journal of Marketing*, 61(3), pp. 1–20.

Stevens, E., N'Goala, G. and Pez, V. (2012). 'Fluidifier les parcours clients'. In P. Volle (Ed.) *Stratégie Clients: points de vue d'experts sur le management de la relation client*. Pearson, p. 155–189.

Turilli, M. and Floridi, L. (2009). The ethics of information transparency. *Ethics and Information Technology*, 11(2), pp. 105–112.

Wetzel, H.A., Hammerschmidt, M. and Zablah, A.R. (2014). Gratitude versus entitlement: a dual process model of the profitability implications of customer prioritization. *Journal of Marketing*, 78(2), pp. 1–19.

Williamson, O.E. (1985). *The Economic Institutions of Capitalism*. The Free Press, New York.

Williamson, O.E. (1993). Calculativeness, trust, and economic organization. *Journal of Law and Economics*, 36(1), John M. Olin Centennial Conference in Law and Economics at the University of Chicago. pp. 453–486.

Wingfield, N. and Pereira, J. (2002). Amazon uses faux suggestions to promote new clothing store. *The Wall Street Journal*, 4 December.

Xiao, B. and Benbasat, I. (2011). Product-related deception in e-commerce: a theoretical perspective. *MIS Quarterly*, 35(1), pp. 169–196.

Further reading

McKinley, M.M. (2011). *Ethics in Marketing and Communications: Towards a Global Perspective*. Palgrave Macmillan, Business & Management Collection.

Searls, D. (2012). 'The intention economy: when customers take charge'. In *The Intention Economy*. Harvard Business Review Press.

Volle, P. (2012). *Stratégie Client: point de vue d'experts sur le management de la relation client*. Pearson.

8

THE DARK SIDE OF BUSINESS RELATIONSHIPS: AN OVERVIEW

Ibrahim Abosag, Dorothy Ai-wan Yen and Caroline Tynan

1 Introduction

Despite the substantial number of theoretical and empirical contributions in the area of business-to-business (B2B) relationships, most studies have largely focused on the positive aspects of relationships that enable business relationships to grow and generate greater value for stakeholders (e.g. Dwyer et al., 1987; Sheth and Parvatiyar, 1995). Existing knowledge and understanding of the dark side of business relationships tend to be too narrow and only focused on one or a few components – e.g. opportunism, uncertainty and conflict. They offer limited reflection on the wider issues surrounding inter-organisational and interpersonal interactions as well as on the process of relationship development.

The studies of business relationships that explore the dark side tend to investigate all the relevant issues from two different perspectives. The first group of studies examines the dark side throughout the process of business relationship development (e.g. Moorman et al., 1992; Barnes, 2005), with the aim of understanding where in the development process of relationships the dark side occurs and also its consequences on the development of business relationships. For example, some studies have argued that the dark side of business relationships is more likely to occur in relationships characterised by long-term development (e.g. Grayson and Ambler, 1999), whereas others found that the dark side is likely to occur earlier in the development process (Barnes, 2005).

The second group of studies tends to focus on the role of certain constructs that can cause negative interaction within the relationship and/or undermine the relationship to varying degrees (e.g. Gaski, 1984; John, 1984). These include conflict, uncertainty, tension and opportunism. They can influence business relationships either positively or negatively at both inter-organisational and interpersonal levels. These two schools of thought are not completely separate from each other; the difference between the two exists in their focus. Having said this, the second school of thought has received significantly greater research attention than the first, for two reasons. First, theories and models of relationship development have faced serious criticism due to their weak explanatory power and lack of ability to predict relationship development. Second, the dynamic development of relationships within different contexts has proven difficult to capture in an accurate manner.

Learning objectives

The chapter aims to examine the existing literature on the dark side of business relationships. When you have read the chapter, you should be able to:

1. Use relationship development models to describe where in the process of business relationship development the dark side could emerge.
2. Recognise the negative consequences of over-developed trust and commitment in business relationships.
3. Discuss how cultural contexts and orientations influence the development of the dark side in business relationships.
4. Explain how interpersonal relationships may contribute to the development of the dark side of business relationships.
5. Critically discuss negative relational constructs such as tension, uncertainty, conflict and opportunism and their damaging impact on business relationships.

2 Route map

This chapter aims to expand, clarify and develop a better understanding of the dynamic development and effects of the dark side of business relationships for students, academics and practitioners. In order to expand the current frameworks of analysis on the dark side of business relationships, the chapter develops four main themes. The first section explains relationship development processes and examines when and where the dark side emerges throughout the development process of business relationships. Existing theories and frameworks of relationship development motivated by key relational constructs, such as trust and commitment, are employed as recent literature suggests that the bright side is not always so, and does not necessarily result in positive relationship outcomes (e.g. Ping and Dwyer, 1992; Halinen and Tahtinen, 2002; Pressey and Mathews, 2003; Johnson and Selnes, 2004; Anderson and Jap, 2005; Noordhoff et al., 2011).

Stemming from the aforementioned point – and in order to better challenge the current belief that relational constructs can either be 'bright' or 'dark' in nature – the second section discusses the negative impact of constructs traditionally perceived as positive, namely trust and commitment. The chapter goes on to explore the tension inherent in close interpersonal relationships between relationship boundary personnel, e.g. sales and procurement staff of different cultural backgrounds within international business relationships, and then considers the key dark side constructs, including conflict, uncertainty and opportunism. Of all constructs considered, 'opportunism' is the most negative and can lead to true negative outcomes for business partners. The chapter then concludes with an overview and highlights areas for future research attention, before finally presenting a case study on cross-cultural expectations and interpersonal styles.

3 State of the art in research on business relationships

The dark side of relationship development

Despite the conflicting findings and arguments about where in the development process darker elements are likely to occur in business relationships, studies of relationship development tend to rely on theories and models of the relationship development process that are not themselves free from criticism. This section explains how different theories and models are employed in explaining the development of the dark side in business relationships.

Models and theories of relationship development

Relationship development theories and models often highlight different approaches and styles of thinking. They not only reflect the brighter and more positive aspects of relationship development, but also identify areas wherein the dark side of relationships can challenge the development of that relationship or completely disrupt relationship development and future interaction. Hence, Van de Ven (1992, p. 174) defined relationship development theory as: 'A theory of process consists of statements that explain how and why processes unfold over time.'

The work of Van de Ven (1992) on the strategic processes of organisations provides a platform for studying relationship development. This framework was later adapted by Halinen (1997) to discuss relationship development in three different ways, focusing on: 1 causal relationship development (input–output models); 2 relational change over time (change models); and 3 processual development (process models). The first input–output model refers to the causal development between independent variables and dependent variables. Research interest has focused on examining the success or failure of a relationship in its phases of initiation, maintenance or dissolution. These input–output models are used in the business relationship literature to examine the antecedents and consequences of development (e.g. Morgan and Hunt, 1994; Chenet et al., 2000).

The second category focuses on 'changes' to a specific variable(s) of the development process, such as a change in commitment or trust over time (e.g. Stumpf and Hartman, 1984; Vandenberg and Lance, 1992). Longitudinal research is commonly used to examine whether a change has occurred or not. For example, Ford (1980, 1982) employed such a change perspective on relationship development by analysing changes in variables such as experience, uncertainty, distance, commitment and adaptation through the development process. Third, the developmental event sequence or processual approach focuses on how changes occur in the development process. Processual research tends to look at the nature of development, sequence, event order and activities over time (Wilson and Mummalaneni, 1986; Dwyer et al., 1987; Wilson, 1995).

These models of relationship development could be congruent with one of two development theories, which are life-cycle theory and evolutionary theory (Van de Ven, 1992). Rao and Perry (2002) describe the life-cycle theory as 'stages theory' and the evolutionary theory as 'states theory'. The life-cycle/stages theory assumes that relationship development goes through a stage-by-stage development process, where the change from one stage to a prefigured stage is assumed imminent. Hence, relationship development is considered a gradual progression, growing in a sequential manner over time (Van de Ven, 1992; Rao and Perry, 2002), following a single sequence of stages in the process. Stanton (2002) calls this theory the unidimensional theory, as it moves in one direction, starting at the input at the end, processing through every stage either serially or in parallel, and finally resulting in the output at the end of the process. Nevertheless, this theory has been criticised for the inherent assumption that relationship development goes through an inevitable and irreversible, progressive one-directional development process (Halinen, 1997; Bell, 1995).

The evolutionary/states theory, on the other hand, reviews the development process as unstructured and unpredictably dynamic. This theory 'explains change as a recurrent, cumulative, and probabilistic progression of variation, selection and retention' (Van de Ven, 1992, p. 179). Processual modelling is commonly used since it captures the dynamics of relationship development, and phasing can be used to simplify the relationship development process. This approach is not necessarily deterministic and is rather dependent on the circumstances at a point in time. Rao and Perry (2002, p. 604) indicate that, according to this theory, '[r]elationship and network development can move forward and backward or even stay in the same state for an undetermined period in the development process'. The strength of this theory lies in its openness and responsiveness to the dynamic nature of relationship development, which may result in the development process taking different directions. Hence, Stanton (2002, p. 177) refers to it as a multidimensional theory because of its interactive hierarchy of processes or stages in which information passes through the system in more than one direction or along more than one axis.

Relationship development is a dynamic process of changes, improvements, maintenance or dissolution over time, between two or more parties that are governed by internal and external influences. The literature on B2B relationship development provides a number of models/frameworks, from both service and industrial marketing. Although these models appear to show universally agreed stages/phases of the development process, the conceptualisation of these models clearly shows otherwise. For example, some models fail to recognise the pre-relationship/awareness stage (e.g. Van de Ven, 1976; Gronroos, 1980; Borys and Jemison, 1989; York, 1990). Other models have ignored the dissolution stage of the relationship process (Van de Ven, 1976; Gummesson, 1979; Gronroos, 1980; Borys and Jemison, 1989; York, 1990; Ring and Van de Ven, 1994; Wilson, 1995; Zineldin, 2002). The time dimension has only been mentioned in a few models (Ford, 1980, 1982; Dwyer et al., 1987; Wilson, 1995), while the integration of relational variables and development process was only conceptualised by Wilson's (1995) model. Most influential models are those of a processual nature (Frazer, 1983; Wilson and Mummalaneni, 1986; Dwyer et al., 1987; Wilson, 1995), while the remaining models are of the less complex 'input–output' and 'change' formats. In general, there is a clear lack of comparability between these models in the literature.

The dark side and relationship development

Research on when and how the dark side emerges through the relationship development process has been very limited. From the handful of studies that examined where in the development process the dark side emerges, leading to serious challenges to the relationship, Moorman et al. (1992) were among the first to claim there is a dark side of long-term relationships that weakens the positive influence of relational constructs like trust. Contrary to common belief, they suggest that the longer the relationship exists, the more it is prone to negative influences because over time both parties gradually increased their expectations of each other's performance. When actual performance fails to meet the increased expectation, it can result in dissatisfaction, thus reducing the positive influence of increased trust and commitment. While the findings of Moorman et al. (1992) were later confirmed by Grayson and Ambler (1999), Barnes (2005) discovered that, in a dyadic context, some negativity is more likely to occur in mid-term rather than long-term relationships, as a degree of complacency creeps into such relationships. Research examining the dark side of relationships is scant and very little has been concluded concerning how such effects can influence future relationship dynamics.

Nonetheless, and despite the apparent lack of studies in this area, it is safe to argue that the dark side of a business relationship can emerge at any point in the development process, depending on relationship contexts, types, interaction dynamics and market conditions. It is also safe to argue that the dark side of relationships is likely to occur frequently in those relationships where uncertainty and physical distance between relational partners exist because of the cross-cultural/cross-national nature of such relationships (Leonidou et al., 2006). What is clear is that more studies are needed on the emergence of the dark side throughout the relationship development process.

Current literature has thoroughly examined relationship ending/exiting/termination/dissolution (e.g. Ping and Dwyer, 1992; Halinen and Tahtinen, 2002; Pressey and Mathews, 2003), which arguably present the conclusion of the process. Various reasons for terminating/ending a business relationship include the impact of personal conflicts (Alajoutsijarvi et al., 2000), lack of mutual trust (Halinen and

Tahtinen, 2002), differences in cultural values between parties (Shankarmahesh et al., 2003; Batona and Perry, 2003), weak relational capital (Li et al., 2006), weak or no relationship-specific assets (Poppo et al., 2008), finding a more capable partner (Bendoly et al., 2010), and the low cost of terminating the relationship (Heide and John, 1988; Morgan and Hunt, 1994). However, none of these studies has examined the termination of relationships as a part of a wider study of the whole development process of business relationships. Future studies are needed for better prediction of relationship development. Thus, issues such as relationship context, nature, historical and potential development need to be considered in order to provide better understanding of how, when and where in the development process of business relationships the dark side can impose significant risk and potentially lead to relationship termination. In this regard, and to increase usefulness, further studies should focus on the early and mid-term development processes.

The dark side of over-developed trust and commitment

Studies have shown that the development of successful business relationships is strongly linked to the development of trust and commitment (Ford, 1980; Dwyer et al., 1987; Wilson, 1995). Studying the dynamic development of trust and commitment can contribute to better understanding of the development of business relationships. Whilst lack of trust and commitment in business relationships are often criticised, it is less widely recognised that excessive levels of trust and commitment in business relationships can cause negative impacts on relationships (Ekici, 2013; Kusari et al., 2013).

Trust and its dimensions

Trust has been defined as a multidimensional construct (Rodriguez and Wilson, 1995; Brashear et al., 2003; Miyamoto and Rexha, 2004; Johnson and Grayson, 2005). Studies often discuss the antecedents of trust at two dimensions/levels (Coulter and Coulter, 2003; Johnson and Grayson, 2005). The first is the dimension of trust, focused on *performance-related trust*, characterised by competence, customisation, reliability/dependability and promptness. The second is *affective-related trust*, characterised by caring, concern, empathy, similarity and politeness. The antecedents of these two dimensions are integrity, honesty, credibility, benevolence and confidence (Miyamoto and Rexha, 2004; Johnson and Grayson, 2005).

Performance/cognitive trust is the confidence, willingness or intention of a party to rely on a partner's competence, reliability/credibility and promptness in meeting their obligations (Anderson and Weitz, 1989; Moorman et al., 1992). Trust emerges from a party's predictions regarding their partner's future action/behaviours to fulfil promises (Zaheer et al., 1998). These predictions are based on accumulative knowledge gained through parties' interaction (Harris and Dibben, 1999) or based on a party's reputation in other relationships (Johnson and Grayson, 2005). Often when a business relationship develops over time, both parties increase their performance trust of each other based on past successful collaboration. However, this is not always the case. Barnes (2005) reveals that during the mid-term of relationships (between two and five years in length), between UK multinational enterprise (MNE) buyers and their suppliers, trust actually reduced over time. Performance-based trust is viewed as an expectation rather than a conviction concerning a partner's future behaviour and thus reflects uncertainty in anticipating this behaviour (Zaheer et al., 1998), providing parties with a degree of freedom to disappoint expectations. This highlights an important issue of trust expectation management.

Over time, a reduction in the level of trust (Barnes, 2005) is particularly likely at the inter-organisational level, where trust needs to be reactivated specifically when parties take on new transactional tasks that have not previously been part of the exchange between partners, to prevent unpleasant surprises arising from changes (Huemer, 2004). While future actions/behaviours imply some degree of risk, the knowledge gained from previous collaborations helps reduce the uncertainty in subsequent transactions (Eriksson and Sharma, 2003). Expectations concerning competence and responsibility are central in performance-based trust. Whilst businesses strive to prove their competence to their counterparts through the demonstration of skills and knowledge, as well as delivering promised performance (Gronroos, 1990), businesses also need to set realistic benchmarks and be aware of the danger of over-promising where those promises cannot be fulfilled.

Affective-based trust is the confidence a party places in another party based on the feelings and emotions generated by the caring, empathy, politeness, similarity and concern for the other party, demonstrated in their interaction (Rempel et al., 1985). Affective-based trust is characterised by '[f]eelings of security and perceived strength of the relationship' (Johnson and Grayson, 2005, p. 501), interpersonal liking (Nicholson et al., 2001), and a 'leap of faith' beyond the expectations that reason and knowledge would warrant (Wicks et al., 1999, p. 100), which means that the relational context will act as a moral control on the behaviour of parties (Granovetter, 1985). Past research reveals that emotional bonds are essential in driving the relationship and nurturing mutual trust (Nicholson et al., 2001). However, whilst it is important to improve business partners' understanding of each other as individuals to create emotional openness, firms need to be aware of the consequence of over-emphasising such affective-based trust in recruiting relationship boundary-spanning personnel. Although personal qualities are important in creating an emotional bond as a basis of affective-based trust that strengthens and reinforces the economic and structural bonds (Nicholson et al., 2001; Svensson, 2004), firms must ensure that relationship trust is not only established at the affective level to avoid the danger that boundary-spanning personnel, especially those in sales and procurement, may take their clients and contacts with them when they leave an organisation.

The debate regarding whether performance-based trust and affective-based trust occur simultaneously in a relationship, or which precedes the other, is still very new. The interactivity between the two dimensions needs to be examined to illuminate this issue. McAllister (1995) and Nicholson et al. (2001) argue that, once strong and affective-based trust exists between parties, the need for performance-based trust may be reduced. In contrast, Chowdhury (2005) argues that performance-based trust may not always develop affective trust and therefore partners may not have shared values or similar perceptions. Empirically, Johnson and Grayson (2005) find a significant and positive relationship between performance-based trust and affective-based trust. However, Rodriguez and Wilson (1995) find that affective-based trust does not affect performance-based trust in an individualist culture, while affective-based trust affects performance-based trust in a collectivist culture.

Commitment and its dimensions

Relationship commitment is seen as an enduring desire to maintain a relationship (Dwyer et al., 1987; Geyskens et al., 1996; Moorman et al., 1992; Morgan and Hunt, 1994). Commitment is 'enduring', with an implicit or explicit expectation that partners will continue the process of exchange into the future (Dwyer et al., 1987; Morgan and Hunt, 1994; O'Malley and Tynan, 1997). However, O'Malley and Tynan (1997) argue that the existence of one committed party in a relationship does not automatically suggest that all parties in the relationship are committed. Gundlach et al. (1995) argue that the lack of mutual or disproportionate commitment between less committed partners can lead to opportunism by the less committed partner. In support of these two arguments by O'Malley and Tynan (1997) and Gundlach et al. (1995), Leek et al. (2002) demonstrates that suppliers are more concerned with gaining and maintaining the commitment of their customers in the relationship than vice versa. Such concerns over the lack of a committed partner can seriously lead to the dark side of the lack of commitment in a business relationship. However, commitment is increasingly important as a focal point in business relationships, comprising two dimensions, namely instrumental/calculative commitment and affective commitment (e.g. Gundlach et al., 1995; Gutierrez et al., 2004).

Instrumental/calculative commitment is variously known as economic commitment (Young and Denize, 1995), constraints commitment (Bendapudi and Berry, 1997), and structural commitment (Williams et al., 1998). Geyskens et al. (1996, p. 304) define calculative commitment as '[t]he need to maintain a relationship given the significant anticipated termination or switching costs associated with leaving'. This type of commitment refers to the investment of relationship-specific assets among partner organisations (Rylander et al., 1997). Instrumental/calculative commitment is viewed as a function of pledges, idiosyncratic investments, sharing of information and allocation of relationship-specific resources (Dwyer et al., 1987; Anderson and Weitz, 1992; Gundlach et al., 1995). Inputs or investments in a relationship are evidence and manifestation of implementing early promises that enhance parties' credibility at the beginning of the relationship and reduce uncertainty and the risk of opportunism (Morgan and Hunt, 1994; Achrol and Gundlach, 1999; Wuyts and Geyskens, 2005). The commitment exists based on the calculation of the costs and benefits of a firm's involvement in the relationship.

In a way, calculative commitment acts as reinforcement to keep both parties within the relationship, based on the mutual understanding that it is more costly to leave the relationship than stay. Some firms use instrumental/calculative commitment to express their willingness to maintain their relationships by making adaptations (Hakansson, 1982) and sacrifices (Anderson and Weitz, 1992; Rylander et al., 1997), abandoning the search for an alternative (Alajoutsijarvi et al., 2000) and initiating trust in the relationship (Dwyer et al., 1987). Although it helps contribute to a long-term relationship, instrumental commitment may hinder businesses in search of more competitive partners to maximise their relational performance.

Affective commitment can create emotional bonds that may drive parties to maintain and improve the quality of their relationship (Bendapudi and Berry, 1997; Fletcher et al., 2000). Unlike calculative commitment, which is based on the perceived constraints that bind parties together in the relationship, affective commitment is based on a set of perceptions, knowledge, beliefs and emotions that link two individuals/managers in their business relationship and motivate them to maintain that relationship. Thus, a social structure is generated through individuals' desires to be psychologically and emotionally consistent throughout their interactions with partners (Meyer and Allen, 1991). This is commonly accepted within the Eastern culture. In fact, the Chinese emphasise a similar concept called *ganqing*, which is established on mutual affection, sentiment and emotion. Similar to affective commitment, *ganqing* focuses on the social relationship between two people or two organisations, as well as an emotional attachment existing among network parties (Yen et al., 2011). Affective commitment is often employed by Chinese firms to secure their business relationships with identified buyers over their competitors (Yen et al., 2011). However, over-emphasis of affective commitment may impair a firm's decisions concerning profit maximisation.

The dark side of interpersonal relationships

A great deal of the literature on B2B marketing has examined business relationships at the interpersonal level. Interpersonal relationships are the underlying social content of inter-organisational relationships (Morgan, 2000). The importance of interpersonal relationships in B2B relationships has long been emphasised (e.g. Ford, 1980; Hakansson, 1982; Dwyer et al., 1987; Wilson, 1995). Statements such as '[p]ersonal relationships and reputations between boundary-spanning members play an important role in facilitating and enhancing inter-organisational exchange' (Weitz and Jap, 1995, p. 316) are not uncommon (e.g. Hakansson, 1982; Dwyer et al., 1987; Ganesan, 1994; Bendapudi and Berry, 1997; Svensson, 2004).

However, the extant literature has rarely considered the negative side of the lack of, or excessive, development of interpersonal relationships in B2B marketing. The work by Haytko (2004) in categorising interpersonal relationships identified three types along a continuum, ranging from a 'lack' of an interpersonal relationship to a more excessive type of interpersonal relationship that exists in business relationships. Such types include 'strictly business', where no interpersonal interaction, no self-disclosure or personal communication exists. Such a strict attitude can be seen as negative, especially by some Western and certainly some Eastern and collectivist cultures, where a degree of personalisation of interaction is essential to building business relationships.

The second type, 'business friends', reflects interactions outside work, wherein personal knowledge is developed and some self-disclosure is made (Haytko, 2004). While this type of interpersonal relationship may be regarded as balanced and useful to business relationships in Anglo-Saxon countries, managers from collectivist cultures may require a higher degree of interpersonal interaction, as demonstrated by the Chinese cultural-specific concept of *guanxi*, wherein close interpersonal connections form the foundation of successful business collaborations (Mavondo and Rodrigo, 2001). This highlights the existence of the third type of 'personal' relationships, characterised by a still higher level of intimate self-disclosure, substantial interaction outside the work environment and full personal knowledge. Social interactions among business parties outside work over leisure activities are often encouraged. Examples of this type are *'guanxi'* in China (e.g. Yen et al., 2011; Barnes et al., 2011) and *'et-moone'* in Saudi Arabia (e.g. Abosag and Lee, 2012; Abosag and Naudé, 2014).

The debate over which type of interpersonal relationship is considered appropriate should be judged within its cultural context. Williams et al. (1998) note that highly interpersonally oriented (collectivist) countries would be very responsive to interpersonal aspects of the business relationship and put more emphasis on social bonding, whilst highly structurally oriented (individualist) countries would be more responsive to structural aspects of the business relationship and put more emphasis on structural bonding of the business relationships. Whilst close personal relationships are encouraged in countries such as China and Saudi Arabia, it is considered unnecessary and a waste of resources by many Western firms, especially those from Anglo-Saxon countries. For instance, Rodriguez and Wilson (1995) find that American managers view socialisation as 'unimportant' and of 'no purpose' in the development of long-term business relationships.

Businesses must be aware of such cultural differences in their interactions with counterparts from different cultural backgrounds. Imagine an urgent matter occurs in a cross-cultural interaction, wherein both sides are required to rectify the problem. The firm from a Western individualist culture may react immediately, focusing on fixing the instrumental and performance elements of commitment and trust. Such a reaction may have the opposite effect on its Eastern counterpart of collectivist cultural origin, as they may respond to the event in such a way as to protect the relationship through an emphasis on the affective aspects of commitment and trust. The danger exists when a firm of Eastern collectivist culture views the reaction by the Western individualist culture as selfish or signifying that it does not care for the relationship. While the reaction from the Western firm seems to be completely normal to its managers, managers from the Eastern firm may have already started to view the relationship with some negativity. This explains why such lack of understanding of Chinese *guanxi* has caused the failure of many Western businesses that attempted to go into the Chinese markets (Yen et al., 2011).

It is important to bear in mind any potential cultural difference when dealing with partners from another country, given that nowadays many firms are involved in international sales and procurement activities. Barnes et al. (2011), therefore, highlight the importance of taking into account both cultural perspectives in developing, maintaining and evaluating hybrid business relationships. After all, there is no right or wrong, brighter or darker, better or worse in judging the cultural values possessed by others. Instead of making a decision to drop a business partner using 'cultural incompatibility' as a reason, managers should spend more time in developing and facilitating boundary-spanning personnel's cultural awareness and developing cross-cultural communication skills.

The dark constructs of B2B relationships

This part introduces key constructs that are typically associated with the dark side of business relationships. These constructs have the ability to change from being a positive influence in relationships to being a negative one, as suggested by the IMP Group's interactive framework (Turnbull and Valla, 1985). Such vacillations can be caused by changes in the relationship dynamic, interpersonal and inter-organisational interaction, distance, context of the relationship and type of relationship. In this section, constructs including conflict, uncertainty and opportunistic behaviour will be discussed.

Conflict

Yandle and Blythe (2000, p. 14) define conflict as a 'breakdown or disruption in normal activities in such a way that the individuals or groups concerned experience difficulty working together'. Similar to trust and commitment, conflicts are also divided into functional as well as emotional conflict. *Functional conflict* has been described as a disagreement between partners (Dwyer et al., 1987) that can be resolved as part of doing business (Anderson and Narus, 1990), when the dispute is resolved amicably, on the basis of the existence of trust. However, in different situations it can terminate the relational exchange between partners. Generally, functional conflict is seen to cause a state of negative affect, tension between partners, disliking and negative behaviour in the working relationships. In comparison, *affective conflict* often occurs between boundary personnel at an interpersonal level. Rose and Shoham (2004, p. 943) define affective/emotional conflict as '[p]erceived/recognised interpersonal incompatibilities within groups, which are based on friction and personality clashes'. Affective/emotional conflict was found to have repercussions on partners' loyalty to their relationship (Plank and Newell, 2007).

Within the channel literature, functional conflict is found to disrupt channel learning and sharing of information (Chang and Gotcher, 2010), as a situation wherein one channel member observes another channel member to be engaged in behaviour that is preventing or impeding him from achieving his own goals (Stern and el-Ansary, 1977). Although some research studies have found functional conflict to be a positive outcome of trust (Morgan and Hunt, 1994), leading to an increase in productivity (Anderson and Narus, 1990), other studies such as Moorman et al. (1992) and Chenet et al. (2000) have tended to identify functional conflict as a negative antecedent of trust. These conflicting conceptualisations and findings are worthy of further investigation. It is likely that functional conflict is an outcome of performance trust because functional conflict occurs when both parties fail to deliver the expected performance, or when disagreement about how to perform a specific task or plan arises. In this regard, Jehn (1994), Bradford et al. (2004), and Duarte and Davies (2003) found functional conflict to impact performance negatively.

Given the significant impact that conflict can have on relationship performance and the future of relationships, most studies concentrate on understanding the source of conflict and resolving conflict (Thomas, 1992). In doing so, studies have focused on understanding attitudes, emotions and behaviour towards conflict. Partners' attitudes towards conflict were found to be either positive or negative (Tjosvold et al., 2003). Partners with positive attitudes towards conflict are able to see its usefulness and the benefits for the relationship (Jehn and Mannix, 2001), whereas partners with negative attitudes towards conflict can feel threatened and may fail to engage in positive discussion with their partner. Such failure to engage and deal with conflict resolution can generate even darker implications for the relationship.

As a result, conflict is considered to be a 'dark' entity that should be avoided, as it creates unwanted stress in the relationship, especially concerning goal setting and execution of functions (Jehn, 1994; Shaw et al., 2003). In addition to this, and because conflict occurs between individuals, partners' own personalities can be a source of conflict; efforts to resolve those conflicts should carefully consider the affective or personality traits of the individuals involved. Although functional conflict may be considered useful in promoting more effective business relationships, the extant literature generally agrees that conflict must be managed, in order to reduce the negative and dark implications for firms' relationships and to ensure that conflict remains under control so that partners can see the usefulness of conflicts to their relationships. However, conflict between partners from different countries/ cultures may cause more damage in the interaction and can impact relationship performance negatively. Both types of conflict are thought to escalate due to cultural differences. Both international partners' dissimilarities and differences in relational context and cultural values can lead to emotional conflict and reduce the ability to perceive and produce conflict usefulness. According to Rose and Shoham (2004), disagreements in international relationships have greater potential to exacerbate emotional conflict and create conditions that prevent conflict resolution. They further argue that international partners are '[p]articularly prone to negative conflict'.

Uncertainty

Uncertainty in the business relationship literature has been studied at two levels. The first is environmental uncertainty, focusing on circumstances caused by the environment within which business relationships exist and influenced by factors such as industry structure, market structure, government intervention and so on. The negative impact of environmental uncertainty on trust and business partners' confidence is well documented in the literature (Geyskens et al., 1998). The second type of uncertainty is relationship uncertainty, which is generated largely by business partners' interactions and communications. Uncertainty is defined as the extent to which a partner has sufficient information to make key decisions, can foresee the consequences of these decisions and has confidence in them (Achrol and Stern, 1988), while business uncertainty reflects the unanticipated changes in circumstances around partners' business exchanges (Noordeweir et al., 1990). Uncertainty in business exchange makes it more challenging to predict partners' demands and requirements as well as foreseeing the outcome of a purchase decision (Kohli, 1989).

Uncertainty is theorised as being a negative outcome of trust (Morgan and Hunt, 1994) because trust decreases decision-making uncertainty. However, the argument here is whether uncertainty actually is an antecedent of trust, rather than being an outcome of it. Morgan and Hunt (1994) measure uncertainty using scales developed by Achrol and Stern (1988). Two dimensions of uncertainty were measured, though Morgan and Hunt refer to uncertainty as a uni-dimensional construct. The first dimension measures whether or not the partners in the relationship have adequate information to make decisions. The second dimension measures the degree of confidence of the decision maker when making decisions. Because these dimensions of uncertainty focus on decision making regarding a business exchange, performance trust is the key antecedent of both dimensions of uncertainty. The relationship between performance trust and dimensions of uncertainty is negative. Furthermore, one can argue that, since uncertainty naturally exists in people's behaviour, uncertainty can be an independent variable that influences trust negatively. Similar to functional conflict, Chenet et al. (2000) found uncertainty to be an antecedent of trust and they found that uncertainty negatively influences the development of trust.

In general, it is accepted that, when uncertainty is low, the business exchange can be predicted, resulting in higher trust. The ability to predict economic benefits and costs can quickly lead to an increase in commitment to the relationship, and can enable a more cooperative attitude to develop in that relationship (Lai et al. 2005). Thus, the realisation of the importance of reducing uncertainty in business exchanges has become crucial to ensuring the smoother development of relationships, especially relationships in the early development stages, during which both environmental and relational uncertainties can be particularly high. The damage caused by high levels of uncertainty in business relationships is well recognised, especially regarding its negative impact on the development of trust, commitment and long-term orientation, as well as the risk of it leading to opportunistic behaviour

(Heide, 1994; Madhok, 1995). However, a study of suppliers in Hong Kong suggested the relationship between trust and commitment is moderated by uncertainty. Lai et al. (2005) found trust to have a positive and stronger effect on commitment when business uncertainty is high, as opposed to when uncertainty is low. While this finding needs to be replicated in different cultural contexts, studies of the bright and positive role of uncertainty in business relationships are generally lacking.

Opportunistic behaviour

Opportunistic behaviour is considered to violate the implicit or explicit promises between buyer and seller, and therefore to inhibit the establishment of trust. Opportunism, by definition, is acting in self-interest with guile (Williamson, 1975). Few studies focus on understanding the drivers of opportunistic behaviour in business relationships. Opportunistic behaviour can include behaviour such as breach of contract, deliberately confusing communication and transactions, cheating, deception, withholding information, avoiding creating value for partners and cutting corners (Anderson, 1988; Heide et al., 2007). The findings consistently suggest that opportunistic behaviour negatively affects trust and commitment. If one business partner has behaved in an opportunistic manner, it is likely to cause a long-term damaging effect to the collaborative atmosphere between the two parties. Nevertheless, existing research shows that opportunistic behaviour is much more likely to occur in a highly uncertain environment (Dwyer et al., 1987; Lai et al., 2005), as both parties seek every chance to defend their own interests and maximise their own competitive advantages for survival.

With recognition of the significant dark influence of opportunism in business relationships, studies on opportunism have shifted from explaining opportunism and its influences on relationships, to finding ways of controlling and reducing opportunistic behaviour in business relationships. For example, what kind of mechanism could be employed by a business to stop its partners acting in a selfish and careless manner? Whilst most of the business collaborations and relationship norms could be regulated contractually, some behaviours are difficult to assess and document, especially when one party purposely acts without taking the other's interests into consideration. Gundlach et al. (1995, p. 81) indicated that opportunism possesses a negative influence, describing an instance in which one party reneges on an agreement or understanding to take advantage of an opportunity. Heide (1994) suggests that partners will not behave in an opportunistic manner when the long-term benefits of cooperation outweigh the short-term and immediate gains from opportunism. John (1984, p. 279) suggests that there are links between social power usage and observed opportunism. For example, the more social interactions that have occurred between two parties, the less likely they will be to engage in opportunistic behaviour. Further, Provan and Skinner (1989) found that power is critical for understanding opportunistic behaviour in a relationship between organisations. The inequality of the distribution of power and the different types of power have different effects on the party's beliefs, attitudes and behaviour (Raven and Kruglanski, 1970).

Conclusion

This chapter reviews and discusses the dark side of business relationships through the lens of the theories and frameworks of relationship development, the negative impact of over-developing trust and commitment, the emphasis of interpersonal relationships across cultures, and a critical exploration of conflict, opportunism and uncertainty, with the aim of broadening the existing understanding of issues and contexts that can impact business relationships negatively. Various empirical studies have been discussed, whilst relevant business implications have been explored. Table 8.1 provides a summary of the key themes discussed.

Overall, it is normal for businesses to watch for signs of growth in the dark side of their business relationships, with the aim of successfully managing their relationships away from any threat that can be caused by dark and unexpected issues. While the dark side of business relationships can cause serious challenges, the spillover from that dark side can have similar severe implications for the wider industry, network and competition.

TABLE 8.1 A summary of the dark side of interpersonal and inter-organisational business relationships

	Section 1	*Section 2*	*Section 3*	*Section 4*
Dark side focus	Where and when dark side emerges during relationship development over time	The over-development of positive relationship constructs	Interpersonal relationships between relationship boundary personnel	Negative relationship constructs
Schools of thought	Relationship development process	Investigation and examination of business relationship constructs		
Level of study	Inter-organisational level		Interpersonal level	Inter-organisational and interpersonal level
Key underpinning or supporting theory	Life-cycle theory, evolutionary theory		Social exchange theory	IMP's interactive model
Key construct	Performance, time, relationship termination	Trust, commitment	Culturally specific interpersonal relationship construct, e.g. *guanxi, et-moone*	Conflict, uncertainty, opportunism

4 New research directions

The above overview of the dark side of business relationships has helped to identify a number of research issues that future studies need to consider in order to advance research in this important area. First, and most noticeably, is the lack of research on understanding the dark side within relationship processes. From the few studies in this area, the findings conflict as some studies find business relationships that in their early development are most at risk of dark influences (Barnes, 2005), whereas others found that long-term relationships are most vulnerable (Grayson and Ambler, 1999). Clearly, more research is needed in this area and consideration needs to be given to the appropriateness and effectiveness of using theories of relationship development to address this issue.

Second, and with regard to studying the influence of relational constructs in the dark side of business relationships, we found that most studies have focused on examining conflict within business relationships. The dark side of other relational constructs – such as trust, commitment, uncertainty and opportunism – needs further attention. Thus, future studies should examine the dark side of trust and commitment in more depth, but also address uncertainty and opportunism. Researchers studying relational constructs need to give special attention not only to the cultural context of business relationships, but also to the sectoral context. Such consideration of the differences and similarities between different business sectors will enrich our understanding of the dark side there, as well as at different local and international levels.

Third, in drafting this chapter, we were able to review the dark side at the interpersonal level and the inter-organisational level, but also cross-culturally. However, cross-sectional studies of the dark side are limited. Thus, future studies would greatly benefit the literature by examining the dark side across different cultures. This should be aimed at understanding the dark side from a development process focus as well as a relational constructs one. Furthermore, research could benefit from studies that aim to explore the dark side of relational constructs within the development process of business relationships. Such successful integration of relational constructs within the development process of relationships already exists in the literature (see Wilson, 1995; Abosag and Lee, 2012). However, these studies have only considered the positive and bright side of relationships. Therefore, future studies could add value through such integration of the dark side of business relationships in both relational constructs and development processes.

5 Practising marketing – a case study: two faces of the B2B relationship (the UAE–UK relationship)

Sami is happy to be in England after the few weeks he spent in a very warm Dubai collecting data for his PhD. In his PhD, Sami aims to understand cross-cultural business relationships and how managers think of their relationships with their overseas partners. He has carried out a number of interviews with managing directors and procurement directors in leading companies in Dubai, and is particularly pleased with the interview with Mr Tamer al-Qamer, who was very appreciative of his business partner in the UK (Mr Charles Moone), with whom Mr al-Qamer has been doing business for the past five years. In that interview, Sami asked Mr al-Qamer about his relationship with his British supplier, Mr Moone.

MR AL-QAMER: He is not the usual English person; he is very friendly, sociable not formal; Charles is a man I can trust; we've been working together for five years. He also delivers what we've asked of him. Charles invited me to his home many times and he visited me here too …
SAMI: How about your business relationship?
MR AL-QAMER: Charles understands my business well; as if he is one of us: he is very flexible. If I'm not happy with anything, I call him and he changes things quickly. Charles is the best partner in my business.

At the end of this interview, Sami asked for Mr Moone's contact details from Mr al-Qamer. A few days after his arrival in England, Sami called Mr Moone and asked to see him. An interview was arranged in the following week, to last no more than an hour, as Mr Moone requested. On the day of the interview, Sami waited outside Mr Moone's office, and ten minutes later he was asked to enter. Sami started the interview by telling Mr Moone about his visit to Dubai and his meeting with Mr al-Qamer. Sami was careful not to tell Mr Moone about his partner's opinion of the relationship. Sami asked Charles to tell him about Mr al-Qamer.

Mr Moone looked at his computer for a while and then said, 'Nightmare, nightmare', and stopped. Sami said nothing, waiting for more …

'He is a very organised person in everything except time; he called me four months ago and told me he will need a large quantity of our products very soon …' The order contains 7,000 flashing hazard lamps, 4,200 solar road stud lamps, 230 solar traffic warning lights, 150 solar arrow lights and 310 solar motorway direction lights.

Mr Moone added: 'He called me yesterday and this morning, and he wants all of these to be delivered urgently … How can I manufacture all of these and deliver them now. Just how?'

In the middle of the interview, after just 20 minutes, the telephone rang and Mr Moone apologised to Sami and told him that he must go. He was not able to finish the interview. Sami asked him if he could come again, but Mr Moone apologised and left.

Discussion questions

1. Why was Mr al-Qamer very pleased about his relationship with Mr Moone?
2. In your opinion, can this relationship between the two partners be considered successful? Why?

3. If you were Mr Moone, would you want to continue the business relationship with Mr al-Qamer over time?
4. Where should Sami start in analysing this relationship? On which key factors do you think he should focus his analysis?

6 Further investigation

1. Why is it important to consider the dark side of business relationships?
2. What are the two main approaches to studying the dark side of business relationships?
3. What are the key relational constructs that contribute to the dark side of business relationships?
4. Discuss the negative consequences of over-developed trust and commitment in business relationships.
5. Using one specific cultural context with which you are familiar, discuss how it might influence the development of the dark side in business relationships.

References

Abosag, I. and Lee, J. (2012). The formation of trust and commitment in business relationships in the Middle East: understanding et-moone relationships. *International Business Review*, 21(6), pp. 602–614.

Abosag, I. and Naudé, P. (2014). The development of special forms of B2B relationships: examining the role of interpersonal liking in developing guanxi and et-moone relationships. *Industrial Marketing Management*, 43(6), pp. 887–897.

Achrol, R. and Gundlach, G. (1999). Legal and social safeguards against opportunism in exchange. *Journal of Retailing*, 75(1), pp. 107–124.

Achrol, R.S. and Stern, L.W. (1988). Environmental determinants of decision-making uncertainty in marketing channels. *Journal of Marketing Research*, 25(1), 36–50.

Alajoutsijarvi, K., Moller, K. and Tahtinen, J. (2000). Beautiful exit, how to leave your business partner. *European Journal of Marketing*, 34(11/12), pp. 1270–1289.

Anderson, E. (1988). Transaction costs as determinants of opportunism in integrated and independent sales forces. *Journal of Economic Behavior Organization*, 9 (May), pp. 247–264.

Anderson, E. and Jap, S.D. (2005). The dark side of close relationships. *MIT Sloan Management Review*, 46(3), pp. 75–82.

Anderson, E. and Weitz, B. (1989). Determinants of continuity in conventional industrial channel dyads. *Marketing Science*, 8(4), pp. 310–324.

Anderson, E. and Weitz, B. (1992). The use of pledges to build and sustain commitment in distribution channels. *Journal of Marketing Research*, 29(1), pp. 18–35.

Anderson, J.C. and Narus, J.A. (1990). A model of distributor firm and manufacturing firm working partnerships. *Journal of Marketing*, 54 (January), pp. 42–58.

Barnes, B.R. (2005) Is the seven-year hitch premature in industrial markets? *European Journal of Marketing*, 39(5/6), pp. 560–581.

Barnes, B.R., Yen, D.A. and Zhou, L. (2011). The influence of Ganqing, Renqing and Xinren in the development of Sino-Anglo business relationships. *Industrial Marketing Management*, 40(4), pp. 510–521.

Batona, G. and Perry, C. (2003). Influence of culture on relationship development process on overseas Chinese/Australian networks. *European Journal of Marketing*, 37(11/12), p. 1548.

Bell, J. (1995). The internationalisation of small computer software firms: a further challenge to 'stage' theories. *European Journal of Marketing*, 29(8), pp. 60–75.

Bendapudi, N. and Berry, L. (1997). Consumer's motivations for maintaining relationships with service providers. *Journal of Retailing*, 73(1), pp. 15–38.

Bendoly, E., Croson, R., Goncalves, P. and Schultz, K. (2010). Bodies of knowledge for research in behavioral operations: production and operations management. *Journal of Operations Management*, 19(4), pp. 434–452.

Borys, B. and Jemison, D. (1989). Hybrid arrangements as strategic alliances: theoretical issues in organisational combinations. *Academy of Management Review*, 14(2), pp. 234–249.

Bradford, K.D., Stringfellow, A. and Weitz, B. (2004). Managing conflict to improve the effectiveness of retail networks. *Journal of Retailing*, 80(2), pp. 181–195.

Brashear, T., Boles, J., Bellenger, D. and Brooks, C. (2003). An empirical test of trust-building processes and outcomes in sales manager-salesperson relationships. *Academy of Marketing Science Journal*, 31(2), pp. 189–200.

Chang, K.H. and Gotcher, D.F. (2010). Conflict-coordination learning in marketing channel relationships: the distributor view. *Industrial Marketing Management*, 39, pp. 287–297.

Chenet, P., Tynan, C. and Money, A.H. (2000). The service performance gap: testing of the re-developed causal model. *European Journal of Marketing*, 34(3/4), pp. 472–495.

Chowdhury, S. (2005). The role of affect- and cognition-based trust in complex knowledge. *Journal of Managerial Issues*, 17(3), pp. 310–326.

Coulter, K. and Coulter, R. (2003). The effect of industry knowledge on the development of trust in service relationships. *International Journal of Research in Marketing*, 20(1), pp. 31–43.

Duarte, M. and Davies, G. (2003). Testing the conflict-performance assumption in business-to-business relationships. *Industrial Marketing Management*, 32(1), pp. 91–99.

Dwyer, F., Schurr, P. and Oh, S. (1987). Developing buyer-seller relationship. *Journal of Marketing*, 51(2) (April), pp. 11–27.

Ekici, A. (2013). Temporal dynamics of trust in ongoing inter-organizational relationships. *Industrial Marketing Management*, 42(6), pp. 932–949.

Eriksson, K. and Sharma, D. (2003). Modeling uncertainty in buyer-supplier cooperation. *Journal of Business Research*, 56(12), pp. 961–971.

Fletcher, G., Simpson, J. and Thomas, G. (2000). The measurement of perceived relationship quality components: a confirmatory factor analytic approach. *Personality and Social Psychological Bulletin*, 26(3), pp. 340–354.

Ford, D. (1980). The development of buyer-seller relationships in industrial markets. *European Journal of Marketing*, 14(5/6), pp. 339–353.

Ford, D. (1982). 'The development of buyer-seller relationships in industrial markets'. In H. Hakansson (Ed.) *International Marketing and Purchasing of Industrial Goods: An Interaction Approach*. Wiley, Chichester.

Frazer, G. (1983). Interorganisational exchange behaviour in marketing channels: a broadened perspective. *Journal of Marketing*, 47(4), pp. 68–78.

Ganesan, S. (1994). Determinants of long-term orientation in buyer-seller relationships. *Journal of Marketing*, 58(2), pp. 1–19.

Gaski, J. (1984). The theory of power and conflict in channels of distribution. *Journal of Marketing*, 48(3), pp. 9–29.

Geyskens, I., Steenkamp, J.E.M. and Kumar, N. (1998). Generalizations about trust in marketing channel relationships using meta-analysis. *International Journal of Research in Marketing*, 15(3), 223–248.

Geyskens, I., Steenkamp, J., Scheer, L. and Kumar, N. (1996). The effects of trust and interdependence on relationship commitment: a trans-Atlantic study. *International Journal of Research in Marketing*, 13(4), pp. 303–317.

Granovetter, M. (1985). Economic action and social structure: the problem of embeddedness. *American Journal of Sociology*, 91(3), pp. 481–510.

Grayson, K. and Ambler, T. (1999). The dark side of long-term relationships in marketing services. *Journal of Marketing Research*, 36(1), pp. 132–141.

Gronroos, C. (1980). Designing a long range marketing strategy for services. *Long Range Planning*, 13 (April), pp. 36–42.

Gronroos, C. (1990). 'Relationship approach to marketing in service contexts: the marketing and organisational behaviour interface'. In A. Payne, M. Christopher, M. Clark and H. Peck (Eds) *Relationship Marketing for Competitive Advantage*. Butterworth-Heinemann, Oxford.

Gummesson, E. (1979). *Models of Professional Service Marketing*. Marknadstekniskt Centrum, Stockholm.

Gundlach, G., Achrol, R. and Mentzer, J. (1995). The structure of commitment in exchange. *Journal of Marketing*, 59(1), pp. 72–92.

Gutierrez, S., Cillan, J. and Izquierdo, C. (2004). The consumer's relational commitment: main dimensions and antecedents. *Journal of Retailing and Customer Service*, 11, pp. 351–367.

Hakansson, H. (1982). *International Marketing and Purchasing of Industrial Goods: An Interaction Approach*. Wiley, Chichester.

Halinen, A. (1997). *Relationship Marketing in the Professional Sector*. Routledge, London.

Halinen, A. and Tahtinen, J. (2002). A process theory of relationship ending. *International Journal of Service Industry Management*, 13(2), pp. 163–180.

Harris, S. and Dibben, M. (1999). Trust and co-operation in business relationship development: exploring the influence of national values. *Journal of Marketing Management*, 15(6), pp. 463–483.

Haytko, D. (2004). Firm-to-firm and interpersonal relationships: perspectives from advertising agency account managers. *Journal of Academy of Marketing Science*, 32(3), pp. 312–328.

Heide, J. (1994). Interorganisational governance in marketing channels. *Journal of Marketing*, 58(1), pp. 71–85.

Heide, J. and John, G. (1988). The role of dependence balancing in safeguarding transaction-specific assets in conventional channels. *Journal of Marketing*, 52(1), pp. 20–36.

Heide, J.B., Wathne, K. and Rokkan, A. (2007). Interfirm monitoring, social contracts, and relationship outcomes. *Journal of Marketing Research*, 44(3), pp. 425–433.

Huemer, L. (2004). Activating trust: the redefinition of roles and relationships in an international construction project. *International Marketing Review*, 21(2), pp. 187–201.

Jehn, K.A. (1994). Enhancing effectiveness: an investigation of advantages and disadvantages of value-based intragroup conflict. *International Journal of Conflict Management*, 5(2), pp. 223–238.

Jehn, K.A. and Mannix, E.A. (2001). The dynamic nature of conflict: a longitudinal study of intragroup conflict and group performance. *Academy of Management Journal*, 44(2), pp. 238–251.

John, G. (1984). An empirical investigation of some antecedents of opportunism in a marketing channel. *Journal of Marketing Research*, 21(3), pp. 278–289.

Johnson, D. and Grayson, K. (2005). Cognitive and affective trust in service relationships. *Journal of Business Research*, 58(4), pp. 500–507.

Johnson, M. and Selnes, F. (2004). Customer portfolio management: toward a dynamic theory of exchange relationships. *Journal of Marketing*, 68(2), pp. 1–17.

Kohli, A.K. (1989). Effects of supervisory behaviour: the role of individual differences between salespeople. *Journal of Marketing*, 53 (October), pp. 40–50.

Kusari, S., Hoeffler, S. and Iacobucci, D. (2013). Trusting and monitoring business partners throughout the relationship life cycle. *Journal of Business-to-Business Marketing*, 20(3), pp. 119–138.

Lai, C.S., Liu, S.S., Yang, C.F., Lin, H.W. and Tsai, H.W. (2005). Governance mechanisms of opportunism: integrating from transaction cost analysis and relational exchange theory. *Taiwan Academy of Management Journal*, 5(1), pp. 1–24.

Leek, S., Naudé, R. and Turnbull, P. (2002). Managing business–to-business relationships: an emerging model. Proceedings of the 18th IMP Conference, Dijon, France.

Leonidou, L., Barnes, B. and Talias, M. (2006). Exporter-importer relationship quality: the inhibiting role of uncertainty, distance, and conflict. *Industrial Marketing Management*, 35(4), pp. 576–588.

Li, S., Madhok, A., Plaschka, G. and Verma, R. (2006). Supplier-switching inertia and competitive asymmetry: a demand-side perspective. *Decision Sciences*, 37(4), pp. 547–576.

Madhok, A. (1995). Revisiting multinational firms' tolerance for joint ventures: a trust-based approach. *Journal of International Business Studies*, 26(1), pp. 117–137.

Mavondo, F. and Rodrigo, E. (2001). The effect of relationship dimensions on interpersonal and interorganisational commitment in organisations conducting business between Australia and China. *Journal of Business Research*, 52(2), pp. 111–121.

McAllister, D. (1995). Affective-and cognition-based trust as foundations for interpersonal cooperation in organisations. *Academy of Management Journal*, 38(1), pp. 24–59.

Meyer, J. and Allen, N. (1991). A three-component conceptualisation of organisational commitment. *Human Resource Management Review*, 1(1), pp. 61–89.

Miyamoto, T. and Rexha, N. (2004). Determinants of three facets of customer trust a marketing model of Japanese buyer–supplier relationship. *Journal of Business Research*, 57(3), pp. 321–319.

Moorman, C., Zaltman, G. and Deshpande, R. (1992). Relationships between providers and users of market research: the dynamics of trust within and between organisations. *Journal of Marketing Research*, 29(3), pp. 314–328.

Morgan, R. (2000). 'Relationship marketing and marketing strategy'. In J. Sheth and A. Parvatiyar (Eds) *Handbook of Relationship Marketing*. Sage Publication, London.

Morgan, R. and Hunt, S. (1994). The commitment-trust theory of relationship marketing. *Journal of Marketing*, 58(3), pp. 20–38.

Nicholson, C., Compeau, L. and Sethi, R. (2001). The role of interpersonal liking in building trust in long-term channel relationships. *Academy of Marketing Science Journal*, 29(1), pp. 3–15.

Noordeweir, T.G., John, G. and Nevin, J.R. (1990). Performance outcomes of purchasing arrangements in industrial buyer–vendor relationships. *Journal of Marketing*, 54, pp. 80–93.

Noordhoff, C.S., Kyriakopoulos, K., Moorman, C., Pauwels, P. and Dellaert, B.G. (2011). The bright side and dark side of embedded ties in business-to-business innovation. *Journal of Marketing*, 75(5), pp. 34–52.

O'Malley, L. and Tynan, C. (1997). 'A reappraisal of the relationship marketing constructs of commitment and trust'. In *The AMA Relationship Marketing Conference*. Dublin, Ireland.

Ping, R. and Dwyer, F. (1992). 'A preliminary model of relationship termination in marketing channels'. In G. Frazier (Ed.) *Advances in Distribution Channel Research*, pp. 215–233.

Plank, R. and Newell, S.J. (2007). The effect of social conflict on relationship loyalty in business markets. *Industrial Marketing Management*, 36(1), pp. 59–67.

Poppo, L., Zhou, K. and Ryu, S. (2008). Alternative origins to interorganizational trust: an interdependence perspective on the shadow of the past and the shadow of the future. *Organization Science*, 19(1), pp. 39–55.

Pressey, A. and Mathews, B. (2003). Jumped, pushed or forgotten? Approaches to dissolution. *Journal of Marketing Management*, 19(1/2), pp. 131–155.

Provan, K. and Skinner, S. (1989). Interorganisational dependence and control as predictors of opportunism in dealer–supplier relations. *Academy of Management Journal*, 32(1), pp. 202–212.

Rao, S. and Perry, C. (2002). Thinking about relationship marketing: where are we now? *Journal of Business & Industrial Marketing*, 17(7), pp. 598–614.

Raven, B. and Kruglanski, A.W. (1970). 'Conflict and power'. In P. Swingle (Ed.) *The Structure of Conflict*, pp. 69–109. Academic Press, New York.

Rempel, J., Holmes, J. and Zanna, M. (1985). Trust in close relationships. *Journal of Personality and Social Psychology*, 49(1), pp. 95–112.

Ring, P. and Van de Ven, A. (1994). Development processes of cooperative interorganisational relationships. *Academy of Management Review*, 19(1), pp. 90–118.

Rodriguez, C. and Wilson, D. (1995). *Trust me!... but How?* Pennsylvania State University Park: Institute for the Study of Business Markets.

Rose, G.M. and Shoham, A. (2004). Interorganizational task and emotional conflict with international channels of distribution. *Journal of Business Research*, 57(8), pp. 942–950.

Rylander, D., Strutton, D. and Pelton, L. (1997). Toward a synthesized framework of relational commitment: implications for marketing channel theory and practice. *Journal of Marketing Theory and Practice*, 5(2), pp. 1–14.

Shankarmahesh, M., Ford, J. and LaTour, M. (2003). Cultural dimensions of switching behaviour in importer-exporter relationship. *Academy of Marketing Science Review*, 3, pp. 1–17.

Shaw, V., Shaw, C. and Enke, M. (2003). Conflicts between engineers and marketers: the experience of German engineers. *Industrial Marketing Management*, 32(6), pp. 489–499.

Sheth, J. and Parvatiyar, A. (1995). Relationship marketing in consumer markets: antecedents and consequences. *Journal of Academy of Marketing Science*, 23(4), pp. 255–271.

Stanton, W. (2002). The dimensions of stage theories. *Current Psychology*, 21(2), pp. 176–198.

Stern, L.W. and el-Ansary, A.I. (1977). *Marketing Channels*. Prentice-Hall, Inc, Englewood Cliffs, NJ.

Stumpf, S. and Hartman, K. (1984). Individual exploration to organisational commitment or withdrawal. *Academy of Management Journal*, 27(2), pp. 308–330.

Svensson, G. (2004). Vulnerability in business relationships: the gap between dependence and trust. *Journal of Business and Industrial Marketing*, 19(7), pp. 469–483.

Thomas, K.W. (1992). 'Conflict and negotiation processes in organizations'. In M.D. Dunnette and L.M. Hough (Eds) *Handbook of Industrial and Organizational Psychology*, pp. 651–717. Consulting Psychologists Press, Palo Alto, CA.

Tjosvold, D., Hui, C., Ding, D.Z. and Hu, J. (2003). Conflict values and team relationships: conflict's contribution to team effectiveness and citizenship in China. *Journal of Organizational Behavior*, 24(1), pp. 69–88.

Turnbull, P. and Valla, J. (1985). *Strategies for International Industrial Marketing*. Croom-Helm, London.

Van de Ven, A. (1976). On the nature, formation, and maintenance of relations among organisations. *Academy of Management Review*, 1(4), pp. 24–36.

Van de Ven, A. (1992). Suggestions for studying strategy process: a research note. *Strategic Management Journal*, Special Issue, 13 (Summer), pp. 169–188.

Vandenberg, R. and Lance, C. (1992). Examining the causal order of job satisfaction and organisational commitment. *Journal of Management*, 18(1), pp. 153–167.

Weitz, B. and Jap, S. (1995). Relationship marketing and distribution channels. *Journal of the Academy of Marketing Science*, 23(4), pp. 305–320.

Wicks, A., Shawn, B. and Thomas, J. (1999). The structure of optimal trust: moral and strategic implications. *Academy of Management Review*, 24(1), pp. 99–116.

Williams, J., Han, S. and Qualls, W. (1998). A conceptual model and study of cross-cultural business relationships. *Journal of Business Research*, 42(2), pp. 135–143.

Williamson, O.E. (1975) *Markets and Hierarchies, Analysis and Antitrust Implications: A Study in the Economics of Internal Organization*. The Free Press, New York.

Wilson, D. (1995). An integrated model of buyer-seller relationships. *Academy of Marketing Science Journal*, 23(4), pp. 335–346.

Wilson, D. and Mummalaneni, V. (1986). Bonding and commitment in buyer-seller relationships: a preliminary conceptualisation. *Industrial Marketing and Purchasing*, 1(3), pp. 44–58.

Wuyts, S. and Geyskens, I. (2005). The formation of buyer-supplier relationships: detailed contract drafting and close partner selection. *Journal of Marketing*, 69 (October), pp. 103–117.

Yandle, J. and Blythe, J. (2000). Intra-departmental conflict between sales and marketing: an exploratory study. *Journal of Selling and Major Account Management*, 2(3), pp. 3–31.

Yen, D.A., Barnes, B.R., and Wang, C. (2011). The measurement of Guanxi: introducing the GRX model. *Industrial Marketing Management*, 40(1), pp. 97–108.

York, D. (1990). 'Developing an interactive approach to the marketing of professional services'. In D. Ford (Ed.) *Understanding Business Marketing*, pp. 347–358. Academy Press, London.

Young, L. and Denize, S. (1995). A concept of commitment: alternative views of relational continuity in business service relationships. *Journal of Business & Industrial Marketing*, 10(5), pp. 22–37.

Zaheer, A., McEvily, B. and Perrone, V. (1998). Does trust matter? Exploring the effects on interorganisational and interpersonal trust on performance. *Organisation Science*, 9(2), pp. 141–159.

Zineldin, M. (2002). Developing and managing a romantic business relationship: life cycle and strategies. *Managerial Auditing Journal*, 17(9), pp. 546–558.

Further reading

Note: readers are recommended to look for the special issue in *Industrial Marketing Management* on 'the dark side of business relationships', which will be published 2016.

Other recommended reading includes:

Fang, S., Chang, Y. and Peng, Y. (2011). Dark side of relationships: a tensions-based view. *Industrial Marketing Management*, 40(5), pp. 774–784.

Finch, J., Zhang, S. and Geiger, S. (2013). Managing in conflict: how actors distribute conflict in an industrial network. *Industrial Marketing Management*, available since 16 August 2013.

Gu, F.F., Hung, K. and Tse, D.K. (2008). When does Guanxi matter? Issues of capitalization and its dark sides. *Journal of Marketing*, 72(4), pp. 12–28.

Massey, G. and Dawes, P. (2007). The antecedents and consequence of functional and dysfunctional conflict between marketing managers and sales managers. *Industrial Marketing Management*, 36(8), pp. 1118–1128.

Mele, C. (2011). Conflict and value co-creation in project networks. *Industrial Marketing Management*, 40(8), pp. 1377–1385.

Meunier-FitzHug, K., Massey, G. and Piercy, N. (2011). The impact of aligned rewards and senior manager attitudes on conflict and collaboration between sales and marketing. *Industrial Marketing Management*, 40(7), pp. 1161–1171.

Skarmeas, D. (2006). The role of functional conflict in international buyer-seller relationships: implications for industrial exporters. *Industrial Marketing Management*, 35(5), pp. 567–575.

Villena, V. and Revilla, E. and Choi, T. (2011). The dark side of buyer-supplier relationships: a social capital perspective. *Journal of Operations Management*, 29(6), pp. 561–576.

Zhou, N., Zhuang, G. and Yip, L. (2007). Perceptual difference of dependence and its impact on conflict in marketing channels in China: an empirical study with two-sided data. *Industrial Marketing Management*, 36(3), pp. 309–321.

9

THE DARK SIDE OF CRM: BRAND RELATIONSHIPS AND VIOLENT EXTREMIST ORGANISATIONS

Michael Breazeale, Erin G. Pleggenkuhle-Miles, Mackenzie Harms and Gina Scott Ligon

1 Introduction

This chapter's focus is a very specific dark side of consumer–brand relationships – the relationship between violent extremist organisations (VEOs) and their sympathisers and supporters. The authors conducted research exploring these organisations' use of accepted branding and customer relationship management (CRM) techniques that further their causes, engage potential followers and enhance their reputations among supporters. This situation is unique in that the organisations in question are not trying to minimise the aspects of their practices that most would consider to be dark sided, but instead choose to highlight those aspects as selling points.

VEOs are not typically the subject of business research, though many comparisons to traditional firms can easily be made. Similar to firms whose primary function is to maximise profit, VEOs profit from increased brand recognition through greater exposure to their target market, share in the benefits of co-branding with other highly visible VEO brands, and see their images enhanced when they release high-profile 'products' (i.e. terror and destruction). Just as more traditional businesses must organise and manage their relationships with their constituencies, VEOs must employ CRM strategies designed to maximise the relationships they have with their constituents. Through effective implementation of these strategies, VEOs shape their followers' decision-making processes, create strong brand advocates, ensure long-term continuation of the relationship and receive actionable feedback.

This chapter explores various brand-building and relationship-management techniques currently employed by VEOs – primarily via social media, where recent estimates suggest that nearly 90% of VEO Internet activity takes place (Weimann,

2012). Just like the traditional business organisations that populate most of the examples in this book, VEOs employ specialised techniques to manage relationships with their followers. Whereas most traditional organisations can openly advertise and promote messages designed to reach and impact their target audiences, VEOs must utilise strategies that allow them to communicate with their customers more surreptitiously. For that reason, social media platforms provide an excellent vehicle for VEO CRM. Comparisons to the same practices as applied by traditional business firms will emphasise the value to the traditional business organisation of efficient implementation. CRM techniques such as treating customers as partners, soliciting customer input, communicating proactively with customers and recognising the importance of service take on additional significance when the customer in question is potentially being asked to sacrifice more than financial resources and the product being promoted is terrorism. The customer of a VEO may actually be asked to give his/her own life to advance the cause; the product of the VEO is often destruction and terror; and the more attention that destruction receives, the more terror produced and the more profitable that product is for the VEO.

The authors find that even the most unlikely types of organisations employ CRM techniques and, when effectively implemented, these techniques produce desirable outcomes for the organisation. Whether the desired effect is a vocal cohort of brand advocates and a strong bottom line or a willing band of supporters prepared to conduct violent acts and increasing donations from like-minded sympathisers, impactful CRM is a common thread. So, the question becomes, if VEOs have adopted techniques utilised by successful businesses, can traditional businesses benefit from studying the implementation of those same techniques by dark side organisations? This chapter explores the various social media tactics employed by VEOs to build and maintain a strong brand image, as well as the CRM strategies that allow them to customise these communications, ensuring a strong customer–brand relationship with their constituents. The unique nature of these strategies allows the authors to recommend some novel techniques that can be employed by more traditional organisations.

Learning objectives

When you have read the chapter, you should be able to:

1. Understand how VEOs employ standard CRM strategies to craft a strong brand identity.
2. Identify how VEOs employ standard CRM practices to encourage their followers to deliver desired outcomes.
3. Critically discuss the similarities between traditional and dark side business strategies, and use this insight to produce guidance on how traditional businesses can utilise dark side approaches to produce noteworthy results.

2 Route map

This chapter explores the intersection of two broad areas of the overall marketing literature: strategy and consumer behaviour. The literature on CRM lies primarily within the strategy domain while tapping into the consumer behaviour literature for some grounding foundations. The literature on consumer–brand relationships lies primarily within the consumer behaviour domain while moving into the area of strategy to discuss applications. The work presented in this chapter represents the overlap of CRM and consumer–brand relationships, discussing the nuances of consumer behaviour and their impact on effective business strategies (see Figure 9.1). The grounding of this research within the domain of violent extremist organisations provides researchers with the ability to examine standard business practices through a unique lens. The perspective this provides allows business academics and practitioners alike to analyse these strategies in a more objective fashion and to better determine which CRM tactics are most effective in the ever-changing marketplace.

FIGURE 9.1 Route map

3 State of the art in consumer–brand relationships

The reality of consumer–brand relationships was first theorised and solidified as recently as 1998 (Fournier, 1998). Although business practitioners prior to this time had anecdotal support for the idea that their customers often developed close bonds with the brand, it was at this time that firms began to act upon their belief that one of the most powerful tools they possess is the relationship they have with their customers. Strong relationships encourage loyalty to the brand (Francisco-Maffessolli et al., 2014), contribute to predictable cash flows (Keller, 2012), allow the brand to profit from brand extensions (Kim et al., 2014), and ensure positive word-of-mouth (Wallace et al., 2014) and brand advocacy by vocal supporters (Lawer and Knox, 2006). A solid brand relationship can also protect a brand's image in the wake of crisis (Keller, 2012). Naturally, marketers have worked diligently to build strong relationships with their customers, while coming to the realisation that creating value in this manner is far from an easy task. Brand relationships evolve over time, and, while they can be encouraged and nurtured, they are also organic and complex in nature. Savvy marketers must carefully craft and tend to the relationships they maintain with their customers while striving to leverage the benefits that come with them. This task is made equally simpler and more difficult by the proliferation of social media – a conglomeration of communication tools that have fundamentally changed the way marketers interact with their customers and the role that customers play in determining brand meaning.

The vast majority of research on consumer–brand relationships tends to focus on the love-like relationships that consumers have with their favourite brands (Batra et al., 2012), but there is another end of the relationship spectrum that receives less scholarly attention. Only recently has there been attention paid to the dark side relationships that produce negative consequences for consumers and the brands themselves (Breazeale and Fournier, 2012). Most research on the dark side of consumer–brand relationships has focused on the brands that people avoid because of negative memory associations (White et al., 2012), or on harmful consumption practices (Breazeale and Fournier, 2012), but no research to date has explored relationships with brands that are as harmful to society, as is the case with VEO brands. VEOs represent an especially unique situation in the brand relationship domain because they represent consumption that is injurious, or even fatal, to many of their consumers, while also promoting a product (terror and destruction) that is equally harmful to those who do not intend to consume it (the public at large). Of course, a significant number of the VEOs' supporters do not view this consumption as injurious and rather as a means to achieving salvation, but the non-supporter members of the public who are impacted by that effort do not share this view.

Consumer–brand relationships and CRM

Until recently, consumer–brand relationship research has diverged from CRM research on one very important point. CRM research has tended to rely on an economics-informed view of the consumer, in which rational consumers attempt to maximise utility in all situations (Nguyen and Mutum, 2012). This view potentially reduces the importance of the consumer in the relationship and stresses the role of the consumer as information provider to the firm (Fournier and Avery, 2011). The implication inherent in the term *customer relationship management* is that customers and their attitudes towards the firm must be managed to ensure that they deliver value to the firm. This is not the case in healthy interpersonal relationships. Neither partner manages the relationship or the other partner. Both choose to be in the relationship because they *want* to be. To suggest that marketers can somehow impose relationships on their most appealing customers is 'akin to the notion of Neanderthal man clubbing and dragging home the Neanderthal woman who seems most likely to provide him with healthy children – it is outdated and impractical' (Breazeale, 2010, p. 54).

More contemporary CRM research has begun to focus on a dyadic relationship between the marketer and the customer, and has placed more emphasis on engaging customers in long-term partnerships based on satisfying the customers' needs (Payne et al., 2009). The marketer benefits from the interaction with the customer and is able to produce a more customised experience, motivating an enduring relationship. Indeed, CRM practised this way not only enhances the customer's perception of the firm, but also increases its profitability (Nguyen and Mutum, 2012). This more individualised approach to CRM necessitates the kind of bi-directional communication that the Internet makes possible. Websites, blogs and social media such as Twitter, Instagram, Facebook and YouTube allow marketers to have conversations with their customers and even to participate in their customers' daily lives in real time. Modern CRM strategies are driven by technology and are dependent upon these tools to create the customised experiences that customers now demand (Nguyen and Simkin, 2011). This technology is even more vital as a CRM apparatus for VEOs.

VEOs as a special case of CRM

VEOs may not look like typical business organisations, but comparisons can easily be made. First, VEOs profit from increased brand recognition through greater exposure to their target market, just as for instance Starbucks' brand recognition increased following its introduction of new channel distribution in supermarkets (see Tepper, 2013). Moreover, a VEO's image is enhanced when it is responsible for a high-profile product (Breazeale et al., 2015). Second, VEOs deliberately co-brand with other prominent VEO brands for the same purposes as traditional organisations. As is the case when Frito-Lay works with KC Masterpiece, or Cinnabon works with Pillsbury (McKee, 2009), legitimacy gains and reputational advantages to partnering are ways for VEOs to build donor support. Finally, just as more traditional businesses must organise and manage their relationships with their constituencies, VEOs must employ CRM strategies designed to maximise the benefits of the relationships they have with their followers. It is through the effective implementation of these strategies that VEOs are able to shape their followers' decision-making processes, create strong brand advocates, establish and develop long-term relationships and obtain actionable feedback.

VEOs utilise proven CRM techniques such as treating customers as partners (VEOs often place calls to action in their social media feeds, sometimes asking for volunteers to provide intelligence regarding intended targets or, in some cases, actively to carry out missions), soliciting customer input (VEOs not only scan social media chatter for relevant customer data but also post questions for their followers in attempts to gauge follower sentiment), and actively communicating with customers (VEOs use social media and well-coordinated networks of supporters both to disseminate and gather information that allows them to share their message and ensure that they are in step with their constituents). The convenience, affordability and broad reach of social media platforms like Twitter, YouTube and Facebook have captured the attention of all types of organisations, and most certainly that of terrorist groups.

VEOs and various media

The second half of the twentieth century witnessed the beginnings of a transformation in the way that humans connect. Increased media coverage of world events produced a global information society that, in many ways, removed national boundaries. As the century came to a close, even greater changes surfaced in the form of the Internet and the communication capabilities produced by that technology. While this transformation in the way people send and receive information has produced many benefits to mankind, it has also opened up new possibilities for those who wish to bring harm and fear to the masses, consistent with the proliferation of many other technical innovations. Indeed, those individuals and organisations that were previously threats to only contained points on the globe now have the ability to become transnational threats to the safety and well-being of all mankind. Prior to the use of social media, VEOs utilised trusted intermediaries and mass media, reluctant to be perceived as tangentially supporting VEO efforts (Grinyaev, 2003), to disseminate information. Today, they can communicate directly with their intended global audience and receive feedback in real time:

> [VEO Al-Shabaab] is using Twitter the way social media experts have always advised – not just broadcasting, but engaging in conversation. Spend some time following the account, and you will realise that you're dealing with a real human being with real ideas – albeit boastful, hypocritical, violent ideas.
>
> (Oremus, 2011)

Partially as a result of the reach made possible by social media, governments around the globe have had to increase their efforts to coordinate activities designed to contain VEOs. One of these efforts, designation by the US government as a foreign terrorist organisation (FTO), indicates that the United States deems these organisations a recognised threat to global security and directs penalties for those who would donate financial resources to the organisations. At time of writing there, were 59 recognised FTOs (www.state.gov), but a search of the World Wide Web indicates that there are more than 9,800 terrorist websites – a number that does not include the various social media accounts maintained by those organisations (Ryan, 2014). While not all of these websites are created or even sanctioned by the groups in question, sympathiser websites do increase the reach of these VEOs. The magnitude of these numbers suggests that VEOs have the tools necessary for 'manipulation of the mass consciousness' (Grinyaev, 2003, p. 86), only made possible by a global communication system. They are taking advantage of this resource.

Some VEOs, especially those with a global scope, rely on social media for the majority of their communications with the broader public. For instance, Al-Qaeda possesses a dominant web presence through the organisation's own public and private websites and social media accounts, as well as through those maintained by loyal supporters. Indeed, thousands of websites are dedicated to this VEO's movement (Jenkins, 2011). However, it is social media such as Twitter, YouTube and Instagram where these groups have their most immediate contact with followers. An Al-Qaeda support account boasts tens of thousands of followers on Twitter (twitter.com/alqaeda), the Taliban has nearly a quarter of that number following their Twitter activity (twitter.com/ABalkhi), and VEOs such as Al-Shabaab amass tens of thousands of followers using Twitter and YouTube to publicise their campaigns (http://bbc.news.com). All of this is made more impressive by the fact that government agencies are actively working to squelch these accounts and are often successful (Jenkins, 2011). When a VEO's social media accounts are shut down or locked due to the actions of governmental regulators, the VEOs are forced to reintroduce new accounts and quickly disseminate the information to their followers. Such coordinated VEO efforts would be daunting to any organisation, no matter its size and the amount of human and financial resources devoted to the social media re-branding. Yet the VEOs prioritise this process because of the benefits that an active social media presence provides. In 2011, Aaron Weisburd, director of the Society for Internet Research, told a Senate Homeland Security Subcommittee on Counterterrorism and Intelligence that social media lend an air of legitimacy to the content produced by VEOs, allowing them to brand their content. 'Branding in terrorist media is a sign of authenticity and terrorist media [are] readily identifiable as such due to the presence of trademarks known to be associated with particular organisations' (Weisburd, 2011).

How VEOs employ social CRM

Ease of accessibility, minimal cost and the virtual anonymity provided by the Internet, and specifically social media platforms, make it an ideal tool for VEOs seeking to brand themselves and manage relationships with their 'customers'. Aside from the missions that inspire VEOs in the first place, the most important goals for these organisations are to spread propaganda, radicalise and recruit new followers, and cultivate donors (Eres et al., 2011). Social media allow the organisations to be part of the mainstream, while reaching out to both existing and potential customers.

An effective brand is an important component of good CRM. As a branding mechanism, social media provide a perfect platform. Branding is – at its core – effective storytelling, and social media are very effective channels for real-time storytelling. Through Facebook and Twitter, VEOs tell their existing followers about their campaigns in real time as they are unfolding and are able to reframe negative press to accentuate their ideological message. Even before traditional media inform the general public about terrorist actions, interested followers of these organisations around the globe have first-hand details. For instance, when ISIS (Islamic State of Iraq and Syria) marched into the northern Iraqi city of Mosul in June 2014, their own Twitter accounts of the violence – accompanied by photos of destruction – preceded news of the occupation from the mass media (*The Telegraph*, 2014). Additionally, these particular social media have a humanising halo effect on the organisations that utilise them (Eres et al., 2011). Increasingly marketers are encouraging their customers to anthropomorphise their brands in an attempt to increase the connection that customers feel with the brand (Aggarwal and Wan, 2015). Through the customisation of messages made possible with social media, VEOs allow their followers the impression of direct interaction with the people at the heart of the organisation and feel a first-hand connection to the 'brand'. For the charismatic leaders at the helm of most VEOs, this is a very important tool for enhancing brand relationships.

Vocal brand advocates are one intended outcome of traditional branding efforts. When consumers believe strongly enough in the merits of a beloved brand, they often reach out to other consumers and encourage them to exhibit the kind of loyalty that they themselves feel. This is especially true for VEO brands. Because followers of these organisations are at times asked to make great sacrifices on behalf of the group, there is a need for intense loyalty and dedication, particularly when operatives are not located within geographic proximity to the organisation's central leadership. When VEO supporters share their strong beliefs on social media, backed up with stories that resonate with readers, potential followers are emboldened and impassioned to demonstrate their devotion as well. In this way the organisations are empowering their followers and involving them in the value-creation process, a prime example of effective CRM.

Of course, the social media accounts of the VEOs also serve to activate and even train lone individuals who previously had no ties to such organisations. VEOs craft special appeals designed to resonate with impressionable young people who make up the largest group of social media users (Eres et al., 2011). By offering a sense of community to disenfranchised young people, these organisations extend their reach and contribute to a sort of 'lone-wolf' terrorism (Ryan, 2014). Recruits do not feel that they are alone when they connect with other VEO followers via social media, and become part of a virtual pack instead. Some of these lone actors have carried out sophisticated acts of terrorism such as hacking into mainstream media accounts and disseminating misinformation or providing the home addresses of VEO targets, becoming 'keyboard warriors' for the cause without ever leaving their homes (Olding, 2014). For instance, ISIS often uses the social media accounts of active followers – dubbed the 'new disseminators' (Townsend and Helm, 2014) – to recruit people willing to carry out further brutal acts on their behalf, with the belief that once someone has committed a violent act in the name of the cause they will be even more committed than before to further sacrifice (Hamilton, 2014).

An example of the lengths to which VEOs will go to further their cause occurred during the 2014 World Cup, one of the most conspicuous sporting events in recent history. In an act of promotional brilliance, ISIS employed the trending hashtag #WorldCup2014 to reach potentially millions of football (soccer) fans worldwide and flood the Internet with information about their cause (Siegel, 2014). The same group has used the hashtag #AMessageFromISIStoUS to directly threaten US citizens with airstrikes in an attempt to spread fear and foster distrust in the US government, by planting the seed in citizens' minds that the VEO can reach them without intervention by the government that is supposed to protect them.

Besides human capital, financial support is equally vital to VEOs. These organisations – just like traditional businesses – need money to be able to maintain their operations. Luckily for VEOs, social media are also an excellent tool for fundraising. While Al-Qaeda cannot realistically initiate a Kickstarter campaign, some of their efforts are equally successful and surprisingly transparent. For instance, in many cases, social media are used to solicit funds for specific causes, while including instructions for wiring those funds to specific banks and even providing account numbers (Rubenfeld, 2014). VEOs actively advertise their needs while soliciting donations and communicating not only with donors but also with the radical recipients of their fundraising efforts. Because the followers of these organisations are so committed to the cause, they willingly provide financing for daily operations of the groups and for the more dramatic terrorist acts as well (Rubenfeld, 2014).

Another less obvious consumer of VEO products is traditional mass media. In a symbiotic relationship with the VEOs, news media rarely support the ideals of these groups, yet the media thrive on coverage of a VEO's exploits. The public anxiously consumes reports of these events, and the purpose of the terrorist organisations – the dissemination of terror – is accomplished. The more afraid the public is, the more they feel the need to watch media reports, and the more the media feel they need to offer such coverage. In this way, the relationship between VEOs and the public represents a network of power in which each party is constantly observing the other (Schmelser, 1993). By courting the media and providing provocative news to report, the VEOs ensure that their message is spread to an ever-wider audience. Even though mass media are increasingly reluctant to be complicit in this way in the acts of terrorist groups (Grinyaev, 2003), the ubiquitous nature of social media guarantees that anxious citizens are easily able to locate and consume the more lurid details of the events that are covered only cursorily by the mainstream media.

As in any worthwhile CRM campaign, VEOs also utilise social media to gather intelligence not only on their targets but also on their own consumers. Through observing and engaging in conversations with their supporters, VEOs gain a better understanding of the causes that are important to their followers, and gauge response to their current and proposed campaigns. Using blogs, online forums and hashtags, VEOs participate in direct exchanges with interested consumers, giving the impression of being customer oriented and highly interactive, in an age when individualised service is highly valued (Nguyen and Mutum, 2012). Increased collaboration allows the organisations to develop even stronger bonds with their followers, while gathering the information necessary to coordinate their promotional efforts with the service they provide. This dyadic learning relationship is key to any successful CRM campaign (Payne and Frow, 2006; Lusch et al., 2010; Galitsky and De la Rosa, 2011).

Of course, the Internet has also provided VEOs with another excellent tool for intelligence by way of free satellite surveillance. Google Earth has been used by VEOs to carry out campaigns successfully, such as the 2008 attack on Mumbai by VEO Laskar-e-Tayyiba, in which more than 150 people were killed (Ryan, 2014). The increasing sophistication of tools such as this one provides VEOs with time-sensitive information that would have been much more difficult to attain prior to the digital age.

Challenges faced by VEOs and implications for any organisation

While the Internet and social media have certainly enhanced the ability of VEOs to maintain and manage relationships successfully with their supporters, mass media and the general public, these organisations still face very real challenges to the way they conduct business. Understanding these challenges and the way that VEOs attend to them provides some interesting insights for any non-VEO organisation that finds itself operating under adverse circumstances.

The very existence of most VEOs is deemed a threat to global security by law enforcement agencies around the world. For this reason, the global community has devoted massive resources, both financial and human, to efforts to eradicate the threat. The United States alone spends over US$16 billion each year on counter-terrorism activities (DeSilver, 2013). Few traditional organisations face this kind of threat to their continuance, yet VEOs manage to thrive in spite of these well-funded efforts to silence their operations. How do they do it?

VEOs understand that a highly motivated customer base, which feels connected to the parent organisation and valued as a supporter, can be a daunting ally even during difficult economic times. By efficiently managing their social media to respond to detractors quickly and to converse with fans regularly, VEOs maintain a two-way dialogue that ensures loyalty even in the face of adversity. The knowledge they glean from their followers – directly and via observation – allows them to stay one step ahead of those who would terminate their operations. These same loyal followers actively evangelise on behalf of the organisations to recruit other sympathisers and ensure a broad foundation upon which VEOs can draw support, both financially and in human capital.

Even the social media accounts of VEOs are threatened on a daily basis. Increasing support exists for the discontinuance of social media accounts of known VEOs. Government agencies and the private sector have made requests to the various social media platforms to shut down accounts of these groups as soon as they are located (Jenkins, 2011). Yet many involved in the fight against terrorism feel that these efforts will prove fruitless. Because the VEOs move quickly to replace any account that is shut down or that they feel has become too closely monitored by counterintelligence agencies, law enforcement ends up playing a game of 'virtual Whack-a-Mole' (Jenkins, 2011), jumping at accounts just as they are closed and missing their replacements as they are opened. This type of well-coordinated social media planning would be coveted by any traditional organisation trying to stay one step ahead of consumer trends and competitor brands that most assuredly monitor each other's social media accounts.

One tool used by many VEOs to aid in these efforts is the darknet, a term used generally to describe all non-commercial sites on the Internet but more specifically to denote 'underground' Internet networks that allow for completely anonymous posting with no tracking of IP addresses. Despite government tracking efforts, VEOs utilise the darknet for communication with key associates, who then disseminate information to their own social media networks. While use of the darknet might not be appropriate for traditional organisations, the idea of maintaining networks of highly motivated brand supporters and equipping them with appropriate tools to communicate messages to their personal networks is quite feasible.

VEOs are able to move so deftly because of the close relationships they have with their consumers. By expertly utilising networks of opinion leaders, VEOs can stealthily monitor the actions of competitors and detractors and can nimbly craft campaigns that utilise rapidly changing social media accounts. As these groups close one account and activate another, their followers have no difficulty locating the new online presence of the brand because of the well-coordinated communication network developed with their supporters. By maintaining a close connection with their network and by using their multiple social media accounts to reinforce each other, they are able to navigate skilfully the most difficult of business environments. Unity of message is made possible by effectively communicating consistent organisational missions and goals to key stakeholders on a constant basis, leading to a strong brand image among followers. VEO supporters never have to wonder what the organisation stands for, because every touchpoint they have with the organisation consistently reinforces the same core ideas.

Another important challenge faced by VEOs is a highly fractured customer base. The contrary nature of these organisations necessitates a far-flung reach for supporters and recruits. Other than near the headquarters of these movements, supporters are not likely to represent a highly visible and concentrated target market geographically. VEOs must cast a wide net to find the kind of customers who are willing to align themselves with groups most would deem radical extremists. They do this successfully by creating vocal brand advocates and by providing them with ample tools to disseminate their message.

Most VEO campaigns involve highly visible and provocative acts. Bombings and hostage taking all represent opportunities to grab mass media attention, as well as the imaginations of supporters and the general public. These kinds of activities, while horrific, are all consistent with the stated missions of the organisations conducting them. In this way, they are practising highly efficient branding. By conducting campaigns that are true both to their reasons for existence and to the belief systems of their followers, they ensure that each violent act sustains their current followers' desire for authenticity and intrigues those who might be moved by such shows of extreme fidelity to a cause.

Perhaps the most daunting challenge faced by VEOs lies in the fact that, other than their supporters, the public at large is highly opposed to and appalled by their actions. As their primary product is fear, they guarantee that non-sympathisers are at a minimum critical of their cause and, at the extreme, advocates for their extermination.

Other than some so-called vice products – such as drugs, tobacco, alcohol and pornography – few brands face this kind of opposition from the majority of consumers. Many brands, however, find themselves in the middle of crises that threaten their reputations and profitability. For instance, BP faced a major public relations crisis in 2010 when an accident on one of its oilrigs, the Deepwater Horizon, claimed the lives of 11 employees and poured millions of gallons of raw crude oil into the Gulf of Mexico. On a different front, automaker Toyota faced public ridicule and potential government action when it issued a massive recall of its cars in 2009–10. The move saw the company's image fall from 83% positive among American consumers to as low as 30%, before beginning a gradual and expensive return to pre-recall numbers (Kelly, 2012).

VEOs face this challenge by confronting their detractors head on. They actively campaign against the very way of life of the people who disagree with them. In so doing, they bolster their own causes and promote an outsider status that only makes them more appealing to the disenfranchised followers who support them.

Tactics such as these would not work for most brands in crisis, but that does not mean there is no lesson to be learned here. When VEOs are faced with opposition, they hold true to their belief systems and mission statements. They represent a united front and encourage their supporters to campaign actively for their causes by publicly accepting responsibility for the actions in question. This demonstrates to their customers that they are in sync with their wishes, and assures detractors that the VEO is indeed a force to be reckoned with. Social media again allow the VEO to reach a broad audience with a message of accountability.

What should marketers take away from this discussion?

We stated at the beginning of this chapter that VEOs possess a great number of similarities with traditional organisations, despite the highly significant differences in their missions. We have provided examples of the highly efficient and effective strategies that VEOs employ in order to thrive in a marketplace that is, for the most part, opposed to their very existence. If these organisations can overcome obstacles that include major threats from competitors (law enforcement or other VEOs competing for the hearts, minds and funds of the same customer base), a distinctly fractured customer base and decidedly negative public opinion, then they must be doing something noteworthy. We believe that the branding and CRM tactics that they employ are in no small way responsible for their success in a hostile marketplace.

By skilfully telling a story that is consistent with their missions, these groups provide an authentic brand around which their customers can gather. VEOs adeptly empower brand advocates to tell their story for them by providing ample resources via social media. These groups also actively recruit and educate new followers by way of a regularly updated online presence that has many channels to accommodate the varying media preferences of their intended audience. Even in the face of governments that would reallocate donations made to them, VEOs provide easy access to supporters who wish to give them money via highly transparent online portals for conducting business. Funds are often provided via charities established by either the VEO or sympathisers, and also via legitimate businesses owned by the VEOs. These organisations also understand the importance of utilising mass media to help publicise their cause and nurture that relationship by providing noteworthy content that will resonate with their target audience. VEOs also regularly monitor social media to gather intelligence on their customers and their competitors, a tactic that allows them to manoeuvre adroitly a highly volatile marketplace.

VEOs represent a side of humanity that many people find particularly unattractive, but they also typify highly efficient marketers who understand the value of strong consumer–brand relationships and the necessity of an effective CRM system to ensure those relationships. See Table 9.1 for key takeaways from this section.

Conclusion

Most business leaders would not look to VEOs as a source of inspiration on any front. When one steps back, though, and examines the activities of these organisations through a purely analytical lens, it becomes apparent that there are indeed parallels that can inform the CRM efforts of any organisation. The challenges faced by VEOs are intensified versions of those obstacles that most businesses face on an ongoing basis – difficulty in locating and accessing customers, vocal detractors determined to see the organisation fail, active competition vying for the same resources and customers, an ever-changing business environment, and often a geographically fragmented customer base and administrative team. By observing the ways that VEOs overcome these obstacles, other organisations can modify the techniques that are effective in the most adverse conditions to inform their own CRM practices, thus creating a stronger bond with customers and impacting the stability of the organisation.

TABLE 9.1 How traditional organisations can enact VEO strategies

Organisational imperative	Method
Authenticity	Unity of message that is consistent with organisational goals and missions is vital to the creation of a strong brand image that resonates with customers. All communications from the organisation, whether they are from the leader or distributed through other customers, need to reinforce the overall identity of the brand
Brand advocates	Authenticity as described above is made possible through the recruitment and empowerment of strong brand advocates. These customers who believe so strongly in the brand that they are willing to evangelise to other customers in their own social networks are a valuable asset and worth the time and effort required to empower them
Recruit and educate	The organisation itself and its brand advocates are in an excellent position to identify those customers who are willing to help spread the message about the brand. Smart organisations equip these vocal customers with the tools they need to communicate effectively. Premiums, pre-announcements and special best-customer events allow the organisation to court a team of advocates who are then well informed themselves
Easy access for supporters	Just as VEOs make it easy for their financial supporters to fund projects, so too must traditional organisations. Multiple channels for obtaining the organisation's products, easily accessible portals for product purchase and return, and informed, energetic customer support representatives make it easier to do business with the organisation
Assistance from mass media	The mass media can be an excellent partner in telling a brand's story when given access to content that is actually newsworthy. Like VEOs, smart organisations court the media to help tell their stories. When an organisation goes out of its way to help its customers or society at large, this is news only if it is done in a way that is highly consistent with the organisation's goals and enacted in a big way. Even small things can be done in a big way, thus increasing their noteworthiness
Use of social media to create dialogues	Social media, when used appropriately, allows an organisation to listen to its customers, detractors and competition in a way that was not possible before their proliferation. Smart organisations use the intelligence they gather to inform policy, procedures and other decisions. Organisations cannot stop at listening, though. It is vital that they participate in dyadic conversations not just with their advocates but also with their detractors. Even though some detractors will not be swayed by the 'personal touch' of social media, the open nature of the discussion allows others to see the brand representing itself well

4 New research directions

Moving forwards, the identification of both successful and *unsuccessful* engagement strategies embodied in the bi-directional communication that is taking place on social media platforms will strengthen our understanding and inform the development of effective CRM strategies. The successful utilisation of social media by VEOs has captured the attention of various governments and agencies, as well as researchers and media around the world (Grinyaev, 2003), and led to funding for research grants to study social media as a new arena in the 'war on terror' (Ryan, 2014). The result is a novel platform on which to inform, extend and apply our theories.

One way forwards is for experts in CRM to provide insight on this phenomenon by interjecting their own voices and evaluations of such trends. Another is for us to continue to study objectively the successful CRM strategies employed by VEOs and further apply them to traditional organisations. Below we discuss Al-Shabaab's sophisticated social media strategy and its execution, and note how it fundamentally changed the way Al-Shabaab manages its 'customers'. What is not discussed is whether this move has also resulted in a loss of customers. How do firms balance new CRM techniques with traditional techniques? Further, do organisations necessarily make trade-offs in pursuing new strategies?

Another key area of research needed in the CRM arena is the study of CRM competitive dynamics. How do organisations respond to new/novel CRM strategies of a close competitor? In what ways are CRM strategies imitated, and at what point will the social media currently being utilised transition to a new communication format? Because of the nuances with which social media platforms allow organisations to interact with consumers, managing customer relationships may prove simultaneously easier and more challenging. While it may be easier than ever to reach and engage consumers, these platforms are accessible to all, suggesting that the only winners will be those who are able to stay current with emerging social media platforms. For example, the group ISIS jumps from social networking site to site, ranging from www.diaspora.com, Instagram, Twitter to askfm.com. This 'early adopter' strategy allows them to remain synchronised with the way their users consume, further adding to their firm relationships and brand identity.

Like traditional organisational leaders, VEO leaders tend to have a magnetic appeal to their followers, and this effect seems to be magnified on social media platforms. Because of the ease of accessibility and personal connection, current VEO leaders tend to release important messages to followers on social networking sites so that they can reach brand community members quickly. Little research has been conducted, however, on the immediate first-order impacts of these messages as transmitted though Internet communication technology. Future research could examine whether the messages from charismatic violent leaders are received similarly in traditional media channels versus social media applications.

Similar to the way we explored the use of accepted CRM strategies here, applying accepted branding models to continue our exploration of the dark side of customer relationships would likely prove beneficial. VEOs have leveraged social media to double their brand communities, raise millions of dollars and communicate strategically to geographically distal operatives (Eres et al., 2011). While the target audience is markedly different, it seems that more conventional organisations could learn from the application of CRM by VEOs in the social media space.

Lessons gleaned from VEO usage suggest three enduring operating principles. First, VEOs seem to use a variety of messengers to distribute their brand messages to consumers. For example, during the Westgate Mall attack in Kenya in 2013, Al-Shabaab had Twitter feeds from a variety of sympathisers all using the same hash-tag. This approach adds to the diversity of customers reached by the group, as well as contributing to the overall notion of firm reputation. Second, VEOs seem to be agnostic with respect to type of platform used. As government and private organisations regularly shut down the accounts due to security concerns, VEO sympathisers will often adopt new platforms to spread their message. This approach to cutting the 'sunk costs' of losing current followers shows an adept, pragmatic and nimble approach to CRM that is not seen in conventional organisations, which tend to rely upon the same platforms across time and customers. Third, VEOs are quite active on social media, yet they do not share scheduled updates or weekly newsletters. Instead, they tend to use social media as a tool for daily communication at random intervals. For example, ISIS tweets current pictures from the battlefield on a daily basis – and sometimes multiple times a day. This constant, variable and seemingly organic communication may work to increase the connection between the brand community and the organisation in a way that conventional organisations may not have realised.

Utilising VEOs as the basis for the study of CRM techniques that are grounded in strong consumer–brand relationships allows those interested in the creation of strong CRM strategies to assess objectively the effectiveness and efficiency of various tactics. In a dynamic marketplace, the insights garnered from such analysis can lead to distinctive competencies that will benefit traditional business organisations via more impactful customer interactions and more profitable intelligence gathering.

5 Practising marketing – a case study

Al-Shabaab, a militant organisation aiming to establish an Islamic Emirate in Somalia, is perhaps the most widely recognised global jihadist group that has gained notoriety for using social media to communicate with the public and promote its ideology. Most notably, Al-Shabaab gained media attention during its attack on Nairobi's Westgate Mall in September 2013, for its utilisation of Twitter to disseminate information over the course of the three-day hostage scenario.

At around noon on 21 September 2013, Al-Shabaab militants entered the Westgate Mall in Nairobi, shooting at civilians and throwing grenades. Despite attempts by the Kenyan Security Forces to re-establish control over the shopping centre, Al-Shabaab's attack on Westgate lasted over 72 hours and resulted in 67 deaths.

Prior to the Westgate attack, Al-Shabaab had faced blatant criticism, both within the jihadist community and the general public, due to increasing attack failures, military and political setbacks and conflict among the top leadership (Ansalone, 2013), and was considered by many to be losing its status as one of the greatest threats to Western interests among global jihadists. Despite its recent FTO designation and official acknowledgement as an affiliate of Al-Qaeda, many felt that Al-Shabaab's peak influence was in the past.

The Westgate attack re-established Al-Shabaab as a top threat among global jihadists. Its success was a product of both establishing control over the hostages within the shopping centre, and maintaining a hold over the media and public through its ongoing Twitter narrative. The media strategy employed by Al-Shabaab during the Westgate attack was considered a novel and revolutionary way to exploit the public and media during crisis scenarios. It not only increased coverage of the event, but also projected a specific ideological message as the attack unfolded in real time.

> The Mujahideen entered #Westgate Mall today at around noon and are still inside the mall, fighting the #Kenyan Kuffar (infidels) inside their own turf.
>
> (Alexander, 2013)

Tweets came from @HSM_PressOffice, another Twitter account opened by the jihadists just a couple hours after the @HSM_Press – Shabaab account was shut down by Twitter:

> #Westgate: a 14-hour standoff relayed in 1400 rounds of bullets and 140 characters of vengeance and still ongoing. Good morning Kenya!
>
> It's slowly approaching the 24-hour mark – the darkest 24 hours in Nairobi – highlighting the sheer fragility of the Kenyan nation.
>
> The Mujahideen are still firmly in control of the situation inside Westgate Mall. Negotiation is out of the question!
>
> We'll not negotiate with the Kenyan govt as long as its forces are invading our country, so reap the bitter fruits of your harvest #Westgate
>
> More than 30 hours have now passed and, like rabbits caught in the headlights, Kenyans are still shell-shocked. #Westgate

Throughout the attack, Al-Shabaab used Twitter in three impactful ways (Ansalone, 2013). First, it promoted a counter-narrative to that of the Kenyan media, describing its Westgate attack as a response to the suffering inside Somalia. Second, Al-Shabaab used Twitter to issue warnings and demands to the Kenyan Security Forces, threatening escalating violence if Kenyan forces were not called out of Somalia. Third, Al-Shabaab utilised tweets to disseminate statements promoting its stability during the attack and undermining the attempts by the Kenyan Security Forces to reduce anxiety among the public. As a result or by-product of this utilisation of Twitter, Al-Shabaab attracted additional media attention, which further enabled it to spread propaganda during the attack, promoting its ideology and recruiting operatives. This tactic also allowed the organisation to ensure that its views were as widely reported to the public as those of mainstream media organisations.

In addition to the content of its tweets, Al-Shabaab is notable in that it was one of the first jihadist groups to appeal to a Western audience through its Twitter campaign. This was done by issuing statements in English, using sophisticated vocabulary and advanced rhetoric (Pantucci and Sayyid, 2013). Simultaneously, Al-Shabaab released audio and written statements to news agencies, both reinforcing the message promoted in its Twitter account, and providing information in its micro-blogs about subsequent accounts once their primary handle faced suspension by Twitter. CBS offered the headline 'Al-Shabaab Showed Gruesome Social Media Savvy During Attack', and J.M. Berger, a US-based terrorism analyst, stated, 'The person who runs their Twitter account has obviously invested a lot of energy in the process of grabbing headlines, and for Shabaab, the account allows them to amplify the message that they wish to send with the attack itself' (CBS/AP, 2013).

In the aftermath of the attack, the leader of Al-Shabaab, Godane, released an official statement about the attack, reinforcing the narrative told through tweets. In conjunction with this statement, Al-Shabaab released English translations both in text and audio formats of the statement, rather than trusting the media to translate the statement and publish the story. In the English version of the statement, a British-accented operative spoke the message from Godane. This tactic, which has been used more recently by ISIS militants in Iraq, establishes camaraderie and familiarity with Westerners and reduces alienation due to perceived cultural boundaries (Ansalone, 2013).

Following the Westgate attack, social media became a primary format through which jihadists communicate with the public and disseminate propaganda (Atsori, 2014). Al-Shabaab's sophisticated use of Twitter to micro-blog its attack was highly novel and effective. Since 2013, other groups have also gained attention for their use of social media (Atsori, 2014). In addition to the widespread implications of this strategy, Al-Shabaab also re-established its global status following previous public humiliation.[1]

Discussion questions

1. Al-Shabaab utilised social media as the primary mode of communication with their 'customers' during this event. How practical is this reliance on a single mode of communication for traditional organisations? How could a traditional organisation use this method effectively during a brand crisis?

2. In this chapter, we have established the importance of two-way communication, yet Al-Shabaab attempted to control the conversation completely during the mall attack by tweeting to all stakeholders, including law enforcement and the media. How can traditional organisations ensure that they effectively manage the message while still listening to their stakeholders?

3. How could law enforcement have used social media in a similar manner to re-frame the message or even to discredit Al-Shabaab with its followers? Are there implications for traditional organisations as they compete for market dominance?

4. Audio press releases from Al-Shabaab utilised an operative with a British accent in order to establish camaraderie and familiarity with Westerners. How important is it for the tone and 'voice' of social media to emulate that of the intended customer? How can traditional organisations ensure that their social media have the same impact on customers?

6 Further investigation

Questions

1. Why does the idea of brand relationships matter in terms of CRM? Is it necessary to maintain relationships with customers in order to practise effective CRM?

2. How does the information that VEOs gather using social media inform their practices? In what ways might law enforcement authorities utilise social media to undermine some of the benefits of that information? Would it be unethical for traditional organisations to use the same kinds of methods to undermine competitors? At what point would it become unethical?

3. In what ways do the social media efforts of the VEOs discussed in this chapter impact on the relationships that their customers (potential recruits, active supporters, donors, the media, etc.) have with the organisations?

4. Some VEOs actually operate legal business entities to provide financial support for their operations. How would it affect the customers of these businesses if they knew that their support of these businesses was actually funding VEOs? What parallels do you see between this situation and when traditional businesses face vocal resistance to some of their charitable contributions?

5. What other types of organisations might face the same challenges that VEOs face in terms of CRM? How do these other organisations overcome those challenges?

Projects

1. Students should divide into two teams and debate the merits of social media utilised as a CRM tool. Use examples from the VEOs discussed to justify and to argue against the use of social media in this way.

2. Choose a legal business organisation and prepare a recommendation for ways in which this business can utilise VEO-style social CRM to benefit from their customer relationships.

Note

1 For additional reading on the attack and Al-Shabaab's media strategy, see Ansalone, 2013.

References

Aggarwal, P. and Wan, J. (2015). 'Befriending Mr. Clean: the role of anthropomorphism in consumer brand relationships'. In S. Fournier, M. Breazeale and J. Avery (Eds) *Strong Brands, Strong Relationships*. Routledge, London.

Alexander, H. (2013). Tweeting terrorism: how Al-Shabaab live blogged the Nairobi attacks. *The Telegraph*, 22 September. www.telegraph.co.uk/news/worldnews/africaandin dianocean/kenya/10326863/Tweeting-terrorism-How-al-Shabaab-live-blogged-the-Nair obi-attacks.html (accessed 9 September 2014).

Ansalone, C. (2013). Al-Shabaab's tactical and media strategies in the wake of its battlefield setbacks. *CTC Sentinel*, 6(3), pp. 12–16.

Atsori, D. (2014). The birth of a jihadist caliphate. *Review of Environment, Energy, and Economics (Re3)*, dx.doi.org/10.7711/feemre3.2014.07.004.

Batra, R., Ahuvia, A., Bagossi, R.P. (2012). Brand love. *Journal of Marketing*, 76(2), pp. 1–16.

BBC (2014). Boko Haram: Nigerian Islamist leader defends attacks. www.bbc.co.uk/news/ world-africa-16510929 (accessed 4 September 2014).

Breazeale, M. (2010). 'I love that store! Toward a theory of customer chemistry'. In *Three Essays on Customer Chemistry*. Dissertation, Mississippi State University, pp. 53–106.

Breazeale, M. and Fournier, S. (2012). 'Where do we go from here?' In S. Fournier, M. Breazeale and M. Fetscherin (Eds) *Consumer-Brand Relationships: Theory and Practice*, pp. 395–414. Routledge, London.

Breazeale, M., Pleggenkuhle-Miles, E., Ligon, G.S. and Harms, M. (2015). 'Branding terror: building notoriety in violent extremist organisations'. In S. Fournier, M. Breazeale and J. Avery (Eds) *Strong Brands, Strong Relationships*. Routledge, London.

CBS/AP (2013). Al-Shabaab showed gruesome social media savvy during attack. 24 September. www.cbsnews.com/news/al-Shabaab-showed-gruesome-social-media-savvy-during-attack/ (accessed 9 September 2014).

DeSilver, D. (2013). U.S. spends over $16 billion annually on counter-terrorism. Pew Research Center, 11 September. www.pewresearch.org/fact-tank/2013/09/11/u-s-sp ends-over-16-billion-annually-on-counter-terrorism/ (accessed 4 September 2014).

Eres, E., Weimann, G. and Weisburd, A. (2011). Jihad, crime, and the Internet: content analysis of jihad forum discussions. United States Department of Justice. 31 October. www.ncjrs.gove/pdffiles1/nij/grants/236867.pdf (accessed 17 September 2014).

Fournier, S. (1998). Consumers and their brands: developing relationship theory in consumer research. *Journal of Consumer Research*, 24(4), pp. 343–373.

Fournier, S. and Avery, J. (2011). Putting the relationship back in CRM. *Sloan Management Review*. April, pp. 63–72.

Francisco-Maffessolli, E.C., Semprebon, E. and Muller Prado, P.H. (2014). Construing loyalty through brand experience: the mediating role of brand relationship quality. *Journal of Brand Management*, 21(5), pp. 446–458.

Friedman, U. (2011). U.S. officials may take action again Al-Shabaab's Twitter account. blog.foreignpolicy.com/posts/2011/12/20/us_officials_may_take_action_again_al_Shabaa bs_twitter_account (accessed 4 September 2014).

Galitsky, B. and De la Rosa, J.L. (2011). Concept based learning of human behaviour for customer relationship management. *Information Sciences*, 181(10), pp. 2016–2035.

Grinyaev, S. (2003). Mass media and terrorism: a Russian view. *European Security*, 12(2), pp. 85–88.

Hamilton, G. (2014). ISIS uses gruesome social media posts to recruit more 'blood-thirsty' jihadis and instill terror in enemies. *National Post*, 11 August. http://news.nationalpost.com/2014/08/11/isis-using-gruesome-social-me…re-blood-thirsty-jihadis-and-instill-terror-in-enemies/?__federated=1 (accessed 14 August 2014).

Jenkins, B. (2011). 'Is al Qaeda's Internet strategy working?' http://homeland.house.gov/hearing/subcommitteehearing-jihadist-use-social-media-how-prevent-terrorism-and-preserve-innovation (accessed 4 September 2014).

Keller, K.L. (2012). *Strategic Brand Management: Building, Measuring, and Managing Brand Equity*. 4th edition. Prentice Hall, Upper Saddle River, NJ.

Kelly, A.M. (2012). Has Toyota's image recovered from the brand's recall crisis? *Forbes*, 5 March. www.forbes.com/sites/annemariekelly/2012/03/05/has-toyotas-image-recovered-from-the-brands-recall-crisis/ (accessed 12 December 2014).

Kim, K., Park, J. and Kim, J. (2014). Consumer-brand relationship quality: when and how it helps brand extensions. *Journal of Business Research*, 67(4), pp. 591–597.

Lawer, C. and Knox, S. (2006). Customer advocacy and brand development. *Journal of Product & Brand Management*, 15(2/3), pp. 121–129.

Lusch, R.F., Vargo, S.L. and Tanniru, M. (2010). Service value networks and learning. *Journal of the Academy of Marketing Science*, 38(1), pp. 19–31.

McKee, S. (2009). The pros and cons of co-branding. *Bloomberg BusinessWeek*. 10 July. www.businessweek.com/smallbis/content/jul2009/sb20090710_255169.htm (accessed 9 September 2014).

Nguyen, B. and Mutum, D.S. (2012). A review of customer relationship management: successes, pitfalls, and futures. *Business Process Management Journal*, 18(3), pp. 400–419.

Nguyen, B. and Simkin, L. (2011). *Effects of Firm Customisation on the Severity of Unfairness Perceptions and (Mis)behaviour: The Moderating Role of Trust*. Paper presented at the Academy of Marketing Conference 2011, Liverpool, UK.

Olding, R. (2014). Home terror threat greatest from Sharrouf's fan base: experts. *Sydney Morning Herald*. 14 August. www.smh.com.au/federal-politics/political-news/home-terror-threat-greatest-from-sharroufs-fan-base-experts-20140813-103nij.html (accessed 18 August 2014).

Oremus, W. (2011). Twitter of terror. *Slate Magazine*. 23 December. www.slate.com/articles/technology/technocracy/2011/12/al_shabaab_twitter_a_somali_militant_group_unveils_a_new_social_media_strategy_for_terrorists_.html (accessed 4 September 2014).

Pantucci, R. and Sayyid, A.R. (2013). Foreign fighters in Somalia and Al-Shabaab's internal purge. *The Terrorism Monitory*, 11(2), The Jamestown Foundation.

Payne, A. and Frow, P. (2006). Customer relationship management: from strategy to implementation. *Journal of Marketing Management*, 22(1–2), pp. 135–168.

Payne, A., Storbacka, K. and Frow, P. (2009). Co-creating brands: diagnosing and designing the relationship experience. *Journal of Business Research*, 62(3), pp. 379–389.

Rubenfeld, S. (2014). Social media as a fundraising tool. *Wall Street Journal*, 11 August. blogs.wsj.com/riskandcompliance/2014/08/11/social-media-emerges-as-terrorism-fundraising-tool/ (accessed 18 August 2014).

Ryan, L. (2014). Why terrorists love Twitter. *National Journal*, 2 June. www.nationaljournal.com/tech/why-terrorists-love-twitter-20140602 (accessed 18 August 2014).

Schmelser, M. (1993). *Panopticism in the Postmodern Pedagogy*. Pennsylvania State University Press, University Park, PA.

Siegel, J. (2014). ISIS is using social media to reach YOU, its newest audience. *The Daily Beast*, 31 August. www.thedailybeast.com/articles/2014/08/31/isis-s-use-of-social-media-to-reach-you-its-new-audience.html (accessed 4 September 2014).

The Telegraph (2014). How terrorists are using social media. *The Telegraph*, 4 November. www.telegraph.co.uk/news/worldnews/islamic-state/11207681/How-terrorists-are-using-soc ial-media.html (accessed 12 December 2014).

Tepper, R. (2013). Starbucks aims for supermarket supremacy with new signature aisle. *Huffington Post*, 26 April. www.huffingtonpost.com/2013/04/26/starbucks-grocer y-store-aisle_n_3157075.html (accessed 9 September 2013).

Townsend, M. and Helm, T. (2014). Jihad in a social media age: how can the West win an online war? *The Guardian*, 23 August. www.theguardian.com/world/2014/aug/23/jiha d-social-media-age-west-win-online-war (accessed 4 September 2014).

Wallace, E., Buil, I. and De Chernatony, L. (2014). Consumer engagement with self-expressive brands: brand love and WOM outcomes. *Journal of Product & Brand Management*, 23(1), pp. 33–42.

Weimann, G. (2012). Terrorist groups recruiting through social media. *CBC News*. 10 January. www.cbc.ca/news/technology/story/2012/01/10/tech-terrorist-social-media.html (accessed 4 September 2014).

Weisburd, A. (2011). How to prevent terrorism and preserve innovation. homeland.house. gov/sites/homeland.house.gov/files/Weisburd%20testimony.pdf (accessed 4 September 2014).

White, A., Breazeale, M. and Webster, C. (2012). 'The brand avoidance relationship: exploring consumer motivations'. In S. Fournier, M. Breazeale and M. Fetscherin (Eds) *Consumer-Brand Relationships: Theory and Practice*, pp. 57–73. Routledge, London.

Wiener-Bronner, D. (2014). Twitter is the preferred social media platform among terrorists. *The Wire*, 14 May. www.thewire.com/global/2014/05/social-media-terrorism-rises/ 370893/ (accessed 18 August 2014).

Wilkinson, P. (1997). The media and terrorism: a reassessment. *Terrorism and Political Violence*, 9(2), pp. 51–64.

Further reading

Ansalone, C. (2013). Al-Shabaab's tactical and media strategies in the wake of its battlefield setbacks. *CTC Sentinel*, 6(3), pp. 12–16.

Breazeale, M., Pleggenkuhle-Miles, E., Ligon, G.S. and Harms, M. (2015). 'Branding Terror: Building Notoriety in Violent Extremist Organisations'. In S. Fournier, M. Breazeale and J. Avery (Eds) *Strong Brands, Strong Relationships*. Routledge, London.

Fournier, S., Breazeale, M. and Avery, J. (Eds) (2015) *Strong Brands, Strong Relationships*. Routledge, London.

Fournier, S., Breazeale, M. and Fetscherin, M. (Eds) (2012). *Consumer-Brand Relationships: Theory and Practice*. Routledge, London.

Ligon, G., Breazeale, M., Pleggenkuhle-Miles, E., Harms, M. and Woracek, S. (2013) *Branding Destruction: Applying a Marketing Framework to the Notoriety of Violent Extremist Organisations*. Working paper.

PART IV

Management

10

THE RIGHT MARKETING TO THE WRONG CUSTOMERS? RETHINKING CONVENTIONAL CRM STRATEGIES

Denish Shah

1 Introduction

Managers are prone to implementing customer relationship management (CRM) practices based on intuition or generally accepted beliefs from past experience (Dane and Pratt, 2007). For example, consider the case of Ron Johnson, who was hired as the CEO of the large retail chain J.C. Penney in the autumn of 2011 to revive the declining revenue of the firm (Tuttle, 2013a). Back then, J.C. Penney's core business model was based on artificially raising the prices of products and later deeply discounting them through heavily advertised sales promotions. Mr Johnson believed that such marketing practices were deceptive. His belief was based on his experience at Apple and Target – two firms where sales promotions are minimal or non-existent. Following his intuition and success from past experience, Mr Johnson discontinued the decades-long practice of sales promotions at J.C. Penney, without conducting any data analyses or market research. The decision proved disastrous for the firm, as discussed later in this chapter.

Implementation of CRM practices may also be misled by generally accepted beliefs that come from easy-to-observe aggregate-level outcomes (Kumar and Shah, 2009; Shah et al., 2012). For example, Shah et al. (2012) interviewed marketing executives from 22 different firms serving consumer and business markets. They found that each of these firms implemented cross-selling based on the aggregate-level observed results that cross-buying customers in general resulted in higher profits. However, does this necessarily hold true for *all* customers of a firm?

In this chapter, we discuss how conventional CRM practices based on intuition, popular managerial beliefs or aggregate-level data analyses can result in firms implementing the right marketing programmes for the wrong customers, adversely impacting on the financial performance of the firm.

Learning objectives

When you have read this chapter, you should be able to:

1. Link customer loyalty to profitability.
2. Design a two-tier rewards programme.
3. Understand the importance of customer habits in the context of recurring customer behaviour.
4. Implement a smart-selling framework to manage customer cross-buying.
5. Direct the right marketing initiatives to the right customer.
6. Appreciate the importance of customer-level data analyses to drive CRM strategies.

2 Route map

Broadly speaking, CRM practices of the firm entail managing a firm's relationship with its customers through firm-initiated marketing interactions. This chapter focuses on reviewing the CRM practices of the firm pertaining to: building customer loyalty; managing profitable customers; increasing customer cross-buy; and managing recurring customer behaviour through firm-initiated marketing. The chapter draws upon the findings from recent empirical research to question the conventional CRM practices that typically result in suboptimal financial outcomes for the firm. Consequently, the chapter discusses different tools and frameworks that marketers can implement to refine their existing CRM practices and hence maximise customer profits and the overall financial performance of the firm. The main arguments of the chapter are supplemented by discussions of a real-world business case study and future research directions.

3 State of the art in CRM strategies

Questioning conventional marketing wisdom

This section questions four popular managerial beliefs that have traditionally guided marketing strategies in both business-to-business and business-to-consumer markets.

Are loyal customers profitable?

Companies spend a considerable amount of resources to cultivate customer loyalty through rewards or loyalty programmes (Kumar and Shah, 2004). In 2012, Americans had a collective total of 2.65 billion loyalty programme memberships (Tuttle, 2013b). These numbers underscore the ubiquity of loyalty programmes and their perceived importance across firms.

Extant research in marketing has reiterated the critical importance of customer loyalty as a valuable asset in competitive markets (e.g. Srivastava et al., 2000). This is especially true in the context of businesses where consumers are not locked in by a contract and hence face lower switching costs (Shapiro and Vivian, 2000). Not surprisingly, customer loyalty is a commonly implemented CRM practice across several industries (Lewis, 1997). This is reinforced by the fact that the potential benefits of customer loyalty are well documented (e.g. Morgan and Hunt, 1994; Sheth and Parvatlyar, 1995).

From a firm's standpoint, investing in resources to develop customer loyalty is justified from obvious financial payoffs expected to accrue from loyal customers. For example, Reichheld (1996) identifies four major benefits of loyal customers: 1 firms incur lower costs to serve loyal customers; 2 loyal customers are less price sensitive and/or willing to pay higher prices for products and services of the firm; 3 loyal customers spend more time with the company; and 4 loyal customers are more likely to give positive referrals of the firm's products and services to other potential customers.

Given the obvious financial benefits and the widely acknowledged importance of customer loyalty, most CRM practices are typically directed at retaining *all* customers of the firm. In a widely cited *Harvard Business Review* article, Reichheld and Sasser (1990) report that a 5% improvement in the retention rate of customers can lead to a 30% to 85% increase in a firm's profits. The study makes a strong argument for firms to strive for a zero defection rate. That is, retain *every* customer of the firm by making them loyal to the firm's products and/or services (Reichheld, 1996).

However, are *all* loyal customers (i.e. customers that stay longer with the firm) necessarily profitable? Reinartz and Kumar (2002) investigate this question by analysing the behaviour, revenue and profits of more than 16,000 individual and corporate customers over a four-year period and across four different firms. They find a surprisingly weak relationship in each of the four firms, with the correlation coefficient of loyalty and profitability ranging from 0.20 to 0.45, as summarised in Table 10.1

The results imply that a substantial proportion of the firm's customers that stay longer with the firm (i.e. appear to be loyal) are not necessarily more profitable. Consequently, firms need to rethink management of customer loyalty and rewards programmes.

TABLE 10.1 Correlation between customer loyalty and profitability

No.	Firm	Correlation between customer loyalty and profitability
1	French grocery retailer	0.45
2	High-tech corporate service provider	0.30
3	US mail order company	0.20
4	German direct brokerage house	0.29

Are the most profitable customers of the firm the most valuable?

One of the fundamental objectives of a firm's CRM practices is to identify differences in customers and subsequently customise marketing initiatives based on individual differences. Individual differences in customers can be identified along several dimensions. For example, customers can be identified along demographic and psychographic characteristics (such as age, income, gender, physical location, household size, attitudes, beliefs, lifestyle preferences, etc.), shopping characteristics (e.g. frequent shopper, holiday shopper, online shopper), propensity to respond to different marketing campaigns, or their value (i.e. total monetary amount spent with the firm).

The majority of firms tend to place a lot of importance on the profitability of a customer as the basis to determine the level of CRM investment in them (Kumar et al., 2006). For example, firms offer special services and privileges to their most profitable customers through their rewards programme. In the airline, hotel and casino sectors, it is common to encounter a hierarchical rewards system, where the most profitable customers of the firm are awarded a 'platinum' or 'diamond' status accompanied by access to special benefits such as early boarding, free upgrades to business class, exclusive access to airport lounges and so on, which typically are not offered to other customers of the firm. Similarly, firms tend to focus on the most profitable customers of the firm for marketing additional products, customer care and retention efforts (Kumar et al., 2006).

There is nothing wrong with CRM practices directed at regarding 'profitable' customers as the most 'valuable' for the firm. The potential problem – and often a serious one – lies in how customer profitability is measured by the firm. One of the widely employed measures of customer profitability is 'past customer value' – that is, the overall worth of a customer is determined on the basis of the total monetary value of profits from a customer to the current period. Another popular measure (especially in the direct marketing and retailing contexts) is the RFM or recency-frequency-monetary value (Hughes, 1996; Aaker et al., 1998). The RFM score for a customer is computed based on a weighted sum of three important dimensions of a customer's behaviour: 1 how *recently* a customer bought from the firm; 2 how *frequently* a customer purchased from the firm; and 3 what the *monetary value* of the purchases was.

Both past customer value and RFM are inherently backward-looking metrics. That is, they capture the historic value of the customer. Relying on the past value of customers – especially when the customer value is likely to exhibit an upward or downward value trend – can lead to sub-optimal CRM decisions. For example, consider the case of Customer X and Customer Y exhibiting a change in customer value over a time period of ten years, as illustrated in Figure 10.1.

Customer X results in an average customer value of US$2,630 per year in the first five years with the firm. If the firm makes a relationship investment decision for this customer at the end of the first five years (denoted by a dotted line in Figure 10.1), on the basis of a backward-looking metric, the firm is likely to

FIGURE 10.1 Backward-looking metrics can lead to sub-optimal decisions

under-invest marketing resources. This is because the customer exhibits an upward value trend with average customer value in the next five years expected to increase by 44%. Similarly, in the case of Customer Y, the firm is likely to over-invest marketing resources. Both scenarios underscore the need for firms to implement a forward-looking metric that can offer the firm the expected future value of the customer. Consequently, firms can invest in the right amount of marketing resources for a customer 'today', in anticipation of the expected value of the customer in the foreseeable 'future'.

Extant research in marketing has shown customer lifetime value (CLV) as the most suitable metric for firms making optimal forward-looking CRM decisions (see Kumar et al., 2006; Kumar and Shah, 2009; Kumar, 2008). For example, Venkatesan and Kumar (2004) found that, when marketing resources are allocated to customers on the basis of CLV, customers offer much higher profits, compared with allocating marketing resources on the basis of backward-looking metrics such as the past customer value and/or previous period customer revenue. Therefore, it is important for firms to understand how to measure the lifetime value of each customer and appreciate the numerous ways in which the CLV metric can help the firm upon implementation.

Is customer cross-buying beneficial to the firm?

Cross-buying refers to the customer behaviour of buying multiple categories of products and/or services from the same firm. Research has documented several positive outcomes associated with cross-buying. For example, cross-buying has been associated with an increase in the relationship duration (Kamakura et al., 2003; Li, 1995; Reinartz and Kumar, 2003), increase in purchase frequency (Reinartz et al., 2008; Venkatesan and Kumar, 2004), and increase in the contribution margin per order (Kumar et al., 2008) of customers. In essence, customer cross-buying has been widely known to have a positive effect (direct or indirect) on customer profit (Kumar et al., 2006; Kumar et al., 2008).

Cross-selling refers to a firm's marketing efforts to sell multiple categories of products and/or services to the same customer. Given the expected positive financial outcome from customer cross-buying, conventional cross-selling practices are typically directed at maximising the rate of cross-buying across customers (Shah et al., 2012). That is, if a customer exhibits a propensity to purchase an additional product (i.e. cross-buy), the respective firm would aggressively market that product (i.e. cross-sell) to the customer concerned, with the overarching objective of increasing profit from the customer in question.

However, anecdotal evidence from the marketplace implies potential downsides of cross-selling. For example, a *Wall Street Journal* article reported that Best Buy (a national chain of retail stores selling electronic products in the United States) discovered that 20% of its customers were unprofitable, despite making multiple purchases from its stores (McWilliams, 2004). Filene's Basement (a US discount clothing store) banned two of its most frequent customers from entering the retailer's 21 outlets, after discovering that they were highly unprofitable (Zbar, 2003). Financial services firms have reported highly unprofitable customers, despite cross-buy (Brown, 2003; Weissman, 2006; Shah and Kumar, 2008). These examples indicate that it is worth investigating whether customers who willingly purchase additional products and/or services from a firm can prove unprofitable. If so, to what extent can cross-buying of customers adversely impact a firm's bottom line?

In a recent empirical study conducted by Shah et al. (2012), the authors analyse the customer data sets of five firms serving business or consumer markets: 1 a *Fortune* 500 financial services firm serving business customers; 2 a *Fortune* 500 IT firm serving business customers; 3 a multinational retail bank; 4 a major catalogue retailer; and 5 a *Fortune* 500 retail chain of stores selling high-fashion clothing. Across all five firms, the study finds that 10% to 35% of the customers who cross-buy are unprofitable. Interestingly, these relatively small proportions of customers account for a significant proportion (39%–88%) of the firms' total loss from their customers. Furthermore, detailed analyses of the transaction behaviour of customers with unprofitable cross-buying reveals four types of problem customer segments (Shah and Kumar, 2012), each characterised by the prevalence of a persistently recurring adverse behaviour:

1.   Service demanders: customers who persistently demand excessive customer service across all channels used by the firm.
2.   Revenue reversers: customers whose actions lead to revenue reversals for the firm. For example, by returning previously purchased products, defaulting on payments and/or early termination of contracts.
3.   Promotion maximisers: customers who recurrently purchase loss leaders or products that are steeply discounted by the respective firm.
4.   Spending limiters: customers who repeatedly spend only a small and fixed amount with a given company. This could be either due to financial

constraints or because customers are spreading their purchases across several other companies. Consequently, total customer revenue seldom increases for such customers after cross-buying.

Cross-selling to customers in any of the four aforementioned problem segments causes the habitual (adverse) behaviour of the customer to extend across a greater number of products and/or services from the firm, thereby decreasing customer profits or increasing customer losses. The adverse financial effect is further impacted by the costs associated with the cross-selling efforts. Consequently, whenever customers from the problem segment engage in cross-buying, they are likely to exhibit a downward spiral of an unprofitable relationship, with the losses increasing (or profits decreasing) with higher levels of cross-buying. In contrast, customers not belonging to any of the problem segments are likely to exhibit the opposite outcome.

For example, consider the case of these two actual customers, taken from a major catalogue retailer's customer database, analysed by Shah et al. (2012). Both customers (Customer A and Customer B) initiate the relationship with the firm in the same month of a year, and engage in cross-buying with the firm over a period of seven years, as illustrated in Figure 10.2. At the end of the first year, neither of the customers engages in cross-buying and they incur the same amount of losses (i.e. $94 and $107, respectively, as illustrated in Figure 10.2).

Over the observation period of seven years, Customer A purchases four products and exhibits a downward spiral of losses, increasing with rising cross-buy levels. Customer B also purchases four products, but exhibits an upward spiral of profits, increasing with rising cross-buy levels. In such a scenario, how can firms distinguish between the two customers? In the next section, we discuss a managerial framework that firms may implement to help in identifying problem customers (such as Customer A) early on, deterring them from any future cross-selling initiatives, so as to minimise the probability of a downward spiral.

Does marketing influence recurring customer behaviour over time?

Conventional marketing mix models are based on the premise that changes in marketing initiatives of a firm will impact on the corresponding change in customer behaviour. For example, a positive impact of direct marketing on a customer's purchase implies that firms can leverage direct marketing as a means to influence positively a customer's purchase in the future. However, would marketing continue to have the same level of effect on recurring customer behaviour over time? Can recurring customer behaviour be governed by other underlying factors?

Recurring behaviour of customers can contribute to the onset of a habit. A 'habit' may be defined as one's psychological dispositions to repeat past behaviour (Neal et al., 2012). Interestingly, about 45% of human behaviour is governed by a 'habit', by virtue of the behaviour being repetitive (Wood et al., 2002). Neuroscientists rationalise habitual behaviour with mental associations. That is, when an

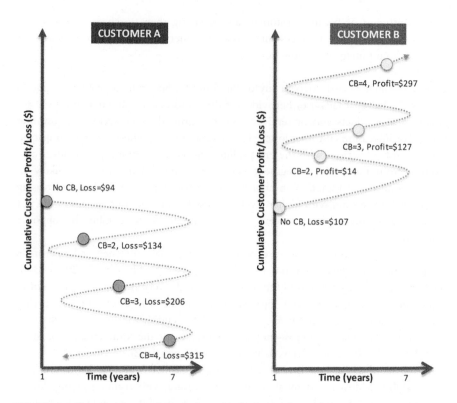

FIGURE 10.2 Cross-buying and profit/loss trend of two illustrative customers

individual repeatedly performs a particular behaviour in a given situation (with a satisfactory outcome) over time, the individual becomes cognitively hard-wired to repeat the same behaviour in the same/similar situation consistently (Muraven and Baumeister, 2000; Marchette et al., 2011). Interestingly, once strong habits are formed, the associated behaviour may even override intentions. For example, Ji and Wood (2007) find that a group of participants consistently repeat their habitual behaviour despite reporting intentions to do otherwise.

The concept of 'habit' is important for marketers, as CRM practices are typically directed at managing repeat customers and hence repeat customer behaviour over time. Assael (1987) describes a model of habitual purchase behaviour where a consumer's satisfaction from prior purchases of a brand is applied as a heuristic to simplify decision making and hence readily applied to buy the same brand in the future, with minimal consideration for alternative brands. In a recently published empirical study, Shah et al. (2014) analyse a large customer data set of a *Fortune* 500 retailer. The study finds that certain customers of the firm are prone to developing a habitual tendency with respect to one or more of the following types of behaviours:

1. Making regular purchases
2. Buying products on promotion
3. Returning previously purchased products
4. Buying low-margin, clearance or loss-leader products.

These habitual behaviours have a direct significant effect on the financial performance of the firm. The study finds that the repeat purchase and promotion purchase habits of customers *positively* impact on the firm's bottom line by \$53.5 million and \$3.9 million, respectively, while the product return and the low margin purchase habits *negatively* impact the firm's bottom line by \$58.9 million and \$61.6 million, respectively, over an observation period of four years.

Collectively, these new research findings underscore the need for marketers to quantify habit formation of different customers over time and hence implement the necessary marketing interventions to ensure profitable outcomes of customers' habits. The next section describes how this can be achieved by marketers.

Tools and frameworks for improving existing CRM practices

Next we will discuss different tools and frameworks that marketers can implement to address issues with conventional CRM practices.

Managing 'profitable' customer loyalty

Segmenting and managing loyal customers

For most firms, customer loyalty is evaluated on the basis of the length of duration of the customer with the firm. However, the correlation between customer loyalty (by that measure) and profitability has been found to be weak to moderate at best. Consequently, firms are likely to encounter long-term customers who are not necessarily profitable and short-term customers who are highly profitable.

Reinartz and Kumar (2002) offer a useful framework through which customers of the firm can be divided into four segments on the basis of their expected lifetime duration with the firm (i.e. short term versus long term) and profitability (i.e. low versus high). Corresponding to the four customer segments, firms should implement a differentiated CRM approach as indicated in Figure 10.3. This would enable firms to manage customer loyalty and profitability simultaneously.

Designing the right customer loyalty rewards programme

Evaluating customer loyalty on the basis of the length of duration of the customer with the firm helps capture only one dimension of loyalty – 'behavioural' loyalty. Another important and often overlooked dimension of customer loyalty is 'attitudinal' loyalty (Kumar and Shah, 2004). Attitudinal loyalty represents a higher-order or long-term commitment of a customer to the organisation that cannot be

HIGH PROFITABILITY CUSTOMERS	
With low lifetime duration	*With high lifetime duration*
• Represents a segment of profitable but variety-seeking or brand-switching customers. • Adopt a tactical approach to profit from every transaction with the customer. • Any marketing efforts to cultivate attitudinal loyalty or long-term relationship with customers in this segment are likely to prove futile and/or wasteful.	• Customers in this segment typically drive the majority of the total customer profits of the firm. • Invest in nurturing long-lasting relationships with customers in this segment through personalised marketing communication and initiatives that are directed at delighting customers and cultivating attitudinal loyalty.
LOW PROFITABILITY CUSTOMERS	
With low lifetime duration	*With high lifetime duration*
• Represents a segment of customers that are a poor fit of the company's products and services. • Cease or limit marketing initiatives for customers in this segment.	• Represents a segment of customers with relatively low profit contribution to the overall customer profits of the firm. • Target customers with marketing initiatives directed at cross-selling, up-selling, and/or increasing the size of wallet of customers in this segment.

FIGURE 10.3 Segmenting and managing customer loyalty and profitability

inferred by merely observing the repeat purchase behaviours of a customer (Shankar et al., 2000). Failure to account for attitudinal loyalty could lead to spurious loyalty (Dick and Basu, 1994) or poor correlation of behavioural loyalty with customer profitability (Reinartz and Kumar, 2000, 2002). Therefore, for customer loyalty to be meaningful for the firm, customers need to exhibit both behavioural and attitudinal loyalty.

Consequently, a firm's customer loyalty rewards programme must be designed to cultivate *both* behavioural and attitudinal customer loyalty. Kumar and Shah (2004) propose a two-tier rewards framework to enable firms to build and sustain attitudinal and behavioural loyalty of their customers.

Tier 1 rewards represent a standard uni-dimensional rewards strategy, where customers are given rewards or points on the basis of their total spending, thereby serving as a means for rewarding behavioural loyalty of customers. Consequently, the terms of earning and redeeming points for tier 1 rewards is the same for all customers. A majority of loyalty programmes in existence today operate at tier 1 and end up primarily rewarding behavioural loyalty of the customers (Kumar and Shah, 2004).

Tier 2 rewards are designed to complement tier 1 rewards (Kumar and Shah, 2004). Tier 2 rewards could be special rewards given to selected customers, to cultivate attitudinal loyalty and/or influence a specific behaviour of a customer in the future, rather than rewarding for behaviour in the past. For example, offering a special discount to a customer for cross-buying in a relevant product category, where the customer has never made a purchase before. Alternatively, tier 2 rewards could be directed at cultivating attitudinal loyalty by offering special privileges to profitable customers, with the objective of cultivating a positive attitude towards the firm. Unlike tier 1 rewards, tier 2 rewards represent highly differentiated rewards, awarded to selected customers of whom the company is interested in cultivating attitudinal loyalty or influencing a specific customer behaviour in the future.

Upon implementation, tier 1 and tier 2 rewards are designed to operate in tandem. Table 10.2 summarises the key differences between the two tiers.

Measuring and implementing the customer lifetime value (CLV) metric

How can the lifetime value of the customers of the firm be measured? The CLV computation entails predicting the future cash flow from each customer by incorporating into one the elements of revenue, expense and customer behaviour that drive customer profitability. This is then discounted by the cost of capital, to arrive at the net present value of all future cash flows expected from a customer, or the lifetime value of the customer.

In general, the CLV for a customer can be computed as:

$$CLV = \sum_{t=0}^{T} = \frac{(p_t - c_t)r_t}{(1+i)^t} - AC$$

where p_t is the price paid by a customer at time t, c_t is the direct cost of servicing the customer at time t and includes all marketing costs, i is the discount rate or cost of capital for the firm, r_t is the probability of customer repeat buying or being an active customer of the firm at time t, AC is the acquisition cost, and T is the time horizon for estimating CLV (Gupta et al., 2006).

Although the basic underlying logic for computing CLV stays the same, several different approaches have been proposed in the literature for modelling and estimating CLV. These methods vary in terms of whether the CLV is computed at the customer level, customer segment level or firm level. While some researchers have employed a finite time horizon of three years (e.g. Kumar and Shah, 2009) or the expected lifetime duration of a customer (e.g. Reinartz and Kumar, 2000), others have used an infinite time horizon (e.g. Fader et al., 2005; Gupta et al., 2004) corresponding to the term 'T' in the equation.

Regardless of the measurement approach, the CLV metric offers CRM managers several strategic benefits for the firm upon implementation. These include: 1 enabling firms to manage customer loyalty and profitability simultaneously (Reinartz and Kumar, 2000); 2 managing and maximising retailer profitability (Kumar et al., 2006); 3 offering a superior means to select customers for marketing communication initiatives (Venkatesan and Kumar, 2004); 4 making firms truly customer centric (Shah et al., 2006); and 5 linking CLV-based CRM strategies to the stock price or the overall financial value of the firm (Kumar and Shah, 2011). Each of

TABLE 10.2 Tier 1 versus tier 2 rewards

		Tier 1 reward	*Tier 2 reward*
1	Main objective	Encourage behavioural loyalty by rewarding customers for past behaviour	Cultivate attitudinal loyalty and/or reward a customer to influence a specific (desired) customer behaviour in the future
2	Level of differentiation	None. Same standard rewarding mechanism for all customers of the firm	Highly differentiated. Reward can vary for each customer
3	Rewards policy	Uniformly applicable for each customer. Terms and conditions are publicly disclosed	Awarded to a specific customer at the discretion of the firm. Terms and conditions may be held confidential by the firm
4	Reward example	– 1% cash back corresponding to the amount of money spent by a customer – Free air ticket or hotel stay after flying 'x' number of miles or staying at a hotel for 'y' number of nights	– Cash voucher to a customer to make a *future* purchase in a relevant product category of the firm where the customer has never made a purchase in the past – Exclusive privileges for a profitable customer with the underlying objective of cultivating attitudinal loyalty

these CRM applications has been documented in the literature as a best practice for maximising the customer value of the firm. Not surprisingly, the critical importance of CLV has evolved from merely being an important metric to a way of thinking and doing business (Yu, 2002).

Smart selling instead of cross-selling

How can a firm desist from cross-selling to customers who are likely to exhibit a downward spiral of decreasing profits or increasing losses, as depicted by Customer A in Figure 10.2? The answer lies in adopting a framework that entails smart selling, or a more selective approach to cross-selling, as depicted in Figure 10.4.

State-of-the-art cross-selling practices apply predictive models to determine which customer is likely to cross-buy what product. Clearly, such an approach is inadequate. Before investing in any cross-selling initiatives, firms need to determine whether the consequence of cross-buying is likely to be profitable. By analysing the underlying behavioural trend of a customer, firms can evaluate whether the customer belongs to one of the problem segments as discussed above.

Membership of a problem segment indicates temporal consistency of adverse behavioural traits and hence relatively high likelihood of the customer engaging in unprofitable cross-buying. If so, the cross-sell decision should be turned into a no-sell or up-sell decision, based on the customer's characteristics and the nature of the

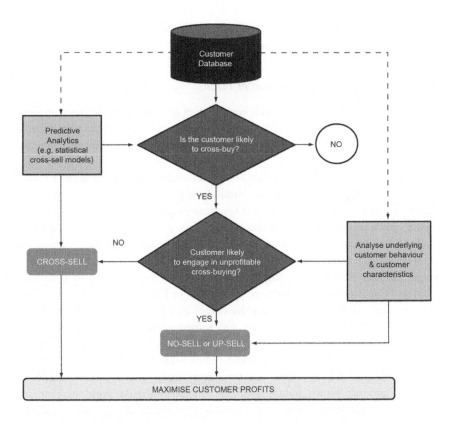

FIGURE 10.4 Smart-selling framework for maximising customer profits

customer's behavioural trend, as depicted in Figure 10.4. For example, if a firm encounters a habitual revenue reverser, who frequently returns previously purchased products, then it may be prudent for the firm to apply a no-sell decision or to exclude that customer from any future cross-selling campaigns. On the other hand, if a firm encounters a habitual limited spender, then the firm may first want to try to increase the customer's current spending with the firm through up-selling, before cross-selling additional products. For example, a retail bank may choose to cross-sell its credit card only after a customer upgrades from a regular current (chequing) account to a premium account, which requires a higher minimum balance. Blindly cross-selling to limited spenders can backfire, as research shows that such customers tend to reallocate their fixed limited spending over a greater number of products (Shah et al., 2012).

In essence, rather than adopting the conventional approach of cross-selling to every customer who is likely to cross-buy, firms need to smart sell. That is, the decision to sell to a customer (who is likely to cross-buy) is ultimately executed as a cross-sell, up-sell or no-sell action, based on the underlying behaviour and characteristics of the customer, as depicted in Figure 10.4. For technical details on how to specify a statistical model to predict the likelihood of a customer exhibiting unprofitable cross-buying, please refer to Shah et al. (2012).

Measuring and managing customer habits

Customers are likely to form a habit with respect to temporally recurring interactions with the firm. Shah et al. (2014) offer a quantitative approach enabling firms to measure the intensity of different customer habits from archived customer transaction data.

At the customer level, knowledge of each customer's habits can help the marketer make strategic resource reallocation decisions. For example, the study by Shah et al. (2014) finds that return and low-margin purchase habits have a negative impact, while promotion and purchase habits have a positive impact on customer profits. Since habits by definition are enduring constructs, firms may strategically move marketing spend away from customers with relatively high return and low-margin purchase habits, reinvesting them in developing purchase and/or promotion habits of other customers of the firm, as depicted in Figure 10.5

At the firm level, firms can assess the extent to which different habitual behaviours are prevalent across customers and subsequently use that information to make major changes in the marketing policy. For example, if a firm discovers that a sizeable proportion of customers' product return habits has a high negative impact on the firm performance, then the firm may implement a more stringent or restrictive product return policy. Similarly, the firm should avoid making any changes to its promotion policy, if a sizeable proportion of the firm's profitable customers exhibit strong promotion purchase habits. In general, firm-initiated marketing directed at cultivating or deterring customers' habits, rather than

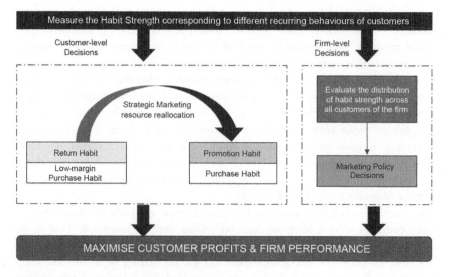

FIGURE 10.5 Measuring and managing customer habits to maximise customer profits

customer behaviour, results in superior performance outcomes for the firm. This is because habits are enduring constructs and often the underlying drivers of recurring customer behaviour.

Conclusion

Evidence from relatively recently published studies debunks four generally accepted managerial beliefs, with substantive implications for the CRM practices of a firm. First, not all loyal customers are necessarily profitable. Therefore, any customer loyalty management initiatives, such as retention efforts, should be contingent upon the profitability of the customer. Furthermore, to achieve true customer loyalty, firms need to rethink their rewards programme, to ensure that they are serving to cultivate attitudinal loyalty in addition to rewarding behavioural loyalty of customers.

Second, CRM decisions based on backward-looking customer value metrics tend to be sub-optimal. A proven superior approach entails the implementation of the CLV metric, to measure the true future worth of a customer and hence implement CRM strategies guided by the future value of each customer or customer segment.

Third, cross-selling a product to every customer of a firm who is likely to cross-buy can adversely impact on the overall financial outcome of the firm's cross-selling efforts. This is due to the prevalence of hidden customer segments with persistent adverse behavioural traits. Cross-selling to such customers results in decreasing profits or increasing losses with the increase in cross-buying levels. Consequently, cross-selling practices of firms first need to identify these problem customers and up-sell or not sell any products/services to them, despite their tendency to cross-buy from the firm.

Finally, customers are prone to developing a habitual behaviour by virtue of their recurring interactions with firms. Habits are enduring constructs with tenacious influence on future customer behaviour. Different customer habits can have a differential impact on firm performance. A firm's CRM practices and policies need to account for the relative prevalence (how many customers) and intensity (how strong) of different habitual behaviours and design marketing interventions accordingly.

4 New research directions

With advances in database technologies and the proliferation of Internet, smart-phone and social media platforms, CRM practices of firms will progressively have access to an increasing amount of rich customer data or 'big data' over time. Richer customer data will offer firms increasing abilities to analyse customer-level information, to refine further their CRM strategies. For example, firms can now monitor their customers' conversations across different social media platforms. Consequently, by analysing the sentiment of the conversation relevant to a firm's brand (positive or negative), a firm can estimate the level of attitudinal loyalty of a customer towards the firm's brand. Future research could investigate how such insights can be applied to enhance a firm's ability to manage profitable customer loyalty.

The accuracy of measuring the lifetime value of a customer can be improved with the help of richer customer-level data. With the proliferation of the Internet and mobile devices, firms can now collect transaction data of customers not only from stores but also online transactions conducted on multiple devices. Future research could develop more sophisticated CLV models that incorporate data from multiple customer touchpoints.

The ability of a firm to 'smart sell' to a customer can be augmented by integrating online and offline purchase transactions of a customer. Future research could evaluate how offline marketing may drive a customer to purchase an additional product (i.e. cross-buy) online and vice versa. Similarly, future research could be directed at understanding changing customer habits with the proliferation of the Internet and social media. For example, customers' purchase habits may gravitate more towards online purchases, rather than those in store. In addition, customers may habitually start relying on product information obtained through social media, rather than conventional marketing communication channels. Such insights could help firms to make the necessary changes to their existing CRM practices.

5 Practising marketing – a case study

In early 2012, Ron Johnson – the newly appointed CEO of J.C. Penney – eliminated the firm's long-standing policy of heavily advertised sales and discounts, in lieu of 'fair and square' everyday low pricing. The change was made in response to Mr Johnson's belief, based on his professional career at Apple Inc. and Target Corp. where sales promotions are minimal, that this would be successful. Intuitively, Mr Johnson's initiatives seemed to make sense. A similar approach – minimal or no sales promotion – had worked favourably for Mr Johnson during his tenure at Apple. Unfortunately, at J.C. Penney it proved to be a classic case of 'right marketing to the wrong customers'. Unlike Apple, J.C. Penney's loyal customers were habituated to purchase only when there was a sales promotion. In the absence of any market research or data analyses conducted prior to the implementation of 'fair and square' everyday low pricing, Mr Johnson grossly underestimated the strength of the customers' shopping habits associated with sales promotions. Consequently, habitual promotion shoppers of J.C. Penney stopped buying from the company. Over a one-year period, J.C. Penney incurred a steep decline in sales that contributed to $985 million in losses (Mattioli, 2013).

The real-world business case study of J.C. Penney underscores the need for firms to undertake data analyses before implementing key CRM strategies. Here is how J.C. Penney could have avoided the marketing missteps by implementing the tools and frameworks described in this chapter.

First, the firm should have measured the lifetime value of each customer and identified the segment of high-value customers. Next, the firm should have quantified the habit strength of different recurring behaviours of customers. The analyses would have indicated that a large proportion of high-value customers of J.C. Penney possessed strong promotion purchase habit. That is, most of the high-value customers of the firm liked to purchase only deeply discounted products (during sales promotions) from J.C. Penney. Consequently, the data analyses would have implied that discontinuation of sales promotion by the firm carried the risk of alienating the high-value customers of the firm.

An alternative and potentially superior approach could have been to apply the CLV information to implement a customer loyalty programme with a two-tier reward system directed at cultivating attitudinal loyalty for the high-value customers, while encouraging low-value customers to purchase more often. The firm could also have employed the smart-selling framework (as depicted in Figure 10.4) to weed out customers exhibiting unprofitable cross-buying. Collectively, these efforts would have helped J.C. Penney to implement a set of data-driven CRM strategies and potentially improve the financial performance of the firm.

Discussion questions

1. What major change did J.C. Penney make with respect to its promotion policy under the leadership of Ron Johnson?
2. How did the change in J.C. Penney's promotion impact on the firm performance? Why?
3. Is it possible to quantify the promotion habit of customers of a firm? If so, how?
4. What other CRM tools could J.C. Penney have applied to improve its financial performance?

6 Further investigation

The research findings and CRM practices discussed in this chapter may be further advanced to address the following questions:

1. How can the digital or online habits of customers be studied?
2. Can a persistently unprofitable customer become profitable over time? If so, how can such a customer be identified early on?
3. How can insights from the social media conversations of customers be leveraged to further refine CRM strategies of the firm?
4. How can 'big data' be leveraged to improve the accuracy of customer behaviour and customer lifetime value models?
5. How can the key lessons learned from this chapter be extended to other CRM strategies of a firm pertaining to customer acquisition and/or customer win-back?

References

Aaker, D.A., Kumar, V. and Day, G.S. (1998). *Marketing Research.* John Wiley & Sons, New York.

Ailawadi, K.L., Lehmann, D.R. and Neslin, S.A. (2001). Market response to a major policy change in the marketing mix: learning from Procter & Gamble's value pricing strategy. *Journal of Marketing*, 65 (January), pp. 44–61.

Assael, H. (1987). *Consumer Behavior and Marketing Action.* Kent Publishing Company, Boston.

Brown, T.K. (2003). The cross-sell cross-up. *Bank Director Magazine.* www.bankdirector. com/index.php/magazine/archives/1st-quarter-2003/the-cross-sell-cross-up/(accessed July 2010).

Dane, E. and Pratt, M.G. (2007). Exploring intuition and its role in managerial decision making. *Academy of Management Review*, 32(1), pp. 519–543.

Dick, A.S. and Basu, K. (1994). Customer loyalty: toward an integrated conceptual framework. *Journal of the Academy of Marketing Science*, 22(2).

Fader, P., Hardie, B. and Lee, K.L. (2005). RFM and CLV: using Iso-CLV curves for customer base analysis. *Journal of Marketing Research*, XLII (November), pp. 415–430.

Gupta, S., Hanssens, D., Hardie, B., Kahn, W., Kumar, V., Lin, N., Ravishanker, N. and Sriram, S. (2006). Modeling customer lifetime value. *Journal of Service Research*, 9(2), pp. 139–155.

Gupta, S. and Lehmann, D.R. (2005). *Managing Customers as Investments: The Strategic Value of Customers in the Long Run.* Wharton School Publishing, Upper Saddle River, NJ.

Gupta, S., Lehmann, D.R. and Stuart, J. (2004). Valuing customers. *Journal of Marketing Research*, 41(1), pp. 7–18.

Hughes, A.M. (1996). *The Complete Database Marketer*, 2nd edition. McGraw-Hill, New York.

Ji, M.F. and Wood, W. (2007). Purchase and consumption habits: not necessarily what you intend. *Journal of Consumer Psychology*, 17(4), pp. 261–276.

Kamakura, W.A., Wedel, M., De Rosa, F. and Mazzon, J.A. (2003). Cross-selling through database marketing: a mixed data factor analyzer for data augmentation and prediction. *International Journal of Research in Marketing*, 20 (May), pp. 45–65.

Kumar, V. (2008). *Managing Customers for Profit: Strategies to Increase Profits and Build Loyalty.* Prentice Hall Professional.

Kumar, V. and George, M. (2007). Measuring and maximizing customer equity: a critical analysis. *Journal of the Academy of Marketing Science*, 35(2), pp. 157–171.

Kumar, V., George, M. and Pancras, J. (2008). Cross-buying in retailing: drivers and consequences. *Journal of Retailing*, 84(1), pp. 15–27.

Kumar, V. and Shah, D. (2004). Building and sustaining profitable customer loyalty for the 21st century. *Journal of Retailing*, 80(4), pp. 317–329.

Kumar, V. and Shah, D. (2009). Expanding the role of marketing: from customer equity to market capitalization. *Journal of Marketing*, 73(6), pp. 119–136.

Kumar, V. and Shah, D. (2011). Practice prize paper-uncovering implicit consumer needs for determining explicit product positioning: growing prudential annuities' variable annuity sales. *Marketing Science*, 30(4), pp. 595–603.

Kumar, V., Shah, D. and Venkatesan, R. (2006). Managing retailer profitability – one customer at a time. *Journal of Retailing*, 82(4), pp. 277.

Kumar, V., Venkatesan, R., Bohling, T. and Beckmann, D. (2008). The power of CLV: managing customer value at IBM. *Marketing Science*, 27(4), pp. 585–599.

Lewis, H.G. (1997). Does your 'loyalty' programme inspire any loyalty? *Direct Marketing*, (June), pp. 46–48.

Li, S. (1995). Survival analysis: just as in life, customers are 'born' and they 'die.' Here's how to prevent their premature demise. *Marketing Research*, 7(4), pp. 17–23.

Marchette, S.A., Bakker, A. and Shelton, A.L. (2011). Cognitive mappers to creatures of habit: differential engagement of place and response learning mechanisms predicts human navigational behavior. *J. Neurosci*, 31(43), pp. 15264–15268.

Mattioli, D. (2013). Penney posts large loss as sales sink further. *The Wall Street Journal*, 27 February. online.wsj.com/article/ SB10001424127887323478304578330632060300820. html (accessed 2 September 2014).

McWilliams, G. (2004). Minding the store: analyzing customers, best buy decides not all are welcome; retailer aims to outsmart dogged bargain-hunters and coddle big spenders; looking for 'Barrys' and 'Jills'. *The Wall Street Journal*, 8 November. www.bc.edu/clubs/gasa/week_8_to_13.htm (accessed July 2010).

Morgan, R.M. and Hunt, S.D. (1994). The commit-ment-trust theory of relationship marketing. *Journal of Marketing*, 58 (July), pp. 20–38.

Muraven, M. and Baumeister, R.F. (2000). Self-regulation and depletion of limited resources: does self-control resemble a muscle? *Psychological Bulletin*, 126(2), pp. 247–259.

Neal, D.T., Wood, W., Labrecque, J.S. and Lally, P. (2012). How do habits guide behavior? Perceived and actual triggers of habits in daily life. *Journal of Experimental Social Psychology*, 48(2), pp. 492–498.

Reichheld, F.F. (1996). *The Loyalty Effect: The Hidden Force behind Growth, Profits and Lasting Value*. Harvard Business School Press, Boston, MA.

Reichheld, F.F. and Sasser, E.W. (1990). Zero defections: quality comes to services. *Harvard Business Review*, 68 (September/October), pp. 105–111.

Reinartz, W.J. and Kumar, V. (2000). On the profitability of long-life customers in a non-contractual setting: an empirical investigation and implications for marketing. *Journal of Marketing*, 64(4), pp. 17–35.

Reinartz, W.J. and Kumar, V. (2002). The mismanagement of customer loyalty. *Harvard Business Review*, 80(7), pp. 86.

Reinartz, W.J. and Kumar, V. (2003). The impact of customer relationship characteristics on profitable lifetime duration. *Journal of Marketing*, 67 (January), pp. 77–99.

Reinartz, W.J., Thomas, J.S. and Bascoul, G. (2008). Investigating cross-buying and customer loyalty. *Journal of Interactive Marketing*, 22(1), pp. 5–20.

Rust, R.T., Lemon, K.N. and Zeithaml, V.A. (2004a). Return on marketing: using customer equity to focus marketing strategy. *Journal of Marketing*, 68, pp. 109–127.

Shah, D. and Kumar, V. (2008). Research before you leap. *Marketing Research*, 20(3), pp. 26–32.

Shah, D. and Kumar, V. (2012). The dark side of cross-selling. *Harvard Business Review*, December.

Shah, D., Kumar, V. and Kim, K.H. (2014). Managing customer profits: the power of habits. *Journal of Marketing Research*.

Shah, D., Kumar, V., Qu, Y. and Chen, S. (2012). Unprofitable cross-buying: evidence from consumer and business markets. *Journal of Marketing*, 76 (May), pp. 78–95.

Shah, D., Rust, R.T., Parasuraman, A., Staelin, R. and Day, G.S. (2006). The path to customer centricity. *Journal of Service Research*, 9(2), pp. 113–124.

Shankar, V., Smith, A.K. and Rangaswamy, A. (2000). Customer satisfaction and loyalty online and offline environments. eBusiness Research Center Working Paper 02-2000. Penn State University, October.

Shapiro, C. and Vivian, H.R. (2000). *Information Rules*. Massachusetts Harvard Business School Press, Boston.

Sheth, J.N. and Parvatlyar, A. (1995). Relationship marketing in the consumer markets: antecedents and consequences. *Journal of the Academy of Marketing Science*, 23(4), pp. 255–271.

Srivastava, R.K., Sherwani, T.A. and Fahey, L. (2000). Market-based assets and shareholder value: a framework for analysis. *Journal of Marketing*, 62 (January), pp. 2–18.

Tuttle, B. (2013a). The 5 big mistakes that led to Ron Johnson's ouster at JC Penney. *Time Magazine*. business.time.com/2013/04/09/the-5-big-mistakes-that-led-to-ron-johnsons-ouster-at-jc-penney/print/ (10 December 2014).

Tuttle, B. (2013b). A disloyalty movement? Supermarkets and customers drop loyalty card programmes. *Time Magazine*. business.time.com/2013/07/11/a-disloyalty-movement-supermarkets-and-customers-drop-loyalty-card-programmemes/ (15 November 2014).

Venkatesan, R. and Kumar, V. (2004). A customer lifetime value framework for customer selection and resource allocation strategy. *Journal of Marketing*, 68 (October), pp. 106–125.

Weissman, R. (2006). Cross-selling: like cholesterol, there are good and bad cross-sales. *The Official Magazine of the Pennsylvania Bankers Association*, 7(6), www.dmacorporation.com/dmarecognized/Cross- Selling%20Article.pdf (accessed July 2010).

Wood, W., Quinn, J.M. and Kashy, D.A. (2002). Habits in everyday life: thought, emotion, and action. *Journal of Personality and Social Psychology*, 83(6), pp. 1281–1297.

Yu, L. (2002). Does diversity drive productivity. *MIT Sloan Management Review*, 43(2), pp. 17.

Zbar, J.D. (2003). When it's time to fire the customer. *Sun Sentinel*, 15 September. articles.sun-sentinel.com/2003-09-15/news/0309120602_1_top-line-growth-bottom-line-client-roster (accessed March 2011).

Further reading

Mittal, V., Sarkees, M. and Murshed, F. (2008). The right way to manage unprofitable customers. *Harvard Business Review*, 86 (April), pp. 95–102.

Nguyen, B. (2011). The dark side of CRM. *The Marketing Review*, 11(2), pp. 137–149.

11

RECOVERY FROM CRM IMPLEMENTATION PITFALLS: INTEGRATING LEARNING BEHAVIOUR FROM FAILURE

Bang Nguyen and Xiaoyu Yu

1 Introduction

Despite growing interest in customer relationship management (CRM) and all the benefits that it offers to companies, various studies reveal high rates of failure when implementing CRM schemes. An urgent problem facing both academics and managers is how CRM expenditure can be more effectively and consistently translated into meaningful business and profits. A study by Nucleus Research (2012) showed that 80% of expected CRM returns are yet to be achieved. These failure rates and lack of key success factors in organisations implementing CRM remain poorly conceptualised and understood. Work with CRM organisations has demonstrated that the indicators of organisations' CRM performance can be developed through a number of factors, such as strategic emphasis, technology and integration of market knowledge. To achieve effective results, firms must combine the richness of information with the rigour of organisational learning and subsequent strategic implementation. However, studies have also revealed implementation pitfalls, or a dark side, leading to failure. These stem from a number of areas, including relationship conflicts, opportunism, dependence and relationship asymmetry (John, 1984; Meunier-FitzHug et al., 2011; Zhou et al., 2007). Few studies have adapted organisational-level research to examine how organisational capabilities can influence firms' pursuit in overcoming the darker side of CRM (Villena et al., 2011).

The purpose of this chapter is to explore how this CRM paradigm – using knowledge and learning approaches – might be adapted to the needs of firms adopting CRM. By employing experiential learning theory, the chapter aims to explain an approach to overcome the dark side of CRM, with the concept of learning behaviour arising from failure, in order to improve firms' CRM performance.

Learning objectives

When you have read the chapter, you should be able to:

1. Describe various CRM implementation pitfalls and the dark side to the organisational management of CRM.
2. Understand how to overcome the dark side with key success factors for implementing CRM, especially those arising from the learning process of previous failures.
3. Determine the distinctive characteristics that can be identified in the key success factors in CRM as highlighted by knowledge management and learning behavioural theories.
4. Highlight the role played by failure in the development of key success factors based on indicators arising from learning behaviour from failure.
5. Offer advice on the benefits or outcomes – such as long-term customer relationships and partnerships – that can be attributed to the CRM learning development process.

2 Route map

Over the past decade, considerable evidence has emerged showing that CRM initiatives are often unsuccessful. For example, Zablah et al. (2004) cite five studies of unsuccessful CRM, with failure rates ranging from 35% to 75%. Frow et al. (2011) report that there are extensive examples of CRM's under-delivery (Osmond and Wood, 2003; Raman et al., 2006; Foss et al., 2008) and undermining of customer relationships (e.g. Colgate and Danaher, 2000). Krigsman (2009) provides a comprehensive summary of CRM failure rates from 2001 to 2009, identifying studies where failure rates range from 50% in 2001 (Gartner Group, 2001, cited in Frow et al., 2011) to 47% in 2009 (Forrester Research, 2009). Clearly, many CRM projects are still failing to deliver the desired results.

Researchers agree that CRM failure cannot be attributed to any one factor, but some common reasons for the poor results of CRM initiatives are evident (Payne and Frow, 2006). Researchers have investigated reasons for the failure of CRM, including quality of data (Abbott et al., 2001), project management skills (Ebner et al., 2002) and technological skills (Croteau and Li, 2003). Other researchers have considered strategic aspects of CRM implementation (Foss et al. 2008; Boulding et al., 2005).

According to Payne and Frow (2006), a substantial amount of CRM failure can be attributed to a lack of clarity regarding what CRM encompasses, which may result in suppliers exploiting customers, mistaking tactically orientated customer management for CRM. Similarly, Reinartz et al. (2004) highlight a severe lack of CRM research that takes a broader and more strategic focus. Thakur et al. (2006) conclude that the absence of a strategic orientation is the chief reason for CRM failures, and that many operationalisations of CRM continue to reflect a tactical rather than a strategic nature (Frow et al., 2011).

This chapter aims to summarise the CRM dark side from the management perspective and explore how organisations can overcome the dark side of CRM by linking varying CRM aspects with the concept of learning behaviour from failure. The outcome of successfully overcoming the dark sides may result in the stimulation of long-term relationships. This chapter thus suggests that the CRM concept has potential to survive and regain its success despite its failings to date, extending the relationship marketing theories. We will reflect on our exploration and implications for CRM, marketing and management, providing implications for the future of CRM strategy.

The first section of this chapter explains the relevance and importance of CRM and its dark side as a research topic. It then addresses the theoretical background regarding the CRM pitfalls and dark side by drawing on the literature on relationship management. The chapter goes on to discuss the primary focus, which is the influence of learning from failure behaviour. This section will also present the theoretical background to failure theory. The chapter next explores CRM recovery from failure. Finally, new research directions related to CRM and learning behaviour from failure are suggested. A case study is provided to illustrate the chapter's broad topics.

3 State of the art in CRM and learning behaviour from failure

CRM is the 'purposive use of customer knowledge and technologies to help firms generate customised offerings on an individual basis, based on fairness and trust, in order to enhance and maintain quality relationships with all the involved parties' (Nguyen and Mutum, 2012, p. 413). CRM is a concept that integrates market knowledge and disseminates knowledge into an organisation, creating a coherent and fast-moving unit that responds rapidly to the needs of the markets. CRM is today considered the forefront of marketing thinking and a key battlefield to gaining sustainable competitive advantage. Due to its all-inclusive nature, CRM encompasses several fields including management, information systems, marketing and strategy.

However, there is a lack of research that examines how the roles of organisational capabilities and micro-environmental factors influence firms' pursuit of successful CRM strategies (Bruton et al., 2010). This represents a gap requiring examination of organisational capabilities and outcomes that influence the management of CRM (Lubatkin et al., 2006; Teece et al., 1997). To date, there have been limited empirical studies in understanding how to overcome these pitfall areas of CRM and reverting this 'dark side' into key factors for success in CRM implementation. Little is known about how CRM pitfalls damage the organisation and how firms and policy makers are able to learn from failures caused by such damaging practices. Existing studies primarily focus on general CRM applications, which is insufficient and often outdated in this fast-changing environment.

In this chapter, we aim to improve our understanding of CRM pitfalls by integrating CRM with learning behaviour from failure. Previous research has identified

CRM as a key enabler of long-term relationships through four CRM aspects: strategic orientation, market (customer-centric) orientation, internal marketing and knowledge management. We identify, as supported by previous work (e.g. Boisot and Child, 1996), that learning behaviour from failure is particularly important for firms using CRM.

Scholars suggest that learning from failure provides unique knowledge from past experiences and aids in improving resources, processes, technologies and market information (e.g. Li and Zhang, 2007). These are critical elements for firms' CRM (Bardhan et al., 2008; Peng and Luo, 2000), yet, in the context of CRM, learning from failure is little researched. For example, since innovation is a high-risk and resource-consuming activity, improved learning abilities provide organisational support to help firms reduce the adverse effects of inadequate infrastructure, often found in firms with failed CRM implementation (Smith et al., 2009; Xin and Pearce, 1996). Thus, firms' CRM is enhanced when they have the ability to learn from failure, as the resources are improved by using existing knowledge (Li et al., 2012; Tsang, 1998).

This chapter highlights four aspects of CRM critical to improving the effects of learning behaviour from failure, as these CRM aspects transform certain kinds of information and resources, so improving firms' internal competitive advantage. This in turn gives the firms the ability to utilise both their social capital and knowledge management to gain full potential of learning from failure, which subsequently facilitates favourable firm performance such as innovation and long-term customer relationships.

CRM and its dark side

The growing interest in CRM lies in the belief that customer data provide an essential source for delivering and customising offerings that meet customers' needs better than the competition, over a prolonged mutually beneficial relationship between the firm or brand and its priority customers. Building relationships enables firms to learn what customers want through continuous interaction, increasing customer intimacy and loyalty intentions. Firms find ways to add value such that customers, as well as businesses operating in those markets, gain from increased competencies and skills, often referred to as 'win-win' situations (Payne and Frow, 2006). These value added skills contribute a coherent CRM strategy, reflecting management, operations, distribution and marketing, providing an opportunity for increased innovation and efficiency. In turn, this generates a significant future income stream, such as cross-sales and up-selling, eventually leading to sustainable competitive advantage. However, scholars increasingly find that there are challenges attached to these practices and to the behaviours of management deploying CRM.

According to Abosag, Yen and Barnes (2014), the limited literature on the dark side of managing relationships follows two different approaches. The first group of studies reports on negative relationship constructs, such as conflict and opportunism

(Gaski, 1984; John, 1984). Studies in this area have predominantly focused on conflict in relation to other areas, such as value co-creation, cooperation, dependence and competitiveness (Meunier-FitzHug et al., 2011; Zhou et al., 2007). Despite the modest increase in understanding business conflict (Skarmeas, 2006; Massey and Dawes, 2007; Finch et al., 2013), the conceptual and empirical examination of uncertainty, opportunism and tension has continued to remain somewhat neglected (Abosag et al., 2014). The second group of studies focuses on the dark or negative side of relationships, with specific reference to the development of relationships over time (Moorman et al., 1992). Grayson and Ambler (1999) and Barnes (2005) discovered in a dyadic context that some negativity is more likely to occur in medium-term rather than long-term relationships, as some degree of complacency creeps in to such relationships. Research examining the dark side of relationships is scant and very little has been concluded on how such effects can influence future relationship dynamics.

In this chapter, we identify two areas of the dark side: upstream and downstream CRM pitfalls. Downstream CRM pitfalls refer to CRM from a marketing perspective, incorporating the misuse of customer data, for instance, to extract customer surplus (Frow et al., 2011). Upstream CRM pitfalls describe the lack of market knowledge and inconsistency in the implementation of CRM within the organisation, causing high rates of failure. As an example of this inconsistency between various organisational departments, we find that the discourse on CRM has produced a rich and diverse set of meanings, causing greater challenges for those implementing the scheme.

There is confusion about what constitutes CRM, which creates a significant problem for adopting it (for more, see Reinartz et al., 2004; Payne and Frow, 2005; Harker and Egan, 2006). On the other hand, many CRM definitions reflect the multifaceted nature of the scheme itself (Buttle, 1996). Despite the lack of consensus in the literature on a definition, as CRM increases in exposure, a growing number of scholars emphasise the need for a holistic approach in order to create a consistent ethos across the organisation (Srivastava et al., 1998; Payne, 2001; Hart et al., 2003). With a clear definition of CRM, it may be possible to overcome the dark side related to inconsistent implementation.

Boulding et al. (2005) have proposed a convergence of CRM on a common definition. According to Boulding et al. (2005), CRM is no longer a customer-focused orientation, but rather an integration of all relationships (e.g. with suppliers and influencers). CRM is the use of systems to collect and analyse data across the firm, linking the firm and customer value along the value chain, in order to develop capabilities to integrate these activities across the firm's network so as to generate customer value, while creating shareholder value. Specifically:

> CRM relates to strategy, the management of the dual creation of value, the intelligent use of data and technology, the acquisition of customer knowledge and the diffusion of this knowledge to the appropriate stakeholders, the development of appropriate (long-term) relationships with specific

customers and/or customer groups, and the integration of processes across the many areas of the firm and across the network of firms that collaborate to generate customer value.

(Boulding et al., 2005, p. 157)

The key elements that CRM emphasises are factors such as the individual-level treatment of key stakeholders, use of data and knowledge and personalisation/ customisation of offerings. The process of partnering with customers and changing/ modifying activities internal to the organisation is also a key trait of CRM (Payne and Frow, 2006; Peppers and Rogers, 2004). Boulding et al.'s (2005) integrated approach to CRM covers two major aspects, which are relevant to learning from failure – namely, the intelligent use of data and technology inside the organisation, and the focus on long-term relationships. Coupled with the notion of maintaining and enhancing relationships, these aspects are pivotal to a firm's CRM offerings, which are the focal point to develop behaviour that can learn from previous failures.

CRM pitfalls and failures

Various studies show, despite all the benefits of CRM, that high rates of CRM failure are in evidence (Nucleus Research, 2012; Prezant, 2013; Rigby et al., 2002). According to Prezant (2013), the CRM failure rate is approximately 35% to 63%, yet, despite such high rates, organisations fail to conduct post-mortems of projects, missing out on the opportunity to learn from their mistakes (Shepherd and Cardon, 2009). When analysing the return on investment of a CRM strategy, some researchers have obtained contradictory results: these seem to vary, both within and between organisations (Bohling et al., 2006). In order to identify and verify what actionable factors are critical to the successful outcome of CRM initiatives, a significant body of research has emerged in the last decade (e.g. Sin et al., 2005).

For example, scholars note that, as over the past decades more advanced CRM schemes have developed, accompanying technologies have been a one-sided development for the benefit of firms. These firms are progressively extracting customer surplus and neglecting the key premise of CRM, which is to create a process of dual value, both for the customers and for the organisation. Public concerns are often directed towards firms' use of customer-tracking systems, both considered necessary to gain market knowledge, but also perceived to induce information mishandling and discrimination of certain customers. This 'dark side' of CRM links with unethical firm behaviour, including manipulation, neglect and unfairness, which are damaging firms' brand reputation.

The two areas of concern, namely upstream and downstream CRM pitfalls, warrant more attention in order for CRM to regain its position at the forefront of marketing and management. From analysis of extant research, it is observed that among the most cited key factors for success in CRM are strategic orientation, technology and organisational factors, including market orientation, knowledge management and internal marketing processes. In this relationship, we suggest that firms adopting CRM should not abandon their efforts, but rather continue to overcome the damage caused by these pitfalls. We propose that firms need to learn from their past failures, as such awareness may provide a source of knowledge unique to the organisation. We thus include in our framework the construct 'learning behaviour from failure'.

Defining failure

There is a challenge in defining failure and a current lack of clarity surrounding its definition, because, while some outcomes can be unambiguously classed as failures or successes, others fall into a grey zone of near-failure or near-success (Rerup, 2005; Ucbasaran et al., 2010). In addition, the challenge is that failure can be defined using both objective and subjective criteria, and at varying levels, including firm, project or individual/personal levels (e.g. Cardon et al., 2011; McGrath, 1999; Singh et al., 2007). Jenkins (2012) suggests in the context of entrepreneurship that three definitions of failure dominate the literature: objective financial criteria; the subjective assessment of alternative options; and personal failure.

Financial criteria

Research suggests that the definition of failure should be focused on firm-level financial criteria (Shepherd, 2003; Shepherd and Wiklund, 2006; Shepherd et al., 2000), as determining failure based on the result of poor performance is measureable. Historically, firm failure was studied and viewed as synonymous with firm exit (Shepherd and Wiklund, 2006). However, researchers have since noted that this does not capture the variance in firm performance when they exit (Headd, 2003; Wennberg et al., 2010). For example, many firms exit for other reasons than failure, such as the owner's retirement, merger and acquisition, or pursuing other strategic opportunities (Headd, 2003; Watson and Everett, 1996). Exit alone should not be considered failure (Davidsson, 2008; Shepherd and Wiklund, 2006; Wennberg, 2009). Thus, to distinguish failure from the phenomenon of exit, researchers suggest that insolvency be used to define financial failure (Shepherd, 2003; Shepherd and Wiklund, 2006; Shepherd et al., 2000). That is, as Jenkins (2012) notes, failure occurs when a reduction in revenues and/or a rise in expenses are of such a magnitude that the firm becomes insolvent and is unable to attract new debt or equity funding. As a consequence, the firm cannot continue to operate under the current ownership and management (Shepherd, 2003).

The subjective assessment of alternative options

The definitions of failure that focus on the subjective assessment of alternative options are based on the perceptions of the firm's performance relative to a benchmark or predetermined goal. McGrath (1999, p. 14) defines subjective failure as the 'termination of an initiative that has fallen short of its goals', which is also considered one of the most commonly used definitions. Ucbasaran et al. (2013, p. 26) define business failure in the context of entrepreneurship as the 'cessation of involvement in a venture because it has not met a minimum threshold for economic viability as stipulated by the (founding) entrepreneur'. Gimeno et al.'s (1997) threshold performance theory underlies these definitions, suggesting that a firm's human capital influences the minimum performance level it is willing to accept (McGrath, 1999). If performance falls below the minimum level, the exit route is likely to occur. For example, Jenkins (2012) states that entrepreneurs with high levels of human capital are likely to have higher threshold levels given the more attractive alternative uses for their human capital. Given the same level of performance, this implies that one entrepreneur may view the firm as being successful while another may view the same firm as unsuccessful (Gimeno et al., 1997).

Personal failure

Although personal failure is not explicitly stated as the definition of failure, Jenkins (2012) notes that it is implicitly mentioned in the sampling frame of previous studies of failure. For example, when operationalising failure, Cope (2011) identifies respondents based on their potential to learn from the experience of failure, and focuses on the impact failure has had on their lives. Whyley (1998) included only entrepreneurs who had suffered financially as a consequence of the failure. This does not mean that the failure construct is only applicable to such a scenario. Indeed, the advantage of using the personal definition of failure is on the *consequences* of failure, meaning that other scenarios involving individuals can make use of aspects pertaining to recovery (consequence). Jenkins (2012) suggests that many of the issues relating to the difficulties of coping with failure and recovering from failure can be identified. Hence, when investigating the negative impact failure can have on the well-being of a firm and individual, the definition is pertinent. Since CRM involves the relationships between individuals, understanding the way in which they deal with failure may lead to further insights into their ability to continue the pursuit of overcoming the dark side and regaining the CRM scheme.

In summary, in the research examining failure, a common theme is that failure can be an important source of learning, especially for entrepreneurs, but also for established CRM firms (Cope, 2003; Corbett et al., 2007; McGrath, 1999; Minniti and Bygrave, 2001; Shepherd, 2003). The interest in learning from failure stems from two inter-related reasons. First, one of the most common causes of failure, such as in the implementation of CRM, is lack of experience (Statistics Canada, 1997). Thus, the skills required for the success of CRM implementation can only be gained by actively engaging with it (Politis, 2005). This suggests that it is possible for firms to learn from failure (Shepherd, 2003; Stokes and Blackburn, 2002). Second, failure can be a rich source of feedback and information for firms about their decision making and its effectiveness (Minniti and Bygrave, 2001), which in turn can provide unique opportunities to gain knowledge that cannot be derived from success alone (Rerup, 2005). Thus, the lessons learned from past failures can be factored into future decision making, improving the likelihood of success in subsequent entrepreneurial endeavours (Cope, 2011; Jenkins, 2012; Jovanovic, 1982; Minniti and Bygrave, 2001).

Learning behaviour from failure

Unique to the study of CRM, we integrate the concept of learning from failure to our framework. Learning behaviour from failure is a dynamic process that involves the use of trial and error (Huber, 1991) to increase knowledge and understanding (Carmeli, 2007). Proactive organisational action is required to learn from failure, as it is a process by which knowledge is acquired and shared, leading to change and improvement (Tian et al., 2013). Learning behaviour from failure is regarded as a unique component of organisational learning (Carmeli, 2007) – a process that implies the movement of knowledge across different levels of action (Crossan et al., 1999). It permeates from the individual to group level, and then to the organisational level and back again (Huber, 1991). Such movement is also a characteristic of learning behaviour from failure, which refers to specific processes to help firms learn from failure by not merely detecting and correcting errors, but also by challenging and exploring their underlying causes (Carmeli, 2007).

With CRM, firms can identify and recognise a failure, stimulating the learning behaviours from such failure. Combined with the acquisition of market knowledge, CRM implementation and performance may be evidenced. Despite high rates of failure, organisations fail to learn from their past mistakes (Shepherd, 2009). Failure is a prospect for organisations to make adjustment and transformation (McGrath, 1999). Aspelund et al. (2005) find that some ventures do not have the capability to explain the obstacles to achieve success. Because of a lack of CRM experience, these ventures have difficulties in identifying failure and are, therefore, unable to learn from it (Shepherd, 2009). Knowledge acquisition – including technology and market knowledge – help the organisation evaluate and stimulate innovative behaviours, organisational targets and learn from failure (Dougherty, 1992; Moorman, 1995; Wang et al., 2009). For example, in acquiring technology knowledge service organisations receive a technological reference, facilitate innovative competencies and enhance their ability to evaluate new materials or production procedures for the CRM project (Shane and Eckhardt, 2003). This in turn stimulates organisations' learning behaviour from process failure in the CRM scheme. We expect that learning behaviour from failure influences a service firm's innovation efforts.

Learning behaviour from failure is a dynamic process involving the use of trial and error (Huber, 1991) to increase knowledge and understanding (Carmeli, 2007). Proactive organisational action is required to learn from failure, as it is a process by which knowledge is acquired and shared, leading to change and improvement (Tian et al., 2013). In the CRM context, we can focus on learning behaviour from failure, referring to specific processes that firms use to learn from failure by both detecting/correcting errors and exploring their underlying causes (Carmeli, 2007). Thus, with CRM, firms identify and recognise a failure, stimulating the learning behaviours from such failures. For firms, it is critical to identify errors and respond to these changes rapidly, so that they are able to commit resources and behaviours to new CRM projects (Shimizu and Hitt, 2004). Learning behaviour from failure implies that firms make strategic decisions more efficiently, and recognise a new business opportunity, threat possibility and maintain competitiveness. These firms use all four CRM processes to transfer acquired resources to firm-specific advantages (Bierly and Chakrabarti, 1996; Dannels, 2002), thus enhancing their strategic advantage.

Firms must be sensitive and maintain attention to constant feedback from dynamic markets (Nguyen and Mutum, 2012). A distinctive characteristic of successful CRM is its flexibility in response to the firm's rapid environmental changes, such as widespread market information, technological uncertainties and competitor activities (Banker et al., 2006; Li, 2012; Shimizu and Hitt, 2004; Yiu et al., 2007). Sanchez (1995) demonstrates that learning from failure depends on available resources. Chamberlain (1968) also points out that an organisation's learning capability is confined to the resources it owns and controls.

According to social capital theory, referring to any aspect of the social structure that creates value and facilitates individuals' actions (Coleman, 1990), one's personal network may affect one's value added behaviour in the organisation (Burt, 1992, 1997; Dubini and Aldrich, 1991; Ibarra, 1995). Social capital contributes to a firm's learning behaviour from failure, as it enables resource management – a defining aspect of such a capability (Blyler and Coff, 2003) – which provides essential information for a firm's resource integration (Cai et al., 2013). To identify and shape opportunities arising from failure, firms must constantly scan, search, explore and collect information about technologies and markets from both inside and outside (March and Simon, 1958; Nelson and Winter, 1982). We posit that firms with better ability to learn from failure enjoy better optimisation of critical technology and market information. These firms may benefit from such learning in a number of areas, including supplies to unique information, technology and support, further enhancing their CRM capability to respond proactively to internal changes (Leiponen, 2006; Tidd, 1995). However, the process of building such capability is also a trial and error process, especially for those firms that lack established affiliations or rich resources (Larson, 1991). Such trial and error may be costly, but, once resolved, the knowledge arising from the process can promote a firm's ability to learn proactively from failure, and identify and evaluate useful information needed for CRM success. In a turbulent environment, such ability supports the reallocation of resources at hand for further CRM activities (Verbruggen and Logan, 2009). However, in many organisations, trial and error runs against the culture and reward system (as a manager is usually rewarded for success, not for trial and error), making it both risky and difficult for these firms to adopt learning behaviour from failure.

In conclusion, Cope (2011) identifies four outcomes of learning from failure, including learning about oneself, the venture (and its demise), networks/relationships, and venture management (Jenkins, 2012; Singh et al. 2007; Stokes and Blackburn, 2002). In terms of learning about oneself, the lessons from failure can be important for developing resilience (Cope, 2011), which is the ability to rebound quickly after stressful encounters (Richardson, 2002). It also reduces over-confidence, giving the individual more realistic expectations about the likelihood of future success (Ucbasaran et al., 2010). Furthermore, specific learning outcomes related to the business failure and the experience of failure can lead to the re-evaluation of how a future business should be managed. For example, Stokes and Blackburn (2002) find that entrepreneurs learn about how they personally manage a business and how they cope with setbacks. Similarly, Cope (2011) finds that individuals are likely to rearrange their entire mental model in relation to how they view business management based on lessons learned from failure. Thus, failure can lead to higher-level learning, which in turn can lead to improved performance in subsequent endeavours (Cope, 2011; Jenkins, 2012).

Recovery from CRM failure

For organisations wanting to overcome the dark side of CRM, a willingness to take risks must be present. For example, these organisations must understand that failure is not the ultimate state and that there is unique knowledge arising from failure. Therefore, they must promote and possibly reward trial and error processes. At the management level, it is important to recognise that individuals must possess the sturdiness and ability to deal with failure. Only then will they be able to rise and learn from failure. Recent research deconstructs prior experience and focuses on how learning from past failure influences current performance (Rerup, 2005; Ucbasaran et al., 2010; Yamakawa et al., 2010). Rerup (2005) suggests that failure triggers mindful applications of past experience in new entrepreneurial ventures, which are characterised by frequent failures. In this context, being mindful is the individual's ability to learn how to modify past failure experiences in order to exploit this knowledge more effectively (Jenkins, 2012). Yamakawa et al. (2010) focus on the relationship between learning and performance, finding that when the individual blamed him- or herself for past failure, s/he was more likely to experience growth in the future. In other words, when an internal attribution process occurs, the individual looks back and considers what went wrong and how the situation might improve in the future (Yamakawa et al., 2010).

Ucbasaran et al. (2010) finds a similar relationship between prior failure experience and comparative optimism. For example, when a portfolio entrepreneur experienced failure because the firm did not meet expectations, he was more likely to express lower comparative optimism in comparison with novice and serial entrepreneurs (Jenkins, 2012). However, this was not apparent when either portfolio or serial entrepreneurs had experienced prior economic failure. Thus, when failure involves unmet expectations, they may be better at fostering learning than economic failure, consequently enhancing the reflection and mindfulness. The feeling of expectations not being met might trigger mindfulness and consideration of what went wrong and why to a greater extent than economic failure (Jenkins, 2012). It is possible that to create CRM success from the perspective of failure, a need exists to have individuals with an entrepreneurial mindset. This is something that requires further investigation and has direct implications on management's ability to recruit such individuals for the benefit of the CRM scheme.

Based on the above discussion, we propose that managers working with CRM need to emphasise understanding failure as felt by the individuals who are able to deal with failure. Researchers suggest that the way in which an individual copes with failure can influence the extent and speed of recovery (Shepherd, 2003; Singh et al., 2007). Shepherd (2003) proposes that oscillating between two alternative methods can result in faster recovery from failure of a project, including: a loss-orientation coping method, which involves confronting the failure and talking about feelings of grief with friends, family or psychologists; and a restoration coping method, which focuses on avoidance of the loss and on secondary sources of stress. This is similar to the emotion and problem-based coping framework suggested by Lazarus and Folkman (1984), which is used as a strategy for coping with failure (Singh et al., 2007).

Cope (2011) breaks down the recovery process into three distinct coping phases: avoidance, confrontation and moving on. Using in-depth case studies, he suggests an initial period of avoidance and stepping back from the failure, as this – similar to the *avoidance* component of the restoration coping strategy – can be important in overcoming the painful emotions associated with failure (Jenkins, 2012). Cope further suggests that *confronting* the failure can be important for accepting and learning from it. This is similar to the loss-orientation and emotion-focused coping strategies, where emotions from the failure are actively processed. Finally, to *move on* from the failure, it is important not to dwell in the confrontation stage. Jenkins (2012) notes that this is similar to the problem of coping and dealing with secondary sources of stress from the restoration coping strategy, where the individual actively takes steps to move on from the failure. Thus, to achieve positive outcomes for CRM failure, especially those opportunities arising from recovery and coping strategies, it is necessary that managers engage in a range of coping strategies to deal with the emotional and financial implications of failure.

This chapter has attempted to fill a gap by developing a more comprehensive theory of CRM, founded in the literature on how to overcome pitfalls and the dark side, expressed recently by academics as an area of great importance (Boulding et al., 2005; Nguyen and Simkin, 2012). This chapter incorporates an additional construct – learning behaviour from failure – to explore the opportunities for the CRM strategy so as to learn how to recover and exploit unique knowledge. It is hoped that new research will confirm the importance of including further constructs in the representation of CRM activities (i.e. the learning from failure construct), as this would create a better operationalisation of CRM, and would provide an explanation for the specific factors that could influence overcoming CRM pitfalls.

4 New research directions

Further studies are needed to explore the business failures in CRM and to consider the difficulties involved in defining and overcoming the CRM dark side and failures in order to regain success. Firms need to develop strategies aimed at maintaining key factors for success, by both overcoming upstream and downstream CRM pitfalls. In establishing these strategies, the literature reveals a number of constructs that can be used to enhance the success of a CRM strategy. These include CRM technology, organisational factors including internal marketing, market knowledge management and innovation processes. In this relationship, we suggest that firms adopting CRM should continue to overcome the damage caused by its dark side. We propose that firms learn from their past failures, which may provide a source of knowledge unique to the organisation. To the best of our knowledge, no studies have explored this relationship and there is little empirical evidence of the effectiveness of these activities in a CRM context.

Research that has empirically examined the pitfalls of CRM is significantly under-played. Further study should be developed to fill this gap by examining how the intra- and inter-organisational CRM dark side – which represents pitfalls at various levels – may influence the way in which an effective CRM strategy is implemented. It is proposed that some CRM aspects will be more important than others in affecting customers, management and stakeholders, due to their different levels of perception in each of the CRM strategies. Accordingly, certain areas may be more effective at overcoming upstream CRM pitfalls, whereas others may be more effective at overpowering downstream ones due to stakeholders' differential perceptions of the influence of CRM. In other words, the two groups may have varying levels of concern towards the different CRM efforts when dealing with a CRM scheme.

Current knowledge is limited in providing insights into the role of CRM as multiple predictors of strategic orientation, market orientation, internal marketing, market knowledge management, learning from failure and business processes in a single model. It is also unclear how the relationships of these factors are correlated in a high involvement context, such as during partnerships, joint ventures and alliances.

To determine the key factors for success in CRM, overcoming internal and external pitfalls could assist in developing a model that explains the way in which organisations can learn from past mistakes when implementing CRM. This literature review has identified aspects of organisational, management and marketing theories, which could be integrated into a CRM context. Further empirical evidence is needed to develop both the dark side study and failure theory further.

5 Practising marketing – a case study

Donnelly et al. (2014) suggest that there is something about experiencing a failure that takes an individual to unusual territory, open for self-exploration, learning and re-envisioning the problem. They note that people who seem particularly adept at learning from their mistakes are founders of small companies. Three examples of learning from failure and turning failure into success are presented.

Zipcar

Zipcar is the world leader in car-sharing, having created this industry in the United States. In 2000, Zipcar was launched with a bang, acquiring its first customer just moments after the website went live. Zipcar received favourable mentions from the Associated Press and on NPR after reporters saw the company's green Volkswagens touring around the Boston area (Donnelly et al., 2014). The company's plan was to lease cars, starting in Cambridge, MA, charging customers a monthly membership along with hourly or daily rates. However, just a few months after the company's launch, founder Robin Chase noticed that her calculations had been wrong: Zipcar was not charging enough to break even. She was left with little choice but to raise the rates.

When Zipcar had to send a notice to its early adopter members to let them know that rates would have to go up straight away, it was a turning point. The company was forthcoming about the miscalculation. Customers generally understood and accepted the reasoning. Even though Zipcar lost a handful of customers, these were soon replaced. The response to the fast pricing change was an early reinforcement that the company had already built Zipcar into a business with strong customer loyalty. The customers viewed Zipcar not only as a way to get around town, but also something that might approach a way of life (Donnelly et al., 2014). These customers were urban cost-conscious consumers who did not like the hassle of car ownership but who wanted the freedom to travel by automobile when they needed to.

Lessons were learned from the early mistakes and, in the process of building Zipcar, Robin Chase became a respected voice on transportation policy and the environment, speaking to think tanks about re-evaluating the entire position on transportation policy for the US government.

Fab.com

By late 2010, Jason Goldberg and Bradford Shellhammer had realised something devastating. Their one-year-old social networking start-up for the gay community, Fabulis.com, had plateaued at 150,000 users and showed no real signs of future growth (Donnelly et al., 2014). They realised that the failure was their fault. Instead of creating something innovative, they had spent their time trying to make the site the gay Facebook, then the gay Yelp, and even the gay Groupon. Shellhammer says that finally admitting their site was not a success gave the duo the confidence to start from scratch. He adds that admitting to utter failure gave them the confidence to go to their board and say, 'Hey, we have your money, but we want to do something completely different'. Once a rather dramatic pivot plan was in place, the duo shut down Fabulis. Three months later, in June

2011, it re-launched as Fab.com, a flash-sales site that sells indie designer home-wares, clothing and vintage items. Since the re-launch, Fab has seen stellar growth and, in July, the company raised $100 million – just seven months after raising $40 million in funding – putting it at a $600 million valuation. Fab says it now has close to 5 million members and plans to achieve $140 million in sales in roughly 20 countries (Donnelly et al., 2014).

Glassybaby

Glassybaby makes colourful hand-crafted candle holders. A venture created by Lee Rhodes, it has a unique business model in that it gives 10% of every sale to chari-table causes. However, that business model was not attractive to investors. Rhodes heard the same business advice from all sides – that manufacturing the candle holders in America and having a profitable business was not possible. Thus, the company outsourced to save money, ordering 150,000 Glassybaby votive holders from China.

Once the Chinese-made votives arrived, Rhodes opened a case, examined the product and then let the rest sit in the warehouse for nine months. They looked close enough in design to the original ones, but accuracy was not the problem, as Rhodes stated: 'I didn't know how to fit them into my story', she says. 'There was no authenticity to them whatsoever.' That authenticity was important as the company had billed itself as a caring purveyor of handmade goods that gave back as much as it could to the local community. Offering some Glassybabys made in China, and others made by local glassblowers, who get health insurance, did not make sense. As there was no opening in the story for the China-made Glassybabys, Rhodes ended up giving them away to hospitals at a loss of $150,000 to the business.

The outsourcing incident showed how important it was for Glassybaby to have a relatable story and to show that it was a company hoping to do more than make money. Rhodes stated that, 'It really cemented the idea that we are made in America', and that 'we support glassblowers'. For a company competing with much cheaper, similar products found in places like Pottery Barn, taking out the locally made angle diminished their story (Donnelly et al., 2014). At least some people have supported the message and not only has Glassybaby expanded to sev-eral cities, including New York City, but Amazon founder Jeff Bezos bought a 20% stake in the company after being impressed by its model. The company is expecting $8 million in sales this year, with plans to expand to San Francisco and elsewhere (Donnelly et al., 2014).

Discussion questions

1. Why were most customers so understanding of Zipcar's price change? What did Robin Chase do right in this case?
2. Do Jason Goldberg and Bradford Shellhammer embody the main characteristics of learning from failure? On what is their success built?

3.   What was the failure of Glassybaby and in what way did Lee Rhodes overcome the failure? What was her new strategy?
4.   In each of the cases, consider and explain from a management perspective how you would encourage the importance and benefits of learning behaviour from failure.

6 Further investigation

1.   What are the major steps that need to be implemented in order to develop an organisation that learns from failure?
2.   Develop an updated definition of CRM that incorporates learning behaviour from failure.
3.   Find examples of organisations that have a systematic emphasis on learning behaviour from failure. In which industries may learning behaviour from failure be more prevalent?
4.   What should be done to encourage organisations to manage more systematically learning behaviour from failure? What type of leadership is needed?
5.   Use an organisation value chain to look at each department and list all the pitfalls related to the upstream and downstream CRM dark side. How can each be avoided and improved upon?

References

Abbott, J., Stone, M. and Buttle, F. (2001). Customer relationship management in practice – a qualitative study. *Journal of Database Management*, 9(1), pp. 24–34.

Abosag, I., Yen, D.A. and Barnes, B.R. (2014). Call for papers: the dark side of business relationships: antecedents and consequences (15 December). www.journals.elsevier.com/industrial-marketing-management/calls-for-papers/call-for-papers-the-dark-side-of-business-relationships-ante/ (accessed 14 December 2014).

Aspelund, A., Berg-Utby, T. and Skjevdal, R. (2005). Initial resources' influence on new venture survival: A longitudinal study of new technology-based firms. *Technovation*, 25(11), pp. 1337–1347.

Banker, R.D., Kalvenes, J. and Patterson, R.A. (2006). Information technology, contract completeness and buyer-supplier relationships. *Information Systems Research*, 17(2), pp. 180–193.

Bardhan, I.R., Gupta, A. and Tallon, P. (2008). Research perspectives on innovation through information technology management in a networked world. *Information Technology Management*, 9(3), pp. 147–148.

Barnes, B.R. (2005). Is the seven-year hitch premature in industrial markets? *European Journal of Marketing*, 39(5/6), pp. 560–581.

Bierly, P.E. and Chakrabarti, A.K. (1996). Technological learning, strategic flexibility, and new product development in the pharmaceutical industry. *IEEE Transactions on Engineering Management*, 43(4), pp. 368–380.

Blyler, M. and Coff, R.W. (2003). Dynamic capabilities, social capital, and rent appropriation: ties that split pies. *Strategic Management Journal*, 24(7), pp. 677–686.

Bohling, T., Bowman, D., LaValle, S., Mittal, V., Narayandas, D. and Ramani, G. (2006). CRM implementation: effectiveness issues and insights. *Journal of Service Research*, 9(2), pp. 184–194.

Boisot, M. and Child, J. (1996). From fiefs to clans and network capitalism: explaining China's emerging economic order. *Administration Science Quarterly*, 41(4), pp. 600–628.

Boulding, W., Staelin, R., Ehret, M. and Johnston, W.J. (2005). A customer relationship management roadmap: what is known, potential pitfalls, and where to go. *Journal of Marketing*, 69(4), pp. 155–166.

Bruton, G.D., Ahlstrom, D. and Li, H.L. (2010). Institutional theory and entrepreneurship: where are we now and where do we need to move in the future? *Entrepreneurship Theory Practice*, 34(3), pp. 421–440.

Burt, R.S. (1992). *Structural Holes: The Social Structure of Competition*. Harvard University Press, Cambridge, MA.

Burt, R.S. (1997). The contingent value of social capital. *Administrative Science Quarterly*, 42(2), pp. 339–365.

Buttle, F. (1996). *Relationship Marketing Theory and Practice*. Paul Chapman, London.

Cai, L., Hughes, M. and Yin, M. (2013). The relationship between resource acquisition methods and firm performance in Chinese new ventures: the intermediate effect of learning capability. *Journal of Business Management*, doi: 10.1111/jsbm.12039.

Cardon, M.S., Stevens, C.E. and Potter, D.R. (2011). Misfortunes or mistakes?: cultural sensemaking of entrepreneurial failure. *Journal of Business Venturing*, 26, pp. 79–92.

CarmeliA. (2007). Social capital, psychological safety and learning behaviours from failure in organisation. *Long Range Planning*, 40(1), pp. 30–44.

Chamberlain, N.W. (1968). *Enterprise and Environment: The Firm in Time and Place*. McGraw-Hill.

Coleman, J.S. (1990). *Foundations of Social Theory*. Harvard University Press, Cambridge, MA.

Colgate, M.R. and Danaher, P.J. (2000). Implementing a customer relationship strategy: the asymmetric impact of poor versus excellent execution. *Journal of the Academy of Marketing Science*, 25(3), pp. 375–387.

Cope, J. (2003). Entrepreneurial learning and critical reflection: Discontinuous events as triggers for 'higher-level' learning. *Management Learning*, 34(4), pp. 429–450.

Cope, J. (2011). Entrepreneurial learning from failure: an interpretative phenomenological analysis. *Journal of Business Venturing*, 26(6), pp. 604–623.

Corbett, A., Neck, H., and De Tienne, D. (2007). How corporate entrepreneurs learn from fledgling innovation initiatives: cognition and the development of a termination script. *Entrepreneurship Theory and Practice*, 31(6), pp. 829–852.

Croteau, A. and Li, P. (2003). Critical success factors of CRM technological initiatives. *Canadian Journal of Administrative Sciences*, 20(1), pp. 21–34.

Dannels, E. (2002). The dynamics of product innovation and firm competence. *Strategic Management Journal*, 23(12), pp. 1095–1121.

Davidsson, P. (2008). *The Entrepreneurship Research Challenge*. Edward Elgar, Cheltenham, UK.

Donnelly, T., Carter, N. and Murphy, B. Jr (2014). 3 brilliant mistakes that built companies. www.inc.com/brilliant-failures/3-mistakes-that-built-companies.html (accessed 10 September 2014).

Dougherty, D. (1992). Interpretive barriers to successful product innovation in large firms. *Organization Science*, 3(2), pp. 179–202.

Dubini, P. and Aldrich, H.E. (1991). Personal and extended networks are central to the entrepreneurial process. *Journal of Business Venturing*, 6(5), pp. 305–313.

Ebner, M., Hu, A., Levitt, D. and McCrory, J. (2002). How to rescue CRM. *The McKinsey Quarterly*, 48.

Forrester Research (2009). Answers to five frequently asked questions about CKM projects. www.forrester.com/Research/Document/Excerpt/0.7211.46432.00.html.

Foss, B., Stone, M. and Ekinci, Y. (2008). What makes for CRM system success – or failure? *Journal of Database Marketing and Customer Strategy Management*, 15, pp. 68–78.

Frow, P., Payne, A., Wilkinson, I.F. and Young, L. (2011). Customer management and CRM: addressing the dark side. *Journal of Services Marketing*, 25(2), pp. 79–89.

Gartner Group (2001). *CRM Economics: Figuring out the ROI on Customer Initiatives*. Gartner Group, Stamford, CT.

Gaski, J.F. (1984). The effects of discrepant power perceptions in a marketing channel. *Psychology & Marketing*, 1, pp. 45–56. doi: 10.1002/mar.4220010306.

Gimeno, J., Folta, T.B., Cooper, A.C. and Woo, C.Y. (1997). Survival of the fittest? Entrepreneurial human capital and the persistence of underperforming firms. *Administrative Science Quarterly*, 42(2), pp. 750–783.

Harker, M.J. and Egan, J. (2006). The past, present, and future of relationship marketing. *Journal of Marketing and Management*, 22(1), pp. 215–242.

Hart, S., Hogg, G. and Banerjee, M. (2003). Does the level of experience have an effect on CRM programs? Exploratory research findings. *Journal of Industrial Marketing Management*, 33, pp. 549–560.

Headd, B. (2003). Redefining business success: Distinguishing between closure and failure. *Small Business Economics*, 21, pp. 51–61.

Huber, G.P. (1991). Organizational learning: the contributing processes and the literatures. *Organization Science*, 2(1), pp. 88–115.

Ibarra, H. (1995). Race, opportunity, and diversity in social circles in managerial networks. *Academy of Management Journal*, 38(3), pp. 673–703.

Jovanovic, B. (1982). Selection and the evolution of industry. *Econometrica* (pre-1986), 50(3), p. 649.

Jenkins, A. (2012). *After Firm Failure: Emotions, Learning, and Re-entry*. Doctoral dissertation, Jonkoping Business School. JIBS dissertation series No. 84 2012.

John, G. (1984). An empirical investigation of some antecedents of opportunism in a marketing channel. *Journal of Marketing Research*, 21(3), pp. 278–289.

Krigsman, M. (2009). CRM failure rates: 2001–2009. http://blogs.zdnet.com/projectfa ilures/?p.4967.

Larson, A. (1991). Partner networks: leveraging external ties to improve entrepreneurial performance. *Journal of Business Venturing*, 6(3), pp. 173–188.

Lazarus, R.S. and Folkman, S. (1984). *Stress Appraisal and Coping*. Springer Publishing Company, New York.

Leiponen, A. (2006). Managing knowledge for innovation: the case of business-to-business services. *Journal of Product Innovation Management*, 23(3), pp. 238–258.

Li, L. (2012). Effects of enterprise technology on supply chain collaborations: analysis of China-linked supply chain. *Enterprise Information Systems*, 6(1), pp. 55–77.

Li, H.Y. and Zhang, Y. (2007). The role of managers' political networking and functional experience in new firm performance: evidence from China's transition economy. *Strategic Management Journal*, 28(8), pp. 791–804.

Li, Y., Hou, M., Liu, H. and Liu, Y. (2012). Towards a theoretical framework of strategic decision, supporting capability and information sharing under the context of Internet of Things. *Information Technology and Management*, 13(4), pp. 205–216.

Lubatkin, M.H., Simsek, Z., Ling, Y. and Veiga, J.F. (2006). Ambidexterity and performance in small- to medium-sized firms: the pivotal role of top management team behavioural integration. *Journal of Management*, 32(5), pp. 646–672.

March, J.G. and Simon, H.A. (1958). *Organizations*. Wiley, New York.

Massey, G. and Dawes, P. (2007). The antecedents and consequence of functional and dysfunctional conflict between marketing managers and sales managers. *Industrial Marketing Management*, 36(8), pp. 1118–1128.

McGrath, R.G. (1999). Falling forward: real options reasoning and entrepreneurial failure. *Academy of Management Review*, 24(1), pp. 13–30.

Meunier-FitzHug, K., Massey, G. and Piercy, N. (2011). The impact of aligned rewards and senior manager attitudes on conflict and collaboration between sales and marketing. *Industrial Marketing Management*, 40(7), pp. 1161–1171.

Minniti, M. and Bygrave, W. (2001). A dynamic model of entrepreneurial learning. *Entrepreneurship Theory and Practice*, 25(3), pp. 5–16.

Moorman, C. (1995). Organizational market information processes: cultural antecedents and new product outcomes. *Journal of Marketing Research*, 32, pp. 318–335.

Moorman, C., Zaltman, G. and Deshpande, R. (1992). Relationships between providers and users of market research: the dynamics of trust within and between organizations. *Journal of Marketing Research*, 29(3), pp. 314–328.

Nelson, R.R. and Winter, S.G. (1982). *An Evolutionary Theory of Economic Change*. Harvard University Press, Cambridge, MA.

Nguyen, B. and Mutum, D.S. (2012). A review of customer relationship management: successes, advances, pitfalls and futures. *Business Process Management*, 18(3), pp. 400–419.

Nguyen, B. and Simkin, L. (2012). Fairness quality: the role of fairness in a social and ethically oriented marketing landscape. *The Marketing Review*, 12(4), pp. 333–344.

Nucleus Research (2012). *CRM: 80% of the Returns are Yet to be Achieved*. Research Note M132, Nucleus Research Inc.

Osmond, L. and Wood, A. (2003). *The Problem of CRM Under-delivery*. Total DM, UK.

Payne, A. (2001). Customer relationship management. Keynote address to the inaugural meeting of the Customer Management Foundation, London.

Payne, A. and Frow, P. (2005). A strategic framework for customer relationship management. *Journal of Marketing*, 69(4), pp. 167–176.

Payne, A. and Frow, P. (2006). Customer relationship management: from strategy to implementation. *Journal of Marketing Management*, 22(1–2), pp. 135–168.

Peng, M.W. and Luo, Y. (2000). Managerial ties and firm performance in a transition economy: the nature of a micro-macro link. *Academy of Management Journal*, 43(3), pp. 486–501.

Peppers, D. and Rogers, M. (2004). *Managing Customer Relationships – A Strategic Framework*. John Wiley and Sons, New Jersey.

Peppers, D., Rogers, M. and Dorf, B. (1999). Is your company ready for one-to-one marketing? *Harvard Business Review*, 77 (January–February), pp. 151–160.

Politis, D. (2005). The process of entrepreneurial learning: A conceptual framework. *Entrepreneurship Theory and Practice*, 29(4), pp. 399–424.

Prezant, J. (2013). 63% of CRM initiatives fail. *Direct Marketing News*. www.dmnews.com/63-of-crm-initiatives-fail/article/303470/ (accessed 14 December 2014).

Raman, P., Wittmann, C. and Rauseo, N. (2006). Leveraging CRM for sales: the role of organizational capabilities in successful CRM implementation. *Journal of Personal Selling and Sales Management*, 26(1), pp. 39–53.

Reinartz, W., Krafft, M. and Hoyer, W.D. (2004). The customer relationship management process: its measurements and impact on performance. *Journal of Marketing Research*, 41 (August), pp. 293–305.

Rerup, C. (2005). Learning from past experience: footnotes on mindfulness and habitual entrepreneurship. *Scandinavian Journal of Management*, 21, pp. 451–472.

Richardson, G.E. (2002). The metatheory of resilience and resiliency. *Journal of Clinical Psychology*, 58(3), pp. 307–321.

Rigby, D.K., Reichheld, F.F. and Schefter, P. (2002). Avoid the four perils of CRM. *Harvard Business Review*, 80 (February), pp. 101–109.

Sanchez, R. (1995). Strategic flexibility in product competition. *Strategic Management Journal*, 16(1), pp. 135–159.

Shane, S. and Eckhardt, J. (2003). 'The individual-opportunity nexus'. In Z.J. Acs and D. Audretsch (Eds) *Handbook of Entrepreneurship Research*, pp. 161–194, Kluwer, Boston.

Shepherd, D.A. (2003). Learning from business failure: Propositions about the grief recovery process for the self-employed. *Academy of Management Review*, 282, pp. 318–329.

Shepherd, D.A. (2009). Grief recovery from the loss of a family business: a multi- and meso-level theory. *Journal of Business Venturing*, 24(1), pp. 81–97.

Shepherd, D.A. and Cardon, M.S. (2009). Negative emotional reactions to project failure and the self-compassion to learn from the experience. *Journal of Management Studies*, 46(6), pp. 923–949.

Shepherd, D.A., Douglas, E.J. and Shanley, M. (2000). New venture survival: ignorance, external shocks, and risk reduction strategies. *Journal of Business Venturing*, 15(5–6), pp. 393–410.

Shepherd, D.A. and Wiklund, J. (2006). Successes and failures at research on business failure and learning from it. *Foundations and Trends in Entrepreneurship*, 2(5).

Shimizu, K. and Hitt, M.A. (2004). Strategic flexibility: organizational preparedness to reverse ineffective strategic decisions. *Academy of Management Executive*, 18(4), pp. 44–59.

Sin, L.Y.M., Tse, A.C.B. and Yim, F.H.K. (2005). CRM: conceptualisation and scale development. *European Journal of Marketing*, 39(11/12), pp. 1264–1290.

Singh, S., Corner, P. and Pavlovich, K. (2007). Coping with entrepreneurial failure. *Journal of Management and Organization*, 13, pp. 331–344.

Skarmeas, D. (2006). The role of functional conflict in international buyer-seller relationships: implications for industrial exporters. *Industrial Marketing Management*, 35(5), pp. 567–575.

Smith, M., Giraud-Carrier, C. and Purser, N. (2009). Implicit affinity networks and social capital. *Information Technology and Management*, 10(2–3), pp. 123–134.

Srivastava, R.K., Shervani, T. and Fahey, L. (1998). Market-based assets and shareholder value: A framework for analysis. *Journal of Marketing*, 62 (January), pp. 2–18.

Statistics Canada (1997). *Failing Concerns: Business Bankruptcy in Canada*. Micro-Economics Analysis Division, Statistics Canada, Ottawa.

Stokes, D. and Blackburn, R. (2002). Learning the hard way. *Journal of Small Business and Enterprise Development*, 9(1), pp. 17–27.

Teece, D.J., Pisano, G. and Shuen, A. (1997). Dynamic capabilities and strategic management. *Strategic Management Journal*, 18(7), pp. 537–556.

Thakur, R., Summey, J.H. and Balasubramanian, S.K. (2006). CRM as strategy: avoiding the pitfall of tactics. *Marketing Management*, 16(2), pp. 147–154.

Tian, Y., Li, Y. and Wei, Z. (2013). Managerial incentive and external knowledge acquisition under technological uncertainty: a nested system perspective. *Systems Research and Behavioural Science*, 30(3), pp. 214–228.

Tidd, J. (1995). Development of novel product through intraorganizational and inter-organizational networks. *Journal of Product Innovation Management*, 12(4), pp. 307–322.

Tsang, E.W.K. (1998). Can guanxi be a source of sustained competitive advantage for doing business in China? *Academy of Management Executive*, 12(2), pp. 64–73.

Ucbasaran, D., Shepherd, D.A., Lockett, A. and Lyon, S.J. (2013). Life after business failure: the process and consequences of business failure for entrepreneurs. *Journal of Management*, 39(1), pp. 163–202.

Ucbasaran, D., Westhead, P., Wright, M. and Flores, M. (2010). The nature of entrepreneurial experience, business failure and comparative optimism. *Journal of Business Venturing*, 25(6), pp. 541–555.

Verbruggen, F. and Logan, G.D. (2009). Proactive adjustments of response strategies in the stop-signal paradigm. *Journal of Experimental Psychology. Human Perception and Performance*, 35(3), pp. 835–854.

Villena, V., Revilla, E. and Choi, T. (2011). The dark side of buyer-supplier relationships: a social capital perspective. *Journal of Operations Management*, 29(6), pp. 561–576.

Wang, L., Xu, L., Wang, X., You, W. and Tan, W. (2009). Knowledge portal construction and resources integration for a large scale hydropower dam. *Systems Research and Behavioural Science*, 26(3), pp. 357–366.

Watson, J. and Everett, J.E. (1996). Do small businesses have high failure rates? Evidence from Australian retailers. *Journal of Small Business Management*, 34.

Wennberg, K. (2009). *Entrepreneurial Exit*. Stockholm School of Economics, Stockholm.

Wennberg, K., Wiklund, J., DeTienne, D.R. and Cardon, M.S. (2010). Reconceptualising entrepreneurial exit: divergent exit routes and their drivers. *Journal of Business Venturing*, 25(4), pp. 367–375.

Whyley, C. (1998). *Risky Business: The Personal and Financial Costs of Small Business Failure*. Policy Studies Institute, Westminster.

Wind, Y. (1982). *Product Policy: Concepts, Methods, and Strategy*. Addison Wesley Pub. Co., Reading, MA.

Xin, K.R. and Pearce, J.L. (1996). Guanxi: connections as substitutes for formal institutional support. *Academy of Management Journal*, 39(6), pp. 1641–1658.

Yamakawa, Y., Peng, M.W. and Deeds, D.L. (2010). Revitalising and learning from failure for future entrepreneurial growth. *Frontiers of Entrepreneurship Research*, 30(6), p. 1.

Yiu, D.W., Lau, C.M. and Bruton, G.D. (2007). International venturing by emerging economy firms: the effects of firm capabilities, home country networks, and corporate entrepreneurship. *Journal of International Business Studies*, 38(4), pp. 519–540.

Zablah, A.R., Bellenger, D.N. and Johnston, W.J. (2004). Customer relationship management implementation gaps. *Journal of Personal Selling and Sales Management*, 24(4), pp. 279–295.

Zhou, N., Zhuang, G. and Yip, L. (2007). Perceptual difference of dependence and its impact on conflict in marketing channels in China: an empirical study with two-sided data. *Industrial Marketing Management*, 36(3), pp. 309–321.

Further reading

Aiman-Smith, L. and Green, S.G. (2002). Implementing new manufacturing technology: The related effects of technology characteristics and user learning activities, *Academy of Management Journal*, 45(2), pp. 421–430.

Anderson, E. and Jap, S.D. (2005). The dark side of close relationships. *MIT Sloan Management Review*, 46(3), pp. 75–82.

Bohling, T., Bowman, D., LaValle, S., Mittal, V., Narayandas, D. and Ramani, G. (2006). CRM implementation: effectiveness issues and insights. *Journal of Service Research*, 9(2), pp. 184–194.

Chang, W., Park, J.E. and Chaiy, S. (2010). How CRM technology transforms into organizational performance: the mediating role of marketing capability. *Journal of Business Research*, 64(8), pp. 849–855.

Crossan, M.M., Lane, H.W. and White, R.E. (1999). An organisational learning framework: from intuition to institution. *Academy of Management Review*, 24(3), pp. 522–537.

Finch, J., Zhang, S. and Geiger, S. (2013). Managing in conflict: how actors distribute conflict in an industrial network. *Industrial Marketing Management*, available since 16 August.

Grayson, K. and Ambler, T. (1999). The dark side of long-term relationships in marketing services. *Journal of Marketing Research*, 36(1) (February), pp. 132–141.

King, F.S. and Burgess, F.T. (2007). Understanding success and failure in customer relationship management. *Industrial Marketing Management*, 37(4), pp. 421–431.

Kolb, D., Boyatzis, R.E. and Mainemelis, C. (2001). Experiential learning theory: previous research and new directions. *Perspectives on Thinking, Learning, and Cognitive Styles*, 1, pp. 227–247.

Nguyen, B. (2011). The dark side of CRM. *The Marketing Review*, 11(2), pp. 137–149.

Nguyen, B., Klaus, P. and Simkin, L. (2014). It's just not fair: Exploring the effects of firm customisation on unfairness perceptions, loyalty, and trust, *Journal of Services Marketing*, 28(6), pp. 484–497.

Rapp, A., Trainor, K.J. and Agnihotri, R. (2010). Performance implications of customer-linking capabilities: Examining the complementary role of customer orientation and CRM technology. *Journal of Business Research*, 63, pp. 1229–1236.

Yu, X., Chen, Y. and Nguyen, B. (2014). Knowledge management, learning behaviour from failure, and new product development in new technology ventures. *Systems Research and Behavioural Science*, 31(3), pp. 405–423.

12

THE DARK SIDE: CUSTOMERS VERSUS COMPANIES

Liz Machtynger, Martin Hickley, Merlin Stone and Paul Laughlin

1 Introduction

We live in a data-rich world, a world in which the actions and even the thoughts of individuals – whether as customers or as people who work in the public and private sector companies that supply them – are visible to others. In a digital age, data that reveal actions, choices and thoughts have extended beyond the classic customer relationship management (CRM) data of transactions, responses, demography and geography, into the social world of commentary and opinion of individuals and groups.

This means that it should be much easier for customers and companies to assess how they are likely to behave towards each other, what kind of fit they are likely to be for each other, and whether they are likely to be 'good' or 'bad' for each other.

This chapter probes this issue in depth. We examine first the issue of good and bad customers, followed by that of good and bad companies. Of course, the two are related, as we shall see. Bad companies can cause bad behaviour in customers and vice versa. Good companies can encourage customers to be good, while good customers can encourage the formation and success of good companies. This subject is often discussed within companies and referred to, though not in the same language, by customers.

The reader will note that there is a strong financial services flavour to this chapter. The main reason for this is because the financial 'bad customer' can do enormous damage to the good supplier, and the financial 'bad supplier' can – as we have experienced in the last few years – do massive damage to many good customers. These issues are not unique to this sector of course. The same patterns of behaviour are visible in many sectors.

Defining good and bad

In this chapter, 'good' and 'bad' are defined mainly according to the supplier's objectives, rather than morally. However, there may be a correlation between the supplier-focused and moral definitions. We considered using the term 'desirable' and 'undesirable', but these words have moral and emotional connotations.

'Good' and 'bad' customer profiles differ by supplier and industry sector. In some cases, it involves illegal behaviour. For example, an illegal bad customer in general insurance may be one who 'expands' a claim (i.e. where the general claim is legitimate, but additional items are added to the claim that are not legitimate). In utilities, a bad customer may be one who tampers with an electricity or gas meter in order to avoid paying for what has been used. In telecommunications, it involves use of network time with no intention to pay. In retailing, a bad customer may be a shoplifter. In the market for holidays, a bad customer may be one who advertises a holiday on the Internet, using the services of a holiday booking website, and then does not provide the holiday (in which case the person becomes a bad supplier to the final consumer). In tax and benefits, it is a citizen who claims for payments to which s/he is not entitled. In all these cases, the action is illegal.

From the point of view of a supplier, bad customers may simply be ones who create a lot of problems for a company; for example, by being a persistent complainer, or by finding clever but legal ways to extract more value from a company without paying for it (e.g. by exploiting a promise to match the best price by searching intensively for a very low price available elsewhere), or by threatening repeatedly to take their business elsewhere unless a subscription is price discounted.

Similarly, from the customer's point of view, a bad company may be fraudulent, by taking payment with no intention to supply, or simply disingenuous, by making promises of quality or conditions of supply that it does not observe, while ensuring that it stays on the right side of the law (though consumer protection and trading legislation is generally becoming much better at making such practices illegal).

Note that whether a given customer is good or bad is determined not just by the individual's underlying characteristics, but is also affected by what the supplier does to the individual via product definition, price, distribution and communication, and how it manages individual customers. Understanding this may be central to the process of product or service definition or marketing communications. A good starting point for marketing managers is the saying, 'You get the customers you deserve'.

Typically, when defining 'good' and 'bad', organisations use indicators that are unlinked to a moral position but based on 'objective' data they have about the customer – e.g. whether a customer has required a very high level of customer service relative to what they have paid.

There are areas where there is no connection with moral issues. For example, some commercial risks relate to the gender of the individual (men live shorter lives and generally are less safe drivers; each gender is more at risk from particular diseases). Companies, particularly insurers, want to take gender into account, but this may be deemed politically unacceptable and now in some countries – such as the UK – has been made illegal, even though some risks vary significantly by gender and this results in low-risk customers paying more for their insurance. In the UK, banks cannot use gender as an indicator to score loans, nor can insurers use gender to discriminate on premiums or terms.

Learning objectives

When you have read the chapter, you should be able to:

1. Understand how the concept of good and bad customers and companies can be applied to different industries.
2. Identify how the existence of significant numbers of bad companies or customers may change best practice in relation to CRM, from the point of view of both customers and companies.

2 Route map

This chapter starts by exploring the definition of good and bad as applied to customers and companies. It then considers the issue posed by the existence of significant numbers of bad customers for companies that are trying to develop policies to improve their management of good customers, including forecasting changes of state from good to bad or vice versa. It then considers how companies may identify which customers should be treated with which initiatives, in order to defend the company from bad customers, and concludes with a series of recommendations as to how to manage bad customers.

This chapter builds on the work of the authors in analysing how companies manage customers and how they should manage them (Stone et al., 2002). In conventional CRM theory as articulated in this work, the term 'customer value' is considered to capture the idea that a customer may be bad and so of negative value. However, CRM theory does not generally consider how to manage this situation, except in considering the issue of trust, which may be completely unrelated to issues of marketing and how customers are managed, being more associated with the general position of a corporation as a responsible entity (e.g. Kang and Hustvedt, 2014). The investigation of trust has been particularly intensive in connection with online CRM (e.g. Angriawan and Thakur, 2008; Noor, 2012), including the relationship with online word-of-mouth, particularly in relation to social media (e.g. Palmer and Huo, 2013) as a way of communicating trust or distrust, and how customers should manage their relationships with bad companies. This chapter fills that gap.

3 State of the art on the dark side: customers versus companies

Background

Technology and data sources now make it possible for companies of all sizes (not just large ones), including government operations, to differentiate much more accurately between 'good' and 'bad' individuals and groups. These developments also make it much easier for these companies to predict likely 'goodness' or 'badness', using a range of statistical indicators. Where use of these indicators is not permitted for some reason, this initiates a search for surrogates for these indicators (for example, the type of car driven as a surrogate for gender of driver or the type of house lived in as a surrogate for social class). Following this approach requires a supplier to define what it means by 'good' or 'bad', and to keep this definition under review according to the performance of individuals or groups.

Who are good customers?

'Good' and 'bad' are relative terms. Their definition changes with time, with laws, and with the strategies and target marketing of companies. In addition, we need to distinguish between character and behaviour. A customer who might naturally be 'bad' for a supplier may be constrained to be 'good' by product design or service management.

Goodness and badness are not necessarily a function of the individual. Wider social and economic forces will at least in part determine goodness and badness. For example, the state of the economy, marital breakdown, life stage or neighbourhood (in an area of high social deprivation or of high relative crime, which sadly tends to lead to shortage of resources relative to need and thence to a propensity to commit fraud).

The state of the economy is particularly relevant because it may have a regionally or even sub-regionally differentiated impact on goodness and badness. The resilience of local economies to a national downturn affects credit defaults (and one could argue other forms of badness as well). These factors are seldom measured or input into models of worth, future value or risk.

In the private sector, good customers are broadly defined as having some or all the characteristics below. However, as noted later, companies can specialise in dealing with customers defined as 'not good' by most others. For example, some store cards are targeted at customers who are less creditworthy, possibly because of imprudence or simply low income. So the list below should be taken more as an example of the spectrum.

- Good net value for the supplier, producing more revenue than it costs to service them, taking into account all costs. Consider the bank customer who keeps a reasonable current account balance, never going into overdraft without permission, and rarely going to the branch, preferring instead to use cash machines. This customer is of higher net value than a customer with the same average balance who constantly moves into a small overdraft and uses branch services often. Even though this customer would pay higher bank charges, these may not compensate for the extra administrative costs triggered by staff constantly checking to see whether the overdraft will be paid off. Although the bank might try to optimise charges to the latter to make the account profitable, it will not always succeed.

- Moral (i.e. non-fraudulent) customers stay on the right side of the law in all their dealings with the supplier. Note that some companies do quite well out of meeting the needs of customers who in other respects are immoral, but adhere to the law while interacting with the supplier – e.g. casinos or betting shops used for money laundering.
- Financially prudent, so that they live their lives within the resources available to them. Note that some companies (such as payday loan specialists) make a very good living out of the imprudent, even if it does necessitate charging very high interest rates.
- Personally prudent or safe – e.g. as a driver or pedestrian and perhaps in sporting habits.
- Healthy in habits – e.g. moderate drinking or not smoking – and perhaps even in genes. This, of course, applies to insurance companies and health providers, but not to providers of food and drink products that are unhealthy when consumed in large quantities!
- Observing rights and responsibilities – e.g. prepared to learn how to work with the supplier to achieve mutual benefit, such as installing security devices, looking after credit cards, following a healthy lifestyle.
- Punctual – e.g. paying bills on time and arriving at transport locations on time.
- Responsive to communications that are accurately targeted at them, by evaluating seriously the possibility of buying the product or service, but do not respond to communications that they receive if they are inaccurately targeted (e.g. promoting products that they are unlikely to want). One of the major problems faced by companies is managing communications cost effectively (whether or not they are solicited in the first place), when they have a low probability of leading to customer retention or development of revenue. Of course, if the communication is solicited, this does not necessarily imply poor targeting, as the customer may respond in other ways than anticipated by the supplier.
- Responsive to other initiatives – e.g. willing to try new products.
- Happy to give relevant and truthful information to the supplier and to update information previously given. This includes complaining only when 'justified', in the sense that poor service actually did occur or that a product was actually of low quality. This means that the supplier can improve its service and reduce later complaints and more generally that the supplier can determine the appropriate 'treatment' for the individual, but also save resources by not offering inappropriate treatment. This also applies to complaints (see below).

- Prepared to recommend to other individuals if a service/product is good. In its most beneficial form (to a supplier), this could take the form of brand defining: if they are the type of customer that would attract other customers like them, due to their profile or how they use social media.
- Loyal – i.e. prepared to buy more products or services from the supplier and unlikely to switch, although this depends on the product. Loyal customers for undertakers are rare (though if the family is the decision-making unit, persistence can exist). However, there are strange bedfellows, so to speak. Loyal customers for wedding wear might also be loyal customers for lawyers, because they can afford to be, hence also good customers for financial services advisers.
- Stable or predictable in their behaviour towards the supplier, so that they do not change state from good to bad or bad to good, and so receive inappropriate treatment. Note, however, that a classic strategy of fraudsters is to build up a record as a good customer before committing fraud.

Several examples have been given of how customers can be good in one domain and bad in another. It is the stability of this pattern, and perhaps more importantly the stability of individuals as members of groups, that allows companies to trade with them profitably. Although in theory all risks can be dealt with by insurance, when it comes to the balance of risk and value, stability may be the key. For example, a town centre retailer setting up a new store may reckon on a particular level of bad behaviour – such as credit default, shop theft, staff fraud or 'de-shopping' (i.e. the deliberate purchase of an item for one-time use and its subsequent return as if it had never been used, common with clothing) – based on its experience with similar stores. As long as each new store displays a similar pattern, the loss level is deemed acceptable and standard control procedures can be deployed. If a new store displays very different characteristics of risk and value, new approaches to customer management may need to be adopted.

Again, we stress the point that these are examples of characteristics that indicate 'goodness' for many companies, but they may also be counter-indications for other companies. In some cases, the combination of attributes is important, rather than the possession of any individual attribute.

Who are bad customers?

Bad customers have characteristics largely the opposite of those listed above. For most companies, the key bad characteristics are current and/or likely future unprofitability, though there are circumstances in which unprofitable customers are highly valued – e.g. as recommenders or as having much higher future value. Companies may include in their definition of bad customers debtors, switchers, liars or those with court judgments against them. However, charities, public sector bodies and certain private sector bodies (e.g. debt collectors) often focus on such customers.

Examples of bad customer behaviour are numerous. It is important that management – and government – understands the origins of 'bad' customer behaviour, as solutions cannot always be found at an individual level. For example, many immigrant communities in Western nations are effectively economic or political refugees. They come from a situation in an emerging or poorer country in which to survive they had to 'look after their own', hiding as much from the government as they could, because they were targeted for 'special attention' by the state. It may take generations before members of these groups adapt their behaviour to the more equitable treatment they receive from the government of their adoptive state. So, for example, they may be reluctant to give any personal information, for fear of it being exploited by the state or the supplier to their disadvantage.

As companies seek to manage customers more as individuals, but remotely, bad customers learn to exploit this tendency. This is most visible in the areas of credit and debit cards and the Internet, but also in insurance and banking. Bad customers learn very quickly because the incentive is often very large (the potential gain) and in some cases transfer their learning very quickly (often to other individuals within an organised criminal network, but sometimes also within their ethnic or professional group or geographical locality). For example, government benefit frauds are often organised within ethnic groups or families. Tampering with utility meters often spreads geographically.

Certain industries always have a relatively high ratio of risk to value at the level of the individual customer. These are typically industries where there is a large insurance, credit or consequential liability element involved. They include:

- Insurance.
- Any industry where maintenance contracts are sold.
- All pure credit industries – e.g. bank loans, credit cards.
- Any continuous supply that takes place under credit terms – e.g. utilities, industrial supplies.
- Any situation in which claims are hard to validate.
- Products where failure or misuse can cause significant damage to the customers, leading to high incidence of product liability claims.

However, other areas of high risk include:

- Service industries where complainers – having taken the service – typically ask for reimbursement of the full value.
- Products or services where the costs the supplier has to incur to serve the customer after the initial purchase may greatly outweigh the revenues, if the customer behaves in a certain way – e.g. cherry picks all the high cost, low or zero revenue parts of the service.
- Situations where entitlement documentation can be forged.

To give the reader an idea of the extent and variety of 'bad customer' situations, and their typical correlates, here are a few examples:

- Certain clothing shoppers buy merchandise knowing that they are going to wear it once, before taking it back to the shop to exploit the shop's liberal returns policy (King and Dennis, 2006; King et al., 2007). Shops develop strategies to deal with this, typically taking the merchandise to the back office and smelling it for signs of body odour, deodorant, perfume, etc. – sure indicators of the garment having been worn for an extended period. If this is suspected, management is called in and the customer is challenged.
- A high percentage of claims on holiday insurance policies are fraudulent, particularly those involving claims of lost cash. Insurers are dealing with this by developing databases of frequent claimers.
- Certain utility users always pay at the very last minute, when they are about to be disconnected or have a pre-payment meter fitted. This is dealt with by keeping records of frequent late payers and asking them to pre-pay.
- Certain customers make a habit of claiming that different types of cleaning and washing fluids damage the item being cleaned – or of course their skin! They are traced by keeping properly computerised records of complainers' identities.
- Customers offered a guarantee of lowest price produce fake quotations from other companies to persuade a supplier to reduce their price.

Bad customers are not to be avoided at all costs. Some companies have as one of their objectives to serve customers defined as bad by these companies and/or by other companies. Examples include police forces, social welfare agencies, charities and payday lenders. Private sector companies can design products for bad customers (tamper-proof electricity meters and phone booths, insurance products with specific risks excluded, service products with pre-payment tariffs). Similarly, slack product or service design can turn apparently good customers into bad customers, and indeed whole markets from good to quite bad. For example, recruitment of customers for cable telephony or motor insurance, irrespective of their propensity to pay their bills or to switch on price, respectively, led to many customers turning bad – as did lending (especially mortgages) to customers whose ability to repay was not proven.

Prediction of good and bad

Risk and worth change over time. Companies decide which customers to accept based on their predicted value or risk. For example, students are low worth and slightly higher risk, yet courted by banks because of assumed future value. Companies need to predict performance, ideally before a relationship begins, rather than observe it in retrospect, and most importantly predict any likely changes in value or status, especially from good to bad. This allows the supplier to price the relationship (e.g. in insurance or banking), change its terms (e.g. pre-payment for utility bills), or simply refuse to enter into it. Once the relationship begins, companies find it harder to change price or terms, and may have to accept the risk. If the customer proves more risky than anticipated, however, the customer may be trapped into continuing to receive supply from the original supplier simply because knowledge of this higher level of risk means that no other supplier will offer the relationship. To avoid such customers, de-marketing may be used – e.g. excluding apparently risky customers from direct marketing campaigns. A related problem is adverse selection, in which a supplier's risk criteria – in particular the omission of a risk factor – become known in some form to consumers who are high risk in relation to that factor, and so tend to choose that supplier.

For a supplier to identify individual bad customers, it must do either or both:

- Acquire data on apparent badness from other companies, typically agencies specialising in credit rating or insurance claims.
- Accept enough apparently bad customers and observe/measure their behaviour, so that the supplier can learn to recognise them and avoid most of them in the future.

As patterns of badness change, companies (whether of data on good/bad customers or of products and services bought by customers) need to refresh their knowledge. The supplier also needs to have enough good customers to enable it to define good, too. To manage and avoid or control bad customers, companies seek indicators not only of which customers are likely to be bad already, but also which ones may turn from good to bad. For credit card companies, this may be a growing outstanding balance with no corresponding increase in monthly repayment.

Also, companies need to distinguish amateurs, whose 'badness' is not systematic or expert, from professionals, who may even make a living from their badness, as in the perpetrators of 'crash for cash', and whether the badness is transferred between groups, as indicated by Table 12.1.

The need for perspective

If a supplier is to predict changes of state, it needs to have a good history of the customer. One of the key benefits of having a well-maintained customer database is the development of a clear history of each customer's interactions and transactions – knowing what changed and when, and in some cases why. Being able to recreate situations and reports, and to analyse the impact of time properly is critical. However, knowledge about customers is often poorly organised inside companies. CRM techniques often assume that there is a single customer database, with each customer uniquely identified. This is rarely so. Knowledge of customers is spread over databases, and some knowledge about likely future customer value (positive or negative) is in the heads of staff who deal with customers – face to face, in the call centre and so forth.

TABLE 12.1 Amateur and professional bad customers

	Individual	Group
Professional	Typically, this is the individual fraudster or near fraudster, determined to gain economically from the supplier, but not as part of a properly organised group. Once detected, the individual problem disappears or can at least be controlled	This is planned group fraud or near fraud. It is hard to detect because 'bad customer' detection systems may rely on identifying a common offender, perhaps even in a given location. Even if the individual is detected, the behaviour will continue unless the whole group is detected. Professional fraud groups use the latest telecommunications and information technology to commit offences, avoid detection, escape or cover their tracks when detected. The Internet has become a conduit for transferring information on how to defraud, and also for recruiting new fraudsters
Amateur	This is usually opportunistic, but may become continuous, with the individual seeking opportunities to make a bit of extra money or pay one bill fewer. However, the scale is usually small	A consumer or individual tells friends and family about the opportunity for fraud. This usually leads to identifiable geographical patterns of fraud, or collusion (e.g. shop theft in which a customer colludes with a shop assistant). This is usually identifiable using simple measurement and detection systems

The portfolio approach

Companies may use the idea of a customer portfolio rather than just seeing their markets as a set of revenues derived from product sales. The aim is to develop a portfolio of customers, with value and risk balanced – either within or between customers. The two may be associated (e.g. customers with large houses may be more likely to be burgled). Indeed, those more at risk may be tempted to make fraudulent declarations in order to obtain insurance coverage at lower prices.

Good value is a net outcome over perhaps several years of buying behaviour and costs of managing customers. For example, a bank customer who keeps a small positive balance, often comes into the branch, complains often and never buys additional services may be of negative value for the bank. However, this same customer might have positive value by changing to using a debit card rather than the branch, or if charges were levied.

The most sophisticated companies develop predictive models, to identify whether an individual not previously known to the supplier is good or bad, and to predict future states and state changes. A good individual turning bad exposes the supplier to risk.

If a company's marketing strategy is one of 'volume marketing', the harder it becomes to 'red line' (avoid completely certain categories of customers) or 'cherry pick' (be selective about which customers to recruit). They may not be able to red line if they have a customer base to which they make a common and simple offer (e.g. sell insurance to bank customers, or electricity to gas customers). This may work against the idea of using carefully defined targeting. One practical approach is to use statistical analysis to identify the determinants of the profitability or value of each group. This produces a set of predictive factors and weights, which can be applied at the point at which a customer targeted for such a mass product or service applies. The customer can then be turned down, although this carries the risk of damage to the company's reputation.

Together with statistical methods for focusing on good customers and managing bad customers come the usual strategies for controlling the risk once bad customers have been accepted. In cases of insurance fraud, it is known that both frequency and size of claim are issues, and there are well-established procedures for identifying likely sinners. Expansion of valid claims is harder to detect and/or manage, but many companies now have specific strategies – e.g. appointing one's own repairers, as in the case of automotive crash damage. However, for areas such as fraudulent holiday claims, specialist loss adjusters use formal and informal techniques (e.g. informal exchange of information with colleagues) to assess whether a claim is likely to be fraudulent and whether to investigate further. A first step is always to see whether a given individual keeps appearing on the 'bad' side of the customer balance sheet. For example, frequent complainers about delayed rail journeys are identifiable once identities are checked and complaints properly logged. This can then be matched against records of whether the trains they complain about were actually late, to identify fraudulent complainers. The importance of companies having strategies for managing bad customers is confirmed by studies that show that fraud is acceptable to many customers. Thus, a study by the US Insurance Research Council in 2013 found that 24% of customers believed it acceptable to expand (or 'pad') a claim (Bramlet, 2013).

It is worth noting that most markets tend to define an acceptable level of moral hazard. Companies in different sectors tend to define a level of fraud or loss due to bad customer behaviour. The level depends upon their degree of exposure. For example, banks and credit card companies make a relatively small margin on payments, so the acceptable level of fraud in relation to the total payment is very small. The same applies to insurance companies in respect of their liability, which can be hundreds of thousands of pounds in respect of a customer paying a few hundred pounds a year. At the opposite extreme, retailers of clothing can accept higher levels, as their exposure is limited to the cost of the item stolen.

Choosing customers for positive – and negative – treatment

A key principle of CRM is that it is hard to meet all customers' needs all of the time. Competitive survival requires meeting the most important needs of the most important customers. Competitive advantage is obtained by doing this and also meeting the needs of customers whose needs are not being met by competitive providers. For this reason, companies aiming to manage customers according to their individual value and risk need to:

- Have a good understanding of the needs of different groups of customers.
- Prioritise customers and needs.

One of the greatest areas of success in the use of statistics in management is credit scoring. This allows all kinds of financial institutions to assess the creditworthiness of individuals. The assessment is based on an analysis of an individual's data, which is compared very quickly with the characteristics of hundreds of thousands or even millions of other individuals, to arrive at an estimate of whether the individual should be granted credit. This credit scoring can be used to identify individuals who are likely to lead to a variety of problems for the lender, from inability to make payments to absolute default.

The automaticity of such decisions has caused some concern in government circles, particularly when the decisions turn out to be based on probabilities that an individual has certain characteristics based on the individual's address and/or postcode. From a commercial point of view, these processes allow many more customers to obtain credit quickly than would otherwise be the case. However, they lead to denial of credit to some individuals – creditworthy individuals living in areas of poor credit behaviour. This is not new. Shopkeepers have always been unwilling to give credit to those they believe unlikely to pay – except at very high interest rates. However, because the main use of automatic decision making is often to exclude customers (from mailings, credit, insurance), and these exclusions are applied to very large numbers of customers, this practice is likely to remain controversial for all but the private sector. The apparent speed of these credit decisions may appear shocking to some – a matter of a few seconds. However, this just reflects technological progress.

Companies are increasingly adding data from a variety of sources to their own databases. For example, in the UK, some data providers offer information gathered from a variety of sources (e.g. household shopping questionnaires, guarantees and direct marketing responses) on very large numbers of households. This supplements data from the electoral roll, credit-referencing data (e.g. past court judgments for debt or bankruptcy), and area-based information from the Census, which can also be bought in pre-digested form, with each household assigned a household type. Industry-specific profiling systems have been constructed, often using data from specially commissioned surveys, to help companies estimate with even greater accuracy the likelihood that a customer will buy a product. Advanced data-mining methods can also be put to use to look for new patterns of behaviour among consumers.

However, the information companies need to manage good and bad customers may grow organically, be spread over many (possibly incompatible) databases and so demand significant efforts (e.g. data warehousing and analytics) to bring the information together into one data set. Making this work at the point of contact with the customer, or the point of decision about how to manage the customer, is not easy. Few businesses – usually green-field direct-only businesses – have the luxury of deciding from scratch about their customer data requirements, and can therefore claim to have the information to hand to manage customers appropriately. Even some of these start off with a clear data strategy, but, as they move into new markets or new products, set up additional databases and start to experience the data-management problems of their more established competitors.

Companies with no clear data architecture underpinning their processes for managing customers are likely to suffer two problems:

- Constant outdating of customer data, due to no update process (many companies have no way of knowing when a particular customer data item was last known to be correct).
- Poor level of compliance with data-protection legislation, because of lack of clarity as to what data are held where and for what purpose.

Lack of data architecture may in turn be due to a lack of process for managing data quality – i.e. no 'data quality architecture'.

Acquiring and housing data are issues, but developing these data is another. As customers' needs and behaviour change – and as marketing and service strategies alter – new data sets are required just to manage customers as well as they were being managed before. Perhaps some data will cease to be relevant (e.g. will cease to be able to explain or predict value, or to help the supplier manage customers better), while other data sets may need to be collected. This may mean 'going back over old ground' with customers – for example, if the major collection point is at the time of customer recruitment, existing customers may need to be re-contacted to acquire more data from them. Incentives may need to be provided.

Making the decision about acceptable exposure and missed opportunity

In theory, the more information about customers to which a supplier has access, the more accurately the supplier can assess customers' current goodness or badness, and the more accurately the supplier can predict future values. The decisions companies have to make range from the simple binary choice – e.g. whether to offer a specific product to a specific customer – to more complex decisions – e.g. which product to offer to which customers and on what terms. However, there are diminishing returns to data, particularly given that each datum collected has to be maintained.

Where risk per customer is high relative to profit per customer, the returns to more accurate information are high. Examples of these industries include consumer markets of general insurance, credit cards or energy, or in business-to-business markets, where customers receive extended credit or where the costs of managing the customer are incurred well ahead of the customer providing revenue.

Similarly, where valuable customers are relatively rare amongst customers for a product, the returns on collecting the data indicating likely future customer value are high. However, before they establish how much data should be collected (and then maintained), companies need an estimate of the link between the costs of data collection and maintenance with the benefits, not only overall but for each datum. 'Classic' direct-marketing companies with long histories of customer management can usually estimate the returns to using particular data, but many companies do not have the stable data and analytical framework to achieve this. The supplier's knowledge about the customer will only become firmed up after customer acquisition (our 'getting to know' stage), when the customer's pattern of transactions, payments, complaints and queries becomes clear. Of course, the pattern is one thing, and knowing the pattern is another – hence the deployment of advanced analytical techniques such as data mining, and the extension of the ideas of knowledge management into customer knowledge management. 'Unless I know what I know, I can't act on it!'

A general rule that applies here is that the more information the supplier has, the better the decision. For example, companies aiming to acquire new customers must balance responsiveness and/or value with risk. This is depicted in Table 12.2.

All of the cells in Table 12.2 are underpinned by personal information. The key sources are:

- Electoral roll names and addresses – to identify whether they really live where they claim to live, improving the economics of direct marketing.
- Derived characteristics, such as household composition or years at address – key in understanding responsiveness and risk.
- Past court judgments – to identify likely future default.
- Negative credit data, usually derived from a closed user group, working under rules of reciprocity, perhaps sharing data through a credit-referencing agency or insurance fraud bureau database.
- Inferred/neighbourhood characteristics, based upon age, income, geodemographic characteristics, which indicate whether the individual comes from a neighbourhood with higher levels of bad behaviour.
- Digital information such as suspicious postings on social media, indicating that the individual is trying to recruit others to participate in a fraud.

TABLE 12.2 Customer risk and responsiveness

Risk	High	Ignore them	Pre-screen them/apply screening throughout sales process
	Low	Incentivise them	Target them
		Low	High
			Responsiveness

This information is used to produce an aggregate score. If, for example, the consumer has opted out of making their entry in the electoral roll available for direct marketing, targeting would be much less accurate, as all the other data would be applied to commercial lists. However, if customers opt out from allowing their personal data to be used, they are less likely to be able to get credit. The current electoral roll declaration mentions this.

Detecting bad customers in practice

We have already stressed the idea that, in an age of mass marketing, moral hazard is harder to detect because the supplier is more remote from the customer. Vital face-to-face contact may be missing, but this deficiency can be made up for with smart software and implementing specific policies to control risk and develop value. Techniques for risk control are fairly well established, ranging from techniques for rapid identification of risk levels and applying clearly formulated policies for matching perceived or forecast risk with the appropriate offer. These include:

- Outright refusal to deal.
- Charging more.
- Asking for deposits.
- Asking for assets to be put up as security.
- Asking for commitments to be underwritten by third parties.
- Gradual escalation of risk accepted as the customer demonstrates a history of staying within risk parameters (e.g. keeping within overdraft limits, paying on time).

Risk and value indicators

One of the most important and difficult exercises companies have to go through is to identify what the actual identifiers or predictors of value or risk are. They usually depend upon the type of customer being marketed to and the product or service type. In general, they are a combination of some or all of the following:

Interaction with the supplier

These include:

- Past and current transaction levels (volumes, prices).
- Past and current risk behaviours towards the supplier (e.g. non-observance of overdraft limits, frequent insurance claims).
- Responsiveness relative to revenues (for example, high responsiveness and low revenues mean the customer incurs high management costs, but delivers relatively little value).

- Propensity to require attention (e.g. frequent complaining or requests for clarifying information).
- Financial value (i.e. income or net assets – perhaps implied by housing type or product purchasing behaviour).
- Court judgments (e.g. conviction for debt).
- Credit records – usually only available from other companies that are members of closed user groups set up to share such data, often via an intermediary, such as a credit referencing agency.

Demographic factors

These include:

- Age.
- Occupation.
- Family or business structure.
- Membership of high-risk groups (areas, certain socio-economic or cultural groups, etc.).

The first set should be held on the supplier's database – though it is not always accessible at the point of customer contact. The second set may have to be obtained from shared data sources. The final set is usually obtained from both these sources. The points we made above concerning holding, tracking and maintaining data all apply here.

Managing group risk

In many cases, it is hard to separate an individual's risk or value from the risk or value of the group to which they belong. For example, in the case of families and small businesses. This may be complicated by the fact that the individual has a position of particular influence in the group, for example:

- The fraudulent individual (perhaps as measured through credit card practices) who creates fraudulent practice throughout the small business s/he owns (a direct contamination effect).
- The worker for an energy utility who persuades his neighbours that gas or electricity meters can be interfered with safely.

In other cases, members of a group share common characteristics of fraud or value because of a less direct influence – e.g. a common outlook or common origin. On the positive side, customers of high value tend to cluster together geographically. Individuals who do not share common characteristics may be treated as if they do – guilt by association or reflected glory. Scoring of individuals tries to find associations between the characteristics of many people and infers individual behaviour or characteristics from this. Associative practices like this are cost effective, but they raise important ethical issues, especially when the prediction carries a relatively low confidence level. However, when several people in a definable group share high-risk/value characteristics, the pay-off to identifying as many members of the group as possible and treating them appropriately is very high. Conversely, if the customer hides membership of the group – e.g. by giving incorrect information – the exposure or missed opportunity is greater.

Managing the risk-value portfolio

Perfect predictions of risk and value are impossible, so companies balance their approach by accepting customers of varying amounts of risk or value. There may not be enough 'ideal' customers for a supplier to supply while achieving economies of scale. Companies may need to be a minimum size to balance risk and value (e.g. by having enough customers to understand patterns, to absorb risks, to obtain reasonable terms for laying off risk on third parties, to supply value economically). This leads to the customer portfolio management approach, in which companies aim to acquire and retain particular numbers of customers with different risk and value characteristics. Customers who are high gross value but high risk (and therefore may turn out to have high negative net value) pose a particular problem. Risk and value may be correlated. Further, a 'risky' customer, whose riskiness is undetected by a supplier, has a strong incentive to develop a high-gross value relationship with that supplier, hoping to turn it to their advantage – e.g. by defaulting on a large loan. This places an extra burden upon companies to identify the characteristics of customers who strategise to outwit the supplier's risk/value selection criteria. The situation can be further confused by the clever customer strategy of 'hard man, smooth man' – e.g. a clearly fraudulent customer who nominates a 'clean' member of the family or group to develop a high-value relationship. This practice happens in state benefit fraud, where the leaders of the conspiracy keep well in the background and hire apparently 'worthy' cases to register for a variety of benefits, in ways that make it hard to detect duplicates.

The positive side of this is valuable customers who recruit further valuable customers, who may have been unidentifiable to companies. 'Member get member' is a very good direct-marketing technique, especially if companies find it harder than existing members to find similar high-value members, perhaps because:

- The recruited customers do not share the normal characteristics of valuable customers.
- The normal characteristics of valuable customers are of the type that cannot easily be detected using available data – i.e. customers are well hidden.
- They do share the characteristics, but are unresponsive to the customer recruitment techniques that worked for existing customers.

The issue of intermediation

Despite worries that advances in IT and electronic communication might reduce the amount of intermediation in the economy, there is no evidence of this. Economic pressures tend to push companies in the direction of specialisation, including in distribution functions. Today, the specialist affiliate acquiring customers online and passing them on to other companies is normal.

The use of individual customer data to estimate value and risk affects the evolution of channels of distribution and channels of communication. For example, if customer recruitment is delegated to an agent whose criterion is value irrespective of risk, while the principal supplier bears the risk, customers recruited will be too risky. Marketing and data-access processes and systems are needed to allow risk and value data to be brought together as appropriate at every level of the distribution channel.

Mutual companies

The origin of most mutual companies is a common view or interest amongst members. Where the mutual organisation develops to deal with issues of value and risk, they survive by excluding as members those consumers whose risk/value profile is out of line with the norm. If they did not do this, the forces of competition would cause those mutuals with weaker membership criteria to be targeted by customers with poor risk/value profiles.

There is a view that, as the world opens up to increasing competition based upon customer data and the Internet, it becomes easier for customers of similar risk/value profiles to combine to negotiate deals for their group that exactly match their risk/value profile. However, this assumes that individuals are better assessors of risk/value than companies. As companies become ever more professional at gathering, managing and interpreting customer data, they may hold the upper hand in these negotiations. This may lead to the formation of customer coalitions or customer clubs (much stronger than the current loyalty-based propositions offered by many companies), where companies are offered the whole deal (e.g. insure the whole group) or nothing at all.

Economic issues

There are clearly great benefits for companies of being able to use individual customer data. These include lower risk, greater ability to target higher-value customers and avoidance of certain communication costs – e.g. not wasting communication budgets on bad customers. However, such data work as both a barrier to entry and a facilitator of entry. Companies with better data about customers and their needs can define offers that are more suitable for these customers and target them more cost effectively. The Internet may reduce the advantage of data, as the new technology makes it easier for good customers to identify themselves and bad customers (and companies) to be identified.

We have already discussed some issues relating to data sharing. It is clear that data sharing can also be used as a barrier to entry (e.g. in airline alliances), or as a way of reducing barriers to competition (e.g. retailers giving access to loyalty card databases to providers of financial services, energy and telecommunications). Knowing who the good and bad customers are means that companies whose processes are attuned to handling these kinds of data can cross industry frontiers more easily. Their skills are in customer management, and all they need to make money in a new sector are the brand and the customer data.

The end result can be a redesigned value chain, as companies desert conventional distribution channels and choose distribution partners because of their customer knowledge. Other effects include the confident outsourcing of a variety of customer-facing activities, as widespread availability of customer data enables the identity and status of individuals to be checked more easily, so that some parts of the process of customer recruitment, retention and development can be outsourced. There are also international effects. Companies entering new markets by acquisition are as interested in acquiring customer databases as they are the physical assets and skills of business. A corollary of this is that the absence of the appropriate data infrastructure and legislative framework may hinder the development of economies.

Social and political issues

The data usage practices of large companies have attracted the attentions of governments, social scientists, consumer watchdogs, moral philosophers and others concerned with the ethics of supplier behaviour. The issues emerging in this area can be grouped broadly under the headings of:

1. Supplier issues – how the supplier can achieve its objectives by using customer data.
2. Public policy issues – the consequences of companies doing this and whether governments should constrain companies' use of data.

The latter issue takes on particular significance in certain situations, in particular:

1. Where the government has a direct influence on industry structure, whether as supplier or regulator (e.g. health-care provision, public or private utilities, financial services).
2. Where there are significant ethical or social issues (e.g. the use of genetic data in life and medical insurance, the emergence of a category of uninsurable individuals or unbankable ethnic businesses who are red lined by companies).

In the United States, red lining in insurance (e.g. in health) caused the government to identify 'pools' of uninsurables. Larger companies were forced to insure people from these pools at reasonable rates, in proportion to their market share.

This made it more profitable for niche cherry pickers, as it forced the larger companies to charge higher rates to cover the additional risk. Heavy-handed government intervention can change industry behaviour to the disadvantage of 'good' customers.

Ethical issues

The world of marketing ethics has been transformed by CRM, in its real and digital versions. Conventionally, discrimination between individual customers took two main forms:

- Creation of different offers according to affordability, so customers could elect into different treatment according to their desire to spend money.
- Vetting – for creditworthiness, fraud, previous claims, etc. – and exclusion of certain customers because of their predicted likely costs.

Some proponents of CRM take discrimination between customers to the ultimate extreme. Their focus is on forecasting individual total customer profitability. In our view, companies cannot afford not to use all available data, or else *they* will be subject to cherry picking of their 'good' customers by competitors, leaving them just with 'bad' customers. The sheer variety of the effects of the widespread use of data on good and bad customers has caused those concerned with the societal effects of this data usage to think very hard about which is the right direction. One reaction has been to try to ban a variety of policies.

The most obvious is the attempt to ban the use of data about an individual, when the individual has not expressly consented to its use for the purpose in question, or when it is used to estimate the probability that a consumer will behave in a certain way. This underlies the drive towards a stronger data-protection regime, and can be considered either very ethical, or by some to be totalitarian. The truth is that governments use these data all the time for controlling 'bad customers' – not necessarily hardened criminals but, for example, those who pay tax late. A related problem is that data collected for one purpose (e.g. to try to improve the health of an individual) or under one set of rules are often very useful for another (e.g. insuring people fairly). This is a theme that recurs throughout marketing – for example, the use of credit data used to include/exclude customers from marketing campaigns or to predict crime.

Behind some of the attempts to restrict the use of customer data is the view that those who hold the data cannot entirely be trusted to use information only for permitted purposes. Putting it simply, some are suspicious of the ethics of companies. Are honest managers honest data users? Are retail staff more likely to abuse data?

Another source of criticism comes from those who know that 'bad' customers (as defined by many companies) are biased towards certain ethnic or religious groups, social classes, geographical areas or even gender. With much political emphasis placed upon reducing bias, the use of customer data that would lead to the exclusion of certain customer types from particular benefits is seen as a back door to discrimination, and to be discouraged. A less radical view here is that bias is built into society and forcing companies not to use data to identify biases that affect them commercially will lead to other strategies which might be more insidious. These include outright red lining of geographical areas because they are known to contain high proportions of risky customers, despite the fact that use of customer data and advanced risk-assessment techniques would allow many customers in the area to be served with low risk.

The current data-protection situation

This is not the place to review in detail data-protection legislation. However, there are two particular difficulties with the data-protection issue:

1. The legislation and guidance given by the regulators only go so far.
2. Discussion adopts terms that are in common use, but which are used precisely in the legislation.

Regulators are constantly trying to catch up with technology and, more importantly, how people use the technology in real life. Guidance has had to accommodate unsecure devices, such as smartphones, some of which have poor security. The legislation and guidance refer to personal information or data, but the definitions are not comprehensive. They ignore a large amount of data at risk to the supplier. Therefore, little is done within the supplier to mitigate the risks. Just fulfilling the legal requirement will not give a supplier the correct level of protection, or the ability to think ahead, and define processes and procedures that the guidance does not cover.

We have to define what the 'personal' of personal information means. It is any datum that can identify (a personal identifier) or be linked directly to that personal identifier for a living human person of any age. It does not apply to deceased people or to any other species, even if they are mentioned in a legal document. It refers not just to information held at any one time on the person, but to all information that may be held over the total time of any relationship – i.e. what can be held in totality. The person is called the data subject, to whom the data refer or are linked. This creates a grey area of interpretation.

Personal data – e.g. name, email, address, age, gender, etc. – in the public domain, to a degree, are considered low risk. Sensitive personal data are higher risk: these data can be used to discriminate against the data subject. For example, information relating to racial or ethnic origin, political opinions, religious beliefs or other beliefs of a similar nature, membership of a trade union, physical or mental health status, genetic data related to health conditions, sexual life, offending behaviour and convictions.

Legislation lags behind the technology, but legislators are aware of this. New European Union laws may come into effect in 2017, with two proposed main changes: 1 notification of breaches to the regulators has changed from 24 hours to

72 hours to 'without undue delay'; and 2 notifying the data subject 'without undue delay' when the breach is 'likely to adversely affect the personal data or privacy' of that individual. Companies that suffer a data breach will need to tell the customer and regulators more promptly. A breach is 'the unrecoverable loss of personal data'. A customer with a high propensity to litigate following loss of their data would be costly. Fraudulent customers might find ways of getting companies to lose their data in order to attain compensation.

The supplier dark side

At the time of writing, the world economy is recovering from a series of bad decisions by governments and financial institutions (often acting closely together), which nearly brought down the world economy. Perhaps it can be argued that many of the decisions taken were for the 'right' reasons, such as extending credit to individuals who previously found it hard to attain it, helping companies that might previously not have been able to fund their investments, or maximising shareholder value. At the heart of the problem, however, were governments and managers behaving badly, and arguably even recklessly.

Many examples of bad behaviour by companies towards customers have been documented, including marketing of dangerous pharmaceuticals, selling unreliable cars, providing atrocious airline customer service, providing fault-ridden software, forcing customers to take financial protection that they did not need. Most readers will be able to put names to the companies that committed these sins against customers. Interestingly, this is one area where the ability of customers to rate companies on the Internet – so that bad companies are avoided – did not help. A case of the 'elephant in the room' or 'not seeing the wood for the trees', perhaps?

The lesson from all this is that competition alone does not guarantee good service to customers; indeed, it can lead to the opposite. A combination of consumer-protection legislation, regulation, ethics and prudence – particularly where there is high information asymmetry – is required. Educating customers may help, but seems to achieve very little when customers are faced with the power of marketing and sometimes the ill-informed opinion of other customers.

The agent problem

At the heart of many of the anti-customer episodes of recent history lies what economists call the 'agent problem'. This may take the form of managers with no direct financial stake in the long-term success of the supplier acting so as to achieve short-term financial gains, irrespective of the longer-term impact of their actions on customers or other stakeholders such as shareholders. Measuring the success of companies with customers should counteract this, but sadly the birth of short-term and rather opaque measures of whether customers really benefit from what companies do – such as the Net Promoter Score (see Grisaffe, 2007) – have made it more likely that the agent problem will continue to cause issues for customers.

Chaos and culture

An additional problem is organisational chaos. It is easy to attribute evil motives to companies that provide poor products or services to customers or fail to listen to them, but this may be due simply to not knowing how to manage customers well. Many companies are learning how to manage customers. Because of waves of innovation in CRM technology (covering first direct mail, then telemarketing, then digital marketing), they are often in a catch-up situation, where they do not know the 'right' way to proceed. Larger companies always have problems of coordination, with one side not knowing what the other side is doing. However, this failure to coordinate can be exploited by managers with bad intentions. If we have no access to data on customer needs, we can sell anything to customers irrespective of their needs.

Some companies face a problem of culture transition (e.g. moving from a production or product orientation to include the customer dimension), including understanding customers and their needs and building trust with them. When faced with a challenge on the product or production front, the customer dimension is all too easily forgotten. Even in marketing departments, the focus on creating successful campaigns and doing so quickly in the digital age often leads to success being judged solely in terms of short-term sales, not acquisition and retention of valuable customers in the long term.

A more sinister aspect of the cultural problem is the deliberate assertion of brand values as being related to customer needs, when in fact the processes, incentives and culture of the supplier all push in the opposite direction – particularly when the managers concerned stand to earn large bonuses from short-term financial success: we are back to the agent problem.

Avoiding being bad

Despite the above, some companies have a good track record of succeeding with customers, products and finances. Sometimes this is because they have brilliant products or services, sometimes because they have focused strongly on understanding and meeting their customers' needs in everything they do (not just products and services), or some combination of the two. In all these successful companies, there is a strong drive from the very top of the supplier that pushes it in the direction of success with customers.

Mergers and acquisitions and down- or upsizing operations have become very common, particularly in financial services. These lead to big changes in processes and decision making. Who was once seen as a good customer might now be considered bad, or vice versa. The culture of the parent supplier, which may include attitudes to customers, might be transferred to the new subsidiary to the detriment of customers.

Another cultural aspect is that a supplier's ability to implement definitions of 'good' or 'bad' throughout the organisation may vary. For example, the marketing function may define it, but sales and service may ignore it, as they want any customers to feel welcome. On the other hand, the definition of 'bad' may be communicated so poorly that front-line employees start to challenge any customer whom they feel might loosely fit the definition.

Conclusions

Identification and management of good customers bring rich rewards, but so do identifying and managing bad customers. Our conclusions for companies are:

- Define good and bad customers, recognising that most customers have a mix of good and bad attributes.
- Remember that bad customers often occur in groups, may work together, may collude with your staff, and grow better and better at being bad if they are allowed to be – they learn. So the picture of 'badness' should not be static.
- 'Think the unthinkable' in terms of how 'badness' may be distributed, but base analyses on hard evidence not prejudice, staying within the terms of the various laws covering data protection, racial and other types of discrimination, employment and specific industry regulations.
- Ensure that databases and data sources allow good and bad customers to be identified.
- Measure business performance in terms of net value from each customer – including all exposures and not just routine costs.
- Estimate net exposure to bad customers and calculate whether it is worth investing in reducing this exposure or risk.
- Ensure that systems at the point of contact with customers allow bad customers to be identified and also to predict whether a new customer will be good or bad.
- Where the data needed for this assessment are elsewhere, obtain them. If legally possible, develop relationships with competitors that allow bad customers to be identified and warnings to be exchanged.
- Develop, test and refine alternative strategies for dealing with bad customers, combining limitations on dealing or refusal to deal with techniques to reduce exposure to bad customers who 'get through'.
- Avoid any focus on discriminating between good and bad customers leading to a corruption of a focus on providing good value to customers.

4 New research directions

The economic problems of 2007 onwards were partly a consequence of many consumers being placed under financial duress, often as a result of the policies of governments, banks and other companies that encouraged them to take financial risks. This has led to interest in how the results of CRM are effectively a result not just of CRM policies, but also of a company's marketing strategy and how it leads to the creation of good or bad customers. This interest has been enhanced by the rise of behavioural economics, which has focused strongly on the incentives that encourage consumers to behave in particular ways, including dishonest behaviour or behaviour designed to harm other consumers. There is now a need for more research into how this thinking should change how companies design and implement their CRM policies, particularly when Internet based, as here the consequences of good or bad behaviour occur very quickly and news travels fast on social media.

5 Practising marketing – a case study

Acknowledgement of the widespread existence of fraudulent and other 'bad' behaviour has led to a concerted response by practitioners in the form of industry bodies whose role it is to combat fraud, as well as companies specialising in data sharing, to help companies combat fraud. In some cases, this has been connected with the fight against terrorism (e.g. because the money required to fund terrorism has passed through money laundering). However, not all these initiatives have been financial. For example, the United Kingdom Revenue Protection Agency focuses on energy theft and works on behalf of the energy utilities to combat such activity. The Centre for Retail Research publishes figures about retail theft. The existence of such bodies means that evidence on 'bad' behaviour in certain sectors is relatively easy to obtain, so that companies designing their CRM and other marketing strategies and policies should always factor this behaviour into their planning.

As this chapter has made clear, in many cases this behaviour is not criminal. For example, in 2007, Sky TV in the UK had a serious problem in that large numbers of consumers were threatening to leave in order to obtain a reduced-price subscription. This led to serious problems of motivation in the contact centre and reduced profit because too many discounts were offered. Sky decided to reduce discounts to customers other than those with legitimate customer service problems and instead to tell customers asking for discounts that they could instead receive better value through low-cost add-ons, such as fixed-line telephony and broadband. This policy led to a temporary rise in customer churn (the rate of customers leaving), but thereafter a much reduced churn rate with increased profit, as shown in Figure 12.1.

Discussion questions

1. Which members of your friends, family and acquaintances do you think would be good or bad customers for: 1 banks; 2 motor insurers; 3 life insurers; 4 telecommunications companies; 5 clothes retailers; and 6 grocery retailers? Why? Do you think they know whether they are good or bad? Does it matter?
2. Can you identify situations in which a company has considered you to be a possible bad customer? What led you to believe that? What do you think the company was trying to do?

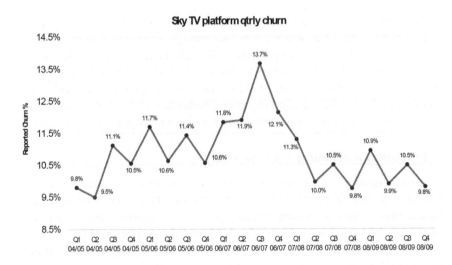

FIGURE 12.1 Sky churn rate

3.   How does your government experience goodness or badness in its citizens? What does it do about it?
4.   Do you think people change as they go through life in their goodness or badness towards organisations that supply them? If so, what causes them to do so?

6 Further investigation

1.   If research is being conducted in a particular industry, identify the patterns of good and bad company and customer behaviour, how they are developing, and what strategies should be used by both parties to improve (ideally) ethical outcomes.
2.   Identify the impact of web and mobile technologies on these patterns.
3.   Identify some case studies of successful strategies and policies, identifying the key principles at work.
4.   Analyse how CRM systems are allowing companies to manage bad customers more successfully.
5.   Examine how social media conversations are being used to identify emerging patterns of bad behaviour by companies and customers.

References

Angriawan, A. and Thakur, R. (2008). A parsimonious model of the antecedents and consequence of online trust: an uncertainty perspective. *Journal of Internet Commerce*, 7(1), pp. 74–94.
Bramlet, C. (2013). IRC report: public less tolerant of insurance fraud. *Claims*, 61(5), p. 9.

Grisaffe, D. (2007). Questions about the ultimate question: conceptual considerations in evaluating Reichheld's net promoter score (NPS). *Journal of Consumer Satisfaction, Dissatisfaction and Complaining Behaviour*, 20, pp. 36–53.

Kang, J. and Hustvedt, G. (2014). Building trust between consumers and corporations: the role of consumer perceptions of transparency and social responsibility. *Journal of Business Ethics*, 125, pp. 253–265.

King, T. and Dennis, C. (2006). Unethical consumers: de-shopping behaviour using the qualitative analysis of theory of planned behaviour and accompanied (de)shopping. *Qualitative Market Research*, 9(3), pp. 282–296.

King, T., Dennis, C. and McHendry, J. (2007). The management of de-shopping and its effects on service: a mass market case study. *International Journal of Retail and Distribution Management*, 35(9), pp. 720–733.

Noor, N.A.M. (2012). Trust and commitment: do they influence e-customer relationship performance? *International Journal of Electronic Commerce Studies*, 3(2), pp. 281–296.

Palmer, A. and Huo, Q. (2013). A study of trust over time within a social network mediated environment. *Journal of Marketing Management*, 29(15/16), pp. 1816–1833.

Stone, M., Machtynger, L. and Woodcock, N. (2002). *Customer Relationship Marketing*, 2nd edition. Kogan Page.

Further reading

Nguyen, B. (2011). The dark side of CRM. *The Marketing Review*, 11(2), pp. 137–149.

Nguyen, B. (2012). The dark side of customer relationship management: exploring the underlying reasons for pitfalls, exploitation and unfairness. *Journal of Database Marketing and Customer Strategy Management*, 19(1), pp. 56–70.

Nguyen, B. and Klaus, P. (2013). Retail fairness: exploring consumer perceptions of fairness in retailers' marketing tactics. *Journal of Retailing and Consumer Services*, 20(3), pp. 311–324.

Nguyen, B., Klaus, P. and Simkin, L. (2014). It's just not fair: exploring the effects of firm customization on unfairness perceptions, loyalty and trust. *Journal of Services Marketing*, 28(6), pp. 484–497.

Nguyen, B. and Mutum, D.S. (2012). Customer relationship management: advances, dark sides, exploitation and unfairness. *International Journal of Electronic Customer Relationship Management*, 6(1), pp. 1–19.

Nguyen, B. and Simkin, L. (2013). The dark side of CRM: advantaged and disadvantaged customers. *Journal of Consumer Marketing*, 30(1), pp. 17–30.

PART V

Conclusion

13

CONCLUSION

Bang Nguyen, Lyndon Simkin and Ana Isabel Canhoto

1 Introduction

There is a distinct gap for a book of this type, reflecting both the maturity of customer relationship management (CRM) deployment and the growing awareness of CRM's dark side. In *The Dark Side of CRM*, we have included original and recent works exploring the current nature of CRM and the darker side of organisations' and consumers' behaviours within this area of marketing. In this final chapter, we discuss the managerial implications of the dark side and the ways in which some of the dark side can be overcome, or at least minimised.

2 Overcoming the dark side

Research into the dark side of CRM and marketing has grown substantially. This literature stream suggests that the marketing landscape today is dominated by consumer suspicion and distrust, often resulting from firms' practices, which include hidden fees, deception, opportunism, manipulation, information mishandling and so on.

In a recent example, Marriott and the American Hospitality & Lodging Association asked the US Federal Communications Commission (FCC) to allow hotels to deploy equipment preventing people from turning their phones into Wi-Fi hotspots while in certain parts of Marriott's hotels. In order to avoid pricey hotel Wi-Fi charges, many guests opt to use their data allotment from their mobile phone provider, connecting their laptops to the Internet via their smartphones. Many customers were outraged by the plan, claiming that Marriott's request for a conference centre Wi-Fi smartphone ban was a veiled attempt to stop access in hotel rooms and lobbies as well. While the hotel chain stated it needed to block Wi-Fi hotspot access in conference centres because attendees could launch cyber attacks on the company's network or disrupt a Wi-Fi service for the conference or guests, it was believed by some observers that the Wi-Fi ban was a way to force guests to use the hotel's connection rates instead. At the time, Marriott's connection rates started at US$14.95 per day. For $19.95, guests received 'enhanced high-speed Internet', which included video chatting, downloading large files and streaming video. Marriott charged between $250 and $1,000 for conference exhibitors and attendees to use its Wi-Fi service. Following the customer outrage, Marriott abandoned the attempt to block the Wi-Fi hotspot use by visitors on their own – already paid for – mobile phone subscriptions (Goldman, 2015). Marriott's motives may well have been genuine, but consumers and those commenting online did not all see it that way, causing Marriott many problems and providing much adverse publicity.

The dark side cases are numerous and many examples have been highlighted in this book. As consumers become increasingly cynical, marketers have revisited and reconceptualised the notion of fairness in marketing and customer management, so that CRM can flourish and progress with further advancements. Especially when dealing with sensitive data, to avoiding further control and imposed regulation. We believe that to succeed in today's competitive markets, it is not enough to focus solely on customers' needs and wants, but also to recognise that to develop long-term relationships firms must adopt a responsible and fair approach to marketing and CRM. This approach calls for the management of fairness in CRM, in order to develop and enhance beneficial relationships not only with customers but also with business partners, communities, employees, governments, regulators and investors (Ghoshal, 2005). The emphasis on fairness among stakeholders reinforces trust, devotion and loyalty, and ultimately long-term success (Nguyen and Simkin, 2012).

In the early 1990s, academics and practitioners realised that there were inherent problems with marketing, which created negative societal consequences. According to Roy and Pratik (2014), bad marketing has severe negative consequences for society and is financially wasteful. They note that the marketing profession, for example, has played a major part in the unconscionable denigration and objectification of women in society. The ways in which women are portrayed in advertising have contributed to many serious problems among teenagers and young women, including eating disorders, feelings of worthlessness, depression, self-injury and even suicide (Kilbourne, 2000). As time has passed, marketers have realised that the adoption of different approaches to marketing is necessary. This leads to the so-called approaches of 'stakeholder theory' (Freeman, 1984), 'enlightened customer management' (Frow et al., 2011) and 'enlightened market orientation' (Roy and Pratik, 2014). The marketing profession has shifted towards a more ethically and socially responsible approach. This is today highlighted by the American Marketing Association's (AMA) Code of Ethics, which emphasises marketers' responsibility towards all stakeholders, including customers, employees, investors, channel members, regulators and the community. The AMA code highlights that marketers' actions and decisions should be of value to all. In addition, the criticism of marketing being unethical has resulted in much research into fairness, trust, social marketing and – in line with this book – the dark side and ways of overcoming it.

Despite increased research, some scholars suggest that the marketing function still suffers from major problems related to both its reputation and effectiveness (Jost and Kay, 2010; Nguyen et al., 2015). For example, researchers have found that the majority of consumers hold negative and even hostile views of marketing. When surveying consumers and business professionals about the image of marketing, Sheth et al. (2006) found that 65% of consumers have a negative attitude towards marketing, 27% are neutral and only 8% positive. Smith, cited in Johansson (2006), conducted a study to examine contemporary consumers' attitudes towards marketing practices and found that an overwhelming majority of respondents held negative attitudes towards marketing, with over 60% saying that their opinion of marketing and advertising had declined in previous years, and 61% describing the amount of marketing and advertising as 'out of control'. When asked to describe what they thought of when hearing the word 'marketing', respondents commonly used words such as 'telemarketing', 'lies', 'deception', 'manipulative', 'gimmicks', 'exaggeration', 'invasive', 'intrusive' and 'brainwashing'. The results are a decline of marketing effectiveness and a decline in productivity of the marketing function (Sheth and Sisodia, 2002).

In response to the extensive consumer criticism of marketing, some researchers have looked into the study of conscious capitalism (Sisodia et al., 2007). Conscious capitalism has two key elements: first, companies should articulate a higher purpose that transcends profit maximisation; and second, companies should be managed for the benefit of all stakeholders in their ecosystem and not just shareholders. The rise of conscious capitalism (Aburdene, 2005; Mackey, 2007) reflects people's higher levels of consciousness about themselves and the world around them. As consciousness is raised, people all over the world place great demands for transparency on companies, using the Internet to accelerate this trend. Sheth et al. (2006) state that, despite its deteriorating reputation, marketing has the capability to solve customers' problems, support their decisions and at the same time build higher levels of trust, accountability and transparency. Thus, marketing has the power to drive conscious capitalism and either enhance or diminish overall well-being in society. That is, with its power and influence, it is suggested that marketing should embrace responsibility and 'stewardship' or trusteeship. The potential for companies to create value and make major contributions to solving some of society's problems are achieved with a greater sense of responsibility and consciousness.

Drawing from the study of conscious capitalism (Sisodia et al., 2007) and customer advocacy (Urban, 2004), Roy and Pratik (2014) developed the concept of 'enlightened market orientation'. Companies that practise enlightened market orientation embody the ideas of fairness and trust, and recognise that long-term survival links profit and prosperity with social justice and environmental stewardship (Nguyen et al., 2015). These firms operate with a systems view, recognising the connectedness and interdependence of all stakeholders. They must tap into deeper sources of positive energy and create greater value for all stakeholders, including customers, investors, suppliers, the environment and societies. By utilising creative business models that are both transformational and inspirational, firms can help solve many of the social and environmental problems faced by the world today. For companies operating with CRM schemes, there are some key practices inspired by conscious capitalism and enlightened customer management (Nguyen et al., 2015).

1. As part of their CRM strategy, firms must identify a higher purpose than simply profit maximisation or shareholder returns. They must realise that business life is not only about creating and exploiting short-term desires, but rather addressing important needs of society and individuals over the long term. A mission and purpose built around fairness, ethics and responsibility will direct the firm towards developing passion and creativity among employees. With an enlightened purpose, the firm may exist beyond its profit-making objective and use CRM to create meaning for all stakeholders. In doing so, the firm attracts customers, motivates employees and inspires investors, who share common belief systems. Every firm must find, articulate and continually renew its unique mission and enlightened purpose through CRM.

2. Firms should exist and be managed for the benefit of all stakeholders. Managers must continually observe, measure and optimise the health of the overall 'ecosystem', recognising the connectedness and interdependence of all stakeholders in the society.

3. Managers must join and align the interests of each stakeholder and develop long-term relationships through their CRM system. This can be accomplished by emphasising value creation for all the involved parties, rather than working opportunistically to increase only the firm's own profits. Such a relational approach will create a win-win situation for both customers and firms alike.

4. Firms should not act opportunistically or engage in exploitation of any kind. They should not take advantage of stakeholders to advance their own interests by misusing people's fears and addictions. Instead, firms must adopt the mindset of stakeholder well-being, in order to serve stakeholders better.

5. Society must be considered as the ultimate stakeholder and marketing should not become a cost but rather a profit or benefit to society. Firms must realise that their responsibility is to advance the well-being of society as a whole. When firms are motivated and have the desire to help solve large societal problems in partnership with governments, other companies and non-governmental organisations, the resulting outcome can only be beneficial for everyone.

6. Firms should emphasise environmental sustainability to improve good will. Hawken et al. (1999) suggest the notion of 'natural capitalism', referring to firms' responsibility for their environmental impact. Such an approach must

be adopted to achieve an enlightened approach. The objective is to do no harm to the Earth and to strive to have a net *positive* impact on the environment.

7. Firms must approach the marketplace with a 'whole pyramid' model that seeks to uplift rather than ignore or exploit the poorer sections of society.

8. Finally, firms must intrinsically believe that doing the right thing ultimately brings improved results. While profit may be seen as a good measure and natural outcome success, the firm must adopt other measures and focus on the overall activities that benefit all stakeholders.

According to Roy and Pratik (2014) and Nguyen et al. (2015), enlightened market orientation recognises the connectedness and interdependence of all the players in the company's ecosystem. CRM, incorporating fairness, has the power and force to benefit society. The larger the company, the more the impact of its marketing on society and popular culture. Marketing and CRM, with a higher level of consciousness about purpose and broader impacts on everyone involved in the process, can be defined as marketing with a conscience. This is about utilising advancements in CRM to drive a primary concern for customers' well-being, rather than a concern with selling as much as possible. This advocates the best interests of not only customers, but of all of the stakeholders involved.

3 Managerial implications arising from the dark side

In this book, we have highlighted ways to overcome the more negative issues linked with CRM. Here we summarise the managerial implications arising from this dark side.

In Chapter 2, Pennie Frow, Adrian Payne, Louise Young and Ian Wilkinson suggest that many types of dark side behaviour can be addressed through a more enlightened and holistic approach to CRM. However, high levels of profitability and the widespread prevalence of dark side practices do little to encourage service providers to address the latter in a timely, socially responsible and ethical manner. A holistic use of CRM processes can help guide service providers away from the 'dark side' and towards a more 'enlightened' practice of CRM. The five key strategic processes of CRM, proposed by Payne and Frow (2005, 2013), are used as a structure to consider how various dark side behaviours can be addressed. At the centre of a more enlightened CRM strategy are strategy development, value creation, multi-channel integration and customer experience, information management and performance assessment. The chapter provides some examples of how successful implementation of each process can facilitate more effective CRM and mitigate dark side practices. The strategy development process is the first in the CRM strategy framework suggested. At the heart of this process is the goal of matching the needs of the customer with the resources and capabilities of the service provider. Issues of customer favouritism and spillover effects are addressed. This framework provides important inputs to the value-creation process.

In Chapter 3, Lan Xia argues that price differentials can easily evoke perceptions of unfairness. While value-based pricing has been shown to be profitable to the firm and may also benefit customers, the potential impact on perceptions of unfairness should be carefully thought through. First, segmentation should not be driven solely by customer willingness to pay. Price differentials should be a natural by-product of different values delivered. Price should be a quality cue instead of a means of taking advantage. Focusing on the values provided will help to switch consumers' attention away from price. Second, consumers care about the offerings given to others (Feinberg et al., 2002) and have a natural tendency to compare. Therefore, carefully setting up price screens will help to minimise comparison and reduce perceptions of unfairness. Customer segments should be accompanied by clear profiles that are sufficiently distinctive, delineating the characteristics of each segment. The dissimilarities will help to form the screens that reduce the propensity to compare. Third, providing a certain degree of control to consumers helps to reduce perceptions of unfairness. Companies can reduce the potential for perceptions of unfairness by offering different price options, having customers tailor their own prices and delivering price increases in a less personal way. Fourth, CRM is about long-term relationships. Therefore, in designing the price structure and prices, it is important to pay attention to procedural fairness. Making the price structure transparent and information regarding price differentials accessible will help. Fifth, a crucial element in a relationship is trust. Sixth, providing an appropriate amount of price-setting information with price differentials is important to guide inferences. Thus, providing information related to price offerings lends more transparency, reducing the chances of evoking perceptions of unfairness. Finally, successful service recovery may require appropriate financial compensation according to a procedure that gives consumers voice and control, as well as courtesy and helpfulness from service employees during the interaction.

In Chapter 4, Adam Rapp and Jessica Ogilvie suggest that social CRM requires organisations to establish, communicate, facilitate, and consistently evaluate and enforce a social media policy. Social CRM failures result from poor organisational culture, absence of managerial support, insufficient staffing and lack of customer engagement (Myron, 2013). Avoidance of the many pitfalls associated with social networks occurs when a firm has aligned, fully integrated and strategically developed social media capabilities to expand and enhance CRM processes. To overcome the pitfalls of social CRM, companies must establish and maintain a customer-centric CRM strategy. Relationship management is no longer about simply extracting information from customer transactions, involving now the co-creation of value with consumers through social media interactions. To do this, firms must set appropriate goals for social media interactions (Andzulis et al., 2012). These customer-centric goals should derive from an understanding of customer expectations and the appropriate integration of social networking into the CRM strategy in conjunction with those expectations. For success in reaching those goals, the strategic allocation of resources should be considered and employees must be trained to perform the tasks necessary for CRM goal attainment. To maintain goal actualisation, constant evaluation of social CRM effectiveness must occur through monitoring and adapting social media's implementation, reflecting the evolution of technologies associated with this phenomenon.

In Chapter 5, Venessa Funches notes that firms are seeking appropriate strategies to reduce or prevent consumer participation in negative word-of-mouth, mis-behaviour and revenge behaviours. Unfortunately, a great deal of consumer parti-cipation in these behaviours is fuelled by the lack of a response from the firm. Addressing negative consumer behaviour is a tricky and sensitive process. Some firms have responded by trying to curtail consumers' ability to convey negative infor-mation, but with little success. Other firms have ignored consumer negative behaviours, often with disastrous consequences. Still others have been over-whelmed by trying to respond to consumer negative behaviours. The primary means for addressing negative behaviours have been education and deterrence. The educational approach seeks to change attitudes and subsequently behaviours through the use of messages designed to strengthen moral constraints. The deter-rence approach uses formal and informal sanctions in order to heighten the per-ceived risks of misbehaviour and thereby reduce opportunism. Unfortunately, there exists very little information as to which approach is the best to use in specific situations. As a result, firms are still trying to determine through trial and error the best ways to respond.

In Chapter 6, Donald Lund, Irina Kozlenkova and Robert Palmatier suggest that commitment, trust, gratitude and reciprocal norms take a central role in the development of successful exchange relationships. Trust and gratitude have shorter-term effects on relational outcomes, while commitment and reciprocal norms have enduring effects that promote relationship success. In order to be most effective, relationship marketing programmes must create clear benefits for the customer. In so doing, all four positive relational mediators will be activated, ensuring the largest impact on relationship performance. The chapter further suggests four different negative relational mediators that can harm exchange relationships: opportunism, conflict, unfairness and complacency. Opportunism and conflict can damage both attitudinal and financial outcomes. Unlike opportunism and conflict, unfairness is perceptual in nature and results in the deterioration of the foundation of a rela-tionship. Complacency, unlike any of the other three negative relational mediators, is completely passive in nature and by definition unknown until some detrimental event occurs. Managers need to be aware of the situations that are likely to cause these negative mediators and take steps to avoid or reduce their influence on the relationship in order to ensure long-term relationship success.

In Chapter 7, Gilles N'Goala discusses how, from a business ethics perspective, customer relationship management is very likely to lead to manipulative and/or deceptive tactics, which opportunistically attempt to exploit relationship asymme-tries and customer vulnerabilities. Following Sher's (2011) analysis, CRM becomes immorally manipulative when marketers disregard their customers' autonomy and dignity, ignore the trust that their customers place in them, take advantage of their customers' weaknesses and vulnerabilities, and/or violate one's general obligation not to harm others. However, not all marketers who manage a customer portfolio can be blamed for using customer data and for marketing products and services based on the resulting insights. Marketers can be blamed, though, for their intentions to manipulate, deceive or exploit their customers; the harm caused to customers or other parties; and the insufficient positive consequences of their decisions. Marketers may be morally blameworthy because they are negligent, reckless, or commit an act that is egregious or harmful to various parties. To overcome this dark side, relationship maintenance (customer retention) and development (increased service usage, cross-buying and share of wallet) are top priorities in CRM. In the long run, companies can effectively influence customer patronage behaviours by leveraging overall customer satisfaction, trust and relationship commitment (Aurier and N'Goala, 2010).

In Chapter 8, Ibrahim Abosag, Dorothy Yen and Caroline Tynan reveal that the dark side of a business relationship can emerge at any point in the development process, depending on relationship contexts, types, interaction dynamics and market conditions. It is also safe to argue that the dark side of relationships is likely to occur frequently in those relationships where uncertainty and physical distance between relational partners exist, because of their cross-cultural/cross-national nature (Leonidou et al., 2006). Studying the dynamic development of trust and commitment can contribute to a better understanding of the development of business relationships. Whilst lack of trust and commitment in business relationships is often criticised, it is less widely recognised that excessive levels of trust and commitment in business relationships can cause negative impacts on relationships (Ekici, 2013; Kusari et al., 2013). For example, over-emphasis on affective commitment may impair a firm's decisions concerning profit maximisation. In addition, which type of interpersonal relationship is considered appropriate should be judged within its cultural context. Williams et al. (1998) note that highly interpersonally oriented (collectivist) countries would be highly responsive to interpersonal aspects of the business relationship and put more emphasis on social bonding, whilst highly structurally oriented (individualist) countries would be more responsive to structural aspects and put more emphasis on the structural bonding of business relationships. Whilst close personal relationships are encouraged in countries such as China and Saudi Arabia, they are considered unnecessary and a waste of resources by many Western firms, especially those from the Anglo-Saxon countries. Thus, businesses must be aware of such cultural differences in their interactions with counterparts from different cultural backgrounds.

In Chapter 9, Mike Breazeale, Erin Pleggenkuhle-Miles, Mackenzie Harms and Gina Ligon suggest that the branding and CRM tactics that firms employ are largely responsible for their success in a hostile marketplace. Most business leaders would not look to violent extremist organisations (VEOs) as a source of inspiration. However, by observing the ways that VEOs overcome their obstacles, other organisations can modify the relationship-building techniques that are effective in the most adverse conditions to inform their own CRM practices, thus creating a stronger bond with customers and impacting on the stability of the organisation.

For example, by skilfully telling a story that is consistent with their mission, these groups provide an authentic brand around which their 'customers' or supporters can gather. VEOs adeptly empower brand advocates to tell their story for them by providing ample resources via social media. These groups also actively recruit and educate new followers by way of a regularly updated online presence that has many channels, so as to accommodate the varying media preferences of their intended audience. Even in the face of governments that would reallocate donations made to them, VEOs provide easy access to supporters wishing to give them money via highly transparent online portals for conducting business. Funds are often provided via charities established by either the VEO or its sympathisers, and also via legitimate businesses owned by the VEO. These organisations also understand the importance of utilising mass media to help publicise their cause and they nurture that relationship by providing noteworthy content that resonates with their target audience. VEOs regularly monitor social media to gather intelligence on their 'customers' and their competitors, a tactic that allows them to manoeuvre adroitly in a highly volatile marketplace.

In Chapter 10, Denish Shah provides different tools and frameworks that marketers may use in order to address issues with conventional CRM practices. Evidence from published research debunks four generally accepted managerial beliefs, with substantive implications for the CRM practices of firms. First, not all loyal customers are necessarily profitable. Therefore, any customer loyalty management initiatives, such as retention efforts, should be contingent upon the profitability of the customer. Furthermore, to achieve true customer loyalty, firms need to rethink their rewards programme, so as to ensure that they serve to cultivate attitudinal loyalty, in addition to rewarding the behavioural loyalty of customers. Second, CRM decisions based on backward-looking customer value metrics tend to be sub-optimal. A proven superior approach involves the implementation of the customer lifetime value (CLV) metric to measure the true future worth of a customer and hence to implement CRM strategies guided by the future value of each customer or customer segment. Third, cross-selling a product to every customer of the firm that is likely to cross-buy can adversely impact on the overall financial outcome of a firm's cross-selling efforts. This is due to the prevalence of hidden customer segments exhibiting persistent adverse behavioural traits. Cross-selling to such customers results in decreasing profits or increasing losses with the increase in cross-buying levels. Consequently, cross-selling practices of firms need first to identify these problem customers and up-sell or not sell any products/services to them, despite their tendency to cross-buy from the firm. Finally, customers are prone to developing a habitual behaviour by virtue of their recurring interactions with firms. Habits are enduring constructs, with tenacious influence on future customer behaviour. Different customer habits can have a differential impact on firm performance. A firm's CRM practices and policies need to take account of the relative prevalence (how many customers) and intensity (strength) of different habitual behaviours, and design marketing interventions accordingly.

In Chapter 11, Bang Nguyen and Xiaoyu Yu explain that, for organisations wanting to overcome the dark side of CRM, a willingness to take risks must be present. For example, these organisations must understand that failure is not absolute or terminal, and that there is unique knowledge arising from failure. Therefore, they must promote and possibly reward trial and error processes. At the management level, it is important to recognise that individuals must possess the sturdiness and ability to deal with failure. Only then will they be able to rise and learn from failure. The chapter argues that managers working with CRM need to endorse understanding of both failure and the individuals who are able to deal with failure. Researchers suggest that the way in which an individual copes with failure can influence the extent and speed of recovery (Shepherd, 2003; Singh et al., 2007). Shepherd (2003) proposes that oscillating between two alternate methods can result in faster recovery from the failure of a project, including a loss-orientation coping method (which involves confronting the failure and talking about feelings of grief with friends, family or psychologists), and a restoration coping method (which focuses on avoidance of the loss and on secondary sources of stress). This is similar to the emotion and problem-based coping framework suggested by Lazarus and Folkman (1984), which is used as a strategy for coping with failure (Singh et al., 2007). Thus, to achieve positive outcomes for CRM failure, especially those opportunities arising from recovery and coping strategies, it is necessary for managers to engage in a range of coping strategies to deal with the emotional and financial implications of failure.

In Chapter 12, Liz Machtynger, Martin Hickley, Merlin Stone and Paul Laughlin explore how some companies have built a good track record of succeeding with customers, products and finances. This might be because they have brilliant products or services, or they have focused strongly on understanding and meeting their customers' needs in everything they do, or some combination of the two. In all these successful companies there is a strong drive from the very top that pushes in the direction of 'success with customers'. Mergers and acquisitions and down- or upsizing operations are very common, particularly in financial services. These lead to big changes in processes and decision making. Who was once seen as a good customer might not be viewed as such by a firm's new management. The culture of the new parent business, including attitudes to customers, might be transferred to the new subsidiary, to the detriment of its customers. Another cultural point is that a firm's ability to implement definitions of 'good' or 'bad' throughout the organisation may vary. For example, the marketing function may define 'bad', but sales and service colleagues may ignore this view, as they want all customers to feel welcome. On the other hand, the definition of 'bad' may be communicated so poorly that front-line employees start to challenge any customer whom they feel might loosely fit the definition. Conclusions for companies are to define the good and bad customer, recognising that most customers have a mix of good and bad attributes; to ensure that databases and data sources allow good and bad customers to be identified; to develop, test and refine alternative strategies for dealing with bad customers, combining limitations on dealing or refusing to deal with techniques to reduce exposure to bad customers who 'get through'; and to avoid a focus on discriminating between good and bad customers leading to a corruption of the focus on providing good value to customers.

4 Conclusion

This book has covered the dark side of CRM across the themes of customers, relationships and management. The wealth of insights and cases is relevant to a range of students, academics and practitioners. The role of CRM managers is to understand this dark side and influence it to the best of their ability, in order to induce fairness for all stakeholders.

Overcoming the dark side of CRM is a complex issue requiring an inherent understanding of laws and regulations, fairness and trust ... and much more research is needed. We have proposed research to highlight the associations between the dark side and discrimination and the perceptions of these: it is important to understand the point at which one becomes the other. Other topics warranting further research include data use infringements, consumer exploitation, implications for the Internet of Things, unethical business practices, fair and trustworthy relationships, consumer welfare and government regulation to mitigate dark side issues. This is a big topic, of strategic importance to the success and viability of firms, yet so many issues are still to be explored.

Let us not forget that customers are treated badly – not all customers and not always, but many are, and often. Some customers are bad and they treat firms badly, so firms have to react. Employees and customers endure the consequences. Such bad behaviours – by firms and customers – have consequences for the perception of trust and fairness, for endorsements and referrals, for repeat purchasing and loyalty, and for profitability and return on investment. The management of customer relationships is core to the success and even survival of the firm. As this book has explored, this is an area fraught with difficulty, duplicitous practice and undesirable behaviour. These need acknowledging, mitigating and controlling. We hope that your practices will benefit from the lessons and proposals discussed in *The Dark Side of CRM*.

References

Aburdene, P. (2005). *Megatrends 2010: The Rise of Conscious Capitalism*, Hampton Roads. American Marketing Association (AMA). www.ama.org/Pages/default.aspx.

Andzulis, J.M., Panagopoulos, N.G. and Rapp, A. (2012). A review of social media and implications for the sales process. *Journal of Personal Selling and Sales Management*, 3, pp. 305–316.

Aurier, P. and N'Goala, G. (2010). The differing and mediating roles of trust and relationship commitment in service relationship maintenance and development. *Journal of the Academy of Marketing Science*, 38(3), pp. 303–325.

Ekici, A. (2013). Temporal dynamics of trust in ongoing inter-organisational relationships. *Industrial Marketing Management*, 42(6), pp. 932–949.

Feinberg, F.M., Krishna, A. and Zhang, Z.J. (2002). Do we care what others get? A behaviourist approach to targeted promotions. *Journal of Marketing Research*, 39(3), pp. 277–291.

Freeman, R.E. (1984). *Strategic Management: A Stakeholder Approach*. Pitman, Boston.

Frow, P.E., Payne, A., Wilkinson, I.F. and Young, L. (2011). Customer management and CRM: addressing the dark side. *Journal of Services Marketing*, 25(2), pp. 79–89.

Ghoshal, S. (2005). Bad management theories are destroying good management practices. *Academy of Management Learning & Education*, 4(1), pp. 75–91.

Goldman, D. (2015). Marriott: you win, we won't block Wi-Fi. *CNN Money*. http://money.cnn.com/2015/01/15/technology/marriott-wifi/ (accessed 15 January 2015).

Hawken, P., Lovins, A. and Lovins, L.H. (1999). *Natural Capitalism*. Little, Brown and Company, USA.

Johansson, J.K. (2006). 'Why marketing needs reform'. In J.N. Sheth and R.S. Sidosia (Eds) *Does Marketing Need Reform? Fresh Perspectives on the Future*. M.E. Sharpe Inc, New York.

Jost, J.T. and Kay, A.C. (2010). 'Social justice: history, theory, and research'. In S.T. Fiske, D.T. Gilbert and G. Lindzey (Eds) *Handbook of Social Psychology*, 5th edn, pp. 1122–1165. John Wiley & Sons, Hoboken, NJ.

Kilbourne, J. (2000). *Killing Us Softly 3: Advertising's Image of Women*. Documentary produced by the Media Education Foundation. www.mediaed.org.

Kusari, S., Hoeffler, S. and Iacobucci, D. (2013). Trusting and monitoring business partners throughout the relationship life cycle. *Journal of Business-to-Business Marketing*, 20(3), pp. 119–138.

Lazarus, R.S. and Folkman, S. (1984). *Stress Appraisal and Coping*. Springer Publishing Company, New York.

Leonidou, L., Barnes, B. and Talias, M. (2006). Exporter–importer relationship quality: the inhibiting role of uncertainty, distance and conflict. *Industrial Marketing Management*, 35(4), pp. 576–588.

Mackey, J. (2007). Conscious capitalism: creating a new paradigm for business. www.flowidealism.org/Downloads/JM-CC-1.pdf.

Myron, D. (2013). CRM – what lies ahead in 2014? *CRM Magazine*, December.

Nguyen, B. and Simkin, L. (2012). Fairness quality: the role of fairness in a social and ethically oriented marketing landscape. *The Marketing Review*, 12(4), pp. 333–334.

Nguyen, B., Simkin, L. and Roy, S.K. (2015). 'Fairness management in India, Pakistan and Bangladesh'. In B. Nguyen and C. Rowley (Eds) *Ethical and Social Marketing in Asia*. Chandos Publishing.

Payne, A. and Frow, P. (2005). A strategic framework for customer relationship management. *Journal of Marketing*, 69 (October), pp. 167–176.

Payne, A. and Frow, P. (2013). *Strategic Customer Management: Integrating CRM and Relationship Marketing*. Cambridge University Press, Cambridge.

Roy, S.K. and Pratik, M. (2014). Enlightened market orientation and consumer well-being. Working Paper. The University of Western Australia.

Shepherd, D.A. (2003). Learning from business failure: propositions about the grief recovery process for the self-employed. *Academy of Management Review*, 282, pp. 318–329.

Sher, S. (2011). A framework for assessing immorally manipulative marketing tactics. *Journal of Business Ethics*, 102(1), pp. 97–118.

Sheth, J.N. and Sisodia, R.S. (2002). Marketing productivity: conceptualisation, measurement and improvement. *Journal of Business Research*, 55(5), pp. 349–362.

Sheth, J.N., Sisodia, R.S. and Barbulescu, A. (2006). 'The image of marketing with consumers and business professionals'. In J.N. Sheth and R.S. Sisodia (Eds) *Does Marketing Need Reform? Fresh Perspectives on the Future*. M.E. Sharpe, Armonk, NY.

Singh, S., Corner, P. and Pavlovich, K. (2007). Coping with entrepreneurial failure. *Journal of Management and Organisation*, 13, pp. 331–344.

Sisodia, R.S., Wolfe, D.B. and Sheth, J.N. (2007). *Firms of Endearment: How World Class Companies Profit from Passion and Purpose.* Wharton School Publishing, New Jersey, USA.

Smith, W.J. (2006). 'Coming to concurrence: improving marketing productivity by reengaging resistant consumers'. In J.N. Sheth and R.S. Sidosia (Eds) *Does Marketing Need Reform? Fresh Perspectives on the Future.* M.E. Sharpe Inc, New York.

Urban, G. (2004). 'Customer advocacy – a new paradigm for marketing?' In J.N. Sheth and R.S. Sisodia (Eds) *Does Marketing Need Reform? Fresh Perspectives on the Future.* M.E. Sharpe, Armonk.

Williams, J., Han, S. and Qualls, W. (1998). A conceptual model and study of cross-cultural business relationships. *Journal of Business Research*, 42(2), pp. 135–143.

INDEX

implementation of 209–10; customer loyalty, value of 201; customer loyalty rewards, design of 207–9; customer profitability, measurement of 202–3; customer profits, smart-selling framework for maximisation of 211; discussion questions 215; easy-to-observe aggregate-level outcomes, accepted beliefs from 199; *Fortune 500* 204; further investigation 215; habit, concept of 206; habitual behaviour by customers 205–6, 206–7; habitual behaviour by customers, measurement and management of 212–13; *Harvard Business Review* 201; improvement of existing CRM practices, tools and frameworks for 207–13; intuition in management implementation of practices 199; J.C. Penney core business model 199; learning objectives 200; loyal customers, profitability of 200–201; loyal customers, segmentation and management of 207, 208; loyalty-profitability correlation, weakness of 201; marketing practice, J.C. Penney and 'everyday low pricing' (case study) 214–15; marketing wisdom, questioning the conventional in 200–207, 213; 'profitable' customer loyalty, management of 207–9; reading suggestions 218; recency-frequency-monetary value (RFM) 202; research directions, suggestions for 213–14; route map to themes 200; segmentation and management of customer loyalty and profitability 208–9, 209–10; smart selling instead of cross-selling 210–12; Target Corp., marketing experience at 199; value of profitable customers 202–3; *Wall Street Journal* 204
Cope, J. 226, 227, 229, 230
Corbett, A., Neck, H., and De Tienne, D. 226
'corner-shop dilemma' 29
cost transparency 127
Coulter, K. and Coulter, R. 155
credit scoring 252
Crosby, L.A., Evans, K.R. and Cowles, D. 101, 102, 103
Crosno, J.L. and Dahlstrom, R. 111
cross-buying by customers 203–5, 206
cross-selling to customers 204–5, 210–12, 213
Crossan, M.M., Lane, H.W. and White, R. E. 227
Croteau, A. and Li, P. 220

cultural vulnerability 137
culture transition, problem of 263
customer lifetime value (CLV) 203, 213; measurement and implementation of 209–10
customer management, identification of dark side behaviours and 6, 14, 21–36, 275; 'Behavioural Insight Team' (UK government unit) 35; co-destiny relationships, mutual reward in 31; communication-based dark side behaviour 26–7; 'corner-shop dilemma' 29; cross-functional strategic approach of CRM 23, 24; customer confusion 26–7; customer favouritism 28; customer management 23–4; 'dark side,' terminology of 24–5; Data Protection Act (UK) 35; dietary habits 30; discussion questions 35; dishonesty 27; ecological impacts 30; enlightened approach to CRM 31–2; financial exploitation 29; further investigation 36; holistic approach to CRM 31–2; information management process 32; information misuse 26; interaction research approach 25–6; learning objectives 21–2; 'lock-in' of customers 28; manipulation of alternatives, dark side behaviour through 28–9; marketing practice, exploitation of customers (case study) 34–5; multi-channel experience process 32; performance assessment process 32; privacy invasion 27; process-based cross-functional conceptualisation of CRM 24; reading suggestions 38; relationship management, CRM and 23–4; relationship marketing (RM) and 21, 22, 23; relationship neglect 28–9; research directions, suggestions for 33–4; research of dark side, CRM and 23–32; route map to themes 22; service provider relationships, dark side of 24–6; side effects and dark side behaviour 29–30; 'small print,' penalties buried in 29; solutions suggested by research 30–32; 'spillover' effects 30; strategy development 32; tactical customer management transactions 24; Target Corp. (US retailer) 35; Tesco Clubcard 34; value creation 32
Customer Rage Survey (2013) 8; negative word-of-mouth (WOM) 74
customer relationship management (CRM): business relationship frameworks and 9, 15, 93–116, 277; business relationships,

moral hazard, risk of 125; opportunism and trust in CRM 125–6; organisational processes, industrialisation of 123; organisational transparency 128; personal data, value of 129–30; persuasion, manipulation by 131; price transparency 127–8; psychological vulnerability 138; rationalisation 123; reading suggestions 149; reckless marketing 141; relationship marketing (RM), CRM practices and 123; reliability of service providers 126; research directions, suggestions for 142–3; route map to themes 124; seduction, manipulation and 132–4; supply transparency 128; technological transparency 128–9; transparency in CRM 126–30; trust, generation of 126; trust, hidden costs of lack of 124–5; trust, marketing literature's emphasis on 122; trust in long-term relationships 138; Zara, sourcing by 141

Wall Street Journal 6–7, 39, 204
Wallace, E., Buil, I. and De Chernatony, L. 177
Walmart: exchange relationships 45, 99; suppliers dependence on 99
Wang, L., Xu, L., Wang, X., You, W. and Tan, W. 227
Wathe, K.H. and Heide, J.B. 111
Wathne, K.H. and Heide, J.B. 107
Watson, J. and Everett, J.E. 225
Weiman, G. 11
Weimann, G. 174–5
Weinberg, B.D. and Pehlivan, E. 60
Weiner, B. 8, 78, 79, 81, 82
Weisburd, Aaron 180
Weissman, R. 204
Weitz, B. and Jap, S. 158
Wennberg, K. 225
Westbrook, R.A. 78
Westbrook, R.A. and Oliver, R.L. 78
Wetzel, H.A., Hammerschmidt, M. and Zablah, A.R. 130
Wetzer, I.M., Zeelenberg, M. and Pieters, R. 76
Whatley, M.A., Webster, J.M., Smith, R.H. and Rhodes, A. 105
White, A., Breazeale, M. and Webster, C. 177
Whole Foods, relationships with 99
Whyley, C. 226
Wicks, A., Shawn, B. and Thomas, J. 156
Wilkinson, Ian xiv, 14, 21–38, 275

Williams, J., Han, S. and Qualls, W. 157, 159, 278
Williamson, O. and Ghani, T. 107
Williamson, O.E. 96, 98, 107, 111, 125, 126, 140, 163
Wilson, D. 153, 154, 155, 158, 165
Wilson, D. and Mummalaneni, V. 153, 154
Wingfield, N. and Pereira, J. 134
Wirtz, J. and Bateson, J.E.G. 78
Wirtz, J. and Kimes, S.E. 43
Wong, A., Tjosvold, D. and Yu, Z.-Y. 99
Wood, J.V. 46
Wood, W., Quinn, J.M. and Kashy, D.A. 205
Wuyts, S. and Geyskens, I. 157

Xia, L. and Monroe, K.B. 40, 43, 46, 47, 50
Xia, L., Monroe, K.B. and Cox, J.L. 7, 40, 41, 42, 43, 44, 46, 48, 51
Xia, Lan xiv–xv, 14, 39–57, 276
Xiao, B. and Benbasat, I. 134, 135, 136
Xin, K.R. and Pearce, J.L. 222

Yamakawa, Y., Peng, M.W. and Deeds, D. L. 229
Yandle, J. and Blythe, J. 160
Yen, D.A. and Barnes B. 222
Yen, D.A., Barnes, B.R., and Wang, C. 158, 159, 160
Yen, Dorothy Ai-wan xv, 150–73, 278
Yiu, D.W., Lau, C.M. and Bruton, G.D. 228
York, D. 153, 154
Young, L. and Denize, S. 157
Young, Louise xv, 14, 21–38, 36n1, 275
Yu, L. 210
Yu, X., Chen, Y. and Nguyen, B. 4
Yu, X., Nguyen, B., Han, S.H., Chen, C. H.S. and Li, F. 12
Yu, Xiaoyu xv, 15, 219–40, 280

Zablah, A.R., Bellenger, D.N. and Johnston, W.J. 220
Zaheer, A., McEvily, B. and Perrone, V. 155, 156
Zara, sourcing by 141
Zbar, J.D. 204
Zeithaml, V.A., Parasuraman, A. and Berry, L.L. 112
Zhou, N., Zhuang, G. and Yip, L. 219, 223
Zineldin, M. 154
Zipcar and learning from failure (case study) 232
Zourrig, H., Chebat, J.C. and Toffoli, R. 77
Zwick, D. and Dholakia, N. 26